REFORMERS ON STAGE

Popular Drama and Religious Propaganda
in the Low Countries of Charles V,
1515–1556

Gary K. Waite

UNIVERSITY OF TORONTO PRESS
Toronto Buffalo London

© University of Toronto Press Incorporated 2000
Toronto Buffalo London
Printed in Canada

ISBN 0-8020-4457-3

Printed on acid-free paper

Canadian Cataloguing in Publication Data

Waite, Gary K., 1955–
    Reformers on stage : popular drama and religious propaganda in the low
    countries of Charles V, 1515–1556

    Includes bibliographical references and index.
    ISBN 0-8020-4457-3

    1. Chambers of rhetoric – Benelux countries – History.   2. Dutch drama –
    Early modern, 1500–1700 – History and criticism.   3. Theater – Religious
    aspects.   4. Reformation – Benelux countries.   5. Theater and society –
    Benelux countries – History – 16th century.   I. Title.

    PT5267.C5W34 2000   839.31'2209'382706   C00-930164-X

University of Toronto Press acknowledges the financial assistance to its
publishing program of the Canada Council for the Arts and the Ontario
Arts Council.

This book has been published with the help of a grant from the Humanities
and Social Sciences Federation of Canada, using funds provided by the
Social Sciences and Humanities Research Council of Canada.

University of Toronto Press acknowledges the financial support for its publishing activities of the Government of Canada through the Book Publishing
Industry Development Program (BPIDP).

To my sweet Eleanor, whose arrival brought joy immeasurable

Also in memory of those whose recent death has brought sorrow:

Grandmothers Annie Waite (d. 1995) and Ethyl Sharpe (d. 1990)
Uncle Stewart Warren (d. 1996) and cousins Jean Walsh (d. 1996)
and Ruby Blake (d. 1997)

Your love lives still in those left behind

Contents

viii   Contents

Acknowledgments

From inception to completion this project on the chambers of rhetoric has occupied for the better part of a dozen years a great deal of my time and energy. While I have begun or continued other research interests during this time, always nagging at my subconscious was the need to give final shape to the manuscript on those fascinating Flemish and Dutch dramatists who entertained and informed their contemporaries and who so often raised the hackles of the higher authorities for their provocative opinions. Thanks to the recent efforts of a handful of scholars, Dutch rhetorician drama is no longer a virtual unknown within the English world, although it still lacks a book-length study in English to do justice to the importance and fame (some would say infamy) of these amateur literary and dramatic societies. Their poetry and drama have been studied from a variety of approaches; here I have taken an unabashedly historical perspective in order to uncover the role played by the rhetorician playwrights and actors in the propagation of reform ideas within the Low Countries of Charles V. This book reveals, among many other things, that their impact was considerable.

Over the course of researching and writing this work I have necessarily incurred a great debt of thanks which can never be fully recompensed by words of acknowledgment. But that, unfortunately, is all I have to offer those who have provided advice or support of one kind or another. I would like to thank here all those who raised questions or points of clarification at the various conference sessions during which I presented sections of chapters or who discussed the topic with me informally afterwards. My colleagues in the Canadian Society of Renaissance Studies / Société canadienne d'études de la Renaissance bore with considerable patience my presentation of no less than four papers drawn from this enterprise, at Quebec City, Quebec, in 1989, Kingston, Ont., in 1991, Charlottetown, P.E.I., in 1992, and most recently at St John's, Newfoundland, in 1997. Audiences in attendence at the Sixteenth Century Studies Conference, St Louis, in 1990, and at the Believer's Church Conference in Fort Worth, Texas, 1989, have had to be less tolerant, if still quite polite, in hearing a paper on what may have appeared at face value as an obscure topic.

In an interesting way this project has marked the transition in my career from PhD candidate at the University of Waterloo to professor of history at the University of New Brunswick. I am, however, still grateful for the rigorous supervision and profound friendship of my doctoral supervisor, Professor Werner O. Packull, who critiqued the original project plan and encouraged me to embark on a vocation of historical scholarship. Yet this study has been completed in a different environment, one that is remarkable for its collegiality and support: the Department of History at the University of New Brunswick. The warm encouragement, listening ears, kind but pointed advice, and various forms of support that I have received from all of my colleagues here have been critical agents in the completion of this book. In this way every member of the department over the last twelve years has assisted in a very real way in creating a stimulating intellectual and work environment. Several of my colleagues have been kind enough to listen to my often lengthy rambles on the chambers or to read papers and chapters relating to the project and I would like to thank especially Professors T. William Acheson, Beverly Lemire, D. Gillian Thompson, and R. Steven Turner for going well above and beyond the call of duty and friendship. Departmental secretaries Elizabeth Arnold and Carole Hines have been tremendously helpful and extremely patient with my all-too-frequent demands on their all-too-valuable time.

Scholars elsewhere have also been willing to read chapters and suggest improvements, and I hope they can see their hands in this work. The four anonymous readers for the Canadian Federation for the Humanities Aid to Publication Programme performed an invaluable service in helping reshape a rather inflated manuscript into a more cohesive discussion, while Professor Benjamin Kaplan (Iowa University) and Robert Baldwin (Connecticut College) were kind enough to make suggestions and to share bibliographies and information. Adriaan Plak (University of Amsterdam Library) and Sol Yoder gave generously of their time to double-check my translations. I also learned a great deal from a brief discussion with Professor Marijke Spies of the

University of Amsterdam, who no doubt is unaware of how helpful her brief meeting was with a visiting Canadian scholar. Professor Piet Visser, Curator of the University of Amsterdam Library, who arranged that meeting, has over the course of the last dozen years become a dear friend and without a doubt the individual most responsible for helping a Canadian scholar with no Dutch background feel at home in Holland. To his family, Janny, Geertje, and Johannes, I owe a tremendous debt of gratitude and friendship for opening their home and hearts to me.

None of this research could have been conducted without generous financial support. The principal source of funding was provided by the Social Sciences and Humanities Research Council of Canada, which awarded the project research funds in 1987 and 1990. Additional financial resources were provided by the University of New Brunswick. A number of archives and libraries opened their doors to me and provided exemplary and friendly service. In particular I must thank the staffs of the Gemeente Archief Amsterdam, the Universiteits-bibliotheek of Amsterdam, the Stads-archief Antwerpen, the library of the University of Antwerp (UFSIA), the Koninklijke Bibliotheek Albert I, Brussels, the Stadsarchief Gent, the Gent Universiteitsbibliotheek, the Gemeente Archief Haarlem, the Haarlem Stadsbibliotheek (especially Henk Duyser), the Koninklijke Bibliotheek in The Hague, and the libraries of the University of New Brunswick, University of Toronto, and University of Waterloo. A most remarkable debt of gratitude is owed to the members of the Haarlem Society 'Trou Moet Blijcken' and their Keizer, O.B. Blaisse, for their gracious hospitality while I perused their rich collection of manuscripts. Not only did they open up their invaluable collection of manuscripts to my scrutiny, but they fêted me in true rhetorician fashion. Bert van't Hof and Jun Pacito, managers of the Hotel de Admiraal, Amsterdam, not only bent over backwards to accommodate me, but became good friends. Most recently, I must also thank Kristen Pederson, Miriam Skey, and Barb Porter for their marvellous editorial assistance and advice.

Family members have had to bear the greatest burden of my scholarly obsessions. For several summers my brother, Brian, tolerated my moving, dog and all, into his apartment in Toronto to be closer to family and research libraries. However, it is undoubtedly my spouse, Kate, and our children, particularly Jessica, who have had to make the greatest sacrifices in their own busy schedules and interests so that I could indulge my desire to 'write that chambers book.' Although they were not present at the beginning of the project, they have since helped create the stimulating atmosphere necessary for its culmination. I am also deeply grateful to Kate for opening my eyes more fully to the importance of life outside of academia. Although delaying the manuscript's completion, the arrival of Eleanor in March of 1995 has, to put it mildly, added a sense of perspective to my writing and existence. She has certainly made our lives much more dramatic and fulfilling.

Although I here acknowledge the help I have received, any remaining errors or omissions in the work are solely my responsibility. Unless otherwise indicated, all translations are mine.

Introduction

Reform Propaganda and Vernacular Drama

This book is a study of the propagandistic function of drama in the Low Countries of Emperor Charles V, whose reign coincided with the early religious reform movement(s) in the Netherlandic provinces. The principal focus of this work centres on the theme of reform, religious and otherwise, as promoted or opposed by the major dramatists of the Low Countries, the members of the chambers of rhetoric. It therefore falls into a cluster of historical investigations which explore the means by which reform ideas were communicated from the major reform leaders, such as the German reformer Martin Luther, to the people, and the alterations made to those ideas in the process of transmission. In the last few decades there has been an explosion in studies on the means of communication in early modern Europe, works that have examined in fascinating detail the various ways in which people communicated their ideas and the effectiveness of these modes of discourse.[1] Luther in particular was a master of popular propaganda and a flood of his own writings, along with those of other Protestant reformers such as the later reformer of Geneva, John Calvin, appeared from the printing presses of Europe in tract and pamphlet form. Oral communication was likewise extremely important, and reform propaganda was presented to audiences in the forms of sermons, debates, drama, songs, and ritual action. The result was a series of reform movements that transformed the religious face of the Holy Roman Empire as people from town and country insisted on change, not always in the direction intended by Luther or his other learned colleagues, as the specific reforms promoted or adopted varied considerably across the regions as well as between countryside and city. In other words, laypeople, both rulers and the ruled, adapted the reform messages to suit their own perspectives and needs.[2] The question remains, how did members of the various social estates, both literate and illiterate, hear and understand the reform messages?

It is now generally acknowledged that prior to the modern era, most people communicated first and foremost by oral and visual means, and that even with the invention of the moveable type printing press and cheap paper, published pamphlets could influence the populace only by intermediary means, as written works had to be read aloud and explained by the literate to the illiterate. Much better were cheap, printed broadsheets that incorporated both pictures and written text.[3] Even so, most people continued to receive their information by listening to others, especially preachers, or discussing the issues of the day in a variety of informal locales, such as taverns.[4] Given this situation, how does the historian gain access to the attitudes and beliefs of the vast majority of people living in the sixteenth century? The major problem is self evident: the vast bulk of accessible source material that has survived from the sixteenth century is in the form of printed works, and these remain an essential source for the scholarly understanding of early modern culture. Obviously the historian cannot come close to fathoming the *mentalité* of early modern Europeans without the written evidence left behind by the educated minority, even though this may distort our comprehension of the beliefs of the illiterate majority. What is required are approaches to the extant material that take into account both the biases of the cultural elites and the attitudes of other laypeople, at least as percolated through the mesh of learned presuppositions.[5] Although there has been a recent preoccupation with the latter, it is extremely important to continue to examine the beliefs and assumptions of the literate minority, for it was they who normally determined the success or failure of a particular reform initiative. The historian must therefore read reform propaganda with both disseminator and audience in mind. Given the nature of the sources at its disposal, this book will necessarily concentrate on the beliefs of literate urbanites, although the notions of others will occasionally appear.

Most of the research into the communication of reform ideas has generally been categorized under the now controversial rubric of 'popular culture.' What is at the heart of recent arguments over this term is whether or not one can make a sharp distinction between popular and elite culture in early modern Europe, between the body of ideas, rituals, and behaviour of the educated world, mostly clerical, and those of the illiterate, peasant majority. What has complicated matters is the growth of an urban society, particularly strong in the Low Countries, where urbanites seemed to have their feet firmly planted in both popular and elite worlds, without truly belonging to either. Their literacy in the vernacular, for example, removed them somewhat from the typical descriptions of popular peasant culture, without allowing them into the fully elitist Latin culture of the universities and higher clergy. For the purposes of this study, then, Richard Kieckhefer's advocacy of a 'common tradition' within which are various 'specialized traditions' is more helpful, although the term 'popular culture' will still be used in general terms to describe the culture and attitudes of those without formal education or excluded from the inner corridors of power.[6]

One collection of sources useful for understanding the beliefs of laypeople is the body of surviving dramatic scripts and published plays from the period. Although these too were the products of educated writers, most of them were intended to appeal to wider audiences and were designed like pamphlets and broadsheets to influence the opinions of both the literate and illiterate. As James A. Parente, Jr, has written of medieval drama, audiences 'from all social strata, many of whom had only a superficial familiarity with Christian dogma, were thus informed of the fundamental tenets of their faith.'[7] Unlike pamphlets, however, drama also served celebratory and humorous functions, attempting to engage the audience by comedic means or to entertain viewers, often with the hope that by so grabbing their attention they would pay better heed to the serious message contained within. Thus these works are at home across the various 'specialized traditions' of a society, in both the so-called popular and elite cultures. Study of sixteenth-century plays within their historical and cultural contexts has so far illuminated many dark alleys in our knowledge of the beliefs of ordinary people.[8] The function of drama as a means of shaping public opinion regarding the religious controversies of the sixteenth-century Reformation has therefore begun to bear considerable fruit, and it is within this framework that this study has been formed.

The people discussed in this study belonged by and large to a relatively small and coherent range of 'specialized traditions,' for most of them were literate artists, artisans, and merchants, citizens of the most culturally sophisticated cities in northern Europe, those of the Low Countries. Their interest in their own culture, especially literature and drama, led them to form or join literary societies called the chambers of rhetoric, for the purposes of honing their poetic skills and providing cultural services to their community. On the strength of this sense of mission, the chambers of rhetoric became the most important performers of popular or vernacular drama in the Low Countries.[9] By the middle of the sixteenth century virtually every city and town of the Low Countries had at least one of these societies, and their popularity is attested to by a multitude of contemporary witnesses.[10] As will become evident in this study, in the majority of cases the messages disseminated in the verses and plays composed and performed by rhetoricians spoke to and for their own interests, and those of their 'specialized traditions': literate artisans and merchants, reflecting the common concerns among those just below the urban religious and secular elites. Whether or not rhetoricians were able to lead or shape public opinion is a more difficult question to answer; the nature of their drama, as a form of the rhetorical arts, meant that their presentations were often composed in a style less accessible to an illiterate audience. This is particularly true of their in-house works, such as the refrains – a particular genre of poetry that followed specific conventions as to rhyme scheme and stanza length[11] – and the serious plays, especially the *spelen van zinne*, literally 'plays of the senses (or mind),' dramatic works that had as their central or sole characters allegorical figures representing elements of human conscience or emotions, and which normally were divided equally between good and evil characteristics. Even so, these plays could range in popularity from the dense and sophisticated to the light and humorous, depending on the particular author and audience. As we shall see, rhetoricians viewed themselves as more than entertainers, indeed as teachers and promoters of good religious and civic virtues; thus their literary productions almost always had a moral or didactic edge, distinguishing them quite clearly from the purely comical entertainments of wandering troupes of players which frequently made the rounds of towns and villages. The *spelen van zinne* are rightly regarded as the epitome of the *rederijkers'* craft, always rhymed, often with double entendre, hidden messages, acrostics, and the like, at times demanding a great deal of their audiences. Rhetoricians also composed and performed simpler works – dinner plays, entertainments, and farces – some involving as few as two actors, and with a more comical purpose. These shorter plays were usually aimed at a less sophisticated audience, had more in the way of slapstick and fools, but still always promoted a moral of some sort. Yet, many of the *spelen van zinne* that we will come across in this study were evidently composed to achieve a broader hearing, to persuade as many urbanites as possible to side with or against a reform message. In fact, most plays of all types written and performed during the first half of the sixteenth century were simple enough to be understood by a wide audience of literate and illiterate viewers, even though many of the subtler allusions or classical and scriptural references may have been lost on some of the spectators. This situation changed after the 1550s, when rhetoricians began imitating Renaissance and classical models of drama and outdoing each other in the inclusion of complex puzzles and acrostics in their literary compositions. Their works thus became less popular stylistically, if more intellectually appealing.

Since many rhetoricians sought to enter the inner corridors of urban politics, they were not likely to write works too terribly scandalous for the city's patricians. However, given the ubiquitous battle between urban governments and ecclesiastical lords, criticism of the higher clergy could be enjoyed by a community's elites as well as by the lower orders. This study specifically asks: to what degree did rhetoricians adopt the reform propaganda and in what ways did they adapt reform messages to accommodate their own concerns about salvation and society? In other words, how were reform ideas strained through the mental filters of Flemish and Dutch urbanites? What did they see as the overriding priorities for change? How was reform propaganda reshaped in the dual contexts of the urban Low Countries and the dramatic stage? The central goal will be therefore the explication of the propagandistic function of the rhetoricians, seen largely from their side of the stage, and the illumination of how rhetoricians believed they were responsible for influencing public opinion on issues of both religious and secular reform. There are many other subjects that could be pursued through the study of Dutch drama, such as gender or marriage, but because rhetoricians do not seem to have promoted these as matters requiring major change, they will not be examined here.

It must not be concluded from the emphasis of this study, however, that rhetoricians did not take seriously their function as entertainers; even the most serious morality play could produce laughter or pleasure, although there are a number of them which when read can only be described as turgid. Unfortunately, we cannot recover the ad lib asides, bodily actions, or facial expressions of the performers, which may have provided spark to such dry scripts. Yet we have enough clues to suggest that the scripts should be read as only the verbal structure around which the real playing occurred. From a distance of several centuries we are at a considerable disadvantage; yet it seems fair to assume that the stage performance of a play would have remained largely faithful to the script, while any actions or ad lib comments would not have substantially contradicted the essential message of the written text.

In spite of the relatively high level of urbanization and literacy in the Low Countries of Charles V, non-literary modes of communication were still essential if the propagandist wished to reach the majority of the populace, which was only partially literate and which was still captivated by ostentatious display and symbolic ritual.[12] For example, Robert W. Scribner recently has suggested that along with the traditional means of communication such as sermons and pamphlets, reform ideas permeated the public consciousness by way of 'a popular cultural acquisition through ritual action, in which Evangelical convictions were assembled and experienced in a form of bricolage, drawing on traditional modes of action.'[13] One therefore ought not to be surprised to discover that the chambers were very important vehicles for the spread of anticlerical and reform opinions. Certainly the authorities acted as if they were.

Understandably the literature on the chambers is immense, although relatively little attention has been paid to the role they played in the incitement of popular passions on behalf of religious and social reform in the first half of the sixteenth century.[14] Instead, the major chronological foci of rhetorician scholarship has been on the periods preceding and succeeding the era of Charles V: the late-medieval Burgundian period, which witnessed the origins of the chambers of rhetoric and the production of a number of quite famous plays, such as *Everyman* (*Elckerlijc*); and the high point of rhetorician activity coinciding with the wars against Spain and the Netherlands's 'Golden Age.' Historical scholarship has rightly concentrated on detailing the activity of rhetoricians in particular communities, and more are in the works.[15] Broadly speaking, recent scholarship has been dominated by Herman Pleij and his students for the early period, and by the school of W.M.H. Hummelen for the later period. For both eras there has been a remarkable number of scholarly works that have examined in considerable detail the development of the style of rhetorician works, especially the later influence of Renaissance classicalism and the transition from the amateur chambers of rhetoric to professional theatres.[16] In both periods, moreover, there has been considerable work in editing the surviving texts and tracing their thematic and stylistic influences, and in examining the role of rhetoricians as artists and cultural experts within the late-medieval and early-modern urban milieu.[17] While in the course of this book we will refer to many of these works, the emphasis here will be on the period between the Burgundian era and the beginning of the revolt against Spanish hegemony. This period, while not receiving the same attention as the other two, has been the subject of increasing attention, and one need only refer to two recent encyclopedias of Dutch literature and drama to see the importance now attached to the era of Charles V in the history of the chambers of rhetoric.[18]

This study is restricted to the time of the early Reformation in the Low Countries during Charles V's rule, roughly 1519 to 1556, and probes the relationship between vernacular drama and Reformation propaganda. It discusses this subject first by comparing developments in Antwerp and Amsterdam, the two most important cities in the southern and northern Netherlands respectively at the start of the Reformation, and second, by examining in a more comprehensive fashion most of the surviving plays known to date to the era of Charles V. From the evidence of surviving plays, it seems that a large number of rhetoricians took it upon themselves to promote a wide range of reform perspectives on the stages of the Low Countries (see appendix). Until 1539 these were dominated by Lutheran or 'Lutheran-minded' outlooks, although Anabaptist, spiritualistic, and other forms were also present to a lesser degree. However, rhetoricians were not simply reflectors of the learned reform proposals of Luther. Instead, they reshaped the reform messages, generally with the hope of bringing in religious reform without unduly disturbing the peace and unity of their communities. The two goals were not always compatible, and in the struggle to resolve the conflict between their economic and social interests and their religious aspirations, rhetoricians often revised or toned down the religious reform rhetoric, aspiring to appeal to as wide an audience as possible without overly alienating their authorities, all with the hope of keeping the peace. The later period (after 1539) witnessed both an attempted suppression of anticlerical drama and an increasing sophistication in how rhetoricians presented reform on stage. It also saw the rise both of Calvinist influence and of spiritualism. In both periods orthodox Catholic playwrights continued to write works supportive of the old faith, but these were only rarely polemical.

In order to deal fairly with all of the major issues relating to rhetorician reform drama, this book is divided into three parts. Part I is intended as an introductory section, providing in the first chapter an overview of society and religion in the Low Countries, especially focusing on the cities of Antwerp and Amsterdam, along with a brief survey of the history of the early Reformation in the Low Countries. As this monograph is the first book-length study of the chambers of rhetoric in English, chapter 2 contributes a general introduction to their history, with special attention to their profound sense of mission. Included here is a brief sketch of the institutional history of the chambers of rhetoric, an analysis of who joined them, and a discussion of the various types of plays they traditionally performed. Part II, also consisting of two chapters, turns to a more detailed analysis of rhetorician activity and religious reform within the specific urban contexts of Antwerp (chapter 3) and Amsterdam (chapter 4). It will become obvious here that an awareness of the specific urban context is essential in properly appraising the reform perspective of rhetorician drama. Part III discusses all of the serious plays known to have been composed during the era of Charles V. It does so by organizing these plays chronologically into three unequal periods, the first (chapter 5) covering the early period of the Reformation, from the first penetrations of Lutheran ideas in the Low Countries ca. 1519, to the eve of the most famous rhetorician event of the first half of the century, the Ghent competition of 1539. Anticlericalism is a dominant theme in this period, even for Catholic playwrights. Although the term 'anticlericalism' on its own says little about the content and extent of antipathy toward the clerical estate, in this discussion we will distinguish between traditional anticlericalism, the expression of sentiment by laypeople jealous of the privileges of the first estate, and 'reform anticlericalism,' the belief that the clerical estate and the ecclesiastical hierarchy needed to be transformed or eradicated. Also prevalent is the assumption that rhetoricians were at the very least the equals of the clergy, certainly in terms of literacy and knowledge of the Bible. Rhetoricians saw it as their duty to use the rhetorical arts to provide religious instruction to their audiences, much to the chagrin of the clerical estate. The next chapter deals in a detailed fashion with the Ghent competition, especially in light of the city's inability to control carnivalesque activity and protest, leading to the populist uprising which convulsed the community mere weeks after the visiting rhetoricians had departed the scene. Although it cannot be said that the plays performed there contributed directly to the revolt, it will become evident that the competition as a whole certainly inflamed passions for change and helped shake devotion to the traditional authorities.

The study then turns its attention to the plays composed during the last fifteen years or so of Emperor Charles V's reign, to see how rhetoricians changed their religious messages and how they presented these after the attempted suppression of rhetorician drama by the imperial government. Here is witnessed the changing face of the Reformation in the Low Countries, as Calvinism makes its initial penetrations after the apparent failure of the earlier Lutheran and Anabaptist forms. What will also become evident is the increasing popularity of the spiritualistic option, of reducing emphasis on religious externals and dogma in favour of an 'inner religion' and religious compromise. The book concludes with chapter 8's detailing of the rhetoricians' concerns relating to the frequent warfare and attendant economic and social disruption. When research for this project was begun, it was not expected that there would be enough plays advocating social and political reform to form a separate chapter. The number of such plays, and the strength of their pleas for peace, economic stability, and social harmony, were a surprise, and are clear evidence of the sincere hope on the part of literate urbanites such as the rhetoricians to express their desire for change in their society without major upheaval. At times these goals were indeed incompatible, leading to conflict with both secular and religious leaders. At the end of the day, most rhetoricians continued to support their authorities, but the stress of religious conflict and economic hardship had very clearly taken their toll not only on the emperor, who abdicated to his son Philip II in 1555, but also on the people of the Low Countries. It can be suggested, in fact, that the inability to find the balance between their desire to implement the correct form of religious faith and practice and their wish to see the end to needless warfare and economic hardship helped develop, by Charles's abdication, an embryonic resistance to Habsburg overlordship and to subservient patrician governance.

With this transition in governance, a new era began, both in the religious Reformation movement and in the history of the chambers of rhetoric. For one thing, the number of surviving manuscript and published plays multiplies in an extraordinary fashion. It was therefore decided to restrict the range of this study to the era of the native-born Charles V. This still left over one hundred plays that could safely be dated to the period. Attention was therefore concentrated only on the 'serious' plays, scripts which specifically addressed religious issues or which advocated or opposed some form of religious and social change, or made critical remarks about some aspect of society beyond the satirical comments of the comical scripts. This criteria still left eighty-four works to analyse, all of which are listed in the appendix, and are summarized at least once in the body of the text. Generally, these plays are described primarily in terms of their central plots and characters; secondary plots and allusions are dealt with only insofar as they contribute to the main thrust of the play. Roughly three-quarters of these plays are available in modern editions; the remaining are still found only in manuscript. Other archival sources that were essential ingredients in the proper evaluation of rhetorician drama were the city account books (*stadsrekeningen*), city council minutes, court records, chamber and guild records, imperial decrees, chronicles, and pamphlets.

A word on currency. There were two major units of exchange in the Low Countries by the end of the fifteenth century: pounds Flemish (the standard coin of the southern Netherlandic provinces) and pounds Holland; pounds Flemish consisted of twenty shillings or six gulden of forty groats each (240 groats). Stuivers were smaller units than shillings, with twenty stuivers to the gulden, hence 120 to the pound. The Holland pound was worth about the same as the standard coin of the realm, the Karolus gulden or guilder, first minted in gold in 1521 and worth about twenty stuivers or forty groats.[19] Unless otherwise indicated, references to curency will be in pounds Flemish or their equivalent.

Following standard usage in Dutch, I have listed Dutch names in the bibliography alphabetically according to the surname, without the preposition (van, de, etc.) while in the text I have included the preposition as part of the surname (Van de Putte, etc.).

List of Abbreviations

AA	*Antwerpsche archievenblad*
ARG	*Archiv für Reformationsgescheichte / Archive for Reformation History*
Belgisch Museum	*Belgisch museum voor de Nederdeutsche tael-en letterkunde en de geschiedenis des vaderlands*
BRN	Cramer, S., and Pijper, F., eds. *Bibliotheca Reformatoria Neerlandica.* 10 vols. The Hague, 1903.
CDIN	Fredericq, Paul, ed. *Corpus Documentorum Inquisitionis Haereticae Pravitatis Neerlandicae.* 5 vols. Ghent and The Hague, 1889–1900.
DAN	Mellink, Albert F., et al., eds. *Documenta Anabaptistica Neerlandica.* Leiden, 1975–. I *Friesland en Groningen (1530–1550).* II *Amsterdam, 1536–1578.* 1980 VII *Friesland (1551–1601) and Groningen (1538–1601).* 1995.
DB	*Doopsgezinde Bijdragen*
JdF	*Jaarboek van de koninklijke soevereine Hoofdkamer van Retorica 'De Fonteine' te Gent.*
MQR	*Mennonite Quarterly Review*
NAK	*Nederlands archief voor kerkgeschiedenis / Dutch Review of Church History*
SCJ	*Sixteenth Century Journal*
TNTL	*Tijdschrift voor Nederlandsche Taal-en Letterkunde*
VHB	*Varia Historica Brabantica*
VMKVA	*Verslagen en Mededelingen van de Koninklijke Vlaamse Academie voor Taal-en Letterkunde*

PART I

Drama and Society in the Low Countries

1

Civic Culture and Religious Reform in the Netherlands

In early modern Europe, drama entertained, informed, angered, motivated to action, and defended the status quo. Audience reaction to a particular stage enactment was inextricably linked to the specific cultural and civic contexts of the play's viewers and performers. After all, the plays performed reflected not only the interests of the playwright and actors, but also the specific needs and goals of the particular guild, fraternity, court, city, or patron which sponsored them.[1] The most important composers and performers of vernacular drama in the Low Countries were without a doubt the amateur literary societies known as the chambers of rhetoric, organizations which were found in most urban centres of the region by 1500. Writing the history of the urban context of drama for the Low Countries as a whole is therefore a daunting task, but one that has borne fruit for historians of many cities and regions.[2] Given the limited goals of this study it will be possible to analyse closely the urban context of only a couple of centres – Antwerp in Brabant and Amsterdam in Holland – for each in turn was the most important and prosperous city for the southern and northern Netherlands respectively.[3] It will become apparent that in spite of the organizational similarity among chambers, their specific developments and experiences during the early Reformation could differ considerably, depending on a wide range of variables. The two examples here highlight only some of the important influences brought to bear on rhetoricians and some of their possible responses. Before embarking on a detailed examination of the history of these chambers in chapters 3 and 4, this chapter will present a contextual overview of the social and political structure of each of these urban communes and will provide a general description of the religious upheaval which confronted both the rulers and the ruled of the Netherlands. It will be followed by a chapter describing in brief terms the history and nature of the chambers of rhetoric and their drama.

Despite local differences in governance, by 1515 both Antwerp and Amsterdam were under the direct lordship of Emperor Charles V and his regent, first his aunt, Margaret of Austria (d. 1530), followed by his sister, Mary of Hungary (1531–55). Imperial administration was in the hands of a central council, which oversaw the conduct of law and finance and which provided the regent with noble advisors.[4] There was in the Low Countries no equivalent to the south German Imperial Free Cities, for urban communes of the north owed their emperor considerable political allegiance and financial tribute. Charles relied heavily on his Netherlandic cities to finance his military campaigns, although such financial burdens had ostensibly to be approved by the cities themselves meeting in their States General, the body representing the landed nobility and urban communes of a particular region. The States General of Holland, increasingly one of the most important of these, sought constantly to resist Charles V's centralizing policies, knowing full well that if he succeeded they would be forced to accede automatically to his financial requests. As a result of their economic power within their provinces, both Antwerp and Amsterdam came to exert inordinate influence within their respective regional governing bodies.

Taking advantage of the economic decline of the previously dominant southern Netherlandic cities of Ghent and Bruges, Antwerp had also by 1515 become the most progressive economic and, to a large extent, cultural centre for the Low Countries.[5] Amsterdam, although a relatively new city, was fast becoming the economic centre for the north. Furthermore, neither city was home to the imperial court, as were Brussels and The Hague; therefore, each lacked the direct influence of the royal family on its cultural activities. Drama produced by rhetoricians of Antwerp and Amsterdam, then, was more likely to represent local burgher interests without the complications of imperial interference.

Antwerp

Antwerp, a fast growing city of nearly 50,000 people by 1500, almost doubled in size in the next sixty years.[6] Its success was based principally on trade and commerce and its port became northern Europe's busiest. Foreign merchants were in abundance in the city's great market squares, dealing in a wide range of precious metals from the New World and Eastern Europe; luxury articles such as silk from Asia; wine, salt, and other foodstuffs from all over Europe; wool from England; and Flemish fine cloth.[7] Antwerp's merchants therefore engaged in a wide range of commercial activity and while the cloth of the nearby Flemish cities was still a major element of their trade, they also had the foresight to dominate the transport of other products as well. The city's commercial success obviously attracted both entrepeneurs and labourers and it seems that the latter fared somewhat better in Antwerp than in most other Low Country towns when it came to living conditions, although real wages generally fell behind the rise in rents and foodstuffs.[8] However, compared to the sluggish economy and high unemployment of Ghent and Bruges, Antwerp seemed a city of endless opportunity. The tremendous population growth that the city witnessed between 1500 and 1567 suggests that at the very least a large number of people believed it to be so.

Governing this burgeoning population was a relatively small and stable political elite dominated by the patricians who had converted their landed noble inheritance or merchant wealth into *renten* investments, allowing them to live like urban gentlemen with the spare time to govern the city without pay. Each year members of these patrician families dominated the two political bodies of Antwerp, the College of mayors (*burgermeesteren*) and aldermen (*schepenen*), and the Broad Council (*brede raad*). The two mayors were elected by their fellows within the College for one or at most two years, with one mayor as 'external mayor' (*buitenbergermeester*), responsible for major political and military affairs, and the other as 'internal mayor,' overseeing matters of internal justice.[9] Advising these two were sixteen aldermen, most of them from the patrician or upper merchant families. In spite of the activity of the larger Broad Council, it was the smaller College that made the important decisions for the city. However, the Broad Council did provide other prominent citizens, such as merchants and prosperous master craftsmen, with a forum in which to express their opinion about or dissatisfaction with the city's governance. Members of this larger body were drawn from the 'privileged citizenry' (*poorterij – rentier* patricians), civic guard, guild deacons, and the district supervisors (*wijkmeesters*). Normally four captains (*hoofdmannen*) of the *poorterij* sat on the council, along with twenty-four *wijkmeesters* (two from each of the city's twelve districts) and a similar number of guild deacons, who were directed by the head deacons of the three most prominent international merchant guilds, the shippers (*schippers*), merchants (*meerse-niers*), and clothmakers (*lakenbereeders*). By and large, Jenny Vanroelen suggests, the *brede raad* represented the welfare of the well-to-do citizens and the middling estates – the upper artisans, shopkeepers, and lesser merchants.[10] While a guild deacon could rise to high positions, such as *wijkmeester* or alderman, the political structure aimed at maintaining the dominant position of Antwerp's old families. As Thomas Brady, Jr., has noted, in most sixteenth-century cities with a combined patrician-guild government, real power lay in the hands of a few patrician families, members of which managed to enter and dominate leadership of the guilds.[11] This appears to have been the case for Antwerp.

The city's social and economic development naturally favoured those involved in commerce and industry. It appears that the city's economic expansion after 1500, which became especially dynamic during the 1540s, provided unusual opportunities for enterprising artisans and retailers, especially those of the so-called middle class (*midden-klasse*), to partake of the city's prosperity and to rise up the social ladder. Wilfrid Brulez chronicles the economic history of Antwerp as one of steady, moderate growth from the end of the fifteenth century to around 1535; a much faster and dynamic rise from 1535/40 to around 1566; a stable plateau to about 1585; and finally a spectacular decline in the next decade.[12] A major but not the sole factor for Antwerp's reversal of fortunes was, of course, the Eighty Years War against Spain, which saw its surrender to Spanish troops in 1585 and the exodus of a large number of its leading entrepreneurs, many of whom were Calvinists. Until the Spanish occupation, however, Antwerp's economic situation was generally very positive. H. Soly, in fact, writes of a 'democratization of business' in Antwerp during the 1540s.[13] At the same time inflation in the cost of foodstuffs and rents outstripped increases in the average labourer's wages, although unemployment was not nearly the problem here as in the Flemish towns. Naturally overcrowding and substandard housing added to labourers' complaints. There were also periodic crises during this relatively prosperous era, usually caused by warfare. For example, the war between Christian of Denmark and Frederick of Holstein in 1531 led to the closure of Baltic trade to all Netherlandic traders. The result was horrendous inflation and hunger throughout the Low Countries which lasted until well past 1532. The following decade also witnessed the unsuccessful siege of Antwerp by the Guelders captain, Martin van Rossum, in July 1542, resulting in serious rural losses.

Overall, those with the means to take advantage of the opportunities were better prepared to cope with the financial crisis which followed in the 1550s. Among other factors, the Valois-Habsburg war of 1551, with the concomitant closure of the waterways, led to a major downturn in trade. At the same time grain prices increased dramatically while the purchasing power of wage earners declined noticeably. The imperial majesty's decision to allow foreign labourers to work on Antwerp's city walls in 1549 and to demand higher excise taxes further exacerbated the population's woes. Finally in 1554 open conflict broke out between the retrenched 'great entrepreneurs' and the the city's middle-ranked artisans and businessmen, whose rising expectations were frustrated by the economic stagnation.[14] Even so, the fact that Antwerp's population waited so long to engage in violent confrontation speaks volumes for the unusually positive economic conditions in the city until 1550; most other Flemish and Brabantish cities had experienced several such uprisings long before the middle of the century.

In spite of the city's relative economic prosperity, Antwerp's rulers were hampered by their inability to raise sufficient revenues to balance their treasurers' accounts. For example, in 1531 the city ended the year with a shortfall of 23,868 pounds Flemish (hereafter £ Fl.), an amount nearly equalling the year's revenues of 24,609£ Fl. This deficit was a result not merely of internal financial matters but largely of the emperor's ever increasing demands on the city's treasury to finance his ongoing wars against France and the Turks. By 1548 the city's debt had become so burdensome that the mayors pleaded with Regent Mary of Hungary for assistance, which she provided by authorizing an increase in the beer excise and a sale of heritable annuities (*erfrenten*) to raise funds. Soon the city's revenues caught up to expenses[15] but Antwerp's prosperity was not to last, for of all major commercial centres in the Low Countries, it suffered the most from the oppressive military actions of Charles V's son, Philip II, during the Eighty Years War, especially when the city capitulated to the duke of Parma in 1585. It was never to regain its earlier ascendancy in trade but was forced to hand that torch over to Amsterdam.[16]

Amsterdam

As a much smaller and younger commune, the north Holland city of Amsterdam was a clear contrast to its older rival of Brabant. Yet both cities had achieved their economic prosperity by monopolizing large-scale trade for their region, although Amsterdam did not come any-where close to achieving Antwerp's status until well after mid century. Moreover, in both cities political life was dominated by the patrician elite, most of whom had made their wealth by commerce. As we shall see, Amsterdam's merchant-patriciate was not nearly as advanced on the road to gentlemanly status as was Antwerp's, a factor that may account for some noticeable differences in policy toward cultural activities and expenses.

In 1514 Amsterdam incorporated some 2,500 houses or roughly 11,000 persons, growing to some 3,000 dwellings by 1543 and to ca. 6,000 by 1565. Long before the immense influx of merchants and artisans from the southern Netherlands, Amsterdam was well on its way to becoming one of the most important cities and economic centres in northern Europe. After 1585 its growth exploded, tripling its population from some 30,000 to over 100,000 by the middle of the seventeenth century and catapulting Amsterdam into the position of dynamo for the Dutch Republic's 'Golden Age' as well as Europe's most important financial centre.[17]

Although paling in comparison to the later dynamism, Amsterdam's growth between 1514 and 1565 was considerable, and like the situation in Antwerp, led to significant strain on the city's housing and charitable institutions. The inflation which accompanied such dynamic commercial expansion hit the artisanal and labouring estates the hardest as wages lagged behind rising rents and grain prices. As in Antwerp the closure of Baltic trade in 1531–2 led to terrible hardship among Amsterdam's artisans and day labourers. The following two years, and again in 1542–4, Holland's merchant shippers were engaged in open naval warfare against their principal Baltic Sea competitors, the merchants of the German Hanse. Closure of the North Sea trade routes hurt Amsterdam's merchant class more profoundly than Antwerp's, for at this point the northern port city's precarious economic prosperity was based almost entirely on the North Sea trade in herring and grain. In 1545 a truce allowed Amsterdam's shippers to ply the northern trade routes in record numbers, reaching a high of 2,140 passages through the Sont in 1566, nearly triple the earlier record.[18] Although the opening of hostilities between the Netherlands and Spain after 1566 led to an immediate decline in such trade, when Amsterdam finally chose the side of the Dutch Republic in 1578, its prosperity seemed assured and after 1585 Amsterdam replaced Antwerp as the great international commercial nexus and considerably diversified its trade.[19]

Unfortunately, not everyone benefited equally from the general prosperity of Amsterdam's merchants. The crisis years, especially of 1531–2 and 1542–4, resulted in considerable unrest in the city, some of which will be discussed later in this study. And while Cl. Lesger notes that employment opportunities were good during the prosperous periods between 1545 and 1569 and after 1578, there was no great demand for labour for most of the first half of the century and wages improved little.[20] With the constant influx of immigrants, rents rose relentlessly as did the price of rye, the staple grain of Amsterdam's wage earners, especially during the early years of the 1520s and 1530s and the middle of the 1540s, 1550s, and 1560s.[21] Overall, then, the vast majority of Amsterdam's population lived a precarious existence during Charles V's reign and in some respects possessed fewer employment alternatives and markets than their Antwerp contemporaries. Certainly there is little evidence of a 'democratization of business' in Amsterdam prior to the last decades of the century.

Despite their city's smaller size, Amsterdam's rulers faced a greater challenge in maintaining peace and order in their commune compared with the magistrates of Antwerp. Not surprisingly, Amsterdam's political structure was organized quite differently from its southern competitor. By the start of the sixteenth century Amsterdam's government was dominated by the office of mayor or *burgermeester*, four of whom governed the city at any particular time and who were elected by the city's aldermen and old mayors without any interference from the count, provincial governor (*stadtholder*), or sheriff (*schout*, the legal representative of the ruling lord). To maintain continuity, one of the old mayors remained a member of the *burgermeester* foursome for an extra year.[22] Although in the fourteenth century Amsterdam's *burgermeesters* were to act as 'helpers and advisors' to the sheriff and aldermen, throughout the following century they had appropriated to themselves most of the tasks of governance: finances; protection of the city's rights; and oversight of public works, ecclesiastical life, and support of the poor. Actual administration of these matters was eventually delegated to colleges consisting primarily of former mayors, such as the *thesaurieren*, which directed financial matters; the *weesmeesters*, who cared for the orphans; and the *accijnsmeesters*, who oversaw the collection of duties.[23] The mayors also appointed all the other important civic officials, such as the city secretaries (*statdssecretarissen*), the pensionary (*pensionaris*), who acted as the city's legal representative in external matters, overseers of the guilds, and the like. Furthermore, all former mayors sat together on the so-called Old Council (*oud-raad*) to act as an advisory body for the current mayors.

All that remained for the sheriff and aldermen was the administration of justice, and even there the *burgermeesters* had to be consulted on capital and other serious sentences. Selection of the city's sheriff, traditionally made by the ruling lord, was leased to the city during most of the sixteenth century. In Amsterdam the *schout* served almost exclusively as president of the *schepenbank* (aldermen's bench), the seat of justice for the city. The aldermen were elected in a somewhat unusual way: first fourteen candidates were selected by the thirty-six members representing the citizenry in the council (*vroedschap*, literally 'wisdom'); then the governor (*stadtholder*) selected seven of these to serve on the aldermen's bench. While membership on the *vroedschap* was originally by yearly election, in the latter half of the fifteenth century its members gained the right to sit for life. The *vroedschap* acted as the principal advisory body for the *burgermeesters*, most of whom also sat on the *vroedschap*, a body which dissented rarely from the direction of the *burgermeesters*. Much more than in Antwerp, the mayors of Amsterdam dominated the governance of the city. In both cities, however, the political structure was an oligarchical one, and the direction of Amsterdam policy, perhaps even more so than Antwerp's, was usually in the direction that best served the patrician elite who dominated all governing organs.[24]

Culture and Society in Antwerp and Amsterdam

The rulers of both Antwerp and Amsterdam were from a similar socioeconomic group – the privileged patricians whose families had established a near stranglehold over political leadership of their respective communities. This does not mean, however, that they necessarily governed in an identical fashion or maintained similar attitudes toward such aspects of urban society as religion, social welfare, or culture. In this respect, the intriguing study by Peter Burke comparing and contrasting the status, wealth, power, lifestyle, and attitudes of Venetian and Amsterdam elites may help illuminate some of the similarities and differences between Antwerp's and Amsterdam's ruling families. While concerned primarily with the long seventeenth century (1578–1719), Burke's description of the differing characteristics of noble and bourgeois elites can be used judiciously in the contexts of sixteenth-century Antwerp and Amsterdam.[25]

According to Burke, the governing elite of Venice was monopolized by the nobility, while that of Amsterdam by commoners, particularly prosperous merchants. Members of the noble estate, not only in Venice but elsewhere in Europe, were concerned with display, ceremony, public splendour, and magnificence in the arts, often regardless of expense.[26] In contrast, the Amsterdam elite had 'no such conscious traditional style,' although their lives were far from uncomfortable.[27] Before Burke's categories can be used here, the caution of Brady, Jr, must be heeded, that in the fifteenth and sixteenth centuries wealthy burghers sought to replicate the leisured lifestyle of the aristocratic gentleman and that the nobility, possessing status but not necessarily the wealth of the upper third estate, sought to enter the business world of the merchant.[28] But our concern is with predominant attitudes, and in the first half of the sixteenth century Amsterdam was a relatively new city, based on the entrepreneurial activity of a vigorous merchant class. Its merchant patriciate did not yet have the opportunity to live like leisured gentlemen from their investment income. Antwerp, however, had been a centre of economic prosperity for several generations and aristocratic practices and attitudes could therefore predominate. It becomes apparent that the Antwerp elite combined noble and bourgeois, or rentier and entrepreneurial, attitudes. In contrast, Burke's characterization of Amsterdam's seventeenth-century elite as predominantly entrepreneurial is even more true of the previous century.[29] A glance at the cities' magistracy confirms this supposition.

As noted above, Antwerp was governed by a combined patrician and guild government; unlike Amsterdam, however, many titled nobleman sat on the city council.[30] Although not the closed aristocratic society of seventeenth-century Venice, in Antwerp too the landed nobility were able to exert considerable influence on the shaping of their city's policies. A survey of the names of burgermasters (two each year) and aldermen (usually sixteen each year) reveals the increasing dominance of the gentry within the city council. Between 1520 and 1529, burgermasters were nobles (*heere, rijder,* or *junker*) twelve times out of twenty (60 per cent) and 18.6 per cent of aldermen positions were filled by known nobles. Noble families which predominated the lists included the Van Liers, Van Berchems, and Van den Werves. Several of the aldermen appear also to have come from cadet lines of these important noble families.[31] Another 19.25 per cent of aldermen bore the title of *meester,* which normally referred to the possession of a law degree, and occasionally to priestly office, noble birth, or university education. Between 1530 and 1539 an average of 75 per cent of Antwerp's mayors were gentlemen and 18.8 per cent of aldermen bore this title.[32] The next decade, however, witnessed an increase in the dominant role played by the Antwerp gentry; between 1540 and 1555, a minimum of 24.7 per cent of aldermen bore the title of *heere* (22.5 per cent more were masters) and nearly all, 84 per cent, of the city's burgermasters were ennobled, although some of these titles could have been newly won.[33] Clearly Antwerp was ruled by an aristocratic faction and even if a number of the noble titles were recent acquisitions, the very fact that they were able to achieve such suggests Antwerp's higher magistracy sought to rule the city along the lines of noble virtues, one of which was patronage of the arts. As already noted, the nobility stressed style, magnificence, and generosity in the use of their wealth.[34]

In direct contrast to Antwerp's elite, we have seen that Amsterdam's government was a strictly merchant-patrician affair, dominated by a small number of extremely prosperous families.[35] There were guilds but they had no significant political influence.[36] While upper-class merchants often desired to achieve the social status and leisured lifestyle of the gentry, their merchant training and experience predisposed them to principles of thrift in financial management. It can therefore be suggested that while Antwerp was governed along aristocratic lines, Amsterdam was ruled by 'upper bourgeois' attitudes. Both Amsterdam's and Antwerp's regents were obviously concerned with mundane matters such as finances and defence. A look at the two cities' account books (*stadsrekeningen*) reveals Antwerp's magistrates' penchant for lavish gifts and ostentatious display and Amsterdam's government's desire to avoid unnecessary or frivolous expenditures.

Each year the Antwerp treasurer recorded the funding of religious and cultural events such as processions and festivals, as well as performances by musicians and rhetoricians. In 1537, for example, the city spent over 207£ Fl. (equivalent to 1,242 guilders) on what can be called cultural activities. While this amounts to approximately .3 per cent of the city's total expenditures (67,430£ Fl.), it is in a league of its own compared to Amsterdam, which spent a meagre 6£ Fl. 6s (not quite 38 guilders) on similar activities, or .06 per cent of its total expenditures of 9,736£ Fl.[37] It is also important to note that from 1530 to 1549 Antwerp ended each financial year with a significant deficit; in 1537 the city was 27,836£ Fl. in debt, not having brought in nearly enough to cover the year's expenses.[38] By 1543 the deficit had increased to 36,015£ Fl. and it was only through the second half of the 1540s, especially after the fiscal reform decrees issued by the imperial government in 1548, that Antwerp's treasurers were able to balance their books.[39] Amsterdam, on the other hand, was not only able to balance its budget, but to pass on to following years a substantial surplus throughout this period.[40] Why did Antwerp's city fathers, clearly in economic difficulty with an oppressive deficit, expend their city's resources so lavishly while Amsterdam's magistrates, working with a substantial surfeit of funds each year, were so stingy when it came to matters of culture? The answer seems to lie, as suggested above, with the differences in attitude between the noble and merchant classes. These differences can also be seen in their respective attitudes to the drama of the chambers of rhetoric. However, before turning to a closer examination of drama in these two centres, there must first be provided a brief overview of another major development that impinged on all facets of life and culture in the Low Countries of the sixteenth century, and that is, of course, the Reformation.

The Early Reformation in the Low Countries, 1519–56

One problem facing the political leadership of not only Antwerp and Amsterdam but of every town in the Low Countries was how to respond to the increasing demands for religious reform that had begun to gather strength only a year or two after the ninety-five theses of the German reformer, Martin Luther, had been circulated in Latin in 1517. Initially vocalized by young humanists, reform-minded clergy, and members of Luther's own Augustinian order, proposals for evangelical reform soon captivated a good number of laypeople in the Netherlands, especially, it seems, those of the artisanal estate. Very quickly city magistrates found themselves in an extremely difficult bind, for their overlord, Charles V, was vigorously opposed to religious schism in his domains and insisted that local lords and civic leaders exert themselves to eradicate the threat. At the same time, city magistrates in particular wished to avoid doing anything to disturb the relative tranquillity of their urban communes, especially since that peace was delicately maintained at the best of times. Moreover, many magistrates themselves were sympathetic to some degree of ecclesiastical reform, especially with the prospect of further secularization of church and monastic property within their walls. A number of civic officials seem also to have been evangelically minded themselves. While they could not openly refuse to obey the numerous imperial mandates against heresy, most of them sought ways to hinder or delay the full implementation of the harsh heresy codes. For one thing, they regarded such heresy placards as little more than another attempt at administrative centralization on the part of the Habsburgs, something that the magistrates and nobility of the Low Countries had been resisting for decades and would continue to do so; such, in fact, provided one of the primary reasons for the later outbreak of the Eighty Years War. At the same time, Dutch magistrates and nobles were often nervous about the social upheaval which seemed to accompany popular religious reform; the disaster of the German Peasants' War of 1524–6 was not something that they wished to see replicated in their own territories.

Compared to the attention paid to the Calvinist Reformation of 1566 and beyond, the subject of the so-called early Reformation in the Netherlands has only recently received significant scholarly analysis. Of course, a major reason for this relative neglect is the simple fact that the earlier attempts at reform, whether conducted by early evangelicals (including the so-called sacramentarians) and Lutherans during the 1520s and early 1530s or the more infamous Anabaptists of the 1530s and 1540s, all failed in the broad aim of establishing significant, widescale religious change. Yet it has become increasingly clear in the important studies of Johan Decavele, A.C. Duke, Albert F. Mellink, James D. Tracy, J. Trapman, and many others, that the later success of the Calvinists owed a great deal to the earlier reform movements.[41] In order to appreciate fully the rhetorician drama composed and performed during the reign of Charles V, it is necessary to provide a brief overview of the religious experience of the Dutch people during the sixteenth century.

The Devotio Moderna

Before the Reformation, the Low Countries had become home to one of the greatest movements of medieval lay religious reform, the *Devotio Moderna*. This movement, formalized in the Brothers and Sisters of the Common Life, emphasized mystical contemplation and the correct inner disposition of the individual when partaking of the sacraments and meditating on Christ's Passion.[42] Its most famous devotional manual, *The Imitation of Christ*, became an immensely popular best-seller, not only in the Low Countries, but all over Europe. Perhaps the most controversial question posed by scholars of the Netherlandic Reformation(s) is whether it was shaped primarily by foreign religious impulses or by the indigenous reforming currents within the Low Countries during the fourteenth and fifteenth centuries.[42] It is not necessary here to review the vigorous debate between Albert Hyma and R.R. Post on whether or not the *Devotio Moderna* in general and the Brothers and Sisters of the Common Life in particular significantly influenced the reforming movements of the sixteenth-century Netherlands. Post's detailed rejoinder to Hyma's positive response still dominates the scholarly scene, and most serious studies tend to describe the *Devotio Moderna* as a late-medieval Catholic reforming movement with little direct connection to the later Reformation.[43] For example, John van Engen recently suggested that

> Broadly speaking, however, scholars are now in agreement that this religious movement, whatever its later influences or permutations, was decidedly 'late medieval' and 'Catholic' in origin, not somehow an early form of the Renaissance or the Reformation. Yet within the later medieval Church, these brothers and sisters sought to work out institutional structures and devotional forms consonant with their particular vision and pursuit of Christian perfection. That effort sometimes brought changes or confrontations resonant of issues raised later in the Renaissance or Reformation.[44]

There is little doubt now that the answers provided by most of the Brothers and Sisters of the Common Life and those suggested by sixteenth-century evangelicals were essentially different. Certainly the quiet reflection on the inner significance of the sacraments as advocated by the Brothers and Sisters was a far cry from the vigorous anticlericalism and iconoclasm witnessed in the Netherlands during the early Reformation. At the same time, the stress on the inner reception of the body and blood of Christ in the Eucharist may have predisposed some to disregard the external observance of the sacrament. Such may have been the case with Cornelis Hoen (ca. 1460–1524), jurist with the Court of Holland, who seems to have rejected the doctrine of transubstantiation after reading some of the writings of Wesel Gansfort on the subject of the Eucharist. Of course Gansfort never denied the doctrine, but as Duke points out, his suggestion that the worth of the sacrament possibly depended on the inner spiritual health of the recipient, 'may have provided the springboard Hoen required to reach his more radical exegesis.'[45]

It is also evident that the general devotees of the *Devotio Moderna* and the members of later reform conventicles and movements shared one important feature: both included laypeople intensely interested in the reform of abuses within the church and the improvement of spiritual life among their contemporaries, both lay and religious. In this sense, then, it is possible to suggest that urbanites of the Low Countries had become quite used to taking responsibility over religious matters and criticizing those spiritual leaders who may not have maintained high spiritual standards. Johan Decavele, in fact, writes of a growing middle class seeking 'religious emancipation' in the Flemish towns.[46] The *Devotio Moderna* may thus have contributed to this predisposition of Netherlandic urbanites to religious activism.[47] Assuredly the rise of religious confraternities and lay-funded altars throughout the towns of the Low Countries also attests to a strong desire on the part of many Netherlanders to be more actively engaged in their religious life. The tremendous burst of anticlerical sentiment in the first years of the early Reformation in the Low Countries (ca. 1519–24) therefore speaks volumes about the religious fervour and sincerity of laypeople. Whatever the later consequences of anticlerical propaganda, it provides no evidence of 'incipient scepticism' among the Dutch populace. Of course there are differing types of anticlerical rhetoric and action, ranging from the mildly sarcastic criticism of devoted Catholics, to the sharper yet still essentially loyal critique of humanists such as Erasmus, to the full-scale attack on the priesthood and the entire sacramental system of the Protestants. Thus the specific meaning of the term 'anticlerical' will be determined by its context; suffice it to say here that once the Reformation was well underway, even the gentle anticlericalism of otherwise orthodox Catholics was regarded with deep suspicion by the ecclesiastical authorities.[48]

On top of this indigenous 'reform activism,' Decavele notes that the major towns of the Netherlands were profoundly open to 'all manner of foreign influences.'[49] For a long time the people of the Low Countries were governed by a foreign ruler who sought to reshape the regions' political institutions in a non-indigenous fashion. This remained true even of Charles V, who, although born and raised in Ghent, tended to use Spanish models of rule, including that of the Spanish Inquisition. Furthermore, the major market towns and commercial ports of the Low Countries, especially Antwerp, were magnets for merchants from all over Europe, bringing with them their peculiar culture and attitudes, whether Italian, French, German, or English, or

Jewish for that matter. The impact of the Low Countries' importance as an international trade nexus is clearly seen in the penetration of Renaissance humanism into the region. At the same time, this new movement of educational and cultural renewal through *bonae litterae*, which originated in the Italian city states, took on a distinctive shape in the context of the Low Countries.

Netherlandic Humanism

According to Jozef IJsewijn, little obvious humanist activity can be discerned in the Low Countries until the second half of the fifteenth century, when Italian merchants began arriving in Bruges and Antwerp bringing with them their humanistic aspirations and ideas.[50] Prior to this period the closest thing to humanist reform of Latin school pedagogy was seen among the Brothers and Sisters of the Common Life, who in a limited fashion supported improvements in the Latin curriculum.[51] It is also clear that the Low Countries' strong current of lay spirituality, of which the *Devotio Moderna* was as much a symptom as a cause, helped stamp Netherlandic humanism with a particular goal of pursuing the humanist program of *humane litterae* not solely for its own sake but essentially as a means of reforming Christian studies and Christendom in the direction of *pietas* and *vita christiani*.[52] One of the earliest serious attempts to combine Italian humanism with the *Devotio Moderna* was made by the Groningen humanist Wessel Gansfort (1420–89), and even Rudolf Agricola of Groningen (1444–85), whose broad goal was to make the Germanic lands more 'Latinate' than the Italian states,[53] struggled to develop a classical education that would develop Christian character, one that showed influence from the writings of the *Devotio Moderna*.[54] After 1490 the number of humanistically trained scholars in the Low Countries increased rapidly and they turned their considerable skill to revamping the educational system, especially the city schools, along classical lines and applying the ethics of Cicero and especially Christ and his early followers as discovered in the ancient manuscripts and original languages.

The epitome of this 'humanistic Christianity' was, of course, Erasmus, justifiably the most famous humanist north of the Alps.[55] Although clearly influenced by the spirit of piety prominent in his homeland, Erasmus disdained much of his early experience in the school residence of the Deventer Brothers of the Common Life as well as his life as an Augustinian monk. He regarded himself instead as a leading member of an international company of scholars. Yet several of his most important writings, especially the *Enchiridion Militis Christiani* (published in 1503), are infused with a piety akin to that of the *Devotio Moderna* and are composed in eloquent humanistic style. His goal was to restore Christendom to pristine Christianity; as he wrote of his homeland: 'Here pupils are taught, here philosophy and eloquence are learned, so that we may know Christ and may celebrate his glory. This is the whole goal of erudition and eloquence.'[56] In large measure due to the dynamic printing industry of the Low Countries, which eagerly took up the publication of humanist works such as those of Erasmus,[57] his influence on Netherlandic scholars, teachers, political leaders, even merchants and artisans was profound, helping to strengthen hope in a peaceable reform of church and society in their lifetime. Such was not to be the case.

Luther and the Early Evangelical Movement

Long before the initial penetrations of Lutheran ideas into the Low Countries, many Dutch humanists and laypeople had taken upon themselves the duty of criticizing the abuses within their church and society. Naturally the cause of educational reform, of replacing the tired, old scholastic curriculum with the new vibrant humanistic one, was at the top of the humanists' agenda. Moreover, humanists and lay-people alike, inspired in part by the devotional writings of the *Devotio Moderna*, increasingly gave vent to their frustration with a church leadership that failed, they believed, to live up to its own spiritual standards. Like Erasmus, many writers also condemned what they saw as the superstitious beliefs and practices of their contemporaries who, in their passion for purchasing indulgences, going on pilgrimages, venerating saints' images, witnessing the elevation of the Host, and so on, neglected the inner significance of these rites and sacraments, approaching a magical notion of their external practice.[58] Writers from both the humanist and *Devotio Moderna* camps sought to counteract this trend by emphasizing the correct inner disposition of the individual toward religious activity and by chiding religious leaders for encouraging a crass popular devotionalism.

Such gentle critique of the religious establishment could be tolerated when there was little threat of popular unrest, as with the case of Wessel Gansfort, whose writings criticizing the sale of indulgences, papal authority, and religious externalism gained serious official attention only after they were reprinted in the 1520s in support of the evangelical cause.[59] The situation changed, however, with publication of the inflammatory writings of Luther. The controversy sparked by the Saxon Augustinian and Wittenberg professor very quickly spread throughout the Germanic lands. A large number of humanists came to see his condemnation of scholastic theology and sale of indulgences as part of the general humanistic crusade to reform the abuses of the church. The church authorities and the emperor himself took another view, soon not only condemning his controversial ideas but also suppressing all critique of the policies of the religious hierarchy. Thus it came about that Cornelius Grapheus, secretary of Antwerp, was arrested in the spring of 1522 for having written and published a year before an introduction to a fifteenth-century treatise opposing monastic vows. In this piece Grapheus had merely continued the humanists' condemnation of the scholastic monopoly on education and promoted the translation of the Scriptures into the vernacular so that the 'philosophy of Christ' (as the core of Erasmus's 'Christian humanism' was called) could be more widely known. In the light of the Lutheran threat, even this mild reform sentiment was now harshly condemned, and on 23 April 1522, Grapheus was forced to recant.[60]

He fared better, however, than many others who dared to express similar views. In November of 1519 the University of Leuven (Louvain) formally condemned Luther's ideas, and the imperial government sought to expunge the Lutheran threat quickly by publicly burning his publications, encouraging the mendicants to preach against his ideas, and arresting any suspected Dutch Augustinians. In February 1522 the prior of the Antwerp house, Jacob Praepositus, was forced to recant, while in the following year two Augustinians were burned at the stake in Brussels and the Antwerp house itself was razed to the ground.[61] These early Augustinian supporters of Luther (many of whom had trained in the same house as he had) probably preached a relatively accurate version of Luther's ideas, such as justification by faith alone. One can only surmise that the further removed a preacher of Lutheran ideas was from the intellectual context of reform-Augustinianism, the less accurately they were presented to audiences.

Other educated propagandists for the Lutheran cause faced a fate similar to that of the Dutch Augustinians or were forced to stop open proclamation of their reform ideas or flee the Low Countries. During the reign of Charles V hundreds of religious dissenters were executed for the crime of heresy in the Low Countries; nowhere else in his empire was Charles V able so rigorously to enforce his heresy edicts.[62] This ferocious attack on religious nonconformism had the effect of driving the reform movement underground and of throwing its leadership into the hands of reform-minded artisans, many of whom had received their initial reform training in small conventicle meetings headed originally by former clergy or teachers.[63] With the virtual disappearance of formally educated leaders (certainly by 1530), reform activity became increasingly turbulent as lay reformers became impatient with the oppressive policies of their higher lords. Although not yet ready to risk sectarianism, absence from obligatory communion services became common among the evangelicals of the Low Countries.[64]

What did lay evangelicals believe? Unfortunately, most of what we know about their beliefs comes from court records, for there have survived in the Netherlands relatively few broadsheets or other examples of popular propaganda, at least compared to the surviving German examples so profitably examined by Robert Scribner.[65] What is discernible from the available sources is that from 1525 on there was an increase in what has been described as 'sacramentarian' sentiment, or the rejection of the sacramental character of the Eucharist and of the Real Presence of Christ in the bread and wine.[66] Although not all Dutch evangelicals held such a view (hence one should avoid using the term 'sacramentarians' to describe all early reformers of the Low Countries),[67] this sacramentarian sentiment was loudly expressed not only in informal sermons and publications, but also in action; in 1526 two weavers of Delft were arrested for threatening a priest with a knife and smashing his monstrance, the ceremonial vehicle which housed the host during processions.[68] Concomitant with this was an increasingly virulent anticlericalism, especially as urban artisans, long fed up with the economically privileged position of urban monastic houses, took over leadership of reform. There also seems to have been disgust with the popular devotion exhibited to the Virgin Mary; the later Anabaptist leader, David Joris, for one was arrested in 1528 for disseminating an anticlerical and iconoclastic pamphlet as well as for openly denouncing those participating in a procession in honour of the Virgin.[69] Also important was the demand of laypeople for the right to read the Scriptures in the vernacular, a demand that printers were more than happy to meet, evidenced by the dramatic growth in the number of editions of the Bible, especially of pocket-sized editions of the New Testament (the printing of which was illegal) in the Netherlands in the 1520s and 1530s.[70] Other reform suggestions, especially from those reform leaders with humanistic education, included a desire to improve funding for education and rationalize the system of charity. The ultimate goal for most was to engage laypeople as fully as possible in their religious faith, purified of both scholasticism and superstition. Here Netherlandic humanism and 'popular Lutheranism' came together; as Duke argues, in the Netherlands:

> Luther's denunciation of works righteousness coincided with, and rein-
> forced, Erasmus's attack on a religion of outward observance: though
> Erasmus and Luther had different objectives, the practical effects of their
> teaching at this point were so similar as to make it sometimes very diffi-
> cult to determine under whose influence an individual acted.[71]

Anabaptism in the Low Countries

Given the horrific persecution, decrease in educated leadership, and increasing level of radical activity within the reform movement by 1530, it comes as little surprise that the proponents of Anabaptism should achieve considerable success in the Netherlands. Duke, among others, has noted that the transition from 'radical sacramentarianism' to Anabaptism was not a major one, for what the so-called sacramen-tarians did to the sacrament of the Eucharist, the Anabaptists did to baptism, by making the worth of the act dependent upon the faith of the recipient.[72] Evidently a goodly number of later Anabaptists, espe-cially leaders such as Menno Simons and David Joris, were able to make the transition, although not without considerable trepidation; unlike involvement in an evangelical conventicle, submitting to adult baptism carried with it a more dangerous level of sectarianism.[73]

The most important Anabaptist preacher for the Low Countries was undoubtedly Melchior Hoffman (1495/1500–43?), a furrier and Lu-theran lay preacher from the south German Imperial Free City of Schwabisch-Hall. Achieving considerable success in his religious mis-sion in northern Germany and Scandinavia, Hoffman's increasing apocalypticism and view of himself as prophet of the Last Day soon raised the concerns of more orthodox Lutherans. In his commentary on the twelfth chapter of Daniel, published in 1526, he announced that the Last Judgment would occur seven years hence in 1533.[74] In 1529 he became acquainted with Anabaptists in Strasbourg, some of whom were visionaries, and the following year his attempt to get the city council to provide the Anabaptists with a church building led to a warrant for his arrest. He brought his apocalyptic message then to Emden in East Frisia, where a large number of Netherlandic religious dissenters had found safe haven from the persecution in their homeland.

The response to Hoffman's preaching here was remarkable, to say the least. According to one of his converts, Obbe Philips, Hoffman personally baptized around 300 persons during his brief stay in the city.[75] Whatever the accuracy of Philip's figure, it is clear that a great number of individuals accepted Hoffman's apocalyptic message and many of them became active Melchiorite proselytizers when they returned to the Netherlands. Among these was Jan Volkerts Trijpmaker, a maker of wooden shoes, who began preaching openly in Amsterdam around Christmas 1530 and soon had baptized a considerable number of residents of the city, making it the centre for Anabaptism in Holland.[76] However, the following year he and nine other Anabaptists were executed in The Hague, sending a shock wave throughout the Melchiorite (or covenanter, as the Melchiorites called themselves) community and causing Hoffman to suspend baptisms for two years in order to stop the bloodshed.[77] Persuaded by a vision recounted to him by a supporter, in 1533 Hoffman re-entered Strasbourg, knowing that he would be arrested, but fully expecting to be released from prison within a short time by Christ himself, who would return to earth to establish his kingdom in Strasbourg. Unfortunately for Hoffman, his deliverance did not take place, and it is presumed that he died in prison in 1543.[78]

With Hoffman in prison, other individuals in Holland sought to take over leadership of the covenanters and to revitalize their flagging zeal. One of these was Jan Matthijs, a baker of Haarlem, who while in Amsterdam during December 1533 proclaimed the end to the suspension of baptism and sent out emissaries throughout the Low Countries and nearby Westphalia to prepare the populace for the return of Christ. In the meantime word had reached Matthijs that the Westphalian city of Münster was undergoing a process of religious reform similar to what the Holland covenanters were seeking, and Anabaptist missionaries were sent there to baptize the city's population and prepare them for the Messianic kingdom; Strasbourg's treatment of Hoffman was interpreted by many to signify that it had lost its preferred status as the city of God. By early 1534, then, Münster had become the central focus for the eschatological hopes of the Dutch and north German Melchiorites, and thousands of them attempted – most without success – to join the Anabaptist kingdom being established there prior to the return of Christ, which Matthijs had boldly predicted for Easter 1534. By this time Hoffman's apocalyptic message had struck such a resonant chord amongst the artisanal and labouring strata of the Netherlands, which were undergoing one of the worst periods of economic hardship to date, that they formed a mass movement on behalf of radical religious reform.[79] At times some of these radical reformers became desperate enough to adopt militant means to achieve the long-awaited kingdom of God; for example, two attempts were made to force the hands of the magistrates of Amsterdam in the direction of radical reformation, while a cloister in Friesland, called Oldeklooster, was briefly occupied by a large band of Anabaptists.[80] However, when Münster fell to the besieging forces at the end of June 1535, Anabaptist leaders in the Low Countries faced disillusionment among their followers and indecision about a future course of action. Many, among them Obbe Philips and eventually David Joris, moved in the direction of spiritualism, of rejecting all preoccupation with establishing an external church or forms of worship – not an unexpected development in the light of the earlier 'sacramentarian' current.[81] Others sought to maintain the militant edge of the movement, a goal that quickly degenerated into the creation of a few roving bands of Anabaptist guerillas known as the Batenburgers.[82]

The most enduring heir of the original Anabaptist impulse was the group that formed around the Frisian priest Menno Simons (1496–1561), whose followers, the Mennonites, created separatist fellowships that eventually achieved informal toleration after the establishment of the Dutch Republic, but which faced frequent bouts of severe persecution under Charles V. Strongest in the rural districts of Friesland and the fishing villages of North Holland, by the mid-1540s Mennonite communities were found in most urban centres as well throughout Holland. In spite of this limited growth, the Mennonites were like their predecessors unable to establish a wide-scale reform of Dutch society and remained a minority sect within the broader populace.[83]

The 1540s and 1550s

By 1540 it had become quite clear that the evangelical and Anabaptist attempts to reform the institutional church of the Low Countries had failed. The imperial authorities continued periodically to pressure local governments to prosecute the heretics in their midst, but as James Tracy has suggested, between 1540 and 1555 'the government of the Netherlands certainly had enough other things to worry about besides the enforcement of heresy laws.'[84] Tracy has furthermore noted that some time before 1542 Mary of Hungary had granted the Marquis of Vere an informal 'permission for Lutheranism' in the wake of his fears that rigorous enforcement of the heresy placards would frighten away German merchants. At the same time the imperial authorities continued their vigilance, especially by attempting to suppress the publication and dissemination of heretical writings and, as we shall see later, by seeking to censure the drama of the chambers of rhetoric.

In spite of the return to a more lenient policy toward heretics on the part of the Court of Holland,[85] throughout the Low Countries during the 1540s and 1550s there continued sporadic bouts of persecution, the results of which are clearly evident from the court records and the Mennonite martyrbooks.[86] Until the late 1540s the most severe outbreaks of official persecution, such as the trials conducted against the followers of David Joris and the so-called Libertine Eligius Pruystinck in 1544/5, were directed against those within the Anabaptist and spiritualist camps.[87] Duke's estimate that a minimum of 1,300 people were executed for heresy in the Low Countries between 1523 and 1566 is a conservative one and he suggests that the total number of those prosecuted for the crime 'may have been five to ten times as high.'[88] Whatever the extact number, such oppression, even in places where it was primarily experienced as a frightening memory, seriously reduced the chance that either the evangelicals or the Anabaptists could offer a realistic alternative to the established church. The apocalyptic emphasis of the Anabaptists which focused on divine deliverance and a revolution engineered by God and his angels, was in this respect already an admission that human attempts to reform Dutch society would likely meet with failure.

Many people therefore found the spiritualists' approach attractive, especially since many of them, Joris included, allowed their followers to practise Nicodemism, or the hiding of one's unorthodox beliefs by outward conformity to approved religious practices.[89] Judging from the response to the dissemination in the Low Countries of John Calvin's tract telling them either to flee their homeland to a place where they could worship openly or face the consequences of a public stand against idolatry, a large number of Netherlanders were quite happy to select the third option of Nicodemism, or at least of not taking an open stand on either side of the religious controversy.[90] Many remained satisfied, it seems, with meeting in secret conventicles for their religious instruction and worship.

At the same time, many reform-minded individuals did not give up hope of a broader reformation altogether, although they realized that without considerable support from the nobility and urban elite as well as from a strong reform community outside of the Low Countries, any attempt to oppose the imperial mandates against religious nonconformism would once again meet with disaster. Thus it was that in 1544 a delegation from Tournai travelled to Geneva to request Calvin to send a Reformed minister to the Netherlands. As Crew notes, many, if not most of the Netherlands's Protestants would not have selected Genevan Calvinism as their first choice for Reform leadership, preferring instead the more irenical outlook of the Strasbourg Reformed ministers.[91] Their turning to Geneva, then, was perhaps an act of desperation, hoping that the discipline of the Genevan ministers might better equip them to face the hostility of the Catholic authorities on the one side and the continued attraction of spiritualism on the other. The full advent of Calvinism into the Flemish-speaking regions of the Low Countries would not take place until the middle of the 1550s,[92] and takes us out of the chronological parameters of this study. However, it is helpful to remember, as Duke points out, that not all Protestants in the Netherlands looked to Geneva for leadership and religious eclecticism remained the favoured approach in the Low Countries.[93]

The following chapters will return to the experience of Dutch rhetoricians during the era of Charles V to see to what extent they mirrored in their drama and activities the religious and social turmoil of their day. For example, is it possible to discern the variations among the reform camps and controversies in rhetorician drama? Did rhetorician playwrights take up their quills to either attack or defend the reform ideas swirling about them? In other words, did rhetoricians act as propagandists for change or as defenders of the status quo? After a chapter introducing the chambers of rhetoric, this study will turn to a comparison of the experience of rhetoricians in two cities, Antwerp and Amsterdam. The four successive chapters will then take a broader look at the available plays that are known to have been composed during the reign of Charles V.

2

Rhetoricians and Urban Culture

To all those who read this present letter or hear it read, especially all princes, factors, deacons and managers (*besorghers*), and all other companions (*ghesellen*) of the noble art of Rhetoric – whose worth no one can adequately praise – in all walled or privileged cities, castles, villages, no one excluded who pledges to perform for the solace of people the most worthy and noble arts of the rhetoricians, praiseworthy above all other arts, which one can justly describe as the queen of all arts ... We, the prince, factor, deacon and managers, guild brothers of rhetoric inside the city of Hulst, ... pledge to perform the most affectionate, pleasant, solacing plays for all gentlemen – religious, secular, noble, commoner, great, middling, of whatever state they may be – with purest pleasure and without any scoffing, and thereby for their own rejoicing ... without anger, but only in brotherly love, solace and purity.[1]

So stated the 'prize card' issued on 7 September 1483, announcing a rhetorician competition for the following month sponsored by the recently established Hulst chamber of rhetoric The Transfiguration (*De Transfiguratie*). Clearly portrayed is the exuberance of a new society holding its inaugural festivity. What is also of note is a strong sense of mission; rhetoricians saw themselves as a cultural elite whose dramatic performances were intended to raise the intellectual, artistic, and devotional standards of their contemporaries of all social standings. In other words, rhetorician drama was much more than a means of diversion from mundane daily routines, especially since rhetoricians were not members of professional troupes whose major concern was to find audiences large or wealthy enough to support their living. Instead, theirs was a loftier purpose – the educational, religious, and moral improvement of their audiences. Judging from even this single document, we can see that the hope was that rhetorician drama would assist in the development of a supportive and cohesive urban commune.

Two examples from the middle of the sixteenth century will help underscore the self confidence rhetoricians expressed about their importance for their society. From the start they saw it as their responsibility to use the stage to instruct their audiences in religious matters. Of course the religious professionals, whether the Catholic clergy or later the Reformed ministers, saw this as interference in their domain on the part of untrained laypeople who naturally would become entangled in heretical notions.[2] Two plays especially present this dispute in a forthright manner. The first of these is a comedy, *Man's Desire and Fleeting Beauty*, probably performed by the Leiden chamber White Columbines (*Witte Accoleijen*) for the 1546 competition in Gouda.[3] This cautious farce praises emperor Charles V and his regent, Mary of Hungary, while at the same time defending the right of rhetoricians to appropriate to themselves the supposed functions of priests. This work typically consists of a play within a play, and in this case the 'outer play' involves three characters who meet on their way to Gouda. One of these is a Woman from Leiden who explains to a sceptical First Citizen – who would rather spend his spare time making money – that she is such a devoted fan of rhetorician drama that she ran from Leiden to make it in time to witness the opening parade, and that in her home city she and her fellow citizens attend all night performances on the great feast days.[4] First Citizen complains to Second Citizen that he finds such plays boring, adding:

> FIRST CITIZEN: Today I think, if truth were told,
> There's too much controversy, interpreting the Bible,
> And such like in these plays. I say it's libel!
> Give me the old ones – they were entertaining.
> SECOND CITIZEN: But surely, even Scripture needs explaining
> (that's obvious) to tell us what it means.
> FIRST CITIZEN: No, no. They simply use it to make scenes,
> And scandalize authority and clergy.

They both agree that such activity is scandalous, but Second Citizen reassures his friend by affirming that because of their earlier reputation all plays of rhetoricians must now be formally approved by the authorities prior to performance:

SECOND CITIZEN: No longer, neighbour. Now they make them clean.
FIRST CITIZEN: Well praise be to God.
SECOND CITIZEN: Before a syllable is moved,
A play must be officially approved.
If they did otherwise, they'd quickly be upbraided.
FIRST CITIZEN: That's good, since people got so agitated
And turned away from truth and good morality.[5]

His fears assuaged, First Citizen agrees to attend the performance and they leave the stage just in time to hear the opening prologue.

Did Leiden's rhetoricians take this caution to heart in their performance in Gouda? Possible inflammatory ad lib comments and visual cues aside, it seems they did, for the theme of this play is quite a traditional one, following in the long tradition of the dance of death literature and its visual depictions. Nowhere in this play do these performers attempt to interpret the Scriptures in an unorthodox fashion. It seems therefore that some rhetoricians had indeed heeded the warning to be extremely careful when presenting plays on religious or moral themes.

Other rhetoricians clearly resented such suppression of their reform rhetoric, viewing it as an attempt to silence the religious leadership aspirations of Holland's literate guildspeople. Such was the case not only with *Man's Desire and Fleeting Beauty*, but with many other plays that we will examine wherein rhetoricians defended their craft against their detractors in humorous asides or tangential comments. However, one surviving play, composed during the reign of Charles V, provides an extremely clear case of rhetorician self promotion: *The Comedy of Music and Rhetoric, Which Art is the Best*, an interpretation of Cicero's *De Oratore (de Rhetorica)*.[6]

In this work, the allegorical characters of the play praise the soothing effects of music but extol most enthusiastically rhetoric as not only a subtle and enjoyable craft, but as the 'daughter of the Holy Spirit,' for as Spirit's Rejoicing (*Gheests Verblijdinghe*) opines:

Rhetoric is most needful to the wise,
A more completely pure art was never known
Whose praise rises to the firmament.
Excellent is she above all the greatest,
For she is daughter of the Holy Spirit;
In all hunting grounds, a prize worthy of the crown.[7]

When two Vices cast aspersions on the rhetorical craft, describing how rhetoricians are usually drunk on Rhine wine and perform little useful service,[8] the Virtues defend Rhetorica, explaining its importance to society. Among many benefits it assists the development of memory and teaches youth discipline and rules, something which has brought it praise from many ancient fathers, both Christian and pagan.[9] Although music is indeed a 'lamp of the holy church,' rhetoric is superior, for it is a 'fountain of wisdom' and a mirror of clarity.[10] Reaching the climax of the argument the Virtues unveil a figure of the fountain of wisdom from which springs seven conduits representing the liberal arts; above this is the Holy Spirit from which flows all arts. The audience is enjoined to study at this fountain prior to reading Cicero's work.[11] That a number of rhetorician chambers were named The Holy Spirit confirms that these dramatists in general viewed their work as specially, perhaps divinely, inspired. It is no wonder, then, that they would take upon themselves the function of religious instruction of the masses, something that irritated not only the Catholic religious establishment, but was also a thorn in the flesh of Calvinist preachers long after the establishment of the Dutch Republic.

With this self-perception we are confronted by one of the most important features of the chambers of rhetoric, one that distinguishes them in some respects from most other dramatists of early modern Europe. Their plays were composed as services to their urban community, within which rhetoricians lived and worked. Amusement of their audiences was one important aspect of this function, but one that seems secondary to their role as teachers and agents of communication between the authorities and the citizenry and between the urban commune and visiting lords and dignitaries, perhaps even between God and the people. The activities and training of the rhetoricians, not to mention the institutional background of the chambers in religious confraternities and militia guilds, helped reinforce the rhetoricians' belief that they were the educational equal of the traditional leaders and moral guardians of society. The themes of their plays illustrate what rhetoricians themselves regarded as the central problems of and desired solutions for their world. These works also offer us clues as to the major preoccupations of their fellow townsfolk, at least as reflected through the prism of these dramatic and literary specialists. By analysing these plays within their historical context, it is hoped that our mental image of the world of the sixteenth-century Low Countries will come into sharper focus. Although those interested in the origins and early drama of the chambers of rhetoric in the fifteenth century now have a number of works to consult,[12] this chapter will provide a brief description of these dramatic societies prior to the Reformation, with an eye to capturing their sense of mission and self-perception. How did they see their social role, and what means did they utilize to accomplish it?

Rhetorician societies arose in the fifteenth century within the strong artisanal and merchant cultures of the mercantile and cloth manufacturing cities of Flanders, Brabant, and Holland. The patricians who governed these claimed to be directed by the 'common weal,' but what this common good meant depended on who was defining the term; patricians, for obvious reasons, emphasized the economic interests of the cloth merchants. In the Flemish cities especially, town government was run to the benefit of the cloth industry, while the majority of townsfolk, especially the numerous wool workers and weavers, had little say in governmental policy.[13] The pervasiveness of popular or guild-sponsored uprisings in late medieval Flanders reveals the frustration felt by the ordinary folk over the policies of their social superiors. Moreover, the desire on the part of the dukes of Burgundy to centralize the government and economy of the various provinces was a goal hardly shared by local merchants and artisans.[14]

To reinforce their stranglehold over political power the urban elites of the Low Countries sought to imitate as closely as possible the leisured life, social etiquette, and culture of the traditional Burgundian aristocracy.[15] By so aping the knightly elite, Herman Pleij has argued, the city fathers of the Netherlands desired to create a sharp separation between their culture and that of the urban commoners, to refashion the traditional medieval hierarchy within the urban environment.[16] One of the aristocratic means taken up by the patricians to accomplish this goal was to act as patrons of arts and letters, thereby determining to a considerable extent the themes and content of their sponsored artwork, promoting especially proper burgher morals such as obedience, loyalty, and religious devotion.[17] As with the other arts, civic-sponsored drama could reinforce patrician attempts to inculcate civic virtues and maintain peace and order in their communes. However, like other forms of media, drama could act both as a promoter of the status quo and as a propagandist for change. Robert Scribner for one has remarked that 'both play and ritual may serve to integrate or to subvert the social order by providing symbolic messages about the nature of social reality.[18] The function of integration or promoting civic harmony and religious orthodoxy was prominent during the first century of the chambers' existence.

As noted by scholars of late-medieval Dutch drama, rhetoricians were historically related to religious confraternities, lay organizations which had assisted the priesthood in encouraging the development of lay piety and charity, as well as assisting in the performance of carnival plays. In these brotherhoods members of the third estate found an outlet for their religious aspirations and asserted a limited self-sufficiency in the religious sphere.[19] Obviously most, if not all, of the plays supervised by the clergy or fraternities were religious in theme while the stated goals of most rhetorician chambers established prior to the Reformation included the injunction to perform drama so as to 'bring the people to better devotion,' to improve the community's worship.[20] For example, Brussel's The Book (*Den Boeck*) chamber was established around 1402 as 'a society, confraternity and brotherhood ... for the most noble art of rhetoric and music,' to the honour of God and to the consolation and instruction of the residents of this ... city.'[21] Judging from chamber names, mottos, and patron saints, it seems many rhetoricians regarded their work as divinely approved, even as inspired by the Holy Spirit; at least nine chambers were named The Holy Ghost or some variant thereof and a number of others had the Holy Spirit either in their motto or as a patron saint. Many of those with secular names had religious mottos, such as Sint-Truiden's The Olive Branch (*Die Olyftack*) with its motto 'God's spirit enlightens,' or Vlissingen's The Blue Columbine (*De blaeu Acolye*) which upheld the slogan 'the spirit examines all.' Another fourteen were named after Jesus Christ or his cross and twenty bore the names of saints; moreover, the majority of those established prior to the Reformation had patron saints, the most popular being the Virgin Mary and saints Barbara and Catharine. Of course, given the late medieval predeliction for allegorical or metaphorical interpretations of the natural world, chambers named after flora or fauna were likewise intended as signifying a higher, spiritual meaning.[22]

Likewise, the formal charters which set forth the rules for each chamber show the importance of upholding the Catholic religion, expressed most visibly in the altars funded by most chambers in honour of the chamber's patron saint. The sovereign Ghent chamber, for example, was established as both a chamber and 'brotherhood of the Balsam' with the dual duties of performing drama to the honour of the chamber's patron, Jesus, and overseeing worship at the altar of the confraternity's patron saint, St Barbara, established in the chapel of the archduke's residence in Ghent.[23] While membership in the formal rhetorician chamber was restricted to fifteen adult men and fifteen male youths, anyone, male or female, rich or poor, could join the chamber's associated religious confraternity.[24] Similarly, no scandalous or blasphemous plays were to besmirch the reputation of Antwerp's The Gillyflower (De Violieren). Composing or performing plays or refrains 'against the Catholic faith' was strictly forbidden and the chamber leadership was to guard against the writing, performing, or publication of any such works.[25] To blaspheme the name of God or 'his dear saints' or to cause any trouble during a worship service would in fact net the offender a ten stuiver fine.[26] These examples provide evidence that patricians supported their rhetorician chambers because they were seen as a means of reinforcing patrician attempts to oversee the spiritual welfare of their residents. Like the confraternities, they were closely linked to the church but under the immediate direction of laypeople and sponsored by civic leaders. By the turn of the sixteenth century it appears most chambers had extracted themselves from direct ecclesiastical control and were instead closely directed by the civil authorities, who used them to promote their city's honour and needs before the higher rulers.[27]

Even those chambers which originated as literary adjuncts to the militia units and as clubs for socially ambitious citizens had a strong sense of religious mission.[28] All chamber members were imbued with the goal of increasing religious fervour and disseminating theological understanding among the Low Countries' populace. The Hague's With Delight (Met Ghenuchten), a chamber with a militia guild origin, promoted religious devotion by establishing a confraternity in honour of the 'Sweet Name of Jesus.'[29] Modelling their drama competitions after the famous contests of the militia guilds, rhetoricians sought 'to encourage and increase unity, friendship and affection among the cities and territories,' a purpose that appears again and again in the rhetoricians' requests for civic support.[30] This intention was without a doubt the principal reason behind Archduke Philip the Fair's establishment of the Ghent chamber Jesus with the Balsam Flower (Jesus metter Balsembloeme), for the archduke was so impressed with the Mechelen competition of May 1493 that he decided to establish the 'noble art' throughout the Flemish-speaking Netherlands. Behind this patronage of drama lay Philip's intention to create a head chamber which would ensure that the regulations of new chambers fell in step with the duke's goals.[31] His witnessing of a rhetorician competition seems to have convinced him that with their interprovincial gatherings and large audiences, rhetoricians could make remarkably effective agents of cultural and political centralization.[32]

As we shall see, rhetoricians did assist in the spread and consolidation of ideas across the Low Countries; however, ducal attempts to control rhetorician drama met with little success. At the same time, such centralization did have its effect on rhetoricians, as it did on the general institutional structures of the Low Countries. Walter Prevenier and Wim Blockmans, for example, suggest that the transformation of the Netherlands from an essentially Burgundian domain to a more properly Habsburg one began most seriously between 1520 and 1550 and was symbolized by Charles V's introduction of a new central government structure after his coronation at Bologna in 1530. Contemporaneous with these institutional developments there also occurred a series of socio-economic crises, a noticeable artistic transition from late Gothic to Renaissance styles, and, of course, the introduction of religious reform ideas and conflict. Prevenier and Blockmans conclude therefore that 'a change took place in the main sectors of the society of the Netherlands, which can be seen as signifying the end of the Burgundian structure and culture.'[33] For this reason we will concentrate on the development and drama of the rhetoricians in the period after Charles V's election as Holy Roman Emperor in 1519. A brief discussion of the organizational structure of rhetorician chambers and their pre-Reformation drama will help set the stage for this more specific analysis.

Rhetorician Chambers

By the start of the sixteenth century, the chambers of rhetoric were prominent in the writing and performing of songs, poems, farces, and, most importantly, the serious allegorical plays (*spelen van zinne*) for which they became most famous.[34] The *spelen van zinne* in particular were didactic in function and moralistic in tone. 'Farces' (*kluchten*), while more overtly comical, often also had a moral edge,[35] and 'entertainments' (*esbattementen*) attempted to convey the didactic or moral lesson in a more light-hearted fashion compared to the allegorical plays. Any of these dramatic works could be performed either in private or public. Private gatherings included chamber meetings which were open only to members and invited guests, and special performances of dinner or gift plays for invited audiences, such as weddings and other ceremonial gatherings.[36] Many of the public plays were sponsored by civic authorities for special events, such as religious holidays, visits of dignitaries, or peace treaties, and could draw thousands of spectators. City fathers would go to great lengths to ensure that the entire population of the commune could witness these performances 'for the common weal.' As the acknowledged experts on drama and literature, rhetoricians were also frequently called upon to lead their community's preparations for a royal entry and to arrange and act in the wagon plays and *tableaux vivants* typical of these occasions.[37]

On top of their didactic functions, rhetoricians also provided comic diversion from the harsh realities of sixteenth-century life. In this respect, their activities increasingly came to replace the less disciplined and more disruptive popular feasts such as carnival and other youth rituals which most cities attempted to suppress in the course of the sixteenth century.[38] In the most extravagant endeavours of rhetoricians, audiences were entertained not only by the comedic elements of the plays, but also by the festivities surrounding gatherings of chambers from different cities. Such inter-city *rederijker* competitions were impressive displays often involving hundreds of lavishly costumed participants who entered the host city riding horseback or performing plays on wagons.[39] If the awarding of prizes is any indication, the highly symbolic ritual associated with the chamber entrances was nearly as important as the performance of the plays themselves. Providing the financial resources for such feasts and prizes was the 'prince' (sometimes an 'emperor'), a ceremonial overlord who was usually from the rural nobility or urban patriciate but occasionally from the clergy or a profession. Managing the personnel and finances of the chambers were the overseers, whose offices and responsibilities resembled those of the craft guilds: for large chambers a captain (*hooftman*) and elders, who conducted meetings, enforced the rules among the members, organized special events and performances, and consulted with other chambers and the civic leadership, and deacons, who kept the books and financial accounts.[40] Smaller chambers would operate with only elders and deacons, or sometimes with deacons only, but all had a prince. However, the soul of a chamber was undoubtedly the factor, who, as the principal poet and playwright, received a salary. For example, the duties and salary of the Antwerp factor Jan Salomon are spelled out in a contract written when he was hired by The Marigold (*Den Goudbloem*) on 22 February 1524. Aside from composing, the factor acted also as director of the plays and drama teacher to the general membership.[41] In return he was to receive a yearly salary of thirty stuivers (one and a half guilders), plus twelve groats for his services on special occasions. On top of these fees, he received a commission of one-half stuiver for every 100 lines of newly commissioned plays or refrains, thus closely tying a factor's salary to his industry; Salomon was expected year round to produce enough dramatic material for chamber members so that 'good time would be spent in learning' and to maintain unity and friendship among the members. If the relationship between the chamber and Salomon soured, notice of the contract's termination, by either the deacons or the factor, had to be made a year in advance.

The protection of the actual plays and verses composed by the factor was not left in the factor's hands. Instead, only the deacon was allowed to have the key to the locked cabinet where the important papers were preserved. The procedure for taking inventory of the chamber's literary works illustrates their nearly sacred character. The deacon provided the factor with a booklet of paper in which he would write or copy the relevant *spelen van zinne,* miracle plays (*miraculen*), or other dramatic work. The factor would maintain possession of the manuscript until after the play's performance, at which time he would return it to the deacon for safe keeping and the factor would be given more paper. Clearly, then, the works composed by the factor under the chamber's commission remained the property of the chamber, and could not be disposed of in any way without approval of the chamber's directors, presumably ensuring that factors did not sell their works to competitors. Undoubtedly the care taken by conscientious deacons was one reason why so many rhetorician plays have survived in manuscript. Several fifteenth-century plays were copied and performed again in the sixteenth century, attesting not only to the enduring popularity of some of their themes and stories, but also to the difficulty in producing new works of enduring value.[42] One only needs to peruse the remarkably rich collection of sixteenth-century folios still housed in the Haarlem Loyalty Must Prove (*Trou Moet Blijcken*) chamber to get a sense of the seriousness with which the chamber's deacons undertook their office.

As seen in this description of the contract of Jan Salomon, the society's managers, the elders and deacons, were also central to the proper functioning of the typical chamber. Fulfilling other specific tasks were the messenger, doorman, costume manager, and the fool. The chamber's general members acted out the parts assigned to them and provided the financial base for the necessary salaries (the messenger was also paid for his services), props, costumes, and, if not financed by the city, the rental of the meeting hall or chamber. Fortunately for us, some chamber ordinances have survived, and their analysis reveals a great deal about how chambers functioned. Generally speaking chamber ordinances were quite stereotypical, in large measure due to the Burgundian attempt to standardize the organization of rhetorician societies, modelled after those of the sovereign Ghent chamber.[43] Examination of just one of these, then, will provide us with a general understanding of the workings of a typical chamber.[44]

In 1480 the St Luke's guild of artists of Antwerp composed an ordinance 'for the support of the rhetorician guild of The Gillyflower.'[45] From its inception this chamber was connected to the artist guild of the city but gained a measure of administrative independence with the issue of this ordinance. Like its sister chamber The Marigold, The Gillyflower was ruled by a prince, captain, elders, and deacons. The prince was chosen by the majority of the chamber's officials for a three-year term one month before St Luke's Day. To celebrate his selection, the prince was to fête the chamber with a blazon (blasoen, an allegorical shield; for example, see illustration 7) or refrain festival, for which he would fund the prizes to a minimum of fifty guilders.[46] This sizeable sum indicates that only those with considerable means would be chosen for this ceremonial position. The Gillyflower also chose two princes 'from the membership,' whose responsibility it was to keep a watch over the activities of the members.[47]

After an examination before the chamber's leaders, the general members swore an oath in the chamber hall, for admission into the society needed to be strictly controlled since most cities established membership limits on their official guilds.[48] Those who were already committed to another guild or society by an oath could aspire only to the position of 'free persons' (vrypersoonen) or amateurs (liefhebbers) in The Gillyflower, not reckoned among the 'privileged' of the chamber and thereby without the right to appointment to any of the chamber's offices. Official membership in a rhetorician guild seems therefore to have precluded membership in any other guild. The members of Ghent's Jesus with the Balsam Flower, for example, were explicitly freed, by royal mandate, 'from all guilds, brotherhoods and societies.'[49]

The rhetorician society, of course, accepted the amateurs' payment of the entrance fees and normal expenses.[50] Members of The Gillyflower, for example, were required to pay eighteen guilders as an entrance fee, tip the messenger one guilder, and contribute a yearly fee of six guilders; first year expenses therefore came to a minimum of twenty-five guilders which in the 1520s could purchase over thirty-five bushels of wheat. On top of the yearly fee members also contributed to the expenses of extraordinary events, such as rhetorician contests and princely entrances. Furthermore, members were to pay four guilders every time they met together for festivals or meals and this fee was to be paid, 'without protest,' even if the member was unable to attend.[51] Absence from any festivals was met with a six stuiver fine if the offending member had received the messenger's announcement. Princes, deacons, and elders were not immune from such fines; for example, if the prince missed any of the chamber's special meetings, he was to pay six guilders, while deacons paid three and elders thirty stuivers. Also meriting significant fines were failing to respond to the roll call at a chamber meeting and bringing unauthorized guests to a chamber meal or performances of private 'chamber plays.' In exchange for all of these costs, members received typical guild benefits: a gift of six guilders if planning a marriage, and burial at death. If a member decided to quit the guild, he had first to pay the twelve guilders 'quit-fee' (*dootschult*) and all other debts.

As befitting the important function performed for their communities by rhetoricians, their activities were strictly regulated, since the public presentation of rhetorician drama was considered far too important to be left in the hands of individual members or factors. Chamber leaders had to approve any performance of plays and refrains and members had to seek the consent of the prince or deacons of the chamber before performing any private marriage, banquet, or other feast plays. Not even the factor was allowed to arrange the performance of a play not approved by the deacons or the prince of the members, who also carefully monitored all cards announcing performances; members were furthermore forbidden from revealing any of the secrets of the chamber. Also regulated were the internal workings of chamber meetings so that peace and harmony would prevail. Judging from the charters, arguments over choice parts in plays or the awarding of prizes were common, as were disputes over business (*coopmanschappen*) or lotteries (item 29 of The Gillyflower's ordinance). The playing of cards or other inappropriate games could elicit similar rancour among the members.[52]

Attendance at regular chamber meetings was required of all members. Shortly after noon on the day of a meeting the messenger would clean and prepare the chamber for the gathering and if the meeting was an irregular one, he was to notify all the members in good time. The members were to arrive at the hall 'in good time, before the hour bell of Our Dear Lady [Cathedral] chimes' and if they were late, the proceeds from the fine of six stuivers were shared between the chamber and the membership, presumably to quell their irritation at the interruption of a performance. Members were furthermore responsible for memorizing and performing their roles 'without any contradiction,'[53] an understandable injunction given that factor and thespians were expected to write and rehearse an occasion play within three to four weeks.[54] On the basis of the financial burdens involved in becoming a member of an official rhetorician chamber and of the restrictions on the size and number of such societies, it seems that rhetoricians could very easily come to regard themselves as a cultural elite within their cities, a status that they believed placed them in the same social class as their neighbours who were privileged members of civic guard units and prominent confraternities.

Aside from their upper-class patrons and well-educated factors, most associates of these literary clubs came from the artisanal and merchant strata of society; such is the conclusion of E. van Autenboer, whose study of the Mechelen chamber The Peony (*De Peoene*) revealed that rhetoricians were recruited from all social strata.[55] Obviously, the love of the literary and dramatic arts is not the sole preserve of any particular estate, although certain levels of education, or familial support, or political aspirations, or work experience were important factors in whether or not an individual was able to find a place within a chamber. For one thing, we have seen that membership in a rhetorician's guild required a modicum of financial resources. Those lacking such could find expression for their dramatic interests in the many non-approved acting groups which also sprang up in the major cities of the Low Countries (see below, chapter 3). Certainly some crafts allowed greater income and time for their practitioners to partake in literary activities. For example, Natalie Z. Davis has shown that printers' journeymen had a higher level of literacy than most artisans and were particularly prone to joining reform groups in France.[56] Was there a similar correspondence between specific trades, literacy, and interest in reform in the Low Countries?

Van Autenboer's thorough study discovered, in accordance with the conclusion of Walter Gibson, that artists were at the forefront of Mechelen's rhetorician activities, totalling thirty-seven of the 191 individuals whose vocation could be discerned from the sources (see table 1).[57] While there were ten priests on the membership rolls, there is a surprising lack of schoolteachers, for only one (a college rector) is mentioned. Quite possibly Mechelen's teachers concentrated on Latin school drama instead of vernacular rhetorician plays. Other professionals were represented, with six doctors and surgeons and ten lawyers, evidence that such professionals and university-educated men found rhetorician chambers an appropriate place to develop their literary interests. Also prominent, naturally, were the nobility, with thirty titled individuals.

Of those in the non-artistic crafts, the fishmongers (*visverkopers*) predominated to an unusual extent, with twenty-one known members. While this figure might merely be a result of the chance survival of the Mechelen *visverkopers* guild records and the loss of comparable records of other guilds, the fact that only seven butchers, five tanners, one fat renderer (*vetterwarier*), and one baker were discovered by Van Autenboer suggests that of Mechelen's merchants, shopkeepers, and guildsmen, the fishmongers were the most interested in drama. Those in the cloth trade were represented by nineteen members, including five merchants, although three of these were old clothes sellers and of the lower ranks of the guild. The metal trades were represented by ten smiths and founders, while construction workers added five stonemasons and one bricklayer. Missing were significant numbers from the lower guilds of the city and its suburbs, with only one gardener appearing in the membership list.

Gazing across the crowd gathered at a rhetorician meeting, one would see a good cross-section of the upper artisanal, professional, and merchant elements of urban society, all of whom shared an interest and talent in the literary and dramatic arts. What one would also survey is a number of men who had experienced membership in confraternities, militia units and perhaps even municipal government. Van Autenboer discovered at least sixteen rhetoricians who at some point held major civic office: twelve or thirteen aldermen, three mayors, and one sheriff (*schout*). Four more had served as city secretary, two as procurators, one as treasurer, and one had held the position of pensionary, the legal representative of the city. At least three more held a licence for the collection of one of the city's excise taxes and two were provided with positions as gate concierge. If Mechelen's case is at all typical, members of a rhetorician chamber could expect to meet and have fellowship with some of the city's social and political leaders; whether this led to a better chance for political advancement on the

TABLE 1: Occupations of Mechelen Rhetoricians

Arts – 37	**Food – 35**
Painters/Artists 28	Fishmongers 20
Glaziers/Glass painters 3	Butchers 7
Musicians (Organist, Composer) 4	Tanners 5
Artsmith 1	Merchant of fish and cheese 1
Noble – 30	Bakers 1
(by title)	Fat renderer 1
Cloth – 19	**Professionals – 23**
Clothmakers 6	Legal profession 10
Collarmakers 4	Medical profession 6
Old clothes sellers 3	Other 7 (3 Masters, 1 Rector, 1 Secretary,
Cloth merchants 2	2 Clerks)
Weavers 2	
Shearers 1	**Metal – 11**
Shoemaker 1	Smiths 3
	Goldsmiths 3
Religious – 12	Bell founders 2
Priests 10	Silversmiths 1
Churchmaster 1	Brass founders 1
Coster 1	Organ maker 1
Others – 18	**Construction – 6**
(4 Merchants, 1 Small merchant, 1 Store	Stonemasons 5
keeper, 3 Innkeepers, 1 Candlemaker,	Bricklayer 1
2 Wardens, 1 Concierge, 1 Messen-	
ger, 2 Women, 1 Soldier, 1 Gardener)	

Source: Van Autenboer, Volksfeesten en rederijkers, 163–207

part of most rhetoricians is a matter for speculation, although hope of establishing useful social or economic contacts must have led some to join a chamber of rhetoric, as it had motivated many to join a civic guard unit. A minimum of twenty-nine of Mechelen's rhetoricians were at some point in their lives known to have been members of one of the city's militia guilds, while another eleven were involved in a confraternity. Membership in one of these privileged societies seems to have been a useful means for an individual seeking to cultivate good social and political contacts and for developing a sense of civic importance and influence among its members.

Those faces visible at a meeting of rhetoricians would almost entirely have been those of men, for it seems that, apart from rare exceptions, membership in a rhetorician society was another privilege of the male sex. Although there is some very limited evidence suggesting that widows of members may have been allowed formal membership, any women present at rhetorician meetings would have been invited guests, or perhaps members of an associated confraternity.[58] The question of rhetorician drama and women is best left to a monograph of its own, but it seems very clear here that the views expressed in rhetorician plays were those of men. We might be able to discover what men thought about women in these plays, but we cannot use the plays to any great extent to discern what women thought.[59]

In general, then, most rhetoricians came from the skilled crafts and professions, and were prosperous enough to afford the various chamber fees. On the one hand *rederijker* chambers were not intended as forums for the poor or dispossessed. On the other, it appears they were places where artists, artisans, merchants, and professionals with sufficient means could meet together and find an outlet for their creative endeavours. Affiliation with the chambers of rhetoric provided literate male citizens with not only a social club serving the honour of their city, but also a cultural outlet which hitherto had been the sole preserve of the first two social estates.[60] Artisans and merchants who participated in rhetorician activities presumably found pleasure in having a popular vernacular counterpoint to the humanists' elitist Latin culture.[61] They also found a place to enunciate their religious devotion and express their criticism of those religious leaders who failed to measure up to the high moral and spiritual standards expected of them. Therefore, while the rhetoricians could and usually did serve as promoters of civic pride and obedience, they also acted as critics of the privileged estates, especially the clergy, and of injustice within their society.

Themes of Pre-Reformation Drama

Although rhetoricians occupied themselves with a range of literary and celebratory activities, their principal function was the performance of drama, both comical and serious. The focus of this book is on the serious plays written and performed during the early Reformation era, with an eye to their propagandistic functions on the major reform issues confronting rhetoricians during the era of Charles V. For the purpose of comparison, it will be useful here to summarize the major themes of serious drama composed by rhetorician playwrights on the eve of the Reformation.

The vast majority of serious plays known to have been performed in the fifteenth-century Low Countries were religious in subject matter.

In his 1912 study of late-medieval art and drama, L. van Puyvelde counted some two thousand references to plays in the available sources. Of these, only thirty were not religious in theme, a proportion comparable to the subject matter of art during the same period.[62] Plays composed prior to the introduction of reformation propaganda around 1519 were dominated by themes prominent within the movements of popular devotionalism of the lower Rhineland. These themes were enunciated in literature and art as well as in drama, and included fervent devotion to the Virgin Mary and to her sorrows as well as those of her son; instruction in the proper attitude toward and use of the seven sacraments; and proper regard for the church, although there appears in this period a rising line of satirical commentary regarding the perceived abuses within the institution of the church and the immorality of the clerical estate. As noted in chapter 1 above, the Low Countries were the centre of the *Devotio Moderna* movement and the intense influence of this Netherlandic lay piety is evident, for example, in the unique character of Dutch humanism, which has been described as Christian humanism or humanistic Christianity. That this emphatic lay piety should appear in rhetorician drama is no surprise.

For example, in 1496 Antwerp's The Gillyflower hosted a contest involving twenty-eight chambers from across the Low Countries, with the assigned question, 'What is the greatest mystery or grace ordained by God for the blessedness of humanity?'[63] As typical for rhetorician competitions, the host chamber set the theme or contest question and distributed invitation cards to possible participants. Chamber leaders would set the process in motion, gain the acceptance of the general membership, and win approval and financial backing from the city magistrates. In this particular case, the answers to the question are revealing of the religious attitudes of those rhetoricians who participated: Lier's Unlearned (*Ongeleerde*) won first place with its response, 'the blood of Christ' or 'the death of Christ.'[64] Reimerswaal came second with its performance of 'Charity,' a theme pursued also by Brussels's Lily (*Lelie*). One of Ghent's chambers placed third with its presentation on 'the death of our Lord'; and Herenthals won a prize with its play on 'the sacrament of the altar,' a topic dramatized also by Dendermonde. Most other chambers performed plays on the incarnation of Christ (Kortrijk, Oudenaarde, Mechelen, Axel, Sluys, Leuven, and Ghent's Bottomless Basket [*Boemloose Mande*]) or on his wounds (Hulst, Ypres, and Brussels's Book [*Boeck*]) and death (Brussels and Leuven). Another of Leuven's plays was entitled in Latin 'super verbum incarnatum verbum, sacramentale verbum in spiritum' ('above the word [is] the incarnate word, the sacramental word in spirit'); while Sevenbergen's was called 'the ordinance of the Father in Council' ('de ordonnantie van den Vader in Consilium'). Interestingly, Oostende performed a play on 'election and predestination,' a topic debated vigorously among late medieval scholastics. The rhetoricians of Walloon Nyvel performed en français their play on 'penitence'; Aelst's dramatists acted out a play on 'truth'; and another of Leuven's chambers performed on the 'peace made by God between father and son.' Winning the prizes for first entrance and most beautiful decorations was Amsterdam's Eglantine (*Engeltraren*), which acted out 'in the beginning was the word' (in principio erat verbum). Presumably not able to decide, Lier's Growing Tree (*Groeyendenboom*) performed 'the faith of the resurrection and charity.' Ghent's Fountain (*Fonteyne*) believed that the act of God creating humanity in his image was the greatest mystery, while Bergen op Zoom's actors chose 'the word enclosed' (het woort by goen, i.e., the word made flesh). These answers fit neatly into the predominant themes of late medieval devotional literature or art.[65]

Although the *spelen van zinne* had its origins in the medieval French morality play,[66] rhetorician plays of the fifteenth century were also quite similar in both style and theme to those produced in other European states; indeed, several scholars, such as Leonard Forster, have noted the tendency of English playwrights to borrow themes or entire works from their Dutch fellows.[67] As in England, for example, residents of the Low Countries would have witnessed a number of mystery plays performed during the special feast days of the Christian calendar, although few of these have actually survived.[68] Examples of these include *The First Joy of Mary, The Seventh Joy of Our Lady,* and *The Play of the Five Wise and the Five Foolish Maidens.*[69] The first two mentioned were parts of a series on the seven joys of the Virgin Mary, and Ramakers discusses the tradition of a yearly performance of 'the seven joys of Mary' in Brussels.[70] Miracle plays seem also to have been popular in the fifteenth-century Low Countries[71] and like the mystery plays drew from a stock of familiar stories of saints and their miracles. One of the most enduring miracle plays is *Mary of Nijmegen (Mariken van Nieumeghen)*, a still popular work that presumably originated within a confraternity as a miracle history. Composed between 1485 and 1510, it involves the story of a particularly Netherlandic miracle which occurred to a young maiden of Guelders who made a pact with the devil in exchange for knowledge of the seven liberal arts, but whose soul was ultimately redeemed through her sincere and unrelenting penance. This story thus reinforces orthodox teaching regarding the means of salvation and it also taps into a current of beliefs and fears regarding the devil and witches.[72]

Despite the enduring popularity of *Mary of Nijmegen*, by the start of the sixteenth century miracle and mystery plays were being superceded in popularity by the comical 'entertainment,' such as *The Entertainment of the Apple Tree* (which also has the confounding of the devil as a central theme),[73] and the *spel van zinne*, the Dutch equivalent of the morality play, with its often entirely allegorical characters. For example, R.A. Potter surveyed eighty-eight Dutch rhetorician plays, discovering that twenty-eight (31 per cent) of them could be classified as biblical dramas, while the great majority, fifty-eight (65 per cent) were strictly allegorical in nature.[74] Toward the end of the fifteenth century many other types of Dutch drama, such as mystery plays, were already adding personifications (*sinnekens*) or allegorical characters to the more familiar biblical characters. According to W.M.H. Hummelen, the *sinnekens* performed a function similar to English Vices, although the Dutch versions 'occur far more frequently and their behaviour exhibits more stereotype elements.'[75] This was the case, for example, in *The Five Wise and Five Foolish Maidens*.[76] Hummelen has most adequately described the nature of the Dutch morality, and we need only reiterate one of his key points. Whether in a morality play or in another form of drama, the *sinnekens* acted very much like the English Vices and Virtues, with the evil *sinnekens* taking over much of the role traditionally reserved for the ever popular devil.[77] Furthermore, *sinnekens* not only initiate temptation but also explain the meaning of such to the audience during what Hummelen describes as 'scenes apart,' bringing to light the 'true, demonic nature of the powers which the *sinnekens* portray,' often in ways that seem to the modern reader of the texts as rather pedantic. However, as Hummelen remarks, 'But in dramatic terms the most important thing is that because of the infernal mirth and demonic mockery these reactions are highly charged emotionally and force the observer to alter his attitude to what he has seen *before* the *sinnekens* appeared.'[78] These 'scenes apart' bring home to the audience the true import of the previous scene – sometimes comical, other times serious – and appear in most rhetorician drama, allowing the actors to bridge the gap between audience and stage, to involve the viewers more intimately in the ideas being portrayed, to draw their attention abruptly to the play's moral.[79] Such attempts at directly involving the audience occurred also with the frequent forays of the devil into the audience or with the stage-whispered asides of a fool.

An interesting example of this approach, as well as of the theological preoccupations of rhetoricians on the eve of the Reformation, is provided by Anthonis de Roovere's play *Whoever Wishes to be Saved* (*Quiconque vult salvus esse*). De Roovere (d. 1482), factor in Bruges, was in 1465 awarded an annual salary of 6£ Fl. by the magistrates of Bruges because he had for many years already served the city by writing many good moralities (*moralithetien*) and honourable entertainments as well as other rhetorician works.[80] It is evident that De Roovere intended *Whoever Wishes to be Saved* to be a work of theological education, reminding his viewers of the Apostles' Creed and explaining its meaning to them. Assisting him on stage are six characters, Jew (*Jeude*), Heathen (*Heydene*), Christian (*Kerstene*), the fool Half Fool-Half Wise (*Half Zot Half Vroet*), and two *sinnekens*, The Law of Grace (*De Wet van gracien*), and Faith (*Ghelooue*). Following the prologue's call for divine assistance for the performance, the play begins with a heated argument among Jew, Heathen, and Christian over the superiority of each of their faiths. After hurling insults at each others' religious beliefs, they are joined by Half Fool-Half Wise, whose presence on stage is not noticed by the other characters. His comments, therefore, are directed straight at the audience in frequently comic and occasionally bitingly satirical asides, helping to involve the viewers in the vigorous debate.[81] The *sinnekins* for their part explain in great detail the meaning of the Christian faith and how to be received into it; they also present a rather sophisticated explication of the Apostles' Creed and the doctrine of the Trinity. Occasionally the playwright provides some comic relief for his audience by having the three original characters renew their name-calling, or by the humorous interjections of the fool, but De Roovere always brings the viewers back to the very serious matter at hand. The moral edge of the play is offered by Heathen who points out the inconsistency of Christians who are supposed to live in peace with each other as a result of Christ's Passion, but who instead 'slay each other, like wolves do to sheep,'[82] a point seconded by the fool who shames the members of the audience with their own hypocrisy, criticizing especially 'usurers' such as storekeepers, merchants, and great financiers, 'who bankrupt the common welfare / with outward evil, openly!' and admonishes them to public penance.[83] Later, Heathen and Jew also criticize Christian and especially the clergy for their lack of charity, a fault that is a major reason why these characters have not converted to the Christian faith.[84]

As in so many Netherlandic plays the climax of this drama is tele-graphed by the unveiling of a painted figure, in this case that of Christ on the cross, and with the admonition to remember the Passion of Christ, do proper penance, observe the sacraments, worship properly, and honour the faith.[85] Thus this presumed Easter play combines orthodox theology, popular devotionalism, and criticism of ecclesiastical and social abuses. We, of course, do not know how well it was received by those watching it. However, the fact that the 'scene apart' format and intermingling of satire with straightforward didactic elements continued to be the major format followed by sixteenth-century factors suggests that rhetoricians deemed their approach to be effective. We have no reason to doubt this belief.

Undoubtedly the most famous Dutch morality play is that portraying the spiritual quest of *Elckerlijc*, or in English, *Everyman*, entitled also *The Mirror of Salvation*.[86] The work of a Brabanter, Peter of Diest, possibly the Carthusian Petrus Dorlandus, *Everyman* has achieved so much fame that it is unnecessary to rehearse its plot here. Its theology is certainly orthodox, and like *Whoever Wishes to be Saved*, supports officially sanctioned acts of devotion and penance, especially as controlled by the clergy. The play centres on Everyman who embarks on a pilgrimage to find someone who will accompany him before the throne of the almighty, who has called him to account for his lack of piety and materialism.[87] Finally, Everyman proceeds through the stages of despair, confession, and self-abnegation, until Contrition advises him to receive the sacrament of extreme unction from a priest, advice confirmed by Five Senses, whose praise of the priestly estate supports the belief that the play was composed by a cleric:

> Yes, Everyman, get thy viaticum.
> No emperor, king, duke, or count
> Received from God such paramount
> Authority as did the meanest priest.
> He carries, ever ready, the keys
> To all the sterling sacraments
> By which man attains heaven's radiance,
> And which God, for a medicine,
> Gave in pain from His heart to mankind,
> To take on earth ere he must hence,
> The seven holy sacraments
> ...

The priest surpasses all that is.
It's they who teach us Scripture, they
Who turn mankind from sins away.
They received from God even greater might
Than the angels in the heavenly light.
For each priest can manifest
God's body, His very blood and flesh,
Upon the altar in the mass

...

O noble priest of great worth,
Thou wouldst deserve that we kissed
Thy footsteps. Those who would resist
Their sins can only be released
Through the ministry of the priest.[88]

Contrition's mild rebuke of the sins of simony and sexual immorality among some of the clergy is quickly rebuked by Five Senses with his comment: 'I hope to God none be of that kind. / Therefore, let us honor the priests / and follow the good things that they teach.'[89] The play concludes with an epilogue admonishing its hearers to rely solely on charity, for all else will desert them in the end. Although plays composed by lay writers tended to be more vigorous in their satire of clerical or ecclesiastical abuses, in broad terms *Everyman's* depiction of lay religious practice and reliance on the sacraments and clerically controlled system of penance is typical of fifteenth-century moralities.

All in all, then, late medieval Dutch drama supported the theological system of the age, even when frequently poking fun at some of the church's representatives. Penance, the seven sacraments, devotion to the Virgin Mary and the saints, meditation on the suffering and crucifixion of Christ, and reliance on the priesthood were all essential elements of religious drama of the era. It can be suggested that promoting or defending these elements of the Catholic faith was a defining characteristic of late medieval religious drama in the Low Countries. In this context of strong support for the central facets of orthodoxy, gentle chastisement of the priesthood for individual failings was not seen as a threat by the authorities. This situation changed dramatically with the start of the Protestant Reformation, when the central tenets and structure of the Catholic church were called into question. Obviously those rhetoricians who decided to side with the reformers to some degree had to reshape their drama and perhaps even craft new plots if they sought to use the stage to promote their religious views. How they did so will provide one focus of the rest of this study. However, those playwrights who wished to remain faithful to traditional orthodoxy had at their disposal a goodly number of popular plays that in the past had supported the Catholic church. Whether they availed themselves of these models to craft vigorous defences of their faith and to counteract the innovations of the reformers will therefore provide another focal point. In other words, did rhetoricians continue to act as spokespersons for the religious status quo or did they become propagandists for the reform of church and society? In the following chapters we shall discuss this and other questions and meet more rhetoricians, especially those in Antwerp and Amsterdam. Obviously the level of criticism or support for reform among rhetoricians varied widely among individual rhetoricians, as well as among chambers. Successive chapters on the rhetoricians in Antwerp and Amsterdam will provide useful examples by which to examine the involvement of rhetoricians in the early Reformation in the Low Countries.

PART II

Vernacular Drama and the Early Urban Reformation

3

The Chambers of Rhetoric in Antwerp

Having sketched in broad strokes the development of a particular sense of mission among Netherlandic rhetoricians and described the political and religious context in which they performed their drama, it is now appropriate to examine in greater detail the experience of some rhetoricians in the sixteenth-century Low Countries. Antwerp's dramatists provide a case study of rhetoricians who, by and large, worked closely with their civic leaders throughout the period of the early Reformation, even though many of them became caught up in the groundswell of reform rhetoric.

The Early History of Antwerp's Rhetoricians, 1480–1519

By 1510 Antwerp was able to boast of three official chambers, The Gillyflower (*De Violieren*), The Marigold (*De Goudbloem*), and The Olive Branch (*De Olijftak*).[1] Although this public support of rhetorician groups was not quite in the same league as in Ghent and Brussels, which supported four each, certainly Antwerpenaars could feel considerable pride in their patronage of three very active drama societies. This support included important financial contributions from the city treasury, which were intended to fund the rental of the chamber itself and to cover special expenses incurred by the rhetoricians for their activity on behalf of the community.[2] Even though there developed considerable arguments about precedence, it appears that The Gillyflower was the first rhetorician society in the city (see illustration 5). In 1480 this chamber was officially created out of the St Luke's artist guild, itself established sometime in or before 1400.[3] It seems, in fact, that St Luke's members had for some time been involved in drama, for the name 'Gillyflower' (*Violierbloem*) was the first name of the St Luke's guild and it shared with the rhetorician society the same motto, 'gathered in goodwill' (*wt Jonsten versaemt*). The description of the chamber's establishment confirms that the artist guild had, prior to 1480, undertaken to perform the city's drama: 'This year our guild brothers won at the *Landjuweel* at Leuven two silver dishes for the highest prize, where Lord Jan de Buysenere, knight, was the prince. Then our chamber was ordained *The Gillyflower* with the motto, "gathered in goodwill."'[4] The Gillyflower kept its institutional connection to St Luke's, although it maintained limited administrative independence by having a prince and captain distinct from the heads of the artist's guild. The deacons of St Luke, however, continued to oversee this chamber.

In 1504 The Gillyflower was awarded the status of one of the city's 'sworn' or 'privileged' guilds, those that directly served the city, such as the various ceremonial guard, marksmen guilds, and confraternities. Among other privileges, these guilds were given the right to precedence over other guilds in processional order. Like the other privileged guilds, the size of The Gillyflower was limited to seventy-five members.[5] Furthermore, its original charter enjoined its companions to perform plays, entertainments, and allegorical riddles (*zinnebeeldische raedsels*) or refrains 'to the entertainment of the community,' and to present to the audience the question or topic of the performance in the form of a large banner or blazon. Moreover, like rhetoricians elsewhere, The Gillyflower's actors were expected to participate in various rhetorician competitions and to bring home their share of prizes for the promotion of their city.[6]

The Marigold appears to have originated shortly after The Gillyflower.[7] Over the course of the late fifteenth and sixteenth centuries, the two chambers vied with each other to bring the greatest glory to their community.[8] The chambers' efforts did not go unnoticed, for after a performance in Antwerp in 1490, both were rewarded with a gift of twelve Rhine gulden, which was recorded on 17 November in Antwerp's treasury book as an annual grant of three pounds Brabant. The city treasurer noted the expenditure in the following terms: 'In order to support Rhetoric to the honour and adornment of the city, to each of these same two societies is granted three pounds groat Brabants every year, for as long as they shall practise Rhetoric, and to assist in the rental of their chamber and other burdens.'[9] Judging from their activities in the following two decades, it appears that these chambers did everything they could to live up to the expectations of the Antwerp magistrates and to support the religious cult of the city. A few examples drawn from the dozens of known activities between 1490 and 1515 will suffice to illustrate the kind of work performed by Antwerp's rhetoricians. In 1493 The Gillyflower (and presumably The Marigold) participated in the major contest for Mechelen called by Duke Philip, who intended to have all rhetorician societies participate.[10] According to St Luke's guildbook, The Gillyflower entered the city on a wagon float depicting the 'glorious castle of Antwerp,' on top of which was shown St Luke painting the Virgin Mary.[11] The following year the St Luke guild celebrated the residence in their city of Mary of Burgundy, now King Maximilian's wife, and the entrance of her husband and son by erecting a statue of Venus, Juno, and Pallas on the market square and by staging *tableaux vivants*; for their part The Gillyflower's members fêted the rulers with a reading of refrains and a tournament (*ternoij spel*) involving forty participants.[12] Obviously rhetoricians did not restrict their organizational ability to strictly rhetorician events but frequently put themselves at the community's service as cultural experts.[13] In this same year The Gillyflower was granted by Pope Alexander VI a confraternity of the 'Seven Woes,' housed in Our Dear Lady Church, for which the chamber performed a play. The following year this chamber performed a long play on the King of Aragon to the pleasure of the city's magistrates,[14] while during 1496 Antwerpenaars witnessed The Gillyflower's major *Landjuweel* described in chapter 2 above.[15]

The following decades saw Antwerp's rhetoricians participating in a wide range of literary and dramatic activities both inside and outside their city. The Gillyflower could boast of an excellent composer of refrains, Mr Jan Casus Wenckart, a master painter and book illustrator, who won first prize at a refrain competition in Mechelen.[16] In 1503 The Gillyflower's leaders regaled their colleagues of Mechelen's The Peony with literary and dramatic performances, for which the latter returned the favour, 'to the friendship of both cities.' This dramatic exchange between the two cities seems to have become an annual affair, normally occurring on Division of Apostles' Day (15 July) in Antwerp and St John's Day in Mechelen, and is recorded several times in the guildbook of St Luke.[17] As already noted, in 1504 The Gillyflower was awarded the status and membership limit of a 'privileged guild' and in 1505 moved from their old premises to a chamber in 'den Bontenmantele,' presumably in a search for a larger and more dignified performance hall in keeping with their higher status.[18]

Not to be outdone, The Marigold likewise took part in regular exchanges with another city's chamber, this time Lier's Growing Tree (*Groeyenden Boom*).[19] Yet it appears that The Gillyflower was the dominant chamber in Antwerp. In 1509 it hosted a refrain contest involving rhetoricians and factors from several neighbouring communities, the expenses of which were borne by their captain, the knight Sir Costen van Berchem.[20] Growing esteem for The Gillyflower appears to have raised the jealousy of the leadership of The Marigold, who, after receiving permission to increase their membership, on 5 August 1510, initiated official proceedings to have the city decide which of the two societies was the most distinguished. Because it was older The Gillyflower was officially declared to be preeminent, although the decision by the magistrates surely did little to calm the feelings of The Marigold's membership.[21] The dispute, however, seems not to have hindered the ability of the two chambers to cooperate when it came to attending major events outside of Antwerp. A mere week after The Marigold initiated the legal complaint, both chambers and guild representatives, totalling over 400 men, made a glorious entrance into Herenthals, one that was reported to have been 'much more costly than the other cities.'[22]

By this year interest in rhetorician events seems also to have increased to the point where the official chambers, with their limitations on membership, could not contain all those wishing to participate. Thus it was that in 1510 a new chamber was officially established, one that perhaps had a less auspicious origin than its predecessors but which would certainly do its part in honouring the city. Originally known as The Unesteemed (*De Ongeachte*), this new society was organized by a Flemish advocate, Joris de la Formanteel, who gathered together a group of young fellows, most of them cabinetmakers, into a 'guild of rhetoric,' which in 1511 was renamed The Olive Branch (*De Olijftak*).[23] While there is evidence that this group had been meeting as early as 1500 to practise the art of rhetoric,[24] it had no formal status until it received its charter ten years later. To celebrate its foundation The Olive Branch performed a play *On Our Dear Lady* on the Saturday following her procession.[25] Their motto was the Latin 'Ecce Gratia' (I am grace), while their blazon depicted a dove with an olive branch in its beak, flying toward the ark of Noah. Aside from providing an outlet for the literary and dramatic aspirations of its members, it is evident that belonging to this chamber was a means by which these young craftsmen could seek to win the social esteem of their fellow burghers.

Certainly given the growing fame of their colleagues in The Gilly-flower and The Marigold, The Olive Branch's members could look forward to greater respect among their fellow Antwerpenaars.

Following its establishment, it appears The Olive Branch took its place in the cultural promotion of Antwerp. All three chambers, in fact, participated in a competition hosted in 1515 by The Peony in Mechelen on Mary Magdalene's Day (22 July), involving a truly impressive opening procession of entrants from fifteen rhetorician societies. Arriving from Antwerp were not only the rhetoricians, but also eight armoured knights of the city, the city's advocates, and 600 men on foot, horseback, or floats (*praelwagens*), led by The Gillyflower's prince, Benedictus sHertoghen, or Ducis, the cathedral organist. All wore the same costume and hosiery and not surprisingly won first prize for the most glorious entrance.[26] Clearly rhetorician contests had broad social and political significance far beyond the heightening of civic pride through success at dramatic contests. Such events provided the rulers of Antwerp opportunities to display visually to their neighbours the rising glory of their city, and perhaps to encourage them to submit to its political leadership.

Not even after the creation of The Olive Branch could the official chambers encompass the dramatic interests of Antwerp's population. Over and above the officially sponsored societies, it seems that other Antwerp citizens formed several unofficial chambers, called '*pap-gilden*,' ('pablum guilds') which performed their unapproved plays in private homes or in the streets.[27] The oldest of these was created sometime before 1533 and was called Lilies in the Valley of Calvary (*Leliken in den Dale van Calvariën*).[28] Presumably building on their education in Latin drama, children likewise put on public performances and residents of different streets competed with each other in the same manner as *rederijkers* at a *Landjuweel*.

Antwerp's Rhetoricians

Who joined Antwerp's three official chambers during the era of Charles V? Although there is not nearly the same amount of information available regarding Antwerp's dramatists as that found by E. van Autenboer for Mechelen's, there is enough data to make a few comparisons. Including the deacons of St Luke's guild, who acted also as The Gillyflower's deacons, a total of 121 rhetoricians who are known to have been associated with one of the three chambers between 1515 and

1556 were identified ·from the sources.[29] The vast majority of those rhetoricians (ninety-two or 77 per cent) whose chamber affiliation could be identified were members of The Gillyflower, a fact explained by the survival of the St Luke's guildbook. A further twenty had joined The Marigold while only four members of The Olive Branch were named in the sources. The affiliation of three more could not be identified. Altogether seventy-eight (65 per cent) of these individuals held chamber office above that of the general membership or actors, including four princes (Aerde de Ruytere, prince of The Marigold in 1524; Benedictus Ducis, prince of The Gillyflower in 1515; Jan de Broeckere, The Marigold's prince in 1529; and Merten Pemels, a German merchant selected as a 'pious prince' in 1555)[30] and three captains (Hr. Anthonis van Stralen, knight and captain of The Gillyflower in 1550; and two captains of The Marigold, Mr Philip de Buekeleer in 1524 and Hr. Philips Gontreel in 1529), whose status was similar to the prince. The identity of five of the city's factors is also known: Cornelis van Ghistele, playwright of The Marigold from 1551; Jan Salomon, who was selected as The Marigold's factor in 1524; The Gillyflower's Jan van den Berghe, who was this chamber's factor for most of the time between 1537 until at least 1551; Frans Fraet, whose chamber membership is unknown;[31] and Willem van Haecht, who seems to have replaced Van den Berghe in 1555. Given the preponderance of chamber leaders in this list, we must be careful not to draw facile conclusions about the 'rank and file' members of rhetorician societies.

A list of those occupations that could be identified illustrates once again that, like their confrères elsewhere, Antwerp's rhetoricians came from a fairly wide spectrum of professions and artisanal occupations (see table 2).[32] Even more than was the case with Mechelen's The Peony, Antwerp's artists dominated the dramatic scene of the city. However, if the deacons of The Gillyflower are momentarily excluded (they were, after all, selected primarily as deacons of St Luke's guild), then no single occupational group dominates the list. One might expect that, given the close connection between St Luke's and The Gillyflower, all or most of the latter's members would have been practitioners of the artistic crafts. This is not the case, for of those ordinary members of The Gillyflower whose occupations are known (sixteen), there were two sellers of old clothes, a tapestry weaver, a drapier, a pinmaker, a barmaker (*staefmaker*), two fine bakers (a *suykerbakker* and a *pasterymaker*), a butcher, a barber/surgeon, a schoolteacher, a brewer (*grootwerker*), a Nuremburg merchant, a sawyer, and a labourer. Only a

TABLE 2: Occupations of Antwerp Rhetoricians

Arts – 51 (50 from The Gillyflower)	**Food – 4**
29 unspecified artistic craft	2 Fine bakers
13 Painters	1 Butcher
3 Glassmakers/Painters	1 Brewery worker (Grootwerker)
3 Goldbeaters/Smiths	**Professionals – 6**
1 each of Sculptor, Lettercutter, Master printer, and Mirrormaker	2 Schoolmasters
	2 'Masters'
Nobles – 2	1 Lawyer
	1 Barber/Surgeon
Cloth – 6	
2 Old clothes sellers	**Metal – 2**
1 each of Drapier, Furrier, Blue dyer, and Tapestry maker	1 Barmaker (Staefmaker)
	1 Pinmaker
Others – 6	
3 Merchants	**TOTAL – 76**
1 each of Sawyer, Bookbinder, Labourer	

single goldsmith could have laid claim to membership in St Luke's guild. Even if all of the other twenty-five members of The Gillyflower whose occupations are unknown were artists, there was still room in this St Luke's–controlled chamber for actors from other crafts.

Rhetorician Activities during the Reign of Charles V

Rhetoricians' promotion of their city and higher rulers continued after Charles of Spain was declared of age and began his rule over the Low Countries in 1515 and over the Holy Roman Empire in 1519. By the time of his imperial election, the Netherlands had received the initial penetration of Lutheran propaganda, and Antwerp was fast becoming an early reform centre. Despite this complication, Antwerp city fathers continued proudly to sponsor the activities of their rhetoricians.[33] Naturally the imperial election of Charles required major festivities on the part of his Netherlandic subjects. St Luke's deacon recorded that in 1519 The Gillyflower's leaders put on a triumphal celebration, 'which cost a great deal,' in honour of Archduke Charles's election.[34] A Latin pamphlet described the event as a great spectacle, noting the wide assortment of painted figures and acted *tableaux* with inscriptions in Latin, Greek, and Hebrew. All of these revolved around the terms '*Fides et Amor*,' declaring the inviolable faith and love of Antwerp towards its sovereign.[35] Albrecht Dürer, visiting the city at the time of the celebration, remarked with considerable admiration on the procession:

> On Sunday after Our Dear Lady's Ascension Day I witnessed the great procession at Antwerp, where the entire city was gathered, of all crafts and standings ... In this procession there were made very many wonderful things, prepared at great expense. For one saw many wagons, plays, ships, and other clever works. There were also in order multitudes of the prophets, followed by the New Testament, also the multitude of the angels, the three kings riding on large camels and on other rare monsters and very nicely equipped, also the flight to Egypt, very edifying.[36]

On top of all this, The Gillyflower lavished the city with an expensive feast 'on the Cauwenberg' (op den Cauwenberg) which cost them 78£ Fl., a debt that required three years to retire.[37]

Frequent were visits to the neighbouring cities of Diest (1521, 1541),[38] Leuven (1529), and Lier (1527). In return Antwerp rhetoricians often hosted other southern Netherlandic chambers.[39] On the last Sunday in May 1525, The Gillyflower held their May festival, which their deacon described in the following terms:

> Item. In the same year the guildbrothers and deacons of our guild celebrated the May festival, the like of which had never before been seen inside Antwerp. To their honour the guildbrothers were given a prize from the gentlemen of the law [magistrates] and from the common people, which triumph shall abide long in memory. Mr Peeter Gielys did the planning.[40]

In 1534 the St Lucas guild complained about the increasing costs of their rhetorician activities, noting that entertaining rhetoricians from other cities, as well as performing 'Lenten plays and other similar things to the honour of this city' were putting an excessive burden on the guild's treasury, which was already under considerable strain as a result of having to support too many poor members and to counteract the presence of numerous foreign artists in the city.[41] Then on 30 April 1531, St Luke's leaders passed an ordinance establishing a poor chest (armen Busse) and on 30 April 1537, requested permission to create a charitable brotherhood (busse en minlicke broederscap) to help their sick and poor.[42] However, these financial problems were resolved by 1538, when the treasurer was able to pay off all the guild's debts,[43] although the deacons would later complain in 1561 about the excessive costs of producing rhetorician drama.[44]

In spite of the considerable costs involved in putting on major dramatic and celebratory events, Antwerp's rulers clearly encouraged their rhetoricians to spare no effort in surpassing their previous accomplishments. Such encouragement could take on very concrete shape; certainly from 1530 on, if not before, the city's account books list yearly gifts of wine to the official chambers to help them celebrate their annual feast day.[45] Again, Antwerp's rulers were not disappointed.[46] On 16 August 1529, they ordered a feast in honour of the Peace of Camerijk, calling upon the city's civic guards, rhetoricians, and guilds to dress in their finest costumes and to produce plays and other costumed performances.[47] It appears that The Gillyflower's contribution to this celebration was a play called *The King of Aragon*.[48]

The usual rhetorician activities continued unabated throughout the 1530s and 1540s, in spite of the frequent periods of hardship caused by the Habsburg-Valois wars and the disturbance of the religious peace of the city resulting from the authorities' attempts to suppress dissemination of Lutheran and Anabaptist ideas. Just a couple of weeks after the crushing of the Anabaptist kingdom in Münster, Antwerp's rhetoricians competed at the Mechelen *Landjuweel*, with The Gillyflower and The Marigold bringing home first prizes. Then, as part of the celebrations surrounding the Armistice of Nice in 1538 The Gillyflower put on a large feast on the Great Market.[49] The civic rulers had in fact proclaimed a city-wide competition for the most beautiful celebration among the city's rhetorician and artisan guilds, with awards of mutton and wine.[50]

The crowning achievement for The Gillyflower's rhetoricians was undoubtedly their success at perhaps the most infamous of the sixteenth-century rhetorician competitions, that held in Ghent in June 1539. While we devote a separate chapter to this contest below, it will be necessary later in this chapter to recount some aspects of The Gillyflower's play, which won first prize in the most prestigious event of the contest, the *spelen van zinne* competition. From the St Luke's deacon's account, however, it would seem that The Gillyflower's garnering of the award for most glorious entrance was of even greater value for the eminence of the society.

In this year there came to us tidings of a glorious festival of rhetoric, established by The Fountain inside Ghent, into which we made our

entrance most triumphantly, with many beautiful figures, characters, etc.,
and with many gentlemen, merchants, and guild brothers, all very costly,
for which we won three cups of four marks, and for the blazon which we
had presented before the stage, we won a lovely silver fountain weighing
three ounces. And we performed there a very good play, for which we
won the highest and greatest prize, four silver tankards, together worth
nine marks. And the factor, for his person, one silver cup of four ounces.
And our fool had for his prize a silver ape of four ounces.[51]

Presumably inspired by The Gillyflower's success at the Ghent competition, leaders of Antwerp's districts or streets in August and September organized formal drama competitions among their children. Given
the prevalence of instruction in classical Latin drama in the Low Countries' city schools, it seems reasonable to assume that Antwerp's youth
were able to compose and perform refrains, dramatic comedies, and
songs.[52]

Although some smaller competitions continued to be run, such as the
one held in Diest in 1541 at which The Gillyflower won first prize and
the other two Antwerp chambers competed,[53] larger contests such as
the *Landjuweel* planned for 1540 in Antwerp were delayed because of the
ongoing state of war and perhaps too as a result of increasing religious
and social unrest in the city.[54] It was, after all, only in the previous year
that Ghent's populace had risen up against its rulers just a matter of
weeks after the rhetorician competition in the city (see below, chapter 6).
Almost at the same time Antwerp's magistrates had their hands full in
negotiating a peaceful settlement with their populace over an unpopular excise.[55] The postponement of the *Landjuweel* was therefore not surprising. That it should be delayed until 1561 speaks volumes for the
level of suspicion that the higher authorities had developed regarding
rhetorician contests as a result of the Ghent competition.[56]

Such misgiving does not appear to have hindered rhetorician performances at the local level. The annual May, Lent, and Epiphany feast
days remained popular after 1539, and the city continued to rely on
their dramatists to help organize civic celebrations. Ironically they
were called upon to do so when in May 1540 Charles V visited the city
after quelling the Ghent rebellion. One can well imagine the members
of The Gillyflower wishing to put extra effort into their preparations so
as to assure their ruling prince that they had no seditious intentions.
Their deacon recorded that for this event The Gillyflower's leaders had
put on a 'triumphal celebration' in front of St Luke's guildhall.[57]

Another example of rhetorician service to the community occurred in 1542, when Antwerp's treasurer noted that 'as the guilds of rhetoric of the city during last Lent, performed their *spelen van zinnen* before my lord and other good men who heard the play in front of the city hall, thus a banquet was prepared for them.'[58] In the same year the treasurer further recorded that the rhetoricians were among those who partook of the festivities in front of the city hall during Epiphany.[59] These rhetorician activities may have had greater import than normal, for this was the year that Charles V's war to bring the duchy of Guelders into his orbit had come to the gates of Antwerp in the person of the Guelders' captain Martin van Rossum. Although the siege did not come to Antwerp until July, distracting the apprehensive residents from their plight and encouraging them to continue support of their ruling prince were undoubtedly the goals in the minds of Antwerp's magistrates when they commissioned these performances (for an example of the Antwerp Treasurer's entries regarding the rhetoricians, see illustration 5).

Throughout the last dozen or so years of Charles V's reign Antwerp's rhetoricians continued to fulfil their cultural services for their community. For example, in 1551 St Luke's leaders expressed great pleasure with the performance of Jan van den Berghe's *The Voluptuous Man*.[60] Not to be outdone, The Marigold's factor Cornelis van Ghistele wrote and produced two versions of the classical drama *Eneas en Dido*, the first performed in 1551 and the second in the following year. Van Ghistele, in fact, regarded it as his duty to translate Latin classics into the vernacular for the instruction of those not learned in Latin, thereby bringing Renaissance humanism's love of the classics to the masses.[61] Finally, in 1556 the city prepared itself for the visit of Philip II, who sought to solidify his claim to the governance of the Low Countries after the abdication of his father. As one can imagine the costs for this extravagant display were enormous, adding an extra burden to Antwerp's already considerable debt load. All citizens of the city were expected to contribute toward the 'twentieth penny' which the *brede raad* had approved on 28 March preceding the entrance, while each guild, both artisanal and ceremonial, also contributed funds toward the considerable expenses.[62] According to one account, nearly 1,160£ Fl. was collected from the major guilds of the city, ranging from a high of 200£ Fl. exacted from the prosperous merchants' guild (*Meerssen*), to a low of 8£ Fl. from the humble peat bearers (*Torfdragers*).[63] Another tally has a somewhat higher figure (1,860£ Fl.), and includes payments of 40£

Fl. each from the three rhetorician chambers and of 50£ Fl. each from two confraternities, The Sacrament Guild and Our Dear Lady Brotherhood.[64] If these figures represent anything like the economic prosperity of each of the city's guilds, then the rhetoricians appear to fit somewhere in the middle, below the wealthy merchants but well above the lowest artisans.

Conflict between Rhetoricians and Militia Guilds

In spite of these ceremonial successes, not all was well within Antwerp's rhetorician communities. Toward the end of Charles V's reign, a new conflict broke out, this time over what the rhetorician leadership regarded as the theft of members from their chambers by the militia guilds of the city. However, it seems that the dispute had also run the other way, for in a letter to the city dated 1 June 1548, the emperor discusses the problem of militia guildsmen who have gone over to The Olive Branch.[65] In other missives now housed in the City Archives of Antwerp, it is apparent that The Olive Branch and The Marigold had both grown in size to over a hundred strong, greatly increasing the rental costs of their chambers, much of which was borne by the city treasury.[66] Judging from the surviving sources, it appears that the dispute was heightened around 1551 as a result of Charles V's desire to improve the fortification and military readiness of the city, which involved the reorganization and strengthening of the various militia or marksmen guilds. In a letter of 8 September 1551, the emperor ordered the guilds' leaders to select four 'qualified citizens' to go through the membership lists of the various confraternities and rhetorician chambers to discover any former members of the militia guilds and present them to the mayors, presumably to encourage their return to their military duties.[67] A year later it had become clear to the emperor and his regent, Mary of Hungary, that Antwerp's militia guilds required new members and they raised the total membership of the six guilds to 460 from 360.[68] The problem was where to find these recruits. Obviously they had to be of the same social standing as the current members and the most obvious place to find them was within the city's other ceremonial guilds.

Not able to find enough potential militiamen through means of persuasion, on 24 February 1555, Philip II ordered the release from their membership oath of seventy-five men each from The Marigold and The Olive Branch, so they could join the militia guilds. This was notwithstanding the fact that The Marigold's membership had been reduced to seventy-five individuals from over one hundred in 1553.[69] This move would leave each of these guilds in dire financial straights, for although they were permitted to find new members to restore their membership lists, they would remain vulnerable to constant raiding on the part of the militia guilds. Furthermore, the chambers' replacements obviously would be of lesser economic standing than those desired by the militia guildsmen, not to mention less experienced in the rhetorical arts. Throughout the rest of the decade these two chambers sent missives of complaint to their rulers, reminding them of their members' privilege of freedom from oaths to the other 'sworn' guilds and petitioning them not only to restore their lost members, but to increase their maximum size by fifty each, and failing that, at least to eighty. Philip II finally decreed in 1559 that each chamber could protect from militia guild interference seventy-five members each.[70] While a far cry from the expansionary goals of the chambers' leadership, the decision allowed for the survival of these two rhetorician societies. Perhaps because of its connection to St Luke's guild, The Gillyflower does not appear to have been touched by the conflict. It might be possible to conclude from these proceedings that there were a number of citizens of relatively high social standing who preferred membership in a guild devoted to the literary and dramatic arts than to one devoted to marksmanship and military drilling. At the same time, it is also evident that the higher rulers regarded the militia units as more important to the welfare of the civic community, at least in times of unrest.

Antwerp Rhetoricians and the Reformation I: Anna Bijns

In spite of this difference of opinion, the activities of Antwerp's rhetoricians were approved and financed by the city fathers, and regarded as beneficial to the city's honour. The ongoing support on the part of the city must have helped to keep the chambers in line when it came to their flirting with the more radical forms of religious heterodoxy. As elsewhere, many of Antwerp's citizens were attracted to the ideas of Luther and other reformers and it is therefore not surprising that many of the city's *rederijkers* were also interested in the Reformation. At the same time, it must be remembered that not all rhetoricians shared reformation tendencies. For example, in 1539 Joris Formenteel, founder of The Olive Branch, established a mass in the Church of St Walburgis on the feast day of the name of our Lord Jesus Christ. Similarly, a few years later, on 22 June 1542, The Marigold founded a mass on an altar in the Our Dear Lady Cathedral.[71] Most likely those founding these masses did so out of more than mere prudence, and may have intended them as a sign of orthodoxy during a religiously turbulent time, made especially so after the rhetorician contest in Ghent in 1539.

By far the clearest example of an Antwerp rhetorician opposing reformation ideas came from the skilful quill of Anna Bijns.[72] Born in Antwerp in 1493, Bijns never married but after 1516 she taught at the primary school opened by her brother, and at his marriage in 1536, established her own single-room school house, teaching until her eightieth year. She died in 1575 at the venerable age of eighty-two, having achieved in her lifetime the status of the most talented composer of rhetorician refrains in the Netherlands and the best-selling Netherlandic author of the sixteenth century. Although Bijns is not known to have been an official member of a rhetorician chamber, Herman Pleij has suggested that she was the 'Antwerp girl of fifteen' who won a prize for her city at Brussels's 1512 refrain competition on the topic of Mary's conception. Pleij speculates that Bijns was allowed to participate in a chamber on a semi-official basis, even travelling to Brussels with the other rhetoricians.[73] One can only imagine the wonder of the other male rhetoricians at the remarkable performance of this young girl.

Unfortunately, no plays have been conclusively attributed to her[74] but there is a considerable corpus of refrains.[75] What these reveal about Bijns's attitude toward the Reformation is considerable, as has been shown in a number of studies and editions of her work, most recently those by Pleij, Aercke, and Hermina Joldersma. According to Aercke, Bijns saw the goal of the poet as twofold: 'as an artist he must let pure devotion yield blossoms of artistic beauty, and as a crusading Christian his task is to apply this art anew in defense of his Church.'[76] This she did with great zeal, characterizing the Lutherans as a damnable sect which has caused more damage to the Low Countries than the infamous Guelders captain, Martin van Rossum.[77] Luther is an 'ignorant heretic' who is worse 'than a Jew,' a 'lying monk,' the true 'messenger of Antichrist'; all who follow him are deceivers of God's people, hostile snakes.[78] Moreover, Luther turned monks and nuns into villains and whores, while now

Scriptures are read in the taverns,
In the one hand the gospel, in the other the stein,
They are all drunken fools; nevertheless by these
Are learned preachers ridiculed.[79]

Bijns furthermore blames Luther for the even worse heresies which, in her mind, plague her homeland: 'Had not Luther spoken out so loudly / We would not have Anabaptism around.'[80] At the same time, she acknowledges that major reasons for the success of the Reformation (against which she fought 'for scanty thanks')[81] were the laxity and immorality of the Catholic clergy who still refuse to show the necessary zeal to push back the tide:

> Alas! They're mostly just dumb dogs.
> They cannot bark – and that is why God's law
> Is now neglected and brushed aside![82]

At the same time, she condemns the easy anticlericalism of the Reformers:

> Is it virtue to invest brazen lies,
> Deride cardinals, bishops, popes,
> Holler and rage against priests and monks
> Leave the straight for the crooked way?
> ...
> Is it a virtue, to insult upright preachers,
> Despise saints and saintesses, the Mother of God?
> If sin be virtue, then Lutherans are saints.[83]

She also defends priests who are 'as human as you and me.'[84] Those whose heresy has split the church she likens to a disgusting disease that was laying waste her homeland.

Not only religious reformers but her male rhetorician cohorts received the attention of her sharp wit and tongue. In a refrain composed on 11 January 1528, ''Tis a Waste to Cast Pearls before Swine,' she castigates rhetoricians for playing down to their audiences, for giving in to 'vulgar conceit' and baser interests:

> Crafty spirits, noble Mercurists,
> Rhetoricians, subtle artists,
> Economize on sterling words.
> Hold in reserve ingenious conceits.
> Men of letters: your cheap artistic claims
> Apply Rhetoric where filthy dung belongs.
> Noble Rhetoric, I weep for the affront

That you bear such verbal disrespects
From whomever and whenever. Shame!
Many a conceited fool you'll find
To whom Rhetoric seems naught but trite.
No need to perform our art soigné
Before vain windbags, tongue-tied themselves.
'Tis a waste to cast pearls before swine.[85]

Given that Bijns's stated goal for the poetical craft is the support of the church, it is very likely that a major reason for her disgust with her contemporary rhetoricians had to do with what she saw as their public support of heresy, or at the very least, of their lack of vigorous opposition to it. As Joldersma notes, 'she was the first, most articulate, and most convincing Catholic voice in Dutch of the century,'[86] but the pessimistic spirit that pervades Bijns's poetry is indicative that she herself thought she was fighting a losing battle.

Antwerp Rhetoricians and the Reformation II: Reform Plays

On top of the refrains of Bijns and others, a handful of plays have survived that are known to have been composed or performed in Antwerp during the reign of Charles V. The most famous of these from a reform perspective was that which won the 1539 Ghent *spelen van zinne* competition. This work, performed by The Gillyflower, was a clearly Lutheran play, yet it had received the official sanction of Antwerp's and Ghent's magistrates.[87] The plays for this contest were composed in response to the assigned question, 'What is the dying man's supreme hope?' and Antwerp's contribution, composed by The Gillyflower's factor, Jan van den Berghe (alias van Diest), answered with, 'the resurrection of the body.' While this play was Lutheran in attitude, it was also directed against the more radical ideas of Loy de Pruistinck, a slater whose quite unorthodox opinions, including his rejection of hell, eternal punishment, and the physical resurrection, as well as his affirmation that the Holy Spirit was none other than human reason resident in each individual, won many followers in Antwerp.[88] An analysis of this script will help illustrate the type of reform message which appealed most to The Gillyflower's members. A brief introduction to Pruystinck will prepare the background for an understanding of the text.

In 1525 Pruystinck travelled to Wittenberg to convince Luther of his pantheistic notions but Luther's response was hardly positive: he hastily dashed off a missive to his followers in Antwerp warning them of this mischievous spirit (*polltergeyster*) and his dangerous notions.[89] Ironically, when in January of the following year Pruystinck and nine of his supporters were arrested for heresy, his crime was identified as 'Lutheranism' (*heresie lutheriane*), something that Luther must have found quite distasteful.[90] On 26 February these heretics took part in a public recantation that exhibited many of the aspects of a formal procession, indeed of a dramatic performance:

> Anno 1526, February 26, a stage was built here, whereupon were the chancellor, members of the council and mayors, the Markgrave, and the aldermen of Antwerp, where the upper priest began a sermon during which entered the ten persons, among them two women, each with a candle, and one carried a torch. And shortly he quit the sermon because of the great noise of the people, and then the general procession began in the market, where stood the marksmen in their armour, from the city hall to the Breederystrate, and the rest of the guilds were in their chambers, and some of the guilds were also in armour. And the great bell sounded, and then the Holy Sacrament came. Upon these people were placed mantles, upon the one stood the Holy Sacrament, upon the other Luther with many devils, and upon some books, and they followed the Holy Sacrament into the church, and from there they went again to the city hall, and had their mantles removed. And each went into the hall, and there these people's books were burned.[91]

As witnessed in this and many other examples, the fulfilment of civic justice was a public display with as many dramatic elements as a rhetorician performance or a *tableau vivant*.

In spite of this public recantation, Pruystinck continued to spread his ideas throughout the city, attracting not only an adoring crowd of poor sympathizers, who bowed down when he passed by adorned in his rags and jewels, but also a number from the middle and upper social strata, including a jeweller and religious refugee from Paris, Christopher Herrault.[92] Although Herrault was interrogated several times in February 1535, he was released.[93] Finally, he and his religious mentor Pruystinck, along with several other Loyists, were arrested and executed in 1544 as a result of the torture-extracted testimony in Deventer of Jorien Ketel, one of the key associates of the Anabaptist/spiritualist David Joris. Ketel confessed to having had discussions with Herrault and other Loyists, presumably to convince them to transfer their allegiance from Pruystinck to Joris, who between 1539 and 1544 resided in and near Antwerp under the protection of Cornelis van Lier, lord of Berchem, and his mother-in-law, Anna van Etten, lady of Schilde.[94] With this added impetus (the authorities seemed more anxious about the heresy of Joris than of Pruystinck), Antwerp's gentlemen of the court took vigorous action to expunge the Loyists from the city. Prior to 1544, however, they seemed quite relaxed about the considerable popular support that the so-called libertines had gained in Antwerp. Perhaps they were hoping that the condemnation of their ideas from the normally divergent quarters of Luther and Bijns would suffice.

It was within this explosive atmosphere that Van den Berghe composed The Gillyflower's entry for the Ghent competition of 1539. This play opens with a verbal battle between two allegorical figures, Examination of the Scriptures (*Schrifs onderzoucken*) and False Meaning (*Verkeerde zin*). Examination chases False Meaning from the stage with his affirmation that the soul's consolation is discovered through the pure, untainted Word of God. Then enters the central character of the play, Dying Man (*Staervende mensche*) who turns to several other allegorical figures in his attempts to find solace in his forthcoming demise.[95] Apprehension over death and the afterlife thus provides the central problem in the play, not surprising given the current debate in Antwerp over Pruystinck's unusual ideas. Reason (*Redene*) directs Dying Man to The Law (*De wet*), who then debates with Self Reliance (*Eyghen betrauwen*) and Dying Man over the question of whether or not Dying Man's good works are sufficient to please God. To Dying Man's plea, 'Have I not done many virtuous works, so that I am righteous?' The Law replies that none are righteous, no one has fulfilled completely God's law in his heart, for human nature has been thoroughly corrupted as a result of Adam's fall.[96] Self Reliance brings up all of the typical objections to Luther's teaching on the depravity of man (such as the unfairness of God making a law that could not be kept),[97] all of which are successfully countered by The Law.

Finally seeing his predicament, Dying Man laments, 'Now all my trusts are gone! How can I flee God's judgment?'[98] Neither Reason nor The Law is able to provide the answer, but at this moment Preacher of the Word (*Vercondigher des woordts*) enters the stage and presents Dying Man with Luther's teaching of salvation by faith alone through the grace of God as proclaimed in the gospel. Preacher's role in the process

of salvation is central, for those who have come to despair as a result of
their sin can find salvation only in hearing the gospel preached, a very
Lutheran emphasis.[99] This character then opens the curtain to show a
painting of God's words to the serpent in paradise. According to
Preacher of the Word, the law's function was to reveal humanity's true
predicament, while the gospel offers forgiveness; 'the law condemns
and the gospel forgives; each has a distinct office, but are bound
together in one book.'[100] Luther's teaching on the role of law and gospel could not be presented more clearly. Supporting this presentation is
another figure, this time the standard one of Christ on the cross, who
bore the sin and suffering of Dying Man.[101] When Dying Man laments
his continuing sinfulness and weakness of faith, Preacher retorts with a
very clear summary of Luther's doctrine of *semper justus et peccator*:

> Sinful you will also remain your whole life;
> But those who believe, God does not reckon
> As sinful, for God places Christ for you
> To wisdom, holiness, and righteousness.[102]

The climax of the play begins with Dying Man's pleading question
of how to receive greater faith. Preacher's response is to reveal another
painted figure of the resurrected Christ triumphant over the serpent
and to affirm the reality of both Christ's resurrection and that of all
believers:

> Stay at rest, and be quiet for a while.
> He is buried, raised on the third day
> In the same condition; so you must be the same,
> For those who are baptized in the good Christ Jesus,
> Have put on Christ and are very sweet
> Members of his body and strong bones.
> So have the believers in the world's garden
> Been richly crucified together with Christ,
> Truly died and buried,
> And also raised with him, for all that he is
> You are too; thus see how Christ is freely
> Living and also triumphant over all.[103]

Dying Man rejoices in this teaching, and Preacher admonishes him to
put on the 'bridegroom's cloak' and thus become a 'new person' that is

'created immortal after God's image,' so that he might finally enter the kingdom of heaven where a place has been prepared for him.[104] Finally getting the point, Dying Man exults in the victory of Christ's resurrection over sin, death, and the devil and its promise for the resurrection of Christians. He then brings Pruystinck's unorthodox opinions to the fore, by asking if the final resurrection of Christians is a spiritual one only.[105] To this Preacher strongly responds:

> So maintain this solution well,
> For the holy, apostolic church
> Believingly confesses (each one take note here)
> The resurrection of the flesh [is] entirely physical.
> And Job also says: I know that I fittingly
> Shall rise up on the Last Day,
> And in my flesh, to my pleasure
> I will see God; and Paul wished also to point out,
> That you on the Last Day will first see
> Death entirely destroyed with its arrows.
> Thus the resurrection of the flesh is, in my narration,
> The greatest consolation for people, for if that did not come,
> So was it all vain of Christ
> All that he has done, and humanity's consolation was gone.[106]

Preacher brings the play to a close by revealing another illustration, this time of the resurrection of the flesh, and by affirming the final judgment after the resurrection.[107]

It is evident that the actors of The Gillyflower and especially the play's author, Jan van den Berghe, were captivated by Luther's doctrines and were not reticent in displaying their opinions on stage. Although some scholars have been reluctant to acknowledge the Lutheran character of this play (and others performed at Ghent), there is little doubt from this summary that it follows quite strictly a Lutheran construction of salvation.[108] That no reprimand was forthcoming from either the Ghent or Antwerp authorities for The Gillyflower's 1539 award-winning play – although the church authorities were understandably irritated by most of the Ghent performances – illustrates that Antwerp's rhetoricians could openly use the stage to inculcate Lutheran doctrines in their audience if they did so in a sophisticated manner. Those who sought to do so in the pulpit or in unapproved channels such as street preaching, or who, like Pruystinck and the

Anabaptists, went beyond Luther's reform program, found the government much less congenial. Perhaps even Catholic magistrates could overlook the moderate unorthodoxy of the Lutheran elements of Van den Berghe's drama because of its usefulness as a tool in countering the more socially dangerous opinions of Pruystinck. Evidently vocal opposition to radical reform was a useful and conscious tool to divert the ire of the authorities from the promotion of less socially dangerous reform ideas, even though still punishable by imperial mandate.

Punished Rhetoricians

Were any Antwerp rhetoricians punished for their reform sentiment? The court records indeed reveal a couple of cases where Antwerp *rederijkers* were disciplined for defamatory actions. One involved a Coppen or Jacob van Middeldonck, who in 1546 was ordered to complete a pilgrimage to Russemadouwe for writing in 1542 a play 'smacking of heresy.'[109] At the time of the performance Middeldonck was only fifteen or sixteen years old and belonged to one of the unofficial chambers, The Damaskflower (*De Damastbloeme*) which, according to his testimony, consisted of other youths. Middeldonck had performed a previously composed play entitled *The Tree of the Scriptures*,[110] which had been earlier enacted in 1539 at the Zeeland town of Middelburg. It was decidedly evangelical and anticlerical in thrust, but no more so than The Gillyflower's Ghent play.[111]

The only member of an official chamber known to have been arrested for heretical opinions before 1556 was the Antwerp schoolmaster Peeter Schuddematte, member of The Gillyflower, who was arrested shortly after Pruystinck's execution in October 1544[112] and executed in 1547 on account of a supposedly scandalous play he had composed.[113] It is unlikely that Schuddematte was involved in any form of radical ideology, for it appears that the local mendicant clergy had become upset about some satirical comments which Schuddematte had made at the expense of Antwerp's Franciscans. Normally magistrates also enjoyed such anticlerical satire, but Schuddematte's efforts came at an unfortunate time when Pruystinck's example provided the Inquisitor with incontrovertible evidence of the dangers inherent in unorthodoxy and anticlericalism. Aside from these two incidents, Antwerp's regents continued to encourage the performances of their official chambers while attempting to check the activities of unapproved dramatic groups.[114]

Van den Berghe's Plays

A survey of the few available scripts confirms that at the most Antwerp's rhetoricians through the decades of the 1540s and 1550s promoted moderate reform. In addition to the Ghent play, two others were composed by Jan van den Berghe: *Hanneken Leckertant*, which won first place at the Diest competition in 1541, is a lighthearted farce (*cluyt*) about two young friends whose attempts to avoid work (spinning) and their mothers' discipline only results in a lesson taught to the both of them by the local Quicksilver.[115] On a more serious level is Van den Berghe's *The Voluptuous Man*, performed to the pleasure of the chamber's leadership in 1551.[116] This long and complex play involving sixteen characters splices a Lutheran theology onto the traditional 'spiritual pilgrimage' format of late medieval plays such as *Everyman*. In this case Voluptuous Man becomes entrapped by the allures of False Faith and Fleshly Mind, the former partly attired as a devil and the latter as death. Whereas in *Everyman* the solution to the central character's dilemma is found in the performance of good works and a return to the churchly means of grace, here Grace of God turns away Wrath of God (dressed in red with a bloody face) from Voluptuous Man by a fervent appeal to God's mercy. There is also considerable expression of vigorous anticlericalism, as when Bad Faith announces to Carnal Lust:

> For most of the clergy follow you.
> They'd rather die then [*sic*] forego you.
> They study mostly for worldly acclaim,
> To 'atch new ideas is their daily aim,
> That's why they argue with all that back-biting,
> Disputing their case with great piles of writing,
> And continuing to grant me their permission,
> In order to retain their superior position,
> Establishing thereby a cast-iron case,
> In which the truth takes second place,
> Twisting right into wrong with disastrous result,
> That's why I, Bad Faith, come into the world.[117]

Not only has Bad Faith inspired the clergy to immoral acts but he confides to his cohort, 'The truth is something I've always abhorred, / and doomed many such to the gallows or stake.'[118]

In line with an evangelical presentation of salvation, Grace of God furthermore reminds Almighty Power that his own Son had taken upon himself the sin of the world. Voluptuous Man makes a plea for forgiveness and the day of tribulation is graciously forestalled. He then turns to the audience to remind those watching of the nearness of that day and encourages his hearers to take up the book of life in which will be found 'trust for poor and rich,' possibly a coded message to take up the Bible in the vernacular, the unauthorized printing of which was illegal while possession of a pocket New Testament was in itself evidence of heresy. Of course, if hauled before the Inquisitor, the playwright could simply respond that the passage was allegorical in intent. Given the tremendous thirst for vernacular Bibles in the Low Countries, it is expected that many hearers of this play would have taken the passage literally.[119] In this work Van den Berghe and his actors have presented in unmistakable fashion an evangelical view of salvation using a traditional dramatic format normally associated with orthodoxy, helping to ease the play's audience into accepting the new and heretical ideas. At the same time, Van den Berghe composed the start of his play in a very humorous, often ribald fashion, presumably to catch and hold the attention of his audience and to make them more receptive to the serious message presented in the second half of the work. One can well imagine the guffaws of the audience at the following repartee:

> CARNAL LUST: Just turn around, you vicious old rake ...
> Let's see what you've got 'idden from view.
> BAD FAITH: I'll show you my arse.
> CARNAL LUST: Ay, you're a devil it's true,
> You're worse than the very 'ound of 'ell.
> BAD FAITH: Let's see you then, letching ne'er-do-well,
> You're no saint, for all your smirks.
> Look in my arsehole.
> BAD FAITH. [*sic* – read Carnal Lust]: Hey, that's where death lurks!
> Is that the wages of all in your pay?[120]

At the same time, such use of scatological language to denigrate one's theological opponents was a frequent technique of Luther himself.[121] Taken together these plays, especially the 1539 Ghent work and *Voluptuous Man*, strongly suggest that the playwright and members of The Gillyflower were using the stage as a forum to promote Lutheran reform.

Frans Fraet's A Present from Godt Loondt

Other rhetoricians within Antwerp seem also to have reflected evangelical notions in their plays. Bringing together the farce and allegorical dramatic forms is a dinner play (usually performed at weddings and similar celebrations) called *A Present from Godt Loondt, Grammerchijs, Besolos Manos* written by the Antwerp printer and factor Frans Fraet for The Marigold.[122] This unusual play begins with some rather sharp dialogue among three characters, a drunken Dutchman, Godt Loondt, a Frenchman named Grammerchijs, and the Spaniard Besolos Manos, each criticizing the other's linguistic abilities (each name is in the language of the particular character and is not readily translated). After filling the first half of the play with bawdy repartee, Fraet turns to the central theme of the play. Each of the characters has arrived with a gift for the audience. To the guffaws of the other characters (with remarks like 'you must be drunk'), and surely of the audience, each of the actors announces that he is presenting to 'these excellent gentlemen' a castle (*casteel*), fortress (*borcht*), or stronghold (*slot*). At this point (and the transition is quite abrupt) the spiritual meaning of these gifts is explained. The castle is the true foundation, the light of the world; the stronghold is the alpha and omega, the Word of God which protects those who observe God's commands from faith; the fortress is that before which all despisers of God's Word will kneel. Clearly, then, the presents offered to the audience are metaphors of Christ, described as the only advocate or mediator for sinful man.[123] Besolos Manos furthermore affirms that the 'faithful, strong lock' strengthens believers against the Whore of Babylon, who, riding on the apocalyptic beast, has become drunk with the blood of the righteous. Far from the opening humour, Manos proclaims 'Woe to you persecutors of sects,' who 'spoil God's Word with sophistry and drunkenness.'[124] At the end Christ, the true *casteel, borcht,* and *slot,* will slay 'the old serpent' with all his servants. Like Van den Berghe's, Fraet's effort was Lutheran in theology, including in this case, Luther's sense of the approaching Last Judgment. Once again Antwerp *rederijkers* used the stage to promulgate reform doctrines to the city's gentlemen. Tolerance for Fraet's opinions did not continue after the accession of Philip II to the throne; in 1558 this factor was beheaded for printing a heretical work.[125]

Clodius Presbiter's Lenten Play

Very similar in style, if not in conclusions, to *The Voluptuous Man* is the undated *A Lenten Allegorical Play How Man's Spirit was Deceived by the Flesh, the World and the Devil*, which was composed by a Clodius Presbiter for The Olive Branch.[126] About Presbiter we know nothing else apart from his motto 'Cool Advice' (*Küelen raet*) and while we know the play was performed on 21 January 1560, it was originally composed for a Lenten performance and according to C.G.N. de Vooys and J.J. Mak was most likely written around mid century. In any event, the central character, Man's Spirit (*sMenschen Gheest*), starts the play clothed in angelic white reflecting his state of inner peace through chastening his body and abstaining from food, the central acts of Lent. While on the way to a sermon Man's Spirit is accosted by Flesh (*tvleesch*) and World (*werrelt*), who successfully turn his mind to things of the world and in this condition Man's Spirit complains that now neither indulgences nor processions will help him rebel from his present masters.[127] He is rescued, however, by the labour of The Love of God (*De liefde Gods*) and Fear of Punishment (*Vreese van plaeghen*), who reveal two painted figures, the first being the seven-headed dragon of the Apocalypse, carrying the Whore of Babylon and the second, the risen Christ, standing victorious over the earth and devil. In this play Presbiter presents a clear flesh/spirit dichotomy and defends the necessity of mortifying the old man and putting on the new, and resisting the flesh. At the conclusion of the play, Man's Spirit places his trust in Christ alone, as his 'only worthy saviour.'[128] While there is no evidence of strictly Lutheran teaching, the author of this play has depreciated the traditional ecclesiastical ceremony and means of grace and highlighted the interior spiritual meaning of religious devotion. There is also a noticeable apocalyptic element in this work that is quite similar to the spiritualistic eschatological notions of a David Joris. Apparently Claudius Presbiter had incorporated some of the ideas of spiritualists into an orthodox Catholic framework.[129]

Classical Plays

Along with these religious plays, after the 1540s Antwerp's rhetoricians began presenting a number of classical works on stage, showing the growing influence of northern humanism. The emphasis in all of these works is to use the classical stories as a means of highlighting the folly of contemporary society and to illustrate the effects of naked ambition or lust. It is not appropriate here to analyse these plays, for they followed fairly closely the familiar classical stories. What will be highlighted instead will be a few of the morals Antwerp's playwrights thought they could draw from classical literature that would apply to their own society. Given Charles V's continuing attempts to suppress religious reform in the Low Countries, presenting classical stories was a far safer means of instructing audiences than performing overtly religious or biblical plays.[130] Four of these classical plays have survived from mid-century Antwerp: *Charon the Hellish Skipper*, possibly performed in Antwerp in 1551;[131] *Mars and Venus*, composed by one 'Smeecken' of Antwerp sometime before 1551;[132] and Cornelis van Ghistele's two versions of Virgil's *Aeneas and Dido*.[133] Taking great liberties with the classical text is the anonymous *Charon, the Hellish Skipper*, a work which recasts the gloomy ferryman of the dead into a humorous god curious about the world outside of the river Acheron of Hades. The moral of this play is one familiar to late-medieval audiences: the spiritual danger of relying on worldly things for happiness for, as Charon warns, 'Behold, you all must enter my boat, which is death' and only those 'who have God as a friend' will rejoice eternally, through the saviour who has brought a higher love.[134] Here we have another work in the 'dance of death' theme that reshapes the classical myths to offer a Christian moral. At the same time, the playwright has not been faithful to the ancient stories, suggesting that the work was not originally a product of mid-sixteenth-century Renaissance classicism but of late-medieval preoccupations.

Unlike *Charon*, the other classical plays are generally faithful to the original mythic characters and broad story lines. The theme of *Mars and Venus* is the familiar account of Venus's unhappy marriage to the ugly Vulcan and her adulterous and tragic affair with Mars, with the unsurprising moral that women are fickle, men faithless, and that having a pleasing marital partner is a blessing. The two versions of *Aeneas and Dido* presumably composed by Cornelis van Ghistele similarly use a familiar classical story to make remarks about the playwright's contemporary society, but in this case in a way that was much more faithful to the ancient myths. Van Ghistele saw it as his duty to bring the classics to the general populace of Antwerp and to provide the public with good moral drama. He therefore supplied his audience with contemporizing clues so that the modern significance of the ancient stories were clearly seen. This was done most effectively in the plays' prologue or by the interpretative comments of the allegorical characters. In the prologue of the first version, performed in May 1551, the characters Rhetorical Spirit (*Rhetorijckelijck gheest*) and Poetical Mind (*Poeetelijck Sin*) praise the art of rhetoric as superior to all others, for it is a divine medium of communication, 'flowing out of the mouth of the Holy Spirit,' the scorn of its detractors (who must have been numerous in Antwerp by 1551) notwithstanding.[135] He argues, in fact, that because of rhetoric's close association with the Spirit of God, it does not contradict Scripture, but instead is able to counteract errors.[136] However, the prologue's characters assert that the main goal of this rehearsal of Virgil's story is to bring praise to God and to the emperor Charles V, who like the king of Troy, rules the Roman empire with a strong and just hand; he also governs with the wisdom of Solomon, the humility of Joseph, and the righteousness of David. Despite this praise, Van Ghistele also makes an oblique critique of Charles V's almost constant warfare, for when Mars rules the land, tyranny and evil are not far behind.[137] On the local scene, the playwright hopes his work will further heighten the virtues of brotherly love, peace, and unity among his fellow citizens of Antwerp.

The prologue of the second *Aeneas and Dido*, which seems to have been composed with the membership of Antwerp's Marigold chamber in mind as the principal audience, likewise tackles those who scorn the rhetorical arts, but it does so in such a way that those opponents become more clearly apparent. The central moral of the story this time is the disastrous effects of unchaste love. What is most interesting about this play, at least for the purposes of this study, is again the humorous repartee of the prologue characters. In this case three are involved: Unlearned Ideas (*Ongheleerdt Begrijpen*), Ignorant Taunts (*Onweetendt Schimpen*), and the honourably attired A Stately Man (*Een Statelijck Man*) discuss whether it is better to dramatize religious truth openly or more subtly. For example, Unlearned and Ignorant both recommend speaking from the plain Scriptures, something that will benefit an audience, both lay and religious. Instead of commending their suggestion, however, Stately Man tells them that they speak unwisely, for a much more subtle approach is called for to reach the current audiences; one best treats the ill with medicine that tastes sweet, he contends, instead of with direct and painful remedies, catching more flies with honey, as it were.[138] But, Ignorant and Unlearned respond, 'Must we not reveal and punish sin directly?' Stately Man's response is that audiences will be able to witness from this classical play how unchastity leads to all manner of evil, just as readily as from a biblical story, and without beating the biblical principles over the audience's head.[139] Many who speak of God like prophets, he reminds his colleagues, are in their hearts far from the Lord.[140] In the end he tells them they are not wanted in Antwerp and that they would find a better audience for their drama in Paris. Although concerned that they would have to learn French, these two irritants agree between them to follow this suggestion and depart the stage, concluding the prologue.[141]

It appears, then, that some rhetoricians came to regard the old style of religious *spelen van zinne* as not sophisticated enough for the cosmopolitan tastes of Antwerp's populace. What might in fact be at the centre of the dispute between these characters is the difference in approach between the Calvinist reformers on one side, who desired the Low Countries' inhabitants to take a much more direct and courageous stand on religious reform, and those who yearned for reform but not at great personal risk or at the expense of civic unity. If so, then Stately Man's suggestion that his compatriots take their act to Paris could be an implicit demand that the French Calvinist preachers, whose presence in Antwerp was causing such a religious stir by 1552, return to their native country and leave Antwerpenaars to conduct their own affairs. It may also reflect a growing attitude on the part of at least some rhetoricians that they could find better ways to instruct the populace without causing civic disturbance.

This has only been a brief overview of the actions and drama of Antwerp rhetoricians between 1520 and 1556. What should be evident is that Antwerp's aristocratic magistrates publicly encouraged and financially supported their city's actors. Even though Antwerp's magistrates took stringent measures against heresy in their city, their rhetoricians were able to use the stage to propagate reformation ideas, in large measure because they advocated moderation in the debate over religious reform and publicly denounced extreme reform proposals.[142] They also wrote plays that were sophisticated and subtle, making it difficult to make heresy charges stick. Antwerp's dramatists therefore only occasionally witnessed the loss of toleration. This was not the case in Amsterdam.

4

Amsterdam Rhetoricians and the Reformation

Compared to that of Antwerp, the history of Amsterdam's rhetorician chambers is a much simpler affair. What will become clear in the following pages is the extent to which rhetoricians could become vigorous proponents of religious reform, much to the chagrin of the authorities. While many of Antwerp's rhetoricians were able to get away with espousing moderate versions of Protestant reform, in part because of their open rejection of the proposals of radical reformers such as Pruystinck, Amsterdam's dramatists provide us with an example of the use of drama to support a level of religious reformation which was clearly linked to social upheaval.

Two chambers are known to have existed in Amsterdam during the first half of the sixteenth century, The Blooming [or bleeding] Eglantine (*De bloeyende Eglantier*) and another, known only by its motto, In Fiery Love (*In liefde vierich*).[1] Eglantine seems to have been established sometime in the 1490s.[2] In 1518 the 'old chamber,' presumably Eglantine, took advantage of the celebrations surrounding the coronation of King Charles V to have its debts, amounting to twenty-nine guilders, taken over by the city. The city treasurer also provided a modest public allowance of 1£ Fl. (six guilders) for the rental of the chamber room.[3] Just prior to the introduction of Lutheran ideas in Amsterdam, certainly during the first quarter of the sixteenth century, the rhetoricians of Eglantine performed a short play on the *History of Piramus and Thisbe*.[4] During the decade of the 1520s there were several public festivities in the city, such as the revelry surrounding the birth of Philip II in 1527, which witnessed 'a general procession and large fires were lit on the streets and a lovely satire [*batement*] was performed.'[5] It is not known, however, if the official chambers were involved in this performance, for militia and craft guilds were also known to put on this type of play. Both chambers were active in the 1530s, as seen in the inclusion of their mottos in *An Allegorical Play on the Sick City*, which dates to the second half of the 1530s.[6] Apparently also dating to this decade is the strictly biblical play, *Lazarus's Death*.[7] The play known as *Saint John's Beheading* was composed by the factor Jan Thoenisz (a city messenger) for In Fiery Love some time before 1552, possibly before 1538.[8] During this decade, perhaps in 1553, an Amsterdam playwright, Jacob Jacobsz, composed a *spel van zinne* entitled *Naboth*.[9] Also before the middle of the century Eglantine performed *A Play to Perform in Times of War with Murderous Work*, an eloquent plea for the end of warfare (see below, chapter 8). Both societies were still going strong in 1559 for in that year they received from the city fathers a gift in honour of their work during the festival marking the peace of Cateau-Cambresis.[10] Furthermore, there are extant a few plays performed by both chambers through to the end of the 1550s. Another surviving play, originating from Thoolen and entitled *An Allegorical May Play of Human Frailty*, was performed in the chamber room of Eglantine in 1551.[11]

Unfortunately, aside from these facts, there is very little information regarding the activities of these chambers, especially compared to what we know of their Antwerp comrades. Prior to 1559 the only mention of official civic support of Amsterdam rhetoricians is the above-mentioned reference from the treasury record of 1518. There is not one mention of either of Amsterdam's chambers in the surviving Amsterdam accounts from 1519 to 1555.[12]

Amsterdam and the Royal Visit of 1549

Moreover, the city's rhetoricians are not once alluded to in the records concerning the extensive preparations for the entrance of Prince Philip of Spain into the city in 1549, even though these involved dozens of craftsmen, musicians, and artists. The importance of this visit for Charles V is described by George Kernodle:

> [I]n order to secure the Italian and Netherland provinces to his son Philip, he presented Philip in one city after another to be received with the usual decorations, triumphal arches, processions, speeches, and *tableaux vivants*. Hence the shows served an important political function while they delighted the populace. They also served to demonstrate the pride, wealth, and splendour of the city to the eyes both of its citizens and of its visitors.[13]

To demonstrate such pride, Amsterdam's city fathers expended an impressive 509£ Fl. (3,054 guilders) on the erection of triumphal arches and statues, for the composition of accompanying verses,[14] for the painting of honorific pictures, for the painting, carving, and printing of coats of arms, for the repair and beautification of the city's buildings, and for all of the necessary material.[15] Not one penny, however, seems to have been expended on drama. The contrast with Antwerp could not be more conspicuous. In spite of this apparent lack of rhetorician support during this major celebration, Amsterdam's regents clearly put aside their normal frugality to fête their Spanish prince. Before altering our conception of bourgeois attitudes toward the arts, it must be remembered that a sixteenth-century ruling prince expected no less. Aside from this one notable exception, Amsterdam's commoner magistrates were hesitant to support extravagant festivals that were not political or civic requirements.

Amsterdam's Rhetoricians and the Reformation

Why were Amsterdam's rhetoricians apparently excluded from even this one moment of extravagance? The answer lies in part in their early involvement in illegal heterodox activities, which further reduced their status in the eyes of city fathers. Presumably acting on complaints about unapproved rhetorician drama, in 1523 the city declared illegal the creation of new chambers.[16] This act does not seem to have stopped the performance of plays critical of the religious or secular authorities, for two years later the Imperial Court at The Hague conducted an investigation into 'certain plays which were performed [in Amsterdam] in front of the city hall and inside certain houses by some rhetoricians; to the confusion, derision and blaspheming of the sacraments of the holy church and other good institutions.'[17] It appears that some of Amsterdam's *rederijkers* had sided with the Reformation, and while it is known that many of Amsterdam's humanistic burgermasters and magistrates also sympathized with the reformers, they were early pressured by the imperial authorities to clamp down on the unorthodox opinions of their rhetoricians. They therefore could not afford publicly to support groups under suspicion of heresy.

Not only did Amsterdam rhetoricians place themselves in the service of moderate reformers and humanists, but there is evidence that in the next decade, at least one group of them was willing to identify with Melchiorite Anabaptism. The followers of the apocalyptic-minded

Hoffman had brought his teaching to Amsterdam in 1530 and this city soon became the Anabaptist capital of Holland. When the more moderate reform leadership was forced to flee the Low Countries as a result of persecution, reform was left in the hands of artisans predisposed to Hoffman's message. In December 1531 Hoffman called his two-year suspension of baptism to avoid further martyrdom, blurring the lines between moderate and radical reformers and it became difficult to distinguish between Anabaptists and other evangelicals until the future prophet of Münster, Jan Matthijs, reinstated adult baptism late in 1533.[18] It is therefore nearly impossible to calculate the number of Melchiorites in Amsterdam, although contemporaries placed it in the range of one to five thousand by 1534.[19] Even though an exaggeration – the estimation may accurately reflect the number of sympathizers – it is certain that the followers of Hoffman were popular and influential in the city.[20] Certainly the authorities became concerned about the rumours that the Anabaptists were planning to bring the Münsterite 'kingdom of God' into Amsterdam. While only a handful of desperate Anabaptists did attempt to force the hand of Amsterdam's civic leaders, leading to the infamous putsch on the city hall in 1535, most of the followers of Hoffman remained peaceable.

Within this context of religious flux, some *rederijkers* were attracted to Anabaptism during the first half of the 1530s. After all, between 1533 and 1535 Anabaptism had taken on the characteristics of a mass movement, attracting devotees from all walks of life, although mostly artisans (see chapter 1 above). Given the predominance of artisans within the rhetorician chambers, it should not be surprising that some turned to Anabaptism for religious identity. It is possible, in fact, that an Anabaptist-inclined chamber of rhetoric was informally created in the city in 1533. As seen in Antwerp with the establishment of The Olive Branch and the various informal '*pap-gilden*,' it was not uncommon for aspiring young actors to establish their own chamber when membership in the official chambers was closed to them. Our information concerning this Amsterdam group, however, comes from the court records, and therefore must be used carefully. In this case, nine *rederijkers* were arrested on 28 December 1533, for having illegally created a chamber and for performing a play without first having it approved by the magistrates. Their performance was apparently critical of the religious estate. Far from being the exclusive domain of Anabaptists, an intense anticlericalism was a predominant theme among all reformers, although Anabaptists often turned their anticlerical ire against Lutheran and Reformed clergy as well as against the traditional target of the Catholic priesthood.[21] While we possess neither the play nor the testimony of those arrested, it is possible to suggest that in this period, when the Reformation in Amsterdam was dominated by the radicals, these performers were most likely Anabaptist sympathizers.

Descriptions of the play by the authorities confirm its radical contents. In February 1534 the Court of Holland requested information about a play 'concerning the last chapter of Daniel, performed publicly in the city of Amsterdam, wherein were narrated many scandalous words.'[22] This passage of Scripture was one of the favourites of Hoffman and his followers, for it provided clues to the dating of apocalyptic events, such as the great tribulation, the ultimate deliverance of the people of God, and the final resurrection and judgment. Hoffman had written and had published a large commentary on this prophetic passage and it is possible that, given the strength of his following in Amsterdam, his commentary provided the major source for this *rederijker* play.[23] Having seen the script, the procurator-general, Reynier Brunt, commented to stadtholder Count van Hoogstraten that it was 'full of blasphemies.'[24] Brunt would probably have said much the same about a Lutheran play, but it would have been unlikely that a Lutheran playwright would have composed a work on this apocalyptic passage during the height of Anabaptist activity. In any event, the magistrates certainly feared the play's potential for disturbing the delicate peace within the city; therefore the actors were ordered to complete a pilgrimage to Rome as part of their punishment.[25] However, the zealous Brunt was not pleased about the leniency of the Amsterdam authorities in this and other cases.[26] After noting the blasphemous nature of the play performed in Amsterdam, he remarks impatiently, 'The actors were exiled to Rome by the [authorities of] Amsterdam without [seeking] any advice from the commissioners. They therefore must be allowed to return.'[27]

Scandalous activities did not end with this investigation. While the actors were away on their pilgrimage, the city authorities had their hands full with other *rederijkers* whose anticlerical plays had further upset the tranquility of their community. In an October 1534 missive, stadtholder Van Hoogstraten made several complaints to the Amsterdam government. Piecing together the various charges, a fascinating scenario can be recreated. It appears that a basketmaker, Adriaen Jacobsz, had hired the artist Peter Rippenz to paint a work which stood outside his home. This painting, according to the Amsterdam magistrates, was a cause of great scandal, for it depicted devils dressed in monks' caps, who occupied themselves by fishing for money.[28] The art-ist's rendition served as a backdrop to a dramatic performance, during which the actors, dressed in costumes identical to those in the painting, performed a satire directed against the clergy.[29] The actors, moreover, had not submitted the play to the court for correction; they claimed that it had not been preserved in writing.[30]

Another incident which evoked the ire of the stadtholder illustrates how *rederijkers* cooperated with other discontented groups in the city. Again the stadtholder complained about anticlericalism in Amster-dam. Members of the marksmen's guild of the city were known to dress 'in the colours of the religious' to show their contempt for the first estate (for a contemporary portrait of the members of one of Amsterdam's militia guilds, see illustration 3). As if that was not enough, during his rounds one of the members of the Halberds guild entered a city church one morning in October, crying out, 'Everyone leave the church. What do you have to do here?'[31] Even those entrusted with the city's defence had been subverted by the new teach-ing. What made matters worse was that the *rederijkers* had performed a scandalous play in the practice field of the marksmen's guild.[32] Pre-sumably influenced by reformation propaganda, rhetoricians, artists, and city guards, at least in these cases, worked together to deprecate members of the religious estate, helping to inflame religious passions in a city already awash with radical reform sentiment.[33] While artists and rhetoricians may have been expected to side with some reform ele-ments, it must surely have been unnerving to the higher authorities to have the reliability of Amsterdam's civic guard called into question.

Amsterdam's city fathers responded to the stadtholder's original charges by conducting an investigation to reveal the veracity of the accusations. Moreover, they managed to recover a copy of the play believed to have been performed in front of the basketmaker's house and they sent it to the president of the Court of Holland, Gerrit van Assendelft.[34] The Amsterdam magistrates were less successful when it came to discovering the text for the 'marksmen's field' performance, for although the rhetorician Jacob Fransz van Leiden confessed to hav-ing put on a performance there, he affirmed that he had done so alone, that it was merely a matter of recreation, that there was nothing evil in his enactment, and, finally, that it was an entirely ad lib performance, for he had written none of it down.[35] In spite of his remarks to the con-trary, it is unlikely that Fransz performed alone; he was probably pro-tecting his confrères.

The offences of the target field and the basketmaker's house *rederijk-ers* went largely unpunished, although Adriaen Jacobsz and his artist were commanded to go on a pilgrimage to Rome. From the perspective of law and order, the oversight may not have been a bad thing, for it appears that the punishment of the group of rhetoricians who had been sent on a pilgrimage in 1533 was only counterproductive. On his return at least one of these actors, Hendrik Hendrikszoon, a tailor, became involved in even more radical activity. He 'became the fore-most leader of the naked runners (*naaktloopers*),' eleven Anabaptists who on 11 February 1535 caused a sensation by running naked through the streets of Amsterdam proclaiming 'the naked truth' upon the city's unrepentant residents.[36] In the list of the captured *naaktloop-ers* Hendrikszoon was regarded as the prophet of the unclothed pro-testers.[37] Whether the other chamber members actually took part in the run through the streets is not known, but there is no reason to doubt the government's report concerning their radical sympathies. The par-ticipation of at least one rhetorician in the rather bizarre ritual raises the question of the nature of the protest being enacted. Was it another dramatic performance rendered this time without costume and using the streets for a stage? Previous studies have regarded the *naaktlooper* incident as merely the action of fanatics deranged by apocalyptic excitement and persecution. Yet, it may also have possessed the char-acteristics of an unstructured and stageless morality play performance.

Rhetoricians and Anabaptist Revolt

As if this incident were not enough, the props of one of Amsterdam's chambers were used in the attempted Anabaptist takeover of the city hall during the night of 10 May 1535.[38] An association between some rhetoricians and Anabaptists therefore appears to have continued after the arrest of the *naaktloopers*. That the chamber referred to here was an official one, possibly The Eglantine, which had its chamber in close proximity to the city hall, is indicated by its possession of a chamber room, drums, flags, and other props.

The rebels had originally planned to accomplish in Amsterdam what Anabaptists had been able to do in Münster – take over city govern-ment by peaceful, even 'democratic' means. The Münsterite Anabap-tist government, after all, was a duly elected one, albeit one so chosen only after many of the more orthodox residents had fled the city. Given the presumed large number of sympathizers in Amsterdam, the militant Anabaptists there assumed that a show of numbers and force would be all that was required to convince the incumbent magistrates to hand over the reins of government to the Anabaptists. When only a few dozen actually gathered for the putsch, the plans took on a more desperate tone. The armed Anabaptists confronted the burgermasters and ceremonial guard, who had been celebrating through the course of the evening, and shots were fired, killing among others one of the mayors – ironically one who had been acquainted with some of the Anabaptists and who had sought a peaceful resolution to their demands. A number of the Anabaptists were able to take possession of the city hall, but most were eventually killed or captured in the ensuing assault. In its aftermath, responsibility for the debacle had to be found. Not only were the Amsterdam Anabaptists, both peaceful and militant, sorely persecuted by the authorities, but primary blame for the fiasco was laid at the feet of the incumbent burgermasters, who were now judged to have been far too lenient, even sympathetic, toward the radical reformers.

The investigation into the revolt uncovered an interesting connection between the rhetoricians and the militants. The humanist-reformer Wouter Deelen, a teacher of biblical languages, is reported to have provided one of the radicals, Frans Frederycxz (Frans in den Trompe) with the chamber key.[39] What were his reasons for doing so? Obviously Deelen was on fairly close terms with Frederycxz. Frederycxz explained the situation during his first interrogation on 15 May 1535:

> He said that he frequently had the key to the rhetoricians' chamber. Said that on Sunday evening Henrick Goedtbeleyt desired that he get the key to the aforementioned hall from Mr Wouter, saying that he desired to go into the *rethorijckerscamer* to see what was there. Then on the afternoon of last Monday he who spoke requested the key from Mr Wouter, who then gave it to him. He then handed over the key to the aforementioned Henrick who was waiting there. But Henrick did not let him in on why he wanted the key, only that he would return it to him who spoke ... Said that Henrick had told him [i.e., Frederycxz] to tell the aforementioned Mr Wouter that his bag had ripped and that he had lost what was in it inside [the chamber].[40]

Apparently Goedtbeleyt, a cohort of the leader of the revolt, Jan van Geelen, provided Frederycxz with an excuse to enter the hall with the story of a broken or forgotten bag, if Deelen should inquire.[41] Although it appears Deelen had been using the chamber hall for his biblical language classes, it may also be inferred from the story that Anabaptists such as Goedtbeleyt and Frederycxz frequented *rederijker* performances or may have been themselves members of the chamber.[42] In any event, while Frederycxz pretended no knowledge of Goedtbeleyt's intentions, his actions during the night of the revolt, witnessed by several citizens, left little doubt in the minds of his interrogators that he had been involved in the planning.[43] Frederycxz also claimed that one of the more important Anabaptist leaders, Jan Matthijs van Middelburg, had stayed with Wouter Deelen in an Amsterdam inn known as the Spain (*Spaengnen*).[44] Deelen may have been unaware of the plot, but he clearly was on close terms with several of the Anabaptists and, if the later governmental report can be believed, his reform proposals had spurred his disciples into even worse blasphemies.[45] Deelen's possession of the chamber key may have been a result of more than his use of the room to teach biblical languages. Rhetorician deacons were jealously to guard their keys to the chamber and to the chests containing scripts and props and to guard the property and secrets of the rhetorician society.[46] That Deelen would be given chamber keys in such a casual fashion suggests either that Eglantine's deacons were irresponsible or negligent in their duties, or that they had good reason to trust Deelen. It is not inconceivable that Deelen himself was a member of the society, or perhaps even a deacon. If such was the case, then Deelen's easy access to the chamber keys becomes more explicable.

Amsterdam Rhetoricians after 1535

In the aftermath of the failed Anabaptist revolt the higher authorities reacted in a reactionary fashion. The tolerant magistrates were deposed and more staunchly Catholic patricians took their places.[47] The changeover was symbolized by a yearly procession every 10 or 11 May 'in thankfulness for the victory of God Almighty over the Anabaptists.'[48] Two craftsmen were placed in charge of adorning the city towers along the route of the procession. Also receiving funds were two priests who carried the host in the procession, the bearers of the Ark and of the incense, the musicians, and the bell-ringers of the Old and New Churches. It is not known whether rhetoricians took part in this procession, and the silence of the *stadsrekeningen* concerning this question indicates once again that no city money was expended on *rederijker* drama.[49] Why did the authorities create this public display? The procession was intended to help restore devotion to the Catholic religion and cult on the part of Amsterdam citizens who had been too intrigued by reformist attitudes and unorthodox opinions. By involving the city in the preparations and enactment of such an event, magistrates hoped that religious energies could be funnelled into orthodox channels. Moreover, the procession also acted as a reminder of the danger and futility of political and religious dissent and of the necessity of civic obedience. It served much the same function as the yearly swearing of the oath or the acts of public humiliation instigated by a ruling lord after a victory over a disobedient community.[50]

Less obviously, the procession may have been intended as a means of restoring cultural groups, such as the chambers of rhetoric, to civilly acceptable functions. Rhetoricians who normally performed their plays during festivals, civic events, and processions were expected to promote religious harmony and civic pride.[51] The use of *rederijker* flags, drums, and props in the Anabaptist uprising of May 1535 and the involvement of at least one *rederijker* in the *naaktlooper* incident must have raised the authorities' suspicions concerning the already questionable loyalty of chamber members. Furthermore, the Anabaptists had already used the occasion of a procession to provide cover for their first planned takeover of the city in March of 1534. The formulators of this abortive scheme apparently had hoped that 'when the procession passed by, they would create a riot in the streets, putting to death all the monks and priests and treading upon the sacrament with their feet. Then they would drive the whole community out of the city and take possession of their goods.'[52] It was therefore important that the Amsterdam authorities remove the association between rebellion and Catholic procession which may have developed in the minds of Amsterdam burghers. If so, the procession was an attempt to control the potential influence of *rederijkers* and redirect their energies to civic betterment, not revolt. Moreover, public displays such as rhetorician plays and processions could be very useful not only in inciting rebellion, but also in cementing the bonds within the civil community and deepening devotion to traditional civic holiness.[53] The yearly procession in honour of the victory over the Anabaptists was a visual reminder that the new Amsterdam city fathers had led their city away from religious reform.

The Plays of Amsterdam Rhetoricians

Further evidence of the vexatious reform activity of Amsterdam's *rederijkers* comes from the available play scripts. For example, the anonymous *Allegorical Play of the Sick City* (ca. 1535) decries the suppression of the Reformation, which has made the central character, a woman named Amsterdam, quite ill.[54] Tyranny (*Tijranije*) acknowledges that he has been responsible for the persecution of those who 'are infected with *luterije*.' He rejoices:

> But the sheriff
> Is very heavily burdened by an oath
> That all suspects must be arrested by him
> And thrown into chains. Hear my motive.
> And if he does not end the lives of such ones,
> Do they remain? Certainly not, but they must flee.
> But they want to be lord over these people.
> This we are glad to see, so that the
> City will have the least peace.[55]

The play also provides further clues to the unravelling of the puzzle of militia guild and *rederijker* cooperation. In this long work, Hypocrisy (*Hijpocrisije*) and Tyranny gloat about their victory over Scriptural Preacher (*Scriftuerlicke Predicatie*) and over those who listened to him, mainly members of the artisanal and guild factions of the city. Here the reform message is seen as most beneficial to the powerless elements of Amsterdam society. Hypocrisy moreover comments, 'Of course we do not quench the Community [i.e., the whole citizenry],' to which Tyranny responds, 'Not: do not the civic guards and guilds choose their own leaders?'[56] In 1522 Amsterdam's burgermasters had appropriated to themselves the right to select the leaders of the marksmen militia guild. Thus began a long and bitter conflict between the marksmen, who were from less influential but still wealthy Amsterdam families, and the city's ruling patriciate, who seemed bent on restricting all political decisions to themselves.[57] The anonymous author of this play lamented also the suppression of *rederijker* activity within the city, a reference to the actions taken against chamber members during the years 1523–35:

> Why do you dismiss from me, Everyone responds,
> The noble rhetoric, and the joyful music,

Which truly do assist me,
In everyone's presence why can't you be reasonable?
Why must they depart, for their sweet eloquence
And artistic invention brought me to excellence,
Of complete credence of God's chosen word.
The hearing of which brought me to magnificence.
But through the uncultured the art will get lost.[58]

Both rhetorician and marksmen's guild members harboured complaints against the Amsterdam magistrates, and both may have vented their hostility to the authorities against the clergy in particular, for the latter did not wield the sword of the magistrate and hence offered a safer target for satire. It is therefore not surprising that the marksmen's and rhetoricians' guilds cooperated at this juncture.

Using apocalyptic language quite familiar to Netherlanders of the 1530s, Community (*Gemeente*) threatens So Many (*Sulck Veel*) with divine judgment,[59] but Hypocrisy tells So Many to blame Erasmus and his Greek New Testament for beginning the heresy which has enfeebled his grandmother Amsterdam. The artisan More Than One (*Meer dan Een*) vigorously denies this charge, arguing that Amsterdam's illness was the fault of the clergy, who have persecuted the truth and who have refused to work with their hands, as all should.[60] At this point More Than One and Community unrestrainedly praise the artisanal work ethic:

Because a lazy hand makes one poor, thus you should hate idleness.
But the working hand gains, according to the Scripture's assertion.
...
Oh, how blessed is the working hand.[61]

Therefore, according to Community, labourers can sleep in peace, while the rich cannot, for the latter did not work to become wealthy.[62]

If Amsterdam's magistrates, Community continues, had made their fortunes in a Christian manner (i.e., like artisans), they would not have been so prone to follow the fulminations of the godless preachers – who know how to play to the pride of the wealthy – and to chase out the city's only hope to avert the judgment of God. They have, in other words, forgotten their principal function – to govern the city on behalf of the common welfare (*gemeen weluaert*).[63] Finally, when a doctor examines the ill Amsterdam, he discovers the root cause of her illness to be 'false religion,' which shows itself in a 'clerical fashion.'[64] The cure that he prescribes is to enforce biblical standards for ecclesiastical leadership and especially to impel the city's preachers to climb into their pulpits and there proclaim only the clear gospel, thus protecting the sheep from the wolves.[65] Further decried in this complex play is the hoarding of grain during the several periods of food shortage during the decade.[66] That Tyranny's cohorts are the wealthy So Many and Finances (*Financij*), and Scriptural Preacher's are More than One (an artisan) and Community (a common burgher), suggests the economic and political stance of the play's author. Obviously Amsterdam rhetoricians used their dramatic skills not only on behalf of religious reform, but to promote political reform in favour of citizens excluded from office, and to decry economic profiteering at the expense of the poor.

Even though not all of their plays were as forthright as *Sick City*, Amsterdam's rhetoricians quite consistently criticized the religious policies of the higher rulers. For example, writing possibly during the early 1530s, at the height of radical reform activities, Jan Thoenisz in *St John's Beheading* uses the biblical account of the death of the prophet John the Baptist (Matt. 14:1–12) to veil his condemnation of oppressive rulers. In the person of Truth's Persecutor (*Waerheits verdructinge*) , the authorities have 'banned and hunted the prophets of the Lord' and have 'murdered so many on account of the truth ... in villages, in cities.'[67] John was executed, his disciples agree in the play, because he did not shy from criticizing spiritual and secular princes, and indeed, Herodius, Herod's wife, warns her husband that the prophet must die, for his sermons will result only in sedition.[68] Although Herod comes in for his share of criticism for this act, it is his wife who is most roundly condemned for the murder. Could this play then have been Thoenisz's means of criticizing the imperial regent of the Netherlands, Mary of Hungary (as well as her predecessor Margaret of Austria), who enforced the emperor's placards against heresy?[69]

Thoenisz also uses the play to defend the rhetorician's art against its detractors. In an intriguing example of contemporizing historical persona, Thoenisz puts the following words into the mouths of Herod's courtiers at the royal banquet:

FIRST GENT: Who could hate the sweet practices
Of instrumental music and rhetoric, full of delicacy?
SECOND GENT: I cannot believe that anyone is so clumsy of condition

To bear envy against such expertise
So noble is the art.
THIRD GENT: It certainly has my favour.
But many a frowned person keeps it restricted
So that no one can understand it.[70]

At this the banqueters break into rhetoricians' refrains and songs.

Also decrying religious persecution is the anonymous biblical play *Lazarus's Death*, most likely composed for the Amsterdam chamber Eglantine around the same time as *Sick City*.[71] What sets this play off from most other *rederijker* works is the complete lack of allegorical characters. It is a strictly biblical play, much like those composed by English and German playwrights. Even without the obvious moralizing of the vices and virtues, however, the playwright manages to get across to his audience his distaste for the persecution of religious dissent. Clearly portrayed through the story of Jesus raising Lazarus from the dead is the conflict between the learned clergy, who seek to suppress the message of Jesus Christ, and the laity, who through their simple faith have accepted the gospel. The message of Jesus presented in this work is quite Lutheran in its emphasis on salvation by faith. When Jesus tells Martha that Lazarus will rise from the dead, Martha responds, 'I know he will rise on the last day.' 'No,' Jesus counters, 'he will rise now,' for

Whoever can believe in me
Even though he were dead, he will also live
Faith brings life, whoever can experience that
Never needs tremble before death again
If you believe this Martha, here in the earthly valley
You will deliver your soul from all mishap.[72]

Several Jews then converse about what they have witnessed. Two of them accept the gospel 'in faith,' while a third one is so aghast at their decision that he leaps into the air and shouts, 'Run from the devil,' for 'I will have nothing to do with heretical things.' He then advises going 'to our learned ones.'[73] Then, one of the two Jews who are converted to Christ remarks to his fellow convert that 'some people are merely thirsty for the blood of their neighbours.'[74] Upon receiving news of the resurrection of Lazarus, the high priest Caiaphus issues a mandate or placard for the death of Jesus and the persecution of his followers, all for the 'common welfare.'[75] The resulting mandate is nearly identical in tone and vocabulary to those issued by Charles V against both the major reformers and the radical sects.[76] While the persecution, the actors maintain, would especially harm the innocent, God allows it to proceed so that the evil ones can earn their future tribulation.[77]

Another solution to humanity's dilemma is offered by *An Allegorical Play on How Many People Seek the House of Peace*, also by Jan Thoenisz.[78] Many Men (*Mennich Menschen*) following the words of St Paul and Christ, is on a pilgrimage, seeking the house of peace.[79] Having been led astray by the Lantern of Trusting in Man, he comes to Night's Castle of Darkness, where he receives the attire of World's Honour and is distracted from his quest by *sinnekins* representing Banqueter, Hypocrisy, and Great Appetite. Quoting from the Epistles of Paul, Morningtime (*Morghenstont*) makes a plea with Many Men to 'cast off the works of darkness for the sake of your piety, / take up heartily the weapons of the light.'[80] Many Men is persuaded by Morningtime's scriptural instruction and realizes that he has been misled by false preachers 'who fill their [money] chests with their false sermons.'[81] Many Men is put on the correct path to the house of peace by the remedy of knowledge of sins, provided by God's grace. Realizing that relying on his own works and wisdom is futile, Many Men is told to turn in faith to Christ for purification from sin:

> MORNINGTIME: True faith give the sinner penance
> Then comes a pure conscience, remember this
> You must trust your Lord your God
> Without any fading, with fiery love
> And you will receive peace.[82]

Painted figures of the transfiguration and crucifixion of Christ finally convince Many Men to 'cling not to a cross of wood or stone, but to the pure, crucified Christ / who alone has delivered us with his blood.'[83] This play, with its emphasis again on the grace of God and faith in the sacrifice of Christ, the only mediator, does contain the odd reference to the Virgin Mary and even a satirical comment on 'the sect of Luther.'[84] In its central theme on the process of salvation, it is, at the very least, moderately evangelical or reformist. For example, explicitly identifying Christ as the sole mediator was a central tenet of Lutherans and other Protestant reformers, who used this phrase as an implicit attack on the Catholic doctrine of the intercession of saints and Mary. The rejection of works in salvation and the admonition to trust solely in Christ are also hallmarks of a Lutheran position, although there were some Catholics who sought to incorporate Luther's salvation by faith alone into a Catholic framework. These rhetoricians appear to have grown cautious in presenting new or untolerated ideas to Amsterdam's citizens after the Anabaptist commotions.

Such caution is more than apparent in the biblical play *Naboth*, based on the story of Elijah's controversy with King Ahab and Queen Jezebel over the execution of Naboth, who had turned down the king's request to sell his vineyard (I Kings 16–21). Although it appears the play was composed in the 1550s (the date 1553 which appears on the title page is by a later hand) by Jacob Jacobsz for Eglantine, Jacobsz, if he is the same person whose motto, 'Wilt Jonk bekeeren,' appears near the end of the play, composed works mainly for Amsterdam's other chamber, In liefde Vierich (In Fiery Love). E. Ellerbroek-Fortuin postulates that for this effort both chambers worked together.[85] The play follows the biblical account fairly closely, and nowhere do there seem to be explicit references to sixteenth-century events – because of the difficult handwriting certainties are not to be had. However, given the story line involving the idolatrous prophets of Baal and the persecution of a righteous individual by a weak king overly influenced by an evil queen who pressures the local authorities to kill Naboth, there is every reason to see this work as a covert condemnation of Charles V's policy of religious persecution. That the local authorities are described as sheriffs (*schouten*) and aldermen (*schepenen*) would have assisted a contemporary audience in making this identification. Even though they might argue they were merely following higher orders, these civic officials remain fearful of the wrath of God for having so 'abused Justice.'[86] At the same time the Vices recommend Ahab go to church, where he will be ministered to by 'Baal's clerics' (*baals clercken*). If this interpretation of the play is correct, then Amsterdam's rhetoricians were making a veiled challenge to their magistrates to follow a higher law rather than the depraved edicts of their king.

The last Amsterdam play to be mentioned here is *Concerning Our Dear Lord's Charity*, written again for The Eglantine.[87] Involving only three characters, this simple work presents the evangelical notion of the centrality of faith and proposals for civic reform in a framework which would have been offensive to few and may have been an attempt to provide a compromise theology between Luther's and traditional Catholicism. At the start, a farmer, Little Trust (*Cleyn vertrou-*

wen), complains to his wife, True Love (*Warachtige liefde*), about their desperate poverty and the difficulty of providing for their children, to which True Love responds that their situation is God's will, for their children belong to the Lord and he will care for them. At this, her rather dull husband sets off to church to speak to the Lord and to receive his financial due for caring for the Lord's children for so long.[88] Pastor's (*Pastoor*) first advice to Little Trust, to trust in God's grace and he will supply, merely confirms the confused farmer's belief that he will be materially rewarded. Eventually Pastor warns his enquiring friend not to be concerned about those who are too rich (*over rijck*) for they have placed their trust in the world's riches and will have to answer for it at the last day.[89] Seeing that Little Trust has been converted from his disbelief, Pastor gives him the shield of Perfect Faith. He then presents him with a painted figure of Complete Hope and tells him to stand fast with his wife, now called Perfect Love, for all three need to be bound together. The Pastor, citing I Cor. 13, shows that without love all is lost, for faith without love and hope is incomplete. Surely Pastor's words were meant as a corrective to Luther's emphasis on faith. At the same time, the play does little to defend specifically Catholic rituals or sacraments. It may therefore originate with an orthodox author who sought to promote reform from within.

Although this appears to be an argument from silence, a brief examination of a play which was probably composed just prior to the onset of Reformation propaganda in the city will provide a useful reminder of how Amsterdam's rhetoricians used to depict the Catholic faith. Composed by a Goosen ten Berch for Eglantine, *Piramus and Thisbe* is ostensibly a play on the ancient theme of young love which cannot be consummated, but which uses a classical story as an allegory for the love of Christ. Following the suicide of the two lovers, two *sinnekens* explain the meaning of this sad tale. Poetical Spirit (*Poetelijck Geest*) remarks to Amorous (*Amoreuse*) that 'he who lives according to the flesh, will die / not only physically but also in the soul.' Yet, he ponders, 'and they also preach to us daily in the city / that love exceeds all other virtues.'[90] His colleague is puzzled by this contradiction until Poetical Spirit explains that it is another love to which the preachers refer. Pulling aside a curtain, Poetical Spirit reveals a scene of Christ hanging on the cross with Mary and John below. He then recites a poem of praise to the love of Christ, showing how Piramus's death for Thisbe represents Christ's sacrifice for his beloved, the church.[91] The play's fountain stands for Christ's wounds on the cross, which are received in the sacraments.[92] Poetical Spirit also describes the doctrine of Original Sin (*origo pecatij*), but in a fashion consistent with a Catholic interpretation, as explained by 'many doctors.'[93] Whereas a Lutheran would then proceed to describe how one can be delivered from the effects of original sin by justification through faith, our playwright instead speaks only of the love shown by Christ in taking human form and sacrificing himself, defeating the devil who thought he had him in his clutches.[94] While the play therefore reflects a Catholic understanding of the importance of love in salvation, it also presents its message in a sophisticated form, once again affirming that even before the Reformation, rhetoricians could have a highly developed understanding of religious doctrines, in many cases equal or superior to that of the lower clergy.

As already suggested, it appears that after the decade of the 1530s, Amsterdam rhetoricians reduced the emphasis on radical reform or separatist sentiments. Instead, the emphasis in these reform-minded plays of the 1540s and 1550s is on redirecting the central beliefs of audiences to a broadly conceived evangelical direction, perhaps hoping that institutional abuses, such as indulgences, might fall away on their own.[95] This is a significant shift in approach from the 1520s and 1530s, when rabid anticlericalism, strong condemnation of ecclesiastical abuses, and the blatant presentation of Lutheran and even Anabaptist reforms apparently resulted in Amsterdam's rhetoricians losing civic support. The tactical shift seems to have worked, as seen in the city's sponsoring of dramatic activities in 1559. Amsterdam's humanist magistrates of the mid-sixteenth century could now appreciate the more moderate tone of their dramatists. The main emphasis of plays dating from this later period is the advice to bear suffering with patience and to turn to the grace of God for forgiveness, a far cry from the rhetorician's involvement in the religious revolt of the 1530s. Yet, in the context of the upheaval caused by the Reformation, even mild reform proposals, when combined with a lack of a vigorous defence of Catholic doctrines and practices, must have reinforced in people's minds the ideas of Luther or other popular reformers.

The Drama of Antwerp and Amsterdam's Rhetoricians

In both Antwerp and Amsterdam, many rhetoricians used the stage to stir up anticlerical sentiment and propagate reform ideas. Presented as they were with humour – often bawdy – outrageous costumes, and brilliant visual effects, these ideas must have had an impressive effect on the attentive populace. Because reform issues were presented in such a popular fashion, they could be absorbed almost subconsciously. While Antwerp's aristocratic magistrates early attempted to suppress the communication of reformation notions through traditional channels such as preaching and the printing press, they tolerated to a large degree the often unorthodox sentiments of their rhetoricians. They continued generously to support their chambers, only reluctantly taking action against one or two heretical actors. Through the first half of the sixteenth century, Antwerp's regents held their dramatic guilds in high esteem. The city's rhetoricians continued to be useful in promoting the honour of their city and denouncing the dangerous ideas of more radical reformers. The moderate reform proposals of many of its rhetoricians could therefore be tolerated.

In the early stages of the Reformation, Amsterdam's magistrates were much more tolerant of the spread of reform propaganda than were their Antwerp equals. Yet they apparently did not encourage their rhetoricians. Perhaps one reason for this lack of support is that Amsterdam's merchant patriciate not only sought to avoid frivolous expenditures, but also distrusted popular culture. What city fathers perhaps feared most was the possibility that the rhetoricians would use the stage to garner popular support in their conflict over political and economic power in the city, a battle which pitted the entrenched patriciate on the one side against the city's guilds, guard, and rhetoricians on the other. Even though rhetoricians normally communicated on behalf of their own semi-elite cohort or specialized tradition of literate males, there was a danger that advocacy of even moderate demands for reform, religious and otherwise, could be interpreted by less sophisticated folk as an implicit criticism of patrician policies or even a call to arms. Some of the leaders of these militia guilds and literary societies were often as prosperous and politically ambitious as their patrician fellows, but lacked easy access to political power. The patricians, therefore, could not allow this conflict to be presented to the general citizenry on stage, for the people were already in a restless mood, to say the least. Suppression of rhetorician drama may therefore have been one means by which Amsterdam's regents sought to control unfavourable propaganda. The period during which it seems Amsterdam's regents did not support their rhetoricians dated from the 1520s to at least the 1540s, coinciding both with the city's internal political struggle and the early Reformation and Anabaptist movements. The religious and social satire of the chambers of rhetoric was evidently perceived by those in power as a dangerous tool in the hands of disgruntled guildsmen or merchants ostracized from the decision-making process.

In turn, because they were excluded from the explicit support of city fathers, Amsterdam's rhetoricians were more likely to turn for support to other disenchanted groups, such as the socially respectable marksmen or artisanal guilds, or even to the revolutionary Anabaptists. Only after two decades of relatively innocuous drama – innocuous from a political, but not ecclesiastical standpoint – did Amsterdam's city fathers see fit to renew support for their chambers of rhetoric. Even then this positive evaluation of vernacular drama did not last; in the next century, new laws were introduced restricting chamber performances which competed with divine services (now Calvinist). Not only were magistrates concerned with the loss of religious devotion when citizens attended plays instead of worship, but these plays merely promoted 'frivolity and vanity (which for the most part is the material of the aforementioned Chamber plays).'[96] Of course rhetorician drama was often characterized by religious leaders of all stripes as frivolous and sometimes the *rederijkers* earned this reputation. However, what really bothered the Catholic and later Protestant clergy was the *rederijkers'* presumption as laymen to engage in the controversial debate over religious reform. The plays we have examined from Amsterdam and Antwerp reveal how seriously rhetoricians regarded religious issues, and like Erasmus, their satirical asides were intended to drive home the seriousness of the need for improvement in spiritual life. Even so, it seems that the distaste for such forms of popular entertainment on the part of Amsterdam's regency had not only hindered rhetoricians of the sixteenth century, but also continued into the Golden Age.

PART III

Reform Themes in Rhetorician Drama, 1519–56

5

Anticlerical Drama and the Reform Controversies in the Low Countries, 1519–38

Having examined rhetorician chambers within the specific urban contexts of Antwerp and Amsterdam, it is now appropriate to cast a broader glance at the drama of these amateur actors. As noted, rhetoricians were drawn from the urban upper artisan, merchant, and professional classes and their plays, particularly those performed in the private chamber halls and those which were never published, reflect fairly accurately the range of views of these literate strata of Dutch urban society, especially as they related to the social and religious controversies of the day. As illustrated by the case studies of Antwerp and Amsterdam, each play presents a perspective specific to the interests of its playwright, actors, and civic context. A broad overview of the surviving play texts will therefore help us understand the various opinions held by rhetoricians on the major controversies of their day: religious reform and allegiance to the higher authorities, especially Charles V. The following description of the drama composed during the early decades of the Reformation will show the tremendous popularity and power of anticlericalism in the urban Netherlands. Even orthodox rhetoricians satirized the clergy, albeit without calling for its dismantling, while all reform-minded plays from the period made the criticism of the clergy a central facet of their reform rhetoric. It will be argued here that even the fairly mild Erasmian anticlerical sentiment of Catholic playwrights, such as Cornelis Everaert, added fuel to the religious tinderbox that was the Netherlands in the 1520s and 1530s.

Rhetoricians and Reform Propaganda

The question of the degree to which these acting guilds influenced the spread of reformation ideas in the Netherlands of Emperor Charles V has engaged scholars for most of this century. Several authors have described the rhetoricians' influence in this regard as considerable, especially with respect to the alarming rise of vigorous anticlerical sentiment, which went hand in glove with popular demands for a form of religion more in keeping with lay aspirations, based in part on Luther's doctrine of the priesthood of all believers. Perhaps the most prominent of these scholars is L.M. van Dis, who argued in his 1937 published dissertation that the rhetoricians were major agents in the rise of reform anticlericalism.[1] His conclusions were supported – with some provisions – by E. Ellerbroek-Fortuin, B.H. Erné, and Johan Decavele, among others, who provided further examples of reform activity on the part of the chambers.[2]

Opposing Van Dis's perspective were scholars who sought to depreciate the reform activity of these cultural organizations, pointing out that only rarely did rhetoricians advocate separation from the Roman Catholic church.[3] Some, such as Enno van Gelder, have therefore argued for Erasmian, rather than Lutheran, influences.[4] This perspective has been supported by those scholars of the Dutch Reformation who have argued that in comparison to Erasmus's program of a scholarly and internal religious reform, Luther's assertive and combative writings were only marginally influential for the early Dutch Reformation. Most recent research into the subject of the early period of reform, however, suggests that this perspective does not do justice to the popularity and spread of Luther's key ideas in the Low Countries.[5] For example, basing his conclusions on the reform career of Gerardus Listrius, Bart J. Spruyt has recently argued that 'the specific influence of Luther on the history and the course of the early Reformation in the Low Countries should no longer be denied.'[6] However, to be a Lutheran in the Low Countries of Charles V was not the same experience as being an associate of Martin Luther in Wittenberg. For one thing, the emperor maintained through his regent a much stronger level of control over his hereditary counties and duchies than he ever could over his imperial domains. From the start Dutch and Flemish Lutherans faced a more persistent and effective opposition than did their German confrères.

It is for this reason that in the Low Countries only the most radical of reformers actually attempted to establish a separate church – based on the institution of believer's baptism – and they were rigorously suppressed as a result. Melchior Hoffman's decision in favour of a suspension of baptism in 1531 was not only a compromise reducing his followers' exposure to persecution, but also a tacit admission that visible separatism was suicidal. More common in the early Reformation era was the establishment of reform conventicles or secret meetings of like-minded individuals. Many regarded their participation in these conventicles as a supplement, not an exclusive alternative, to membership in the *Corpus Christianum*. It appears that especially after the failure of the Anabaptist uprisings in Münster and the Low Countries in the summer of 1535, Nicodemism – outward conformity to approved religious practices while maintaining one's true beliefs in secret – became a favourite approach among Dutch urban religious dissenters. Such a practice is evident within a wide spectrum of dissent groups, including early Lutherans, Anabaptists such as David Joris (who developed it into a fine art), and idiosyncratic spiritualists such as Hendrik Niclaes who founded the House of Love.[7]

The question of separation aside, it is evident that it was not only in Amsterdam that rhetoricians frequently espoused reform ideas from the stage. J.B. Drewes, for example, has recently shown that a careful analysis of many plays, traditionally thought to have promoted a Roman Catholic or orthodox perspective, in actual fact were advocating Lutheran ideas.[8] What this ongoing debate shows is the elusive and subtle nature of the presentation of reform ideas by the rhetoricians, a common-sense precaution in the age of Charles V's often rigorous proto-Inquisition. Rhetoricians, after all, prided themselves on their ability to insert into their plays puns on words, double meanings, hidden acrostics, and the like. Many of the surviving plays are indeed quite sophisticated, possessing more than one possible level of meaning. This seeming ambivalence in rhetorician reform drama noted by modern scholars also indicates that rhetoricians in many cases refused to follow the strict lines of either Catholic or Lutheran orthodoxy, and instead sought reform in some form of compromise solution or in a fair degree of intellectual independence.

As we have noted earlier, rhetoricians had developed a special sense of mission, one in which they played the parts of entertainers, teachers, and preachers and one which they believed gave them the divine right publicly to address issues the authorities thought best left to the clergy. From the start their drama and refrains revolved around religious themes, and were presented to their audiences for their religious instruction and moral improvement. Given the generally low state of clerical education in the early sixteenth century and the likelihood that many rhetoricians were more literate, perhaps even better informed in theology than the average priest, *rederijkers* could justifiably have developed the idea that they were better religious instructors than those with the official office. Certainly this high evaluation of the religious abilities of educated laypeople and depreciation of the clerical estate mesh well with what we know about the pronounced level of anticlericalism in the Low Countries and elsewhere in Europe during the fifteenth and sixteenth centuries.[9] Were not rhetoricians the literary elite of their society, imbued with a unique calling and inspired by the Holy Spirit? Was their mission not one of improving the religious knowledge and faith of their audiences? Complaints by preachers – first Catholic and later Calvinist – that rhetoricians were seeking to usurp the office of preacher, confirm this supposition.[10] For rhetoricians to take up the anticlerical cudgel was a result more of their deeply felt religious mission than of incipient scepticism or callous disregard for the faith. In other words, they saw themselves as independent religious commentators, able to construct or combine reform proposals to best suit the situation of their particular community. What will become obvious from the following survey of reform themes in rhetorician drama is the eclectic creativity of rhetoricians as they sought innovative solutions to the religious and social problems of their day, which at the same time would not destroy the civic unity of their communities.

Several criteria for the identification of the ideological affiliation of rhetorician plays have been suggested by Drewes. Orthodox plays emphasized and supported traditional Catholic doctrines, such as the accent on hope and good works (as opposed to faith) in salvation; the sacrifice and sufferings of Christ; the mediation of Mary and the saints; the centrality of the seven sacraments and the priest's role in their operation; and the personal uncertainty of one's salvation. These were, after all, the central components of rhetorician religious drama prior to 1519. Yet only a few of the surviving scripts defended the Catholic church and priesthood to the extent of *Everyman*. Plays composed by a playwright influenced by Erasmian humanism could be expected to criticize the well known abuses of the church without calling for root and branch change; they would also show a wariness with respect to Protestant ideas of the bondage of the human will, predestination, and the rejection of good works in salvation. Plays which deliberately defended Luther's reform message highlighted his doctrine of justification by faith alone; his belief in the continuing sinfulness of the justified believer; his distinctive position on the relationship between law and gospel; his support for predestination and concomitant bondage of the will; and his affirmation of the certitude of salvation. A playwright writing from the so-called sacramentarian or Zwinglian position would combine the main doctrines of Luther with a symbolical interpretation of the Lord's Supper. Even when it is not possible to identify a play as specifically Lutheran, sacramentarian, or Swiss Reformed, expression of an intense anticlericalism which rejected not only bad priests, but the necessity of a priestly caste itself, is sufficient evidence to describe that play as 'reform-minded,' as beyond the gentler critique of Erasmian reform. Such denial of the priesthood and of the sacramental system is a clearly identifiable sign of a generally Protestant reform perspective and cannot easily be accommodated to an orthodox Catholic position.

Drewes also identified several plays which could be described as spiritualistic, emphasizing a strong spirit/flesh dichotomy, the depreciation of external aspects of religious devotion, and a concentration on the work of the Holy Spirit in salvation (as opposed to Luther's Christocentrism). Given the strength of the mystical tradition in the Lower Rhine region and the *Devotio Moderna*, such spiritualism is expected. What distinguishes sixteenth-century spiritualism from its predecessors was its implicit or explicit disregard for religious dogma, doctrinal controversy, and divisive items of external worship and religious practice. Thus a Catholic spiritualist would, like Thomas á Kempis, emphasize the proper inner disposition while participating in the Mass. A Protestant spiritualist would instead focus exclusively on the inner meaning of the memorial supper. Similarly, any Anabaptist-inclined plays could be identified by reference to the distinctive ideas of Melchior Hoffman (or later on of David Joris and Menno Simons) such as believer's baptism, a fervent apocalypticism, and the doctrine of the heavenly flesh of Christ (against which teaching one orthodox rhetorician composed a polemical play; see below). Analysis of plays composed from a radical reform perspective is complicated both by the wide array of Anabaptist factions after 1535 and by the frequent blending of Anabaptism and spiritualism in the Low Countries. The common practice of Nicodemism further muddies the water.[11]

Using these rough criteria, a beginning can be made in the categorization of the seventy-nine plays – mostly *spelen van zinne* or allegorical plays – known to have been composed between the years 1520 and 1556 (see appendix).[12] Of these, twenty-three (29 per cent) dealt primarily with secular matters, such as the harmful effects of warfare on trade and the populace, the celebration of notable civic events, or the defence of the craft of rhetoric.[13] Of the fifty-eight religious scripts, seventeen could be identified as Lutheran, with nine of these originating from the Ghent *spelen van zinne* competition of 1539 (see below, chapter 6). Ten more of these religious scripts could be described as generally Protestant reformist, as criticizing the church beyond the limits acceptable to ecclesiastical or secular authorities, with four of these showing some influence from the ideas of John Calvin. Thus a total of twenty-seven plays, nearly half of all religious scripts (47 per cent), were Protestant, displaying the rabid anticlericalism about which the authorities continuously complained.[14] At least five of these plays, moreover, focus on their disgust at the persecution of religious dissenters.

On the other hand, only twenty of the fifty-eight religious plays (34 per cent) could be identified as fashioned from a traditional Catholic perspective and most of these (thirteen) were drafted by only one factor, Cornelis Everaert. Apart from his works, only two other plays vigorously defended orthodox Catholic beliefs against the advances of the Reformation – Reynier van den Putte's *The Incarnation of Christ*, and Christianen Fastraet's *The Play of St Trudo* (unlike Everaert, these other two Catholic playwrights were likely clerics). If the surviving scripts represent the range of views held by rhetoricians in general at all, then reformist rhetoricians used the stage more aggressively to promote their perspective than did their Catholic confrères.

While not receiving much attention in the scholarly literature, spiritualist plays accounted for 12 per cent (seven plays) of all religious scripts, exhibiting the relative popularity of an inward, individualistic, or private religion among Dutch urbanites. Two further scripts could only be described as independent, for their ideological perspectives did not fit any of the other categories. It is therefore clear from the available evidence that rhetoricians not only vigorously promulgated reform ideas from the stage, but they also demonstrated a remarkable degree of intellectual independence from the major reformers as well as a willingness to deal creatively with the controversial issues of their day. The following discussion, then, will illustrate this point by examining most of the surviving plays datable to the early Dutch Reformation on the subject of reform. This chapter will examine plays from the first two decades (1519–38) of the Reformation, while the two succeeding chapters will discuss in turn the plays of the Ghent competition in June 1539 and those performed during the later years of Charles V's reign, from August 1539 to 1555.

Cornelis Everaert and His World

Roughly a third (eighteen) of the surviving religious plays were composed during the first twenty years of the Reformation in the Low Countries. Only six of these were Lutheran or reformist, while eleven of the early religious plays were composed by the prolific Cornelis Everaert (1480/5–1556), factor of two of Bruges's rhetorician chambers, Three Saints (*Drie Sanntinen*) and Holy Spirit (*Helichs Gheest*). He was also a cloth fuller and dyer, as well as clerk for the Bruges Archer's guild; one of his plays, in fact, was performed during an archery guild competition in Ghistele.[15] Everaert was thus intimately connected to the socio-economic elite of his city and one might expect his plays to reflect their attitudes. Yet one must not neglect the potential influence of other members of a chamber on a play's contents, nor the pressure to appeal to the lower social orders so as to win over a broader audience. Another ingredient in the mix is the interference of frequently censorious rulers who kept their ears open for potentially seditious propaganda, especially during the era of the early Reformation. Obviously, then, a playwright such as Everaert had to walk a fine line when it came to presenting critical ideas on stage. Before examining how he did so, it would be helpful to describe briefly the situation of Bruges as it existed at the time of Everaert's dramatic career.[16]

Still a sizeable city of some 35,000 souls, Bruges was a city in desperate straits by 1500. It had been the economic star of Flanders but in the fifteenth and sixteenth centuries its famed textile industry was experiencing stiff competition from the English and Brabanters. Faced with the ravages of warfare, epidemic disease, and the ruinous taxation policies of the Burgundian and Habsburg lords, the Flemish found themselves at a loss as to how to restore economic viability to their homeland. The merchants of Bruges had managed to forestall economic catastrophe by enforcing monopolies on certain categories of foreign trade and by trying to develop more locally based industries which catered to the domestic market.[17] Yet luck was against the city, for the higher rulers' frequent debasement of coinage made it very difficult for the Flemish to compete with other foreign merchants. Thus Bruges came to rely increasingly on commercial tolls exacted on the international merchants, who in great numbers moved to Antwerp where the financial and trade inducements were unbeatable. Finally, in 1500 the German Hanse, the last foreign merchant house to support the city, abandoned it.[18] By the early sixteenth century the economic situation of the city had seriously deteriorated, and the number of unemployed and poor, already high, reached dangerous levels.[19] Residents of Bruges looked to their civic leaders to provide answers to their current quandary. In this climate rhetoricians could play a very important role indeed.

Fortunately for the historian, Everaert usually identified the specific occasions for which his plays were created, thus providing the celebratory context which is so important in interpreting rhetorician drama. For example, his *Welcome of the Dominicans* was composed for a major meeting of Dominicans in Bruges in 1523. Its praise of the charitable, educational, and inquisitional work of the brothers is therefore effusive, in contrast to the Erasmian style of anticlerical satire in his other plays.[20] Naturally Everaert knew how to play to an audience. Even so, he manages to bring to the gathered dignitaries' attention the problems being experienced by his city, which in former times had been loved by merchants, learned men, and clergy but now felt deserted.[21]

It seems Everaert attempted both to represent the opinions of his audience, so as to ensure their participation and identification with his drama, and to criticize or seek to change some of those attitudes when he thought it appropriate. Everaert provides us with a very useful case study in this respect not only because he left behind such a large corpus of plays but also because several of his plays concentrate on what can be described as 'secular' subjects, such as war and peace and the harmful effects of currency devaluation and loss of business.[22] Here we will examine Everaert's plays to see what he and his colleagues viewed as the social and religious problems of their community and where solutions might be found. In this way we can better understand the social context of the religious plays of Everaert and other rhetoricians. Everaert's and his fellow playwrights' opinions regarding war, peace, and the higher authorities are the central subject of a number of plays and therefore merit a fuller discussion later (see chapter 8).

Everaert lived and worked among the socially respectable members of Bruges society, and his plays reflect quite clearly their social attitudes. Merchants, shopkeepers, and artisans appear in a favourable light in his plays, although Everaert does suggest that responsibility for the woeful economic situation of Bruges is to be shared by all members of its society. Reform of the abuses and sins that had brought his beloved city to its knees was therefore at the forefront of Everaert's mind as he composed his pieces. At the same time, he criticizes his fellow citizens with considerable gentleness, unlike the venomous attacks that he could direct at foreign rulers. For example, in *The Play about the High Wind and the Sweet Rain,* composed in 1525 to celebrate the victory of Charles V over Francis I at the battle of Pavia, Everaert gently reminds the merchants and shopkeepers of Bruges that the activities of both are essential to the welfare of the city, especially in time of war, while harshly condemning the king of France as an overblown ruler who has condemned to ruin much of Europe merely for his false pride. Everaert has an international merchant Any (*Eenich*) arguing with a local shopkeeper Many (*Menich*) over whose business has been most damaged by the long warfare. In the end, Everaert affirms that both have suffered and enjoins them both to pray for the emperor and to seek common cause against the French enemy.[23]

Everaert therefore depicts the international merchants and local shopkeepers and artisans of Bruges as facing a common dilemma which they can do little about, except to pray and learn to appreciate and work with each other. Everaert apparently opposes any attempt to change the social structure of his society, even though it placed an enormous economic burden on the so-called third estate, the common, hard-working citizenry of the town. In a farce entitled *Humble Community and Tribulation,* Everaert presents the perversely unfair situation faced by the typical urban citizenry who, by hard work and sacrifice, must support both their social superiors and the lesser folk. In one passage Tribulation (*Trybulacie*) chastises Humble Community (*Scamel Ghemeente*) for his covetousness and for attempting to live beyond his means, reminding him that

> You have too much to support.
> The noble estate and spiritual prelates
> Humble folk, poor of estate
> Are supported by you here, upon the earth.
> Rabble of little value
> Must sometimes be fed by you too.[24]

In other words, the working members of a civic community must willingly subsidize both the socially privileged and the desperately poor, at the same time being careful not to waste their precious resources on frivolities. Everaert presents no other realistic alternative to this quandary, advising his audiences merely to bear their burdens in patience, remembering that whether one wears a simple cloak or extravagant clothing, 'we must all together return to the earth.'[25] In the long tradition of the 'dance of death,' Everaert regards death as the only true social leveller and no more immediate solution to the unfair burdens faced by him or his 'humble community' is offered.

These points Everaert reiterates in several other plays, such as the farce *Poor in the Chest* of 1529. In this work Poor Chest (*Aerm inde Buerse*) laments the loss of his business and his workers that has forced him to seek advice from Everyman (*Elckerlyc*), a profligate counsellor who spends all his wealth on his own lusts, leaving nothing for the less fortunate who must rely on alms. Everyman recommends that Poor Chest take Profuse Consumption (*Couvre Gebruuckynghe*) as his wife, but she rejects Poor Chest's proposal wishing instead for a 'fat husband.' 'How can I win your love?' Poor Chest implores. 'Become a man like Peace and Prosperous Business' is her response, for one who is 'poor in the chest destroys profuse consumption.'[26] Along with hoping fervently for peace to restore trade, Everaert chastises his employed contemporaries for their wasteful consumption and lack of concern for those even worse off than themselves, a criticism he directs at both women and men.

The causes and damage of unemployment are the focus of attention in three further plays composed by Everaert during 1529–30, a particularly difficult time for his city as a result of the Habsburg-Valois wars, which were only temporarily subdued with the signing of the Peace of Camerijk in 1530. In *The Play about the Dissimilar Money*, performed for Easter 1530, the character Such Rhetorician (*Sulc Rethorisien*) finds that instead of cheering up the merchant Many Folk (*Menichte van Volcke*), her art merely increases his state of depression. The reason, she finds, is that Many Folk's business is in danger of destruction as a result of the activity of Dissimilar Money (*DOnghelycke Munte*), a woman dressed in money who represents the devaluation and revaluation of currency resulting from the war contingencies of the imperial ruler. Those who suffer most directly, Everaert continues, are the normally solid citizens – merchants and guildspeople – whose businesses keep bread on the table of The Humble Labourer (*Den Scaemelen Aerbeyder*). Every deflation of currency leads many of those represented by Many Folk to sell their businesses and lay off their workers. This should be a matter of great concern to ordinary labourers, The Daily Chatterer (*Den Daghelicxschen Snaetere*, a woman selling apples) suggests, for if the city's economic elite and guildspeople suffer, the result will be even greater hardship for the lower social strata of the city.[27] The spectre of widespread unemployment should be sufficient to quell the increasing dissension between the city's labourers and employers, a dispute that Everaert has arbitrated by Daily Chatterer, perhaps as a humorous means of deflating the rising tension between the protagonists. For example, when Humble Labourer tells Many Folk that the latter's seemingly callous business decisions could throw Humble Labourer and his family into a life of begging, Daily Chatterer points out that a prolonged illness, or a loss of trade, could do the same to Many Folk:

> LABOURER: Many Folk, with heart and mind
> You owe me, Labourer, day and night
> Homage, with all your might.
> For from you, Many Folk, small and great
> Must I, Humble Labourer, earn my bread.
> I have no other income except by working.
> And when the work fails, so I have to send
> Wife and children, with desperation of hunger
> Immediately to your doors
> To obtain from you relief of their anxiety.

To which Daily Chatterer responds:

> By the way you behave
> It seems that all your desires are directed to finery.
> Such a Humble Labourer wants to go about with such finery
> As any solid citizen [*poorter*] or rich person.
> He too lets himself become haughty and proud,
> As if he were powerful and rich.
> But when he falls ill in bed,
> Or is deprived of business for a year,
> Poverty immediately forces him to revert to his
> Former habit and clothes.
> LABOURER: I would happily go about honourably like anyone else,
> Although Many Folk thinks to disdain me in this.
> CHATTERER: You might indeed go about honourably in your state.
> It would be better for you to have a mouldy penny
> Than you rise above your estate extravagantly.[28]

Daily Chatterer's goal, then, is to ensure that Humble Labourer remains contented in his estate, not resorting to social disturbance, especially against his employer, in a time of economic hardship that was caused by factors outside of the civic leadership's control. To reinforce this position, Reasonable Sentiment (*Redelic Ghevoel*) hands a cane named 'patience' to Humble Labourer and a scroll inscribed with the motto of Everaert's chamber (The Three Saints), 'the sufferer will overcome' (*die lydt verwint*). Reasonable Sentiment is confident that Emperor Charles V will soon restore the stability of the currency, and thus both labourer and employer should work together for the benefit of the Christian empire. Furthermore, those with means should, even in hard times, remember the virtue of charity and not be overly attached to worldly goods.

This conclusion is reinforced in Everaert's play, performed for the signing of the Peace of Camerijk, 24 April 1530, entitled *Great Labour and Sober Growth*. Briefly, two artisans act as the major characters of the play, discovering to their chagrin that while the obvious cause of their unemployment may be the warfare that interrupts normal trade and living, their sins, especially those of covetousness and murmuring, are ultimately responsible for bringing divine punishment upon them.[29] The solution, provided by Prudence of Wisdom (*Beleedt van Wysheden*), is to be patient, trust the Lord, and to 'keep suffering secretly concealed in the heart.'[30] Presumably Everaert is expressing a middle and upper class hope to avoid social upheaval or revolt by advocating that the lower orders of the city practise patience and serenity during a difficult period of unemployment and inflation. Unfortunately we do not know how any journeymen or day labourers in the audience might have responded to this message.

Another of Everaert's secular plays is *Common Trade*, a work which reveals most clearly the bitter poverty of Bruges during this difficult economic period, reflecting on the sad decline of the city's cloth industry. Performed to celebrate the joint feast of The Holy Spirit and The Three Saints chambers, probably sometime during 1529 or 1530, the play consists of three major characters: Common Trade (*Ghemeene Neerrynghe*), a woman cloth merchant; Such Humble (*Sulc Scaemel*), Common Trade's labourer; and Everyman (*Elckerlyc*), who represents those merchant guilds of the city able to profit during the difficult time, such as the shippers, as well as the higher clergy. Common Trade's complaint that Everyman has stopped buying local textiles,[31] is compounded by Everyman's taking advantage of the poor state of the local cloth market to shop for bargains elsewhere, such as Antwerp, further exacerbating Bruges's plight. As a result, Such Humble is out of work, although Common Trade promises to do what she can to help him, 'out of compassion.' For his part, Everyman, instead of showing his concern for his own community in practical ways, such as by spending his profits at home and by living in moderation, reveals a constant desire for new and exotic products, an affront to the drapers and labourers of the city.[32] Instead, Everyman should not only be satisfied with the local product but regard it his civic duty to purchase only Bruges's cloth. Finally Common Trade brings her case to Justice and Provision (*Provysie*), complaining that Everyman, with his constant demand for new products, is at fault for Bruges's economic turmoil.[33] Justice's decision is that the fault is indeed Everyman's, who has shown little love for either God or his fellows and has earned the wrath of God and brought his neighbours into hardship. Justice's recommendation is that Everyman 'must improve himself, if trade is to return.'[34]

More than in the other scripts examined here, Everaert in this play criticizes the prosperous of the city. Surely any of the audience from the city's lower orders would have added their assent to this chastisement of their economic and social betters. By so criticizing the city's economic elite, Everaert was able in this instance to help vent some of the social pressure which must surely have been causing great anxiety to Bruges's rulers. Of course there was always a delicate balance between 'letting off steam' and being seen to encourage social revolt; as with carnival festivities, the balance could be easily tipped in the direction of disruption.[35] At the same time we must not assume that Everaert was a cynical agent of the social hierarchy; like Erasmus he was not reticent to point a critical finger at the upper orders of the church and society. Overall then, Everaert's critical blade cut both ways without drawing much blood. He warns both workers and employers to behave in a spirit of community-mindedness and to be ready to sacrifice immediate needs for the broader good of the community. That he demanded more sacrifice from the poor than from the rich may not have been noticed by those watching an individual play. Nonetheless, his goal for his beloved Bruges is a return to commonweal, to a public spiritedness that can look beyond immediate needs and problems to see the greater good of the whole community. Unfortunately for Everaert and his fellow townsfolk, there was little they could do to offer any real solution to their society's social and economic problems, aside from some stop-gap acts of immediate amelioration. It is in this spirit of ultimate social despair that Everaert and many of his fellow rhetoricians turned with great hope to the religious reform movements, presumably in the hope that such a Christian revival would revive the spirits of charity and public sacrifice which alone could restore social harmony and peace within Bruges and for Europe as a whole.

Everaert's Religious Plays

Judging from Everaert's extant works, this resolution of societal ills was not likely to be led by the clergy. Our playwright is clearly ambivalent toward the priesthood, both affirming the necessity of the church and its sacraments and strongly chiding the spiritual weakness and moral corruption of those who monopolized the religious office. Like Erasmus, Everaert also satirizes the excessive saint's days and the innumerable regulations about fasting and abstinence from work which only engender hypocrisy; this is the theme of one of his short comedies, *Vigilance*, composed in 1526.[36] At the same time, Everaert composed plays to honour specific religious orders, such as *Jubilee*, a table play performed in 1534 in celebration of the fiftieth anniversary of the profession of a Franciscan monk. In this work there is no evidence of anticlerical sentiment of any kind.[37] Everaert's ambivalence is perhaps best seen in *The New Priest*, composed for the ordination of a priest some time between 1520 and 1533.[38] In this piece the playwright refers to traditional Catholic authorities such as St Bernard, St Augustine, St Ambrose, and St Thomas in order to vigorously defend the clerical estate against its many detractors. Doubting Mind (*Twyffelic Zin*) dressed as a fool, presents the reformers' objections to honouring priests, reminding the audience that priests sin often and are infamous for their womanizing and heavy drinking. Inward Reason (*Inwendeghe Redene*) responds not by denying the charges, but by arguing that such a life is forbidden the priesthood and that each priest should be a mirror of virtue for the lay people.[39] In spite of this chastisement of wayward priests, Everaert fervently defends both the doctrine of transubstantiation and the essential role of priests in the sacraments, affirming that with the priest's words of consecration the elements of the Eucharist are transformed into the body and blood of Christ. Christ himself took on the 'priestly state' which in the words of Old Testament (*Houde Testament*) stands 'above the angelic state.'[40] As New Testament (*Nyeuwe Testament*) affirms, God's power rests upon the 'priestly order':

Just as he has taught them at the Lord's Supper,
That wine, bread will be transformed
Through the power of his word every time
Into the specie of his holy body divine,
Perfect, just like Mary received him.[41]

Therefore each priest, according to Inward Reason, 'holds between his honourable hands / God and man, blood and flesh' which he can then consecrate.[42] Whoever despises priests are to be pitied as fools,[43] for not even the most excellent emperors and kings 'have been given such power upon the earth.'[44] Inward Reason does admit that many priests do not fully realize the great honour that God has placed into their hands, turning instead to sinful acts.[45] However, Old Testament counters with a story from Constantine, who, if he saw a priest committing a public sin, would cover him with his own imperial cloak rather than allow him to become the object of scorn, for priests are the protectors of people's souls.[46] Everaert's critique of the religious estate, therefore, was like that of Erasmus, intended as a reform from within, by reminding priests of their high calling and returning the recalcitrant to their original duties of teaching, praying, and spiritual correction.[47] However, by exposing the failings of individual priests in even this mild and humorous fashion, Everaert certainly contributed to the popularity of anticlericalism in Flanders, a charge laid also at the feet of Erasmus by his many critics.

Another traditional dogma defended by Everaert was the doctrine of the apostolic succession of the papacy. In *Saint Peter Compared to the Dove*, performed in 1531 in the village of Steevoorde, Everaert asserts that St Peter, the head of the apostles, bore Christ's missives, guarded the Scriptures, and acted as Christ's stadtholder, an evident defence of papal authority.[48] In several plays Everaert promotes also the Virgin Mary's role in salvation and the necessity of obedience to the church, not surprising considering Bruges was regarded as one of the major centres for the Mary cult.[49] In such works as *Mary Compared to the City of Jerusalem* (1527), *Mary Likened to the Throne of Solomon* (1529), *Mary Compared to a Ship* (1530), and *The Rose Wreath of Mary* (1530), he affirms that Mary, the sinless Mother of God, was now elevated above the angels as 'Queen of Heaven.' For example, in *Mary Likened to the Throne of Solomon*, composed for Veurne's Poor in the Chest (*Aerm inde Buerse*) chamber and performed at a competition in Ypres in 1529, Everaert takes as his task the awakening 'by figures' of the devotion of the people to God and to Mary.[50] The central figure is a scene of the throne of Solomon, which remains visible for the whole play, offering an allegorical interpretation of the throne as a symbol of the Virgin. Supporting the doctrine of her Immaculate Conception, Mary is likened to this 'unspotted throne' because Christ, the second Solomon, for nine months 'took his rest there' to become man.[51] Mary's purity will endure forever in heaven above that of mere mortals, since she received it as a gift from God so that Jesus could have a mother as pure as his father.[52] Interpreting the six steps leading to the throne as the twelve virtues of Mary, the play focuses on her humility, a virtue all women should cultivate, leading them to obey their husband's commands.[53] Women, Everaert continues, should follow Mary in her sobriety, in willing poverty, avoiding all excess, working with their hands.[54] Because of her meekness, Mary was able to act as a mediator between the apostles whenever disputes arose:

> Mary was also meekly spiritual.
> For when any questions arose
> Between the apostles, so she proved herself
> To be humble, as a lesson.
> Thus was Mary the apostles' mistress
> In this way teaching them strength in the faith.[55]

She has been rewarded with the status of 'Queen of Heaven' and 'Lady of the World,'[56] and acts now as mediatrix between God and humanity. Three Virtues then turn their praise to the Virgin:

> RHETORICAL DELIGHT: Thus you are, according to custom,
> The true mediator, this is the true conclusion.
> SCRIPTURAL PROOF: That above her is God alone.
> Beneath are we humans, in the earthly meadows.
> Thus is Mary the go-between for both
> Between God and us poor creatures.
> JOYFUL DESIRES: For this reason we call to her at any hour
> As advocate, for our consolation.[57]

Everaert's affirmation of Mary's elevated status in heaven is depicted visually in the 1527 play *Mary Compared to the City of Jerusalem* with a painted figure of the Virgin surrounded by the sun's rays, with her feet on the moon and a crown of twelve stars on her head.[58]

Judging from these Mary plays, we see that Everaert's attitude toward the role of women in society is quite traditional. Mary was the role model for women, who were therefore expected to be humble and submissive.[59] At the same time, his reference to Mary acting as mediator in apostolic disputes – albeit by her virtue rather than by her words – alludes to a possible function for women in theological discussion. By so extolling the six attributes and twelve virtues of Mary and defending her Immaculate Conception, as well as by advocating (in the *The Seven Wounds* of 1530) Christ's physical suffering as a panacea for tribulation, Everaert places himself firmly in the popular devotional tradition promoted by Franciscans and northern humanists during the late fifteenth and early sixteenth centuries. While he evidently took the side of Franciscans and humanists in the often acrimonious debate surrounding the doctrine of Mary's Immaculate Conception, he was still able to compose drama honouring their Dominican opponents. This flexibility, combined with his apparent support of humanistic forms of piety and anticlerical satire, suggests that Everaert became a Catholic reformer along the lines of Erasmus of Rotterdam.[60] Even this clearly orthodox rhetorician, whose plays are regarded as models of Catholic drama, was dissatisfied with the ecclesiastical status quo.

Given its title, Everaert's *The Seven Wounds* would seem to promote a crassly externalized religious devotion but it emphasizes instead the inner meaning of the wounds and suffering of Christ. Composed as a gift play to the honour of the chamber's king, the two characters offer the 'men and women seated here' – proving that women were present during some indoor chamber performances[61] – seven vessels each with a different type (*specien*) of blood drawn from Christ. Instead of a grisly display, however, the audience is provided with a discussion of the spiritual meaning of the wounds which provide comfort to believers; for example, the nails which pierced Christ's limbs stand for virtue against sin.[62] Another gift play, *The Mountain*, performed on Good Friday shortly after the proclamation of a peace treaty (perhaps Madrid in 1526 or Camerijk in 1530), has as its lead character a pilgrim who has brought home with him not crass relics but a metaphor of a mountain of peace.[63] After the two other characters fail to guess its identity, the pilgrim reveals the central message that the true mountain of peace is the Mount of Contemplation, the death of Christ which brought perfect peace to humanity. This peace, the play concludes, is transmitted through the Lord's five wounds by means of the sacraments.[64]

There is also evidence of considerable intellectual and stylistic development on the part of Everaert, seen in a comparison of his earliest known play with those dating to the 1520s and 1530s. This reveals a loss of some of his earlier religious naïvety and a movement to a more sophisticated position as both friend and critic of the priesthood. His first play, *Mary of the Rose Wreath*, composed in 1509 presumably for a Dominican-sponsored Confraternity of the Rosary, combines a medieval miracle play in the second half with a more 'modern' *spel van zinne* in the first half. In this transitional work between medieval and early modern forms of drama, Everaert's religious attitudes are quite orthodox, with the play extolling the virtues of the Virgin and of the cult in her honour. At the same time, even at this early stage, Everaert seeks to replace the more materialistic aspects of this cult with a prayerful rosary devotion.[65] His later plays avoid miraculous stories altogether, presumably as Everaert became better acquainted with the writings of Erasmus. Moreover, if Erné is correct in his argument that Everaert was the playwright of Bruges's contribution to the 1539 competition in Ghent, then by that year Everaert had moved to a Lutheran position (see chapter 6 below).[66] Evidently he had come to espouse Lutheran ideas some time between 1534 – the year of his last dated religious play (*Jubilee*) – and 1539.[67] If this conclusion is correct, then Everaert (or his chamber) progressed from a devout Catholic critical of some materialistic aspects of religious observance, to an Erasmian reformer, to a Lutheran. Even during his 'Erasmian reformer' stage, Everaert only rarely criticized Protestants such as Luther or condemned their ideas. Instead, he focused on buttressing the Catholic faith and emphasizing the true meaning of its ritual. This approach is clearly evident in a play entitled *The Vineyard*, performed on 25 March 1533, during the Lenten feast of Mary's Annunciation. In this work he promotes fasting, listening to sermons, giving alms, and attending confession. He also castigates the sin of heresy, but in such a way that the specific heresy condemned is unclear. Based on Jesus' command to work in the vineyard (Matt. 20), Everaert's play confirms that this vineyard is 'the holy faith, the Christian church,' which unfortunately has been afflicted with the 'leprous sin of heresy.'[68] All three estates, Everaert affirms, must be involved in the work of pulling out the weeds, for the protection of the church against heresy is one that must engage the 'common folk' as much as the 'spiritual prelates' and the noble estate.[69] The closest Everaert comes to describing this heresy as a doctrinal issue comes when Willingly Follows (*Ghewillich Volghen*), a farm labourer, describes his work as pulling out the weeds of heresy, which are 'half green, half dry in God's teaching' and which one can 'hardly make them turn away / from their evil, audacious opinions.'[70] But even worse than the weeds of heresy, the master of the vineyard suggests, are the unfruitful tendrils which choke the vines.[71] The emphasis is therefore not on countering heretical ideas, but on promoting good Lenten behaviour on the part of the audience, especially attendance at sermons and devotion to the Virgin. It is possible to argue, in fact, that the heresy Everaert combats in this work is more akin to the traditional mortal sins, such as sloth, or of not practising the Christian virtues of late medieval devotion.[72] The work is also heavily laden with scriptural references which, combined with his emphasis on lay action against heresy, shows that by 1533 Everaert is advocating a much more prominent role for Bible-literate laypeople in the reform of the church than was desired by ecclesiastical authorities. It is conceivable that in his deep concern over the spiritual health of his society Everaert finally became frustrated with the continuing lack of reforming zeal on the part of the Catholic hierarchy and therefore turned to a more dynamic reform camp.

An Anti-Anabaptist Play

One polemically orthodox rhetorician play survives from this early period of the Reformation, Reynier van den Putte's *An Allegorical Play on the Incarnation of Christ*, which was composed sometime in 1534 when Anabaptism still dominated the popular Reformation in the Low Countries (see illustration 4).[73] Not surprisingly, Van den Putte affirms in this work that forgiveness of sins is mediated only through the Catholic church and its sacraments. His central target, however, is the Anabaptist doctrine of the 'heavenly flesh of Christ' – that Christ had brought with him to earth his own 'heavenly flesh' and had therefore received none of his humanity from Mary. Van den Putte, perhaps trained in the Franciscan tradition, is both highly knowledgeable about Catholic theology and well informed about the essential beliefs of Melchior Hoffman and his Dutch followers.[74] Interestingly, the peculiar Melchiorite doctrine of Christ's heavenly flesh was a hallmark of Anabaptist and later Mennonite factions, but Van den Putte seems to have been the only rhetorician of his era to mention it.

Opening this orthodox script are the Vices Killing Letter (*Doodende letter*) and Misuse (*Misbruyck der schrifteren*), disreputable peddlers who provide the malevolent inspiration for the Melchiorite teachers, Self

Wit (*Eygen vernuft*), Rejector of Knowledge (*Waenende weten*), and Stiff-necked (*Hertneckich*). Like all heretics the literacy of these laypeople[75] has led them to misinterpret the Scriptures and to forsake the corner-stone of Christ.[76] Furthermore, their aim, according to Killing Letter, is among them to 'do more evil / in the world than all the sorcerers together,' a bold statement on the part of Van den Putte during a cen-tury when witches were increasingly viewed as the most heinous min-ions of Satan and both witches and Anabaptists were burned at the stake for their supposed evil.[77] These Anabaptist preachers confront the simple commoner Many Innocent Men (*Menich onnosel mensch*) and his wife Simple Trust (*Simpel trouwe*), the latter praying that the Holy Spirit will 'teach us / the most sincere manner of faith.'[78] (As was often the case in rhetorician drama, the wife is depicted as a more religiously sta-ble and intelligent person than her husband.) Simple Trust laments the confusion brought on by a multitude of new beliefs, among which is the horrible blaspheming of the sacrament, with some saying the host is no more than 'baker's bread,' others that it is 'merely a sign' (Zwingli), while still others hold the bread in their vile hands while believing it to be true God and man (Luther); they all despise religious images as idol-atry.[79] In the midst of their confusion enter the Melchiorites proclaim-ing their divine mission to convince the simple couple to 'leave this evil generation' with its pagan ways, abandoning possessions and family, even to the point of separating from one's unbelieving spouse. Then the Anabaptist preachers promise to teach the couple the true faith and afterwards baptize them according to the correct fashion.[80] Although Simple Trust and Many Innocent attempt to defend the orthodox view of Christ and his virgin birth, the two preachers present the Melchiorite view as the only biblical position. Many Innocent begins to doubt the traditional doctrine of Christ's Incarnation, although his wife remains firm in the old faith.[81] Rescuing this simple couple from the teachers of error are the friars Spiritual Understanding (*Geestelijck begrijp*) and Scriptural Meaning (*Schriftuerlijcke zin*), who remind the couple of the biblical warnings about false teachers and warn them that the sup-posed good works and miracles of the Anabaptists are nothing more than hypocrisy.[82] By expounding the traditional interpretation of Christ's Incarnation and Mary's role in it, the orthodox preachers over-power the literalist interpretation of the Melchiorite characters. An inner play of Gabriel making his announcement to Mary confirms the orthodox position, and Many Innocent Men returns to his ancestral faith.[83] The play proper concludes with the husband praising Christ and the wife extolling the Virgin Mary, leading to the climactic unveiling of the image of Christ on the cross.[84]

As an epilogue, Killing Letter and Abuse discuss where they might find refuge. One suggests heading to East Frisia, although his partner doubts its current safety.[85] The other counters that he would like to go to Münster, but again his friend warns him that 'the entrance there is guarded.' Killing Letter then secretly tells his fellow of another refuge, and they both set off for it, ending the performance. The play clearly dates from the period when the Anabaptist kingdom at Münster was still under siege and the disciples of Hoffman and Matthijs were proselytizing through the Low Countries. Among his rhetorician fellows, Van den Putte seems to have been alone in directly confronting Anabaptism during its popular phase, although Anna Bijns had composed some refrains against the multiplicity of sects brought about by Luther.[86] Moreover, his obvious disdain for the practice of laypeople interpreting the Scriptures for themselves must surely have reduced the popularity of his play when performed for the highly literate audiences of Dutch cities.

Reform-minded Plays

Christian Church

Those plays written from a 'Protestant' perspective during the first decades of the Reformation provide important insight into the elements of reformation thought which Dutch urbanites found most appealing. The plays from these years range in tone from those which present reform ideas so subtly that they have been mistaken as orthodox Catholic, to those which so flagrantly denounce the ecclesiastical authorities that public performance would have been extremely dangerous. An example of how carefully rhetoricians could craft reform drama is afforded by *Christian Church*. Composed by a prosperous bookbinder and rhetorician of Utrecht, Reynier Pouwels, this very serious play focuses on the nature of the Christian faith. As in many other plays, Pouwel's perspective is hinted at in the list of characters and their attributes: the virtuous characters are the doctor Sincere Scriptural Proof (*Vprecht Scriftuerlijck Bewijs*); the burgher Desires to Know the Best (*Gharen tbest willen weten*); Christian Church (*Cristenkercke*), an honourably dressed woman; Sincere Simple Faith (*Vprecht Simpel Ghelouen*), a beautiful young maiden, clothed honourably in blue; the nightwatchman Scriptural Guard (*Scriftuerlijcke hoede*); and The Loving

Heart (*Het minnende herte*), dressed like the Son of God; while the Vices are the pimp Blinded Will (*Verblinde Wille*), his cousin Stiff-necked Heart (*Hertnackich herte*), and Thinks Highly of Himself (*Selfs goet-duncken*), a knight wearing a prelate's cap. The only cleric who appears in this drama is therefore the subject of satire.[87] Beginning in the prologue the play emphasizes the preaching of the Word of God and the centrality of faith for salvation. Understandably, considering that Utrecht was the ecclesiastical capital of the northern Netherlands, the play contributes to the promotion of reformation ideas more by intimation than by explicit proclamation. Simple Faith begins the work by defending the doctrine of the Trinity and affirming that the Scriptures teach that salvation is only through grace. Then he describes the bread of God as the Word, not as the host:

> Which bread, word, body, the enemy's iniquity
> With foolish scandalous writings
> Yea, with blind, stiff-necked rage
> Would like to extirpate,
> But Lord, they shall fail by your strong hand.[88]

The reference to the enemy's fearsome attempts to exterminate the word of God is something that Lutheran and other reformist writers frequently accused the Catholic authorities of desiring to do, and it was the emperor and the Catholic hierarchy which used violent means to put an end to the Lutheran threat. It is illuminating indeed that in his discussion of salvation Pouwels ignores the traditionally central means of grace, the seven sacraments, and the priesthood, which were so clearly defended in Everaert's productions. Here too it is laypeople who discuss the means of salvation. For example, Desires to Know remarks to Simple Faith that there are two approaches to the Scriptures, each following a different path – a clear allusion to the controversy between Lutherans and Catholics. Simple Faith disagrees, for there is only one approach to the Scriptures. The confusion has arisen, he notes, because of the strange opinions of clerics:

> There is but one way in the Scriptures,
> But these hypocritical clerics make this error
> Throughout the world very clever in their choice,
> For they make the Scriptures a waxen nose,
> Bending it to their strange opinions.[89]

'How then can one stand firm on the Scriptures?' Desires to Know asks his friend. It is at this point that Simple Faith provides an answer that on the surface appears orthodox:

As the word, so the deeds,
And have the right feelings toward the Christian church,
Submitting yourself as an obedient child.[90]

Simple Faith's explication of what this obedience means, however, lends itself much more to a Lutheran interpretation, for the emphasis is on sincere faith according to St Augustine: knowing the Apostles' Creed is not enough, for one needs faith, and then one can love God and neighbour.[91] When Desires to Know asks Simple Faith what he thinks of these 'new evangelicals' who disregard works and rely upon faith alone, his friend replies that while works might strengthen faith from the outside, it is most important to have an interior faith from which will spring good deeds.[92] Love of neighbour, he continues in accord with Luther, is merely faith at work.

Two Vices then enter complaining that they, Baal's prophets, have been banned from all courts, making it possible for Simple Faith to become deaf to their learned sophists, teleologists, logicists, and legalists, whose teaching has never erred but was now a heretical subject.[93] They therefore set out to deceive Simple Faith by means of their subtle arguments. Before they can do so, Christian Church appears praising the Virgin Mary, although without reference to specifically Catholic teachings about her immaculate conception, elevation as Queen of Heaven or function as mediatrix.[94] Then Christian Church turns to the religious, telling them:

You religious, appear now,
Show now the true shrine of the Scriptures.
Say, stop the wringing of your hands.
You be exempt from false doctrine
Praise now the Lord, the only head of divine beings,
According to the spirit and truth's domain.[95]

In spite of these words, Simple Faith is seduced by the Vices, with the assistance of 'Silly Devotion' (*ghecke deuocie*) and 'Hypocritical Appearance' (*gheveijnst bescouwen*), and by enticing him with all of the world's knowledge and glosses, 'adorned devotion,' and fleshly freedom, all of which destroys 'the Spirit's freedom.'[96] When Scriptural Guard arrives, he castigates the impious who have so despised God's Word, 'the true sacrament.'[97] He warns Simple Faith to get off this new path which leads to the deception of heresy, stop adorning the Word of God with false opinion, and return to the path of charity.[98] To show the way, Scriptural Guard has with him the lantern of the knowledge of sin and the candle of the gospel,[99] the two key ingredients for bringing people to a Lutheran understanding of salvation. He also tells Simple Faith to leave his fleshly delights, become obedient to the church, maintain the covenant (*verbont*), and place the fear of God above all else. Phrases such as 'maintain the covenant' and 'the fear of God' were prominent not only among the early Lutherans in the Low Countries, but also the Melchiorite Anabaptists, who called themselves 'covenanters' and who esteemed the fear of God above all else.

The play clearly blames priests for many of society's ills, for they have mixed the bitter with the sweet in their sermons, sung in Baal's name, pursued idols, and, reminiscent of the Amsterdam play *Naboth*, killed Naboth and persecuted Elijah.[100] Loving Heart then tells Sincere Faith that he must be obedient to the Christian church and reject all errors, for God will soon destroy this diabolical idolatry of the Antichrist (Antiochus).[101] Although there is much ambiguity in the identification of the actual targets of this apocalyptic wrath (in words reminiscent of many early Melchiorite writings),[102] toward the end Thinks Highly comes closest to a clear description when he remarks that 'all heretics'

Capped, shorn, without understanding, always reading in books
Have become known by her deceit [i.e., that of 'inflated false
   presumption'],
All opinions have been blinded by Scriptural Guard
Which are at present still strong in vigour in the world.
In all arts heresies like to sing the dominant tone beautifully.[103]

The modern editor of the play, G.A. Brands, argued that because in his play Pouwels tells his audience to submit to the Christian church, the work must be interpreted along Catholic lines.[104] But most reformers, including Lutherans, also believed that their religious community deserved the distinction of being called the 'Christian Church.' The apocalyptic sentiment also better reflects a reformist perspective and not just an Anabaptist one; Luther was quite adept at calling down apocalyptic judgment on his opponents.[105] Reading Pouwel's play, one becomes convinced that the playwright was writing for a very well-read audience which was sympathetic to Luther's thought and able immediately to empathize with the author's choice of biblical passages and understand his use of innuendo. When he talks about heretics, for example, his reference to their sophistry and mixing of strange, learned opinions with the Scriptures and their 'hooded, shorn' heads leads one to conclude that the heretics are the monks and theologians of the Catholic church and not the simple folk who follow Luther.[106] Pouwels has therefore thrown the charge of heresy back into the faces of those responsible for the religious persecution. Given his subtle presentation of reform rhetoric in this play it comes as no surprise that Pouwels received little more than a slap on the wrist when on 10 November 1540, he himself faced charges of binding and selling an unorthodox book of sermons, 'forbidden by the imperial majesty's placard.' It seems Utrecht's council accepted his explanation that he had received the book from his son; he was therefore ordered merely to ask for forgiveness from the members of the council.[107]

Multiformity of Deceit

It is also in the years before the Ghent competition of 1539 that rhetoricians most flagrantly vented their anticlerical sensibilities. Opposition to salvific works such as indulgences, pilgrimages, and images, and to the priests who controlled them, appears in all of the reform-minded plays from this period, such as the anonymous dinner play *The Multiformity of the Deceit of the World*.[108] Like most dinner plays, this is a simple work with only two characters, both of them Vices. In this case the audience of *Multiformity of Deceit* was most likely an 'in-group,' made up of people who probably shared the ideological perspective of the author and who were able to follow the satirical insinuations of the performance. It is not inconceivable that this play was performed in front of members of one of the many popular reform conventicles, the presence of which so incensed the authorities.

In this play the two allegorical vices, Origin of Sins (*Oerspronck der sonden*) and Manifold Deception (*Menichfuldich bedroch*) are travelling merchants. At the very beginning Origin of Sins calls out for local merchants as customers for his wares: jewels, recipes, letters, and herbs all of which he has brought from 'Lady Venus's mountain' (*vrou Venus berch*), which, apart from its obvious sexual connotations (something the playwright does not develop), purports to be a mythical place which imbued its visitors with magical ability.[109] Origin of Sins' wares, therefore, possessed magical properties, as this character himself notes: 'I have come from lady Venus mountain / where one, without effort, can handle all sorts of arts.' His colleague is amazed and wants to know more:

Have you lodged in the mount of lady Venus
Where are adorned many strange cures
Tell us all about it![110]

Throughout the remainder of the play Origin of Sins displays and explains each of the magical jewels, herbal cures, and talismanic letters which he has brought back from that mountain poised between the dead and the living.[111] Evidently this unknown playwright knew how to grab his viewers' attention, keeping them on the edge of their seats trying to figure out how he was going to interpret these magical items in the expected moral and religious direction. They did not have to wait long, for Origin of Sins' first item is the herb 'error of discord' (*Discordich erroer*), followed by 'forceful will' (*Forsighe will*), 'finance' (*Fynancie*), 'whoredom' (*houerdye*), and the like. His supposedly magical wares become figures of the ills of the church and society. Two of his herbs, 'hate and anger' have been responsible for the slaughter of the prophets and Christ himself. Manifold Deception then suggests that 'there is no shortage among the conventicles / or among the spiritual people, mark my words,' to which his friend responds 'all those who work according to the Spirit of God / are spiritual clergy, according to God's knowledge.' Manifold agrees, for

All who love the Spirit of God
Are spiritual people in God's presence
What, do you think that God inquires about any differences
In tonsure, habit, or other fashion?[112]

Another herb for sale is 'self interest,' a very useful item which bends justice, inspires hypocritical sermons, sticks many people into cloisters, produces many false and quarrelsome articles, and establishes idols, all 'contrary to brotherly love.'[113] A further magical herb is 'hired office,' the foremost of all herbs, which can perform wonders, such as oppress labourers and persecute believers:

Hired office does scatter the sheep
Out of the true sheepfold, to their impiety
When they see the wolf coming from afar
They begin to fear, and start running.[114]

These hired officials are found in great number at Leuven, Cologne, Paris, and Rome, all bastions of ecclesiastical power and orthodox universities. The Vices then proceed to lament the decrease in the use of letters of indulgences, pilgrimages, and images, which they as travelling merchants sell, and the lack of esteem for their servants, the higher clergy. When praising the spiritual power of indulgences, for example, the Vices note that through these letters 'many have received grace,' many have 'ridden on mules and horses,' and many have 'built fine buildings,' hardly the intended spiritual benefits of the treasury of merits. However, Manifold Deception is convinced and purchases one for himself.

Obviously written from a strongly anticlerical and reform posture, the play highlights the spiritual folk who worship God through the love and gifts of the Holy Spirit. Manifold Deception commiserates with the sorrow of the learned clergy, 'who break their heads with earnest study,' while 'dull laymen, who do not know what they say, proclaim that they have received God's gifts from the Holy Spirit.'[115] This critique of higher learning and emphasis on spiritual laypeople meeting together under the direction of the Holy Spirit suggests that the work originated in a lay reform conventicle, illustrating the lack of clerical or educated leadership among reformers by 1530. It is possible that such a group had developed spiritualistic tendencies (there is no mention of Anabaptist baptism).[116] The contrast between a debased and useless clerical estate and a spiritual layfolk could not be more clearly presented.

Priest, Sexton, and Weaver

A similar anticlerical perspective is expressed in another anonymous dinner play from the southern Netherlands, *Priest, Sexton, and Weaver* which, although printed in 1565 seems to reflect the ideas and attitudes of the 1530s, especially with its references to Lutheranism. A plausible scenerio can be conceived if the play was composed in the 1530s and preserved in manuscript until it was safe to print it in time to assist the rising tide of antiplacard and iconoclastic sentiment in the 1560s.[117] In this work the playwright depicts the clergy not only as ignorant and greedy – typical characteristics in reform plays as in all anticlerical literature – but also as hostile to literate laypeople, especially to their reading the Scriptures and deciding religious issues for themselves.[118] Priest (*Prochiaen*, who represents 'self-satisfied,' *Eygen Ghemack*) admits that even with his clerical education he can hardly understand his breviary; how is it possible for 'rude ignorant men' to discover the wisdom of the Scriptures? Weaver (*Wever*) should leave the Scriptures to those equipped to interpret them and adhere instead to the faith of his forefathers.[119] Receiving the brunt of the Priest's and Sexton's (*Coster*) criticism are Lutherans, who, among other things, not only refuse to honour the church, its teachings, sacraments, images, saints, or priests, but also disobey the secular authorities and ignore good works. Furthermore, the reformers reject priests as scribes and Pharisees, claim that priests could marry, and depreciate the value of the whole sacramental system, especially the Mass and purgatory. What is worse in the view of the Priest is that these 'Lutherans' desire to teach their opinions to everyone and appear more than willing to suffer martyrdom.[120] Weaver, speaking on behalf of evangelical reform (while rejecting Sexton's assertion that he was an Anabaptist),[121] counters the Priest's assertion that 'a weaver should weave, a mender should mend, but leave us to watch over the Scriptures,' affirming instead that all believers have been called to proclaim the gospel. Because priests have been too preoccupied with 'selling their wares,' they have not only ignored Christ's command to preach the gospel, but have the audacity to persecute those who do. Among other things the Weaver rejects is the need for clerical confession (confession is best made only to Christ) and the office of pope, identified here as the Antichrist who has robbed God of his honour:

> How dare you blaspheme the Spirit of God,
> That you have exalted the holiness of the pope?
> Was he not also born in sin,
> And conceived in sin, just like other men?
> Why are we concerned about his weeping and wishes,
> About his benedictions or curses?
> I regard them all as arts of sorcery,
> For he seeks nothing but money and worldly honour.
> ...
> He can do it through the power of the great Antichrist,
> Which he himself is and eternally remains.[122]

The papal hierarchy could hardly be treated any more severely, charged with the most heretical of crimes, sorcery.

Other aspects of early reform anticlericalism are detailed in this play. For one thing Weaver criticizes the regulations regarding fasting and holy days, which gave unfair advantage to monastic institutions, such as the rule allowing pastry cooks to work on holy days when other cooks were forbidden to do so. Priest replies that they perform necessary work, a comment that earns this scathing remark from Weaver:

> Yes, but it is to fill your dainty mouths,
> Therefore you say it is necessary, you canons,
> For it is truly a food for priests and monks,
> And not for weavers, furriers, or smiths,
> Who are happy merely with a piece of cheese,
> And coarse bread and water, as is the rooster.[123]

Since Christ has fulfilled the sabbath, Weaver believes all artisans ought to be able to work on holy days, which, he adds, were instituted only for the financial benefit of the clergy.[124]

The Mass is likewise idolatrous, according to Weaver, for 'simple folk' have been led to believe that it contained magical power and that if they have heard a Mass, no harm would come to them on that day.'[125] Only the Spirit, Weaver argues, not external things, can make one holy.[126] Clerical celibacy is also condemned by Weaver, who suggests to Priest that the clergy have been forbidden to marry so that 'you can live your fleshly lives. A fresh whore every day pleases you well!'[127] What is worse, the artisan continues, is that priests and monks do nothing of value to earn their bread. When Weaver finally manages to win Sexton to his position, the latter gives up his life in the church so that he can take up the occupation of weaving.[128] As a corrective to the wasteful life of the clergy, this play promotes a strong artisanal work ethic, for as laypeople took on the religious responsibilities of the priesthood, the clergy were to accept the necessity of labouring for their bread.

Another contentious issue – during the 1520s and 1530s as well as the 1560s – was that of images in the church. When Sexton supports them as the books of the unlearned, Weaver responds angrily that they are instead idolatry and an excuse for the clergy to avoid their responsibility of teaching the laity according to the Word of God.[129] In the late-medieval Netherlands, as elsewhere, religious art served the dual function of beautifying sacred places and informing the illiterate on the essentials of the Christian faith.[130] By the first quarter of the sixteenth century, however, the proportion of laypeople who were literate had increased dramatically in the cities of the Low Countries, thanks in large measure to the establishment of city schools for the children of socially ambitious artisans and merchants and to the labours of the Brethren of the Common Life, whose residences provided opportunities for poorer boys to attend school. During the early Reformation in the Netherlands a number of laypeople were brought to account for iconoclastic statements or actions. Among those charges brought against David Joris at his trial in 1528 was that he had denigrated the saints' images by suggesting they merely misled the people and led them to spiritual destruction.[131] Joris's punishment, although considered too light by the procurator-general of the Court of Holland, involved a three-year banishment from his home and the boring of his tongue. Certainly the authorities sought to counteract such iconoclastic propaganda. The persistence of such sentiment, however, is clear in the court records from the 1520s and from the much more massive and organized iconoclastic riots of 1566.[132]

It seems that urbanites increasingly found didactic art an insult to their reading ability. As suggested by Thomas A. Brady, Jr, it may also have been the case that because religious art tended to be sponsored by the ecclesiastical and patrician aristocracy, its presence in churches was doubly resented.[133] If Weaver's remarks are reflective of literate reform-minded Dutch folk, then we see here their continuing sense of frustration at being restricted to the same visual and aural means of receiving religious knowledge as was available to generally illiterate peasants and lowly regarded labourers. Apparently the remarkable increase in civic-supported preacherships and lay religious confraternities was not sufficient to satisfy the longing of some to participate in religion on a level equal to the clerical elite. Evident too is a dissatisfaction with officially approved means of religious devotion which our playwright regarded as superstitious magic. What the author of this play finds most offensive about the church of his day is that there was little room in it for ambitious layfolk who not only could read, but who were desirous of a more active role in the religious life of their community and insulted by the condescending attitude which the clergy often displayed toward them. Reinforcing this sentiment on behalf of freeing laypeople from the tutelage of the clergy is the aforementioned Amsterdam play *Sick City*, which condemned the Catholic clergy who not only refused to work with their hands but had the temerity to persecute the true, scriptural preachers. Instead, the playwright recommended that the city's magistrates force its preachers to proclaim only the gospel.[134] Such a call for clerics to preach solely the gospel was a central feature of the urban Reformation throughout Europe.

Biblical Plays

Such blatant criticism of the ecclesiastical and secular authorities was dangerous, especially after the suppression of the Anabaptist uprisings in 1535. It could, however, be maintained at little risk if hidden in biblical dramas, in which the actors portray biblical kings and priests in such a way that the audience could, with a little imagination, recognize their contemporary authorities.[135] Three examples of such drama survive from the decade of the 1530s: *St John's Beheading* and *Lazarus's Death*, described in chapter 4 above, and *The Acts of the Apostles, Chapters 3, 4, and 5*, a work which brings together both biblical and allegorical characters.[136] By using the New Testament story of the healing of the crippled beggar by the apostle Peter and the resulting investigation of the apostles before the Sanhedrin, the play is able to present Luther's major doctrines and condemn the persecution of religious dissenters, identified here as those who follow the teachings of the 'German doctors,' a typical nomenclature for Lutherans. Moreover, the apostles proclaim the Lutheran doctrine of justification by faith alone. After John tells the Cripple that the law of Moses has been fulfilled by Christ,[137] Peter states 'it is faith in Christ which we teach you ... Believe in Christ, your soul's pledge / you will be saved, as the Scriptures clearly say.'[138] Later on Peter makes it very clear that the Word of God is the sole source of true knowledge and salvation.[139] According to the playwright, it is the learned who suppress the truth of God's Word by means of persecution.[140] A contrast to the apostles is provided by the Vices, False Prophet (*Valsch Propheet*) and Beautiful Hypocrite (*Schoon Ypocrijt*), the former carrying a merchant's pack full of pictures and the latter displaying on his white robe virtues such as poverty, humility, devotion, and fasting, while under the cloth he is dressed as a devil, with a roll displaying the vices. They complain that the German doctors' lay disciples audaciously spread their teaching everywhere:

But these new preachers
Who like scoundrels dishonour our Lord

And add to the gospel with their teaching,
Thus, by infecting it, mislead the simple community.[141]

Hypocrite describes their preaching as 'it is all Christ before and Christ after. Is this not a great abuse? For they believe they receive salvation only through Christ.'[142] What concerns them is the dramatic spread of Luther's teaching, especially justification by faith. Most frightening about this trend is the loss to their religious business, which they were experiencing at the hands of unlearned artisans (ambachten) who received their knowledge not from the approved schools, which have the law, but from the Holy Spirit.[143] At this point False Prophet exclaims, 'What, is God so ignorant to send his Spirit to laypeople?'[144] Their only option to ending this threat is to use physical coercion against the reformers. The prominent Jewish rabbi Gamaliel's advice to the Sanhedrin (Acts 5: 34–9) that they should let the new teaching run its course is rejected by Caiaphus, who insists on seeing the heretics' blood flowing on the earth, and on destroying all of them with torture, fire, or prison.[145] At the same time, the Cripples decide to turn from their learned instructors to the apostles, for the former have merely covered over the treasure of God with false instruction and hatred.[146]

Reinforcing in the minds of the play's audience the negative image of the clergy as oppressors was the intentional comparison of the sixteenth-century clergy with the Jewish leaders who supposedly had conspired against the early Christians. The evil nature of the learned clergy is further made visual by the unrolling of two pictures, the first revealing Hypocrisy's and False Prophet's patron saint, Saint Lupus, a wolf wearing a tiara and devouring homes and farms. The two Vices then discuss how they might keep their representative, the high priest Annas – described as 'Ons Pontificates' and 'Dominus Pontifex' – faithful to their goals. They decide to send him a vision, presented to the audience in the form of the second painting, depicting the Babylonian Whore astride the dragon of the Apocalypse (Rev. 17) and drunk with the blood of the martyrs. The visual and verbal descriptions make it quite clear that the intended target of this vivid derision is the pope.[147] The apostles pray for deliverance from the 'teeth of the bloodthirsty wolf' in full expectation that God's grace will soon make their enemies obedient.[148] It is also the case that the residents of the Low Countries who witnessed this play were more than familiar with the early Lutheran and Anabaptist apocalypticism which typically portrayed the papal authorities in such light. Evidently sick of the bloody suppression of such reform movements, the playwright concludes his work with the encouragement to end religious persecution, for 'to hate each other is no virtue, but true virtue lies in patience,'[149] a sentiment shared by the author of *Lazarus's Death*, which highlights the contrast between a persecuting clergy and laypeople who have accepted the gospel by faith. The persecutors of Jesus' disciples, one of the characters suggests, 'are merely thirsty for the blood of their neighbours.' God permits such persecution, the playwright argues, so that the enemies of the gospel can earn their future reward.[150]

It is not surprising that Charles V's policy of persecuting religious dissent was extremely unpopular in Dutch cities, even if some local authorities were more vigorous in persecuting religious dissenters than was the proto-Spanish Inquisition.[151] It clearly raised the ire of several rhetorician playwrights who found literary ways to express in their dramatic works their dissatisfaction over the mistreatment of some of their religiously active fellow citizens. The strength of popular opposition to Charles V's placards has generally been overshadowed both by the positive image of the emperor's personal appeal to his countrymen and by many historians' concentration on the role that opposition to Philip II's placards played in the beginnings of the Dutch revolt. However, it should be noted here that already by the end of the 1530s Dutch urbanites had tired of a religiously oppressive and economically burdensome clergy whose religious functions they believed they could perform in a much more satisfactory fashion. With their sense of mission as religious leaders, it is only natural that rhetoricians should have been at the forefront of this critique. Judging just from the biblical play described above, we can see that Netherlandic playwrights had the confidence not only to prepare dramatic versions of biblical stories but also to interpret these in potentially dangerous directions. As noted, the 1530s and early 1540s witnessed both the most radical reform movement in the Netherlands and a horrific suppression of such heterodoxy on the part of the authorities. At the very least, whether or not they openly took up the gauntlet in defence of the Reformation, during the first twenty years of its appearance in the Low Countries the majority of rhetoricians fought on behalf of a religion no longer dominated by a special caste of priests. Instead, they were inspired by a vision of a church in which laymen played leading roles – much as they did on the rhetorician stage – and whose minds and talents were fully exploited.

6

Popular Ritual, Social Protest, and the Rhetorician Competition in Ghent, 1539

The relationship between popular ritual and social protest has provoked some of the most fascinating scholarly studies in recent years. That under certain social circumstances carnivals of the early modern era could turn into rebellion was shown by Emmanuel Le Roy Ladurie's intriguing work on a carnival in Romans.[1] Also relevant to France is the seminal work of Natalie Z. Davis, whose discussions of popular ritual and protest in early modern France have informed the work of a generation of historians.[2] Before his untimely death, Robert Scribner had pursued the nature and impact of popular ritual during the Reformation in the German states in several fascinating essays,[3] while late medieval popular culture and literature in the Low Countries have also received attention, most notably in the works of Herman Pleij.[4] Recently, Pleij and several other Netherlandic scholars have examined the phenomena of carnival and charivari in early modern Netherlandic culture, helping to examine the role of popular ritual and culture in the promotion, and indeed reshaping, of social and religious reform.[5] Among other things, Pleij has shown that late medieval rhetoricians acted primarily as agents of an 'elite culture,' suggesting that their form of drama was at least one stage removed from more popular – i.e., less literary – forms.[6] However, rhetoricians spoke most particularly for the literate urban artisan/merchant tradition, and while their poems and plays usually supported patrician policies, these dramatists often sought broader or popular support for their own causes, occasionally in conflict with their superiors. An examination of the events in Ghent, Flanders, leading up to the major rhetorician contest of 1539, suggests that in certain circumstances the relationship between ritualistic satire, popular religious reform, rhetorician drama, and political uprising could become quite intimate indeed.

This suggestion also finds support in Davis's and Scribner's research on the way certain aspects of popular culture, particularly carnival, could be manipulated as reformation propaganda. For example, Scribner's study of twenty-two incidents in which carnival activities were used on behalf of the Reformation in Germany between 1520 and 1543 led him to argue that the theme of inversion, or the 'world turned upside down,' provides the key to understanding the relationship between evangelical reform and carnival actions. Carnival offered an 'alternative world' which temporarily overturned established authority; as a 'ritual of rebellion' carnival upturned the structure of accepted rule and hierarchy, presented an alternative form of communication to that of the established order, and overthrew the established hierarchy of sacred persons and objects by its ritual desacralization. Overall, carnival met a 'collective psychological and social need of the new faith in its early stages. For the individual believer such a radical change of opinion would not have been possible without extreme tensions and mental stress. By drawing on the collective resources of the community, carnival made possible the transition from the old to the new.'[7] Carnival, like other forms of popular culture, provided participants with a relatively safe means to 'play out' new social or religious relationships before adopting them in their daily lives. While Scribner's conclusions were based on German sources, it is possible that they applied to the Low Countries as well.

Although rhetoricians typically spoke on behalf of a proto-elite, for those just below the ruling class of their communes, their audiences, trained in the traditions of carnival satire and inversion, may have interpreted rhetorician plays as contributing to the desacralization of the established religious hierarchy, and perhaps even of the very political elite that supported rhetorician drama.[8] The 1539 *rederijker* contest in Ghent, preceded as it was by disruptive carnival festivities and followed by a political revolt, provides an intriguing case in which to test the applicability of the theories of Scribner and Davis for the Low Countries.

Events in 1539 signalled a new stage in the promotion of reform by the rhetoricians. It was in that year that one of the most important meetings of rhetorician chambers was held in Ghent, the traditional Burgundian capital of the Low Countries.[9] The notoriety which this competition, along with the published editions of its plays, gained for its quite remarkably open advocacy of religious reform ideas led to closer scrutiny of the activities of *rederijker* chambers on the part of the imperial government. Moreover, the timing of the competition was crucial in shaping imperial response to further rhetorician performances. Held during the summer of 1539, the dramatic festivities ended just weeks before Ghent's guilds and labourers overthrew the city government in protest against the payment of an imperial tax. With an imposing armed force an angry Charles V arrived in Ghent in February 1540 to declare an end to most of the city's privileges and freedom.[10] Some contemporaries, in fact, blamed this *spelen van zinne* competition for encouraging the rebellion. The English merchant Richard Clough remarked that 'those plays waas one of the prynsypall occasyons of the dystrouccyon of the towne of Gannt.'[11] Before examining in detail this *rederijkerfeest* and its broader impact, we will first discuss the experience of Ghent's rhetoricians prior to 1539 and especially their relationship with Ghent's city fathers, who supported the contest. It will also be instructive to look at the correlation between other forms of popular culture and drama and demands for reform in the city leading up to the famous events of 1539.

A Rebellious City

Ghent had been one of the most prosperous cities in northern Europe in the late Middle Ages, and it remained into the sixteenth century one of the most impressive and densely populated urban communities, with some 60,000 to 80,000 residents.[12] Directing the city was the Broad Council (*brede raad* or *collatie*), which included representatives from the 'three members' – the patrician citizenry (*poorterij*), the weavers, and the small craft guilds. But the interference of the hereditary rulers of Flanders was never far removed; the sheriffs acted as the representative of the counts of Flanders and, under Charles the Bold, chose the city's officers and guild leaders. At the count's death in 1477, Ghent's traditional political rights were restored, but the city's further resistance to the centralizing policies of Maximilian of Austria led to a harsh repression symbolized by the Peace of Cadzand in 1492. With this act Maximilian's official representatives gained complete control over Ghent's magistracy, and most odious for the city's labourers, his sheriffs were once again given the right to choose Ghent's guild deacons.[13]

Compounding this political interference were Ghent's economic woes. The vitality of the city's most important industry, the production of fine cloth, had been sapped by English competition, and only the shipping and grain monopolies over Flanders held by the city's elite merchants kept it economically viable. In contrast to the prosperity of the upper burghers, most of Ghent's guildsmen and journeymen experienced long periods of unemployment. The members of the weaver's guild, already feeling the brunt of the city's economic decline, became further incensed in early 1515 during the celebrations of the joyous entry of Charles I of Spain (later Charles V) as Flanders's new count. Instead of renouncing his power to select their guild officers as they had hoped, Charles strengthened the harsh terms of the Peace of Cadzand as a further act of centralizing his government. The resulting document, called the 'vellum' (*calfvel*), became a particular target for feelings of discontent. Charles also expected the cities of Brabant and Flanders to pay for most of his military campaigns in Italy and France and called upon them frequently for the 'voluntary' taxes known as the *bede*. While most cities complied, Ghent's magistrates, still irritated by the humiliating *calfvel*, complained with each request that they could not afford to pay their share, and in 1537 refused outright.[14] Negotiations with the imperial representatives and threats from the government failed to produce the desired results, and the city became polarized between the supporters of princely centralization – the *poorterij* and the privileged guilds members, including the merchant shippers, butchers, and fish merchants (all of whom prospered from the few remaining monopolies of the city) – and the proponents of urban particularism, the small craft artisans and the weavers. Clearly then, social and political discontent were common features of life in Ghent during the reign of Charles V.[15]

Adding to this ferment were the actions of religious reformers. There were in the city during the 1530s at least two currents of religious reform – those who adopted a form of Lutheranism, best described as evangelicals, and Anabaptists. Both groups successfully propagandized among Ghent's dissatisfied artisans and labourers, mainly by means of informal preaching (indoors and out) and meetings in private residences. According to A.L.E. Verheyden, there was a sizeable Anabaptist community in the city in the 1530s, although the execution of five leaders in 1535 and 1536 caused a considerable exodus of covenanters from the city. However, another circle soon formed, led in part by the peddler Mahieu Waghens. Waghens apparently had blamed Ghent's magistrates for the prevailing ecclesiastical abuses, such as the yearly consecration of the city bells, and warned them that 'soon his numerous followers would make an end to these abuses,' possibly with violence.[16] When one of these Anabaptist leaders, Martin Valcke uit Poperinge, was caught in the summer of 1538, his confession led to a severe repression, surely adding to popular disaffection with the imperial government and the city's ruling elite. Verheyden remarks that during the social and political unrest of 1539–40, Ghent Anabaptists became even more radical, adopting a form of community of goods, perhaps with the hope that the kingdom of God would soon be established in their city.[17] After the repression of the revolt by Charles V, Anabaptists in Ghent, as elsewhere in the Low Countries, turned to more peaceful forms of Anabaptism, such as that developed by Menno Simons.

Evangelical groups also gained popular support. This is evident in the reform circle around Martin Hueriblocq, a member of one of Ghent's old families, who in 1540 was named the overdeacon of the privileged fish merchants' guild after the incumbent had been unseated during the revolt. Members of his religious reform circle included a former monk, at least seven tailors (*kleermakers*) and two linen weavers, a wagonmaker, cobbler, pipe maker (*bollepijpmaker*), city messenger, baker, and an innkeeper's son.[18] Hueriblocq was arrested on 17 April 1545, and shortly after another fifteen of twenty-seven suspects were captured. The authorities burned Hueriblocq at the stake on 8 May, while three of his companions were also executed.[19] During his interrogation, one of this circle, Gillis Damman, confessed to having made several scandalous remarks, suggesting that, among other things, confession is nothing and that all confessionals should be burned, affirming that he could make a saint out of wood, and ridiculing those who pay respect to priests or who listen to their sermons.[20] As we shall see, this anticlerical and iconoclastic sentiment was not uncommon in the city. Imperial suppression of heresy was also a particular vexation for Flemish cities intent on excluding any trace of ecclesiastical interference in their domain. Ghent's magistrates and citizens, moreover, seem to have been influenced by the writings on religious toleration composed by Erasmus and other northern humanists.[21]

While from the perspective of the imperial government Ghent's rebellion had begun with its refusal to pay even a reduced *bede* in 1537 (what Johan Dambruyne has called the legal phase of the rebellion),[22] events took a decidedly radical turn in July 1539. On the seventh and eighth of that month the city's rulers met to decide whether or not to send a delegation to Spain to work out a compromise with the emperor on the payment of the *bede*. The Broad Council, against the *poorterij*, voted unanimously against the mission, while small craft guilds and weavers denied the funding required for the trip. Moreover, suspicious of 'secret agreements' which many believed had been made between the emperor and the *poorterij*, the popular elements of the government wanted the publication of Ghent's privileges in the vernacular. The division within the city's governing circle continued throughout July. On 15 August, with the issue still unresolved, came time for the yearly election of new guild officers. The craft guilds refused to nominate the required candidates until there was an investigation into the rumours of secret agreements. Four days later the beleaguered high sheriff, Frans vander Gracht, was pressured by the small guild representatives to arrest some of the old magistrates suspected of making secret deals. On 21 August the Broad Council, small guilds, and the weavers made several new and more radical demands, which included destroying the *calfvel* of 1515, forbidding grain exports from Flanders, excluding monastic houses and peasants from doing business within three miles of Ghent, collecting all the possessions of those suspected city leaders who had fled, handing over the keys to the secret chamber where the city documents were stored, and creating a more broadly representative committee of nine to control city finances.

It was at this time that the common folk became entranced by the demagogic preaching of populist guildsmen who now controlled the civic government.[23] These included the goldsmith Willem de Mey, who apparently acted as the new government's spokesperson; the old city secretary Laurent Claeys, who had earlier been banned on account of heresy; Sim Borluut, an advocate with the Council of Flanders; Lieven d'Herde, the deacon of the cabinet makers; and Lieven Hebscap, a wood merchant and master builder. Supporting this new administration were the 'screamers' (*creesers*), poor day labourers whose meagre and sporadic wages were only partially supplemented by civic alms. On 23 August a mob forced the high sheriff to proceed with the torture of one of the arrested suspects, Lieven Pien, the seventy-five-year-old former overdeacon of the small craft guilds (1536–7).[24] Five days later the unfortunate Pien was put to death. Under mob pressure the *calfvel* was taken from the secret room to in front of the city hall where it was cut into tiny fragments. A new oath was created which excluded any mention of the Peace of Cadzand. To ameliorate the distress of many of the city's residents, the new committee of nine began selling grain at reasonable prices to the impoverished day labourers.

In September, in response to these pressures, Regent Mary of Hungary granted several concessions to the new administration but demanded that the city's workers return to their jobs. Concurrent uprisings in Oudenaarde and Kortrijk on the part of guildsmen and labourers, which involved similar demands for the publication of civic documents and wider guild representation on councils, as well as acts of iconoclasm, led the imperial government to conclude that concessions would only fan the flames of rebellion to all of Flanders. On 13 October Mary of Hungary wrote to the emperor, requesting his return to his native city. Warned of this new development, Ghentenaars became divided over what to do. The weavers and *creesers* refused to give up their hard-earned gains. But when the committee of nine stopped both the supply of cheap grain and the work clock because of the bad state of the city's finances, the *creesers* on 5 November occupied the city's cloisters and many of the houses of rich burghers (most of whom had already fled the city), demanding food and threatening to trade places permanently with the rich.[25] Now the more prosperous leaders of the administration turned their support away from the rebels to the emperor; they had no intention of changing the social hierarchy in the city. On 11 November the regent declared a procession, calling upon God to protect Charles V on his return to Ghent. Most guildsmen returned to work, and the rebellion was, in effect, ended.

Ghent's Rhetoricians

In this tumultuous context it would not be surprising if Ghent's rhetoricians expressed popular dissatisfaction in their plays. Unfortunately, while the activities of Ghent's four rhetorician chambers – Fountain (*Fonteyne*), Saint Agnes (*Sint-Agnete*), To Honour Mary (*Mariën Theeren*), and Saint Barbara (*Sint-Barbara*) are among the best documented for the first half of the sixteenth century, only one play is known to have survived from this period.[26] The material that we do have suggests that Ghent rhetoricians were extremely important in the many celebrations on behalf of Charles V. In his comprehensive history of Ghent's chambers between 1500 and 1539, M. Vandecasteele marshals an impressive number of references to rhetoricians in the *stadsrekeningen* and other official civic documents for virtually every year of his study.[27] At the start of the century, for example, rhetorician drama aided the marking of several events, including the birth of Charles in 1500 and of his sister Isabella in the following year, the signing of the Treaty of Lyon in 1501, the trip of Philip the Handsome to Spain in late 1501, the birth of Ferdinand, Charles's brother, in 1503, and the glorious entry of Philip the Handsome into Ghent on 27 February 1504. For this last event the rhetoricians played the parts of the figures in the *tableaux vivants* and organized drama competitions, which may have included dramatic performances on the part of Ghent's neighbourhoods.[28]

Prizes for all contests and funds for most public *rederijker* performances were provided by the city's magistrates for the next several decades. For example, the peace between the emperor and king of France formulated in 1516 was the occasion for festive plays which included prize-winning contributions from three of Ghent's *rederijkerskamer*. The arrival of the emperor in Spain for his coronation in the following year saw the four chambers perform several comedies and serious allegorical plays, for which the chambers received 1£ Fl. each for their costs.[29] In August 1529 the *rederijkers* helped celebrate the Ladies' Peace of Cambrai and presumably commemorated Charles V's formal coronation as emperor in February of the following year.[30] The joyous entry into Ghent of Charles and Mary of Hungary on 24 March 1531, may have included, along with a tournament, a rhetorician contest organized by the city's chambers, although the evidence is sketchy,[31] as it is for a possible drama competition which may have taken place in 1535.[32] On 4 August 1537, the end of another military campaign was likewise applauded with comic plays. All of the chambers were rewarded for their civic service in 1532–3 when the city government granted them each a yearly subsidy of 3£ Fl.[33] In return, each chamber was to serve the city by performing two wagon plays a year; by providing the actors for the *tableaux vivants* and plays enacted during the Joyous Entry of princes and princesses or the celebrations of peace treaties and official welcomes; and finally, by creating a *tableau vivant* to be displayed in front of the city hall during the yearly Corpus Christi procession.[34]

Such civic support of drama shows that magistrates believed rhetoricians were useful in the appeasement of their prince, who frequently resided in Ghent. Plays composed for Charles's peace treaties and military victories presumably extolled the young ruler's virtues and strength. It is difficult to imagine plays critical of the emperor being performed in the market squares of the city and funded by a magistracy dominated by a pro-Charles *poorterij*. There is also no direct evidence that Ghent's rhetoricians were publicly presenting the new religious reform ideas in the 1520s and most of the 1530s, although it seems that some rhetoricians expressed anticlerical sentiment during a wagon-play performance in 1537 by suggesting that monks and friars were the true fools.[35]

Popular Culture, Carnival, and Protest

While the city's magistrates supported *rederijker* drama, they experienced considerable difficulty in controlling unapproved dramatic presentations on the part of ordinary citizens. For some time before 1539 the city council attempted, it seems without success, to reduce popular disturbances surrounding religious processions and carnival and Epiphany plays, especially on the part of the city's youth. On 27 April 1514, the magistrates forbade parents from 'allowing their children to perform *connighinnefeesten*' plays,[36] in which the youth chose a king or perhaps, in light of the feminine gender of the term, a queen, in the tradition of the 'world turned upside down' discussed by Davis and Scribner.[37] Whereas in other Flemish cities these particular festivities had been ended for some decades,[38] it appears that Ghent's populace had not given up the traditions. As carnival and Epiphany plays were frequently the media by which young people (especially bachelors) were able to vent their frustration at their powerlessness, it may be possible to suggest that such ritual protest remained popular in Ghent because of its general social and economic difficulties. If so, the city's magistrates presumably allowed such satirical acts to continue into the 1530s in order to provide the city's restless population with a ritualistic 'safety valve' against the rising social pressures.[39] While Ghent's rulers found it necessary to reissue the mandate against children performing the *connighinnefeesten* plays in 1517 and 1519, it seems that it was the undisciplined acts of youths that they were most concerned about. The carnivalesque excesses of youth, whose flirting with unorthodox ideas was often 'winked at' because of the immaturity of the participants, could frequently break the bounds of approved carnival, resulting in a dangerous rejection of the established religious order and social values. In other words, the 'safety valve' did not always work.[40]

Carnival celebrations continued to receive governmental support, as in 1523 when the city, 'according to custom,' financed three days of music and song by the 'fellows of the arts' (*ghesellen vander cuenste*).[41] For carnival, 1527, the city magistrates ordered a carnival play to welcome the emperor as he entered the city on 24 February.[42] Interestingly, the celebrations for that event also included a 'fool's competition' sponsored by the city's authorities who obviously were hoping they could control carnival energies.[43] Most chambers seem to have had a fool, and there were a number of 'fool's competitions' or 'feasts of fools' in the Low Countries in the sixteenth century. These had their origin in the acts of ritualized inversion of the clerical hierarchy put on by cathedral chapters and lower clergy in the late Middle Ages. Originally intended as a means of 'letting off steam,' by the fifteenth century their biting satire had developed to the point where church leaders sought to suppress them.[44] Although the selection of a fool, such as an 'ass pope' or bishop (*eselpaus* or *eselbiscop*) was a common feature of carnival, Ghentenaars turned the satirical event into a major 'Feast of fools,' organized along the lines of an intercity *rederijker* contest.[45] Spectators of the opening procession witnessed a parody of an imperial entrance into a city that included the mock emperor and his court, along with 'high dignitaries' from other Flemish communities. Under normal circumstances, such 'role reversal' helped alleviate tension within a community, and perhaps might have dissipated the anxiety surrounding the emperor's presence in the city. That these tensions were present is indicated by the council's act forbidding anyone carrying burning torches, long knives, halberds, armour, or any other unapproved weapons where the carnival play was to be performed.[46] The behaviour of the audience was also strictly regulated: 'So we forbid as above anyone to carry, cover, or disguise himself in order to enter the abovementioned play, or anyone with bundles of straw (*stroebanden*) or anything else to impede or surround these members [i.e., of the carnival guild] and in this fashion to prevent their members a free way, but instead questioning them, etc.'[47] It seems that what Ghent's magistrates were attempting to supervise were the attempts of ordinary (and presumably young) Ghentenaars to reappropriate carnival and to counteract the government's control of popular, ritualized protest. In any event, it is not farfetched to imagine Ghent's guildsmen and cloth workers experiencing something more than the usual glee at the sight of the reversal in position of their secular and religious authorities. It is also not difficult to conclude which of the events, the officially sponsored play or the various mirthful satire of the gathered fools, garnered the most popularity.

The last few years of the 1530s witnessed the climax of the cultural and ritualistic life of Ghentenaars. On 23 November 1537, the council proclaimed for the birth of Juan, Charles's son – who died some months later – a general procession in the morning to be followed by the performance of some comedies at the magistrate's building. Then each district and neighbourhood of the city was to participate in a competition for the cleanest streets and most joyous celebrations and festivities.[48] While these civic-sponsored celebrations were clearly intended to promote cooperation and civic-mindedness among the general citizenry, it is also evident that ordinary Ghentenaars were quite used to participating in and leading celebratory and competitive ritual in their city.

It seems that the government's struggle to regulate carnivalesque activities became increasingly difficult in the following two years. On 8 January 1538, the city again attempted to rein in the boisterous actions of the city's youth, who apparently organized themselves into gangs, perhaps similar to those in French cities described by Natalie Davis.[49] The magistrates heard of groups of youth and children in several districts of the city who were holding large gatherings, running about with banners, striking each other with them or with sticks, fighting amongst themselves, and throwing stones, ruining the peace and tranquillity of the residents.[50] While the council members forbade any further gatherings of youth, especially those involving running or gambling, it becomes clear from the records that they experienced little success in controlling boisterous behaviour. An act in the following month (23 February 1538) once again attempted to restrain seemingly spontaneous satirical events which interfered, in the minds of the magistrates, with the officially approved carnival play performed by the gentlemen of the carnival (*vastenauont heeren*) and their performers. Apparently some Ghentenaars used this performance as an excuse to march into the city's churches, playing musical instruments and drums, 'hindering the divine services.'[51]

Further disruptive events continued through the course of 1538 and 1539. In an act of 6 May 1538, the council again sought to reduce the disturbances surrounding *connighinne feesten* plays, whether performed by adults or by 'their children.' From the magistrates' description of the events, it seems that as the scenes passed by on wagons, some of the spectators – men, women, and especially children – caused a terrible disturbance with their taunts and shouts and by not allowing the players to pass 'unmolested.'[52] Also forbidden in 1538 was the shooting of muskets or bows in the beguine house (*begijnhof*) of St Elizabeth on the part of 'youths, men, or servants (*knechten*).'[53] In June the magistrates expressed their concern over commotions during the procession of the physical remains of St Lieven (one of the patron saints of Ghent) and forbade spectators from carrying knives or other weapons.[54] The following summer the magistrates reissued this decree.[55] This very popular procession had frequently provided a forum for ordinary Ghentenaars to vent their anger over the loss of their rights.

For example, Charles the Bold's Joyous Entry in June 1467 corresponded with the St Lieven procession, during which the procession's participants returning from St Lievens-Houtem broke into the tax collector's office to remove documents relating to a recently added financial burden. They then took St Lieven's reliquary to the Friday market where they swore an oath to revoke the count's regulations based on the Peace of Gavere and to punish those who had governed the city so badly.[56] It was at this point that the duke had withdrawn many of the city's privileges of self-government as a punishment for so threatening his 'public claim to uncontested sovereignty.'[57] P.J. Arnade has described how Ghentenaars were able to challenge the duke's authority by 'rallying around a competing source of local authority: the relics of Saint Lieven,' and it required similarly ritualistic acts of punishment to subvert the saint's power and restore the duke's.[58]

If the Ghent magistrates' records are any indication, it seems that during the last years of the 1530s acts of youthful exuberance, carnivalesque parodies, and religious satire were on the increase. It is not difficult to surmise the effects of these popular expressions of inversion on the minds of the populace of Ghent. The incidents involving the procession of the remains of St Lieven strike one as a parallel to the acts of 'desacralization' associated with the popular reformation in Germany and with iconoclasm.[59] The desacralization of sacred objects and persons (including saints, priests, and the Catholic hierarchy) was a major goal of evangelical preachers and pamphleteers, and an important element of evangelical ritualized protests, including carnival. As Scribner has pointed out, such 'scandalous' actions, when spread orally through a community as rumour, also helped to create a public opinion, for the 'propaganda value of such incidents was considerable, since they incited to imitation: they were forms of agitatory communication.' This collective outlook, in Scribner's perspective, enabled community members to 'engage in concerted action.'[60] If this was the case in Ghent in 1538 and 1539, it seems that the formally approved rhetorician contest may have been performed to audiences ready to interpret even mild reform ideas presented on stage as a clarion call to more vigorous deeds.

The Ghent Competition of 1539

It was in this context of popular disturbance that Ghent's rhetoricians staged their major competition in 1539. The contest's organizers were the members of the Fountain chamber, who justified civic support for such an expensive event on three grounds: first, as a belated celebration of the Armistice of Nice of June 1538; second, to augment trade and employment, 'which is very small here'; and third, to encourage the art of rhetoric in the cities of the other participants.[61] In other words, it would provide political, economic, and cultural benefits. On 3 February 1539, the Regent, Mary of Hungary, signed the decree officially approving the rhetorician contest. Invitations were sent to the chambers of other cities in Flanders, Hanault, Artois, Brabant, Zeeland, and Holland. As with all rhetorician contests, performances were outdoor affairs intended to draw as large and widely representative an audience as possible and the authorities naturally hoped for plays that would ease the rising tension within the city. Prior to the formal *spelen van zinne* contest, a refrain competition was held on 20 April 1539.[62] The question for one of the refrain contests was, 'Which people show the greatest foolishness in the world?' a topic custom-made for the anticlerical sentiment already prominent among rhetoricians. According to A. van Elslander, the rhetoricians of Leffinge, Antwerp, Tienen, Ypres, Nieuwpoort, Axel, Edingen, and Deinze were particularly stinging in their critique of the clergy, while some of them also satirized ecclesiastical practices such as pilgrimages and the veneration of saints.[63] Elslander found most noteworthy the reform-minded sentiment in the contributions of Antwerp's The Gillyflower, especially in its complaints that the Scriptures have been covered over by the 'false teachers full of hypocrisy.'[64] Agreeing with the Antwerp author was Tielt's poet, who also complained bitterly about religious persecution.[65] Such hints of reform sentiment among rhetoricians were further developed in the more serious *spelen van zinne*.

With less than two months before the major rhetorician contest, the magistrates enjoined their citizens to clean the streets, while the cities of the participating chambers spared no expense to prepare their entries and to impress the people and leaders of Ghent.[66] *Spelen van zinne* festivities began on 1 June with an impressive competitive entry of the participating communities. The concern of city fathers that popular carnivalesque acts would mar the rhetoricians' festivities is again evident from the regulation book. On that same day Ghent's magistrates issued a regulation stating that because of 'the danger of the horses' and for 'the execution of the plays' no one was to come inside the area of the newly constructed stage (see illustration 1).[67] Two days later, on 3 June, the council took further action. To forestall any disturbances, it ordered its citizens not to impede, nor in any way disturb, by words or actions (such as throwing objects), the performances of chamber fools.[68] Lasting from 12 to 23 June, the *spelen van zinne* competition was preceded by the government's orders that only approved officials and notables be found on or near the stage and the official seats.[69] In spite of the fears of the magistrates, it seems that the rhetorician plays were performed in front of the city hall without major incident and to the pleasure of both the audience and participants. However, during the procession of St Lieven, which took place a mere four days after the last rhetorician performance, some residents of the city committed acts of 'rudeness' and of 'disgraceful things' to the remains of St Lieven, some shouting for the celebrants to 'open the reliquary' before the time appointed for it (were these 'hecklers' part of a reform circle?). Some also appear to have brandished lit torches and long knives, while others intentionally drove their wagons in front of the procession.[70] It is not inconceivable that the critique of the old religion presented on stage by many of the visiting rhetoricians acted as a further stimulus to acts of desacralization and popular satire, perhaps raising disrespect for traditional authority figures. An analysis of the plays themselves might help to validate this suggestion.

The Plays of the Ghent Competition

Far from providing the Habsburgs with the hoped-for occasion to bring Ghent's often rebellious residents into line with their centralizing policies (this must have been a major reason for their approving the event), the rhetorician competition of 1539 became infamous for its advocacy of religious reform and implicit criticism of the authorities. As in most *rederijker* contests, the Ghent meeting had an assigned question, 'What is the dying man's greatest consolation?' and with this topic the chambers would have found it extremely difficult to avoid taking sides on the religious controversy of their time. Certainly Charles V's inquisitors found the plays offensive, placing the published edition of the nineteen plays on the 1540 index of forbidden books and more rigorously enforcing the censorship of all rhetorician drama after that occasion.[71]

Just how innovative and controversial the Ghent plays were can be seen by comparing the chambers' responses to the assigned question with those of an earlier rhetorician festival. As noted above, in 1496, twenty-eight chambers met at Antwerp for a *Landjuweel* which centred on the question, 'What is the greatest mystery or grace ordained by God for the blessedness of humanity?' a topic similar to the later Ghent meeting. The answers at this late fifteenth-century competition were typical of popular late medieval devotionalism – the Incarnation of the Lord, the death or wounds of Christ, the sacrament of the altar, and charity. In the generation or so between the two competitions, the religious focus of rhetoricians in the Low Countries had clearly changed.

Orthodox Plays

Only three of the Ghent plays – those of Kaprijke, Leffinge, and Tienen – unmistakably champion what can be regarded as the traditional Catholic response to the assigned question: hope in the mercy of God based on the death of Christ and the meritorious works of the believer.[72] Only one of these three, however, presents Catholic dogma in a way that can be described as overtly polemical or defensive; on the whole they are reminiscent of rhetorician plays performed before the onset of the Reformation.

The strongest presentation of Catholic teaching was provided by Leffinge's rhetoricians. Relying heavily on medieval theologians such as Augustine, Lombard, Bernard, and Gregory, their play defends the doctrine of free will, the value of good works in justification, and the importance of confession and penance – elements of the traditional faith most attacked by reformers.[73] The Kaprijke play, on the other hand, is in the tradition of the late medieval *Everyman*, but does not once mention the sacraments, church, or priesthood.[74] Its central character is The Man (*De mensche*), a young pilgrim who is turned back from his travels on the easy path of sin and returned to the true path of salvation by four *sinnekens*: two representing his conscience and reason and the other two as religious instructors named Blessed Teaching (*Zalyghe Leerijnghe*) and Hope (*Hope*); all of these fight against Vices representing youthful lustiness. Even this play, with its central theme of 'hope in God's mercy,' highlights the Word of God and trust in God as two key supports of Man on his pilgrimage. Despite these aids, Man falls into a dark hole, which has been enchanted by the Vices to appear like an inn. Hope at first is unable to bring him out, for Man fears God only as a strict judge (much as had Luther prior to his 'Reformation breakthrough'). She then unveils two figures, one of the grace of the king of Israel shown to Benhadad of Syria as a sign of God's mercy for all men, the other of the prodigal son. Man is convinced, returns to his apparel of innocence, and sets off once again on the difficult path. According to Erné, this play features not a sophisticated theology, but a presentation of salvation based on a 'simple folk's faith.'[75]

The third orthodox play was provided by Tienen's playwright, who like his Kaprijke counterpart has a normally pious young man as his central character.[76] This youth, Dying Man (*Stærvende Mensche*), finds assistance in the typical allegorical helpers, Scriptural Sense (*Schriftuer-lic Zin*) and Figurative Proof (*Figuerlic Bewijs*), both dressed as religious, with the former instructing by the word and the latter through images and likenesses, a good illustration of the orthodox Catholic position against Luther's *Sola Scriptura*. At the same time, the two Vices are also dressed as monks, who promise salvation to Dying Man if he will quickly come into their order. Instead, he is buttressed by the helpful *sinnekens* who give him a lantern of the light of charity which reveals a banner of a crucified Christ bleeding from his five wounds, under which Dying Man must fight against the devil;[77] a staff of faith; and a breastplate of love. With these he is able to remain steadfast, living in a Christian fashion and trusting in God's mercy. Tienen's factor illustrates the importance of hope in the mercy of God with a deathbed scene which includes Dying Man receiving the sacrament of extreme unction. At the same time, he satirizes hypocritical monks who, among other faults noted, take advantage of the dying by hoodwinking them out of their possessions.[78]

These three orthodox Catholic plays generally followed the older style of religious drama, supporting the popular form of piety dominant in the late Middle Ages, without taking any overt stance against the new ideas promulgated by Lutherans, other evangelicals, and Anabaptists. They also participate in a mild and quite traditional form of anticlericalism. Thus, it can hardly be said that there was a strong Catholic presence on the Ghent stage in 1539.

Lutheran Plays

In contrast to the relatively weak defence of Catholicism, nearly half (nine) of the nineteen plays are identifiable as Lutheran, the best example coming from the quill of Jan van den Berghe, factor of Antwerp's The Gillyflower. That Antwerp's presentation won the competition with one of the clearest displays of Lutheranism speaks volumes for the level of support for the Reformation among Ghent's literate elite.[79] Answering the competition question with 'the resurrection of the body,' the play presents Dying Man, who learns through Reason and The Law that his good works are useless for salvation, which must come instead through Luther's teaching of salvation by faith alone through the grace of God as proclaimed in the gospel. According to Preacher of the Word, the law reveals humanity's sinful condition, while the gospel presents forgiveness; 'the law condemns and the gospel forgives; each has a distinct office, but are bound together in one book.'[80]

The eight other Lutheran plays – those of Bruges, Mesen, Ypres, Nieuwkerke, Nieuwpoort, Brussels, Lo, and Edingen[81] – demonstrate in unmistakable form the German doctor's formula of justification by faith alone. The principal character in the Edingen play, Man (*Mensche*), for example, is led by Scriptures (*Schriftuere*) and Evangelical Teacher (*Evangelisch Leeraer*) to trust no longer in his own damnable merits and to affirm instead that the gospel's only answer is faith. God then makes the sinner worthy, who then desires to sin no more but to live in love as a new man.[82]

However, the Nieuwpoort playwright emphasizes that both faith and love are gifts of grace, perhaps attempting to provide a compromise between Lutheran and Catholic conceptions of justification. There is some dispute as to the essentially Lutheran character of the Lo contribution: Erné describes the text as 'an orthodox play,' while Drewes argues much more convincingly that its overwhelming emphasis on faith in Christ alone is essentially Lutheran or 'lutheranizing.'[83] The play promotes only two sacraments, those of baptism and the Eucharist, and it clearly rejects traditional good works such as the purchase of indulgences, trusting in papal bulls or burial in a monk's habit.[84] There is no mention of the priesthood, and the passage to which Erné refers as supportive of the sacrament of confession – 'Confessing openly all your sins' – instead affirms confession to Christ, not to a priest:

> Oh brother, cling to Christ for your comfort,
> Confessing openly all your sins;
> He, as your treasure of free grace
> Will not despise you.[85]

The play therefore best fits a Lutheran conception of the church.

Furthermore, those plays of Edingen, Brussels, Ypres, and Nieuwkerke declared the distinctive Lutheran formula of the role of law and grace in salvation.[86] A good example is provided by the Brussels playwright who opens his play with a dispute between two allegorical characters, the 'natural man,' Human Understanding (*Menschelic Verstandt*), who is on a pilgrimage to the heavenly Jerusalem and is assisted by the 'spiritual man' Spiritual Sense (*Gheestelic Zin*), who tells him that he is still leaning far too much on his staff, 'many written books' (*veil ghedichte boucken*), composed by foolish church theologians.[87] In order to find the true way, Spiritual Sense continues, one must humble oneself and immerse oneself in the Bible, instead of in human writings. There is then revealed an inner play of Dying Man (*Staervende Mensche*) and how he comes to receive grace. The Vices tell him to rely upon the established ecclesiastical customs, something which brings only fear to Dying Man's heart, and soon he finds himself lying mortally ill on the 'bed of discontent.' At the last moment he calls upon God for help and a series of painted scenes highlight Dying Man's discovery of the true means of finding peace: first is a scene of Jesus as The Living Word (*Dlevende Woordt*) giving Dying Man the gospel, at which he stands up and breaks his crutches of 'doubt and weak hope' by the staff of 'God's promise'; second is a paradise scene wherein God damns the serpent and proclaims the coming of Christ; third is a depiction of God's promise to Abraham, which illustrates how the law of Moses was merely a helper, for now through faith people stand under the law of grace; fourth is a view of Christ on the cross bearing human sin and proclaiming victory over death and hell, before which Dying Man feels his burden lighten somewhat; fifth is a scene of the breaking open of hell and the binding of Satan; sixth is a figure of the resurrected Christ chasing death with his cross; seventh is a scene of Dying Man receiving the mantle of Christ as a new covering and witnessing the flight of death; finally, Christ is seen at God's right hand and Dying Man appears before him, now at peace. As a result of these scenes Human Understanding throws away his books, because the 'promises of God are the mightiest stone for the dying man.'[88]

Several of the Lutheran plays also reinforced the Protestant belief of Christ as sole mediator by rejecting the invocation of saints and the intermediary works of priests.[89] Moreover, the unnamed playwright of the Bruges contribution (probably Cornelis Everaert as it is his chamber, Holy Ghost, which is performing), affirms Luther's teaching that even though believers have been made righteous by their faith, they still remained sinners[90] – a view shared by the Brussels rhetoricians who use Luther's phrase of 'wearing Christ as a cloak'[91] – and defends his teaching that one is predestined not because God had foreknown one's good works, but merely by the grace of God through faith. These plays also affirm Luther's conception of the church and sacraments as empowered not by the words of a priest but by the power of Christ.[92] In the Bruges play, Doubting Sense (*Twiffelic Zin*) is a layperson concerned about the religious controversy but who wishes to remain with his simple faith and leave the Bible to theologians: 'Is it not enough that the learned know, / so that they might warn us of practices / wherein we sin?'[93] His question is answered by Reasonable Opinion (*Redelic Ghevoelen*), a layman, and two 'reverends' (*eerwaerdel*), Scriptural Trust (*Schriftuerlic Troost*) and Spiritual Proof (*Gheestelic Bewijs*), all of whom are learned in the Bible and make it plain to Doubting Sense that the question posed by the rhetorician competition cannot be answered without the Scriptures, both the law and gospel. Scriptural Trust responds,

> Hear Paul speak:
> All that is written, far or near,
> Is truly written for our instruction;
> And someone else gives us understanding,
> That all may take books in hand
> And read, reread wherever they go,
> Until they, through much reading, understand these,
> Thus obtaining a firm faith.[94]

When Doubting Sense suggests that his works, such as pilgrimages, fasts, prayers, hearing Mass, funding altars, and placing candles before the saints, play a part in salvation, Spiritual Proof reprimands him with the typically Lutheran response:

> 'All that is not done out of faith is sin,'
> Further he [Paul] says to another nation:
> 'You are made righteous through grace
> And not through your works' ...[95]

Instead, only Christ is righteous and he makes righteous those who believe in him.[96] Humans are born sinners, eternally damned, and it is only through the sacrifice of Christ that they can be delivered from their fate; there is no other mediator.[97] Assisted by eight painted figures, Scriptural Trust and his cohorts explain the history of salvation to

Doubting Sense, including the Lutheran view that those saved by faith remain sinners, although delivered from the power of sin.[98] After explicating the meaning of Romans 8 and unveiling several figures depicting how God kept his promises to the Israelites, the Virtues reveal the play's answer to the assigned question: faith in Christ destroys the power of sin and the fear of death. If the Bruges play was composed by Everaert, as seems likely, this prominent factor had moved from an Erasmian to a Lutheran perspective on reform.

Compromising and Spiritualistic Plays

Attempting to provide a compromise between Luther and more traditional Catholicism were two of the chambers at the Ghent competition, St Winoksbergen and Tielt. As Erné has suggested, their strong similarity both in style and content may suggest that they had the same author – smaller chambers often shared one factor. In any event, the plays performed by these rhetoricians emphasized both the justification of believers by faith in the death of Christ and the importance of the sacraments as a means of grace. They also highlighted more strongly than their Lutheran-minded confrères the need for Christians to perform good works.[99] The author, furthermore, argues against Luther that faith is a gift of the Holy Spirit, not of Christ. Even though the plays stress the post-justification performance of good works more than did Luther, the Winoksbergen contribution adds that the believer's works are made virtuous only through Christ.[100] What also keeps these two plays from entering fully into the Lutheran camp is their point that people cannot expect perfect certitude of salvation, but must hope in the trustworthy signs.[101] The author, like Erasmus, was therefore most concerned about the practical effects of Luther's doctrine of certitude; the maintenance of a virtuous lifestyle after the acceptance of justification was critical.[102] In fact, the positive or negative impact of the new theology on the life of the civic community was a prominent feature of both Lutheran and Catholic drama in the Netherlands.

The three spiritualistic plays from the competition – those of Kortrijk, Menen, and Oudenaarde – develop this preoccupation with personal sanctity and love of neighbour, underpinned by a strong antimaterialism. All three answer the assigned question with the response that the Holy Spirit is the dying person's best consolation, for it is the personal assurance of the Spirit, not Luther's doctrine of justification nor the traditional Catholic means of grace, which provide certitude of salvation.[103] For example, in the Menen play, Scriptural Approbation (*Schriftuerlicke approbacye*) goes through a number of potential answers to the assigned question: works of mercy, faith alone, faith working through love, trust in God's grace, the suffering, resurrection, and mediation of Christ, and the fruits of the Holy Spirit. All of these spiritual benefits merely testify that God has blessed humanity. Only the outpouring of the Holy Spirit on the individual provides ultimate consolation.[104] An illustration of the importance of the individual work of the Spirit is provided by Menen's actors through the example of a lawbreaker who appeals a sentence to the emperor. The lawbreaker's friends tell him that because of his previous service the emperor will be gracious, but this assurance only provides partial peace. Only when he is able to confirm this assurance in his heart will he gladly appear before the judge. In the same way, the playwright affirms, the grace spoken of in the Bible provides each sinner who fears God's judgment with perfect peace only when the Holy Spirit gives it directly to him or her. Such confirmation centres on believers' certitude that they have become 'God's elect children.'[105] To further illustrate this point, the Menen playwright uses the example of two sick persons. The first one trusts in the Word of God and in the promises of Christ, yet he is still terrified by death. The other 'triumphs spiritually,' because he is inspired by the Spirit's inner working and filled by an inner peace which allows him to look forward to death.[106] Oudenaarde's playwright likewise emphasizes that it is only the Holy Spirit that can prepare a believer for death and make his or her works acceptable to God.[107]

In a similar fashion the Kortrijk work has the lead character, Many Wit (*Menygherande Ingien*) assisted by three Virtues: the priest, Cleric's Word (*Clærckelic Wten*), the Word of Truth (*Dwoordt der Waerheyt*), who represents the gospel, and Spiritual Enlightenment (*Gheestelicke Verlichtijnghe*), who reveals God's secrets by the inspiration of the Holy Spirit. The play's theme focuses on the conflict between the spirit and the flesh. Cleric's Word is not able on his own to resolve the controversy, for Word of Truth and Spiritual Enlightenment are also necessary to discover the biblical answer; individuals have to immerse themselves in the Bible and allow themselves to be led by the Spirit to discover God's hidden meaning, namely that the sinner will receive mercy if he converts. Salvation by God's grace alone without human works, and divine election, are pronounced features of this play,[108] although there is also great stress on the spirit subjugating the flesh after salvation.

God sends his Spirit to believers, Cleric's Word and Spiritual Enlightenment affirm, like an overflowing fountain, revealing the secrets of
God.[109]

Such spiritualism was not uncommon in the Low Countries of the
late 1530s. The inwardly turned piety of the late medieval *Devotio Moderna* had helped predispose many Netherlanders in this direction. Furthermore, several important Anabaptist leaders, in particular Obbe
Philips and David Joris, had turned by the late 1530s to an individual-
ized inner religion. Joris in particular won a number of followers
among Dutch urbanites, which included some of the nobility and a few
wealthy patrons.[110] Like the Menen playwright, spiritualists rejected
the theological disputations of the reformers and Catholics – which
often resulted in bloodshed – in favour of an emphasis on inner sanctity and love of neighbour. Often their disregard for external religious
trappings led many to a Nicodemite posture, allowing themselves to
attend the mainstream church while secretly maintaining their true
beliefs. Moreover, one of Joris's central themes in his many writings
was the pouring out of God's Spirit onto believers, which he depicted
visually in his *The Wonder Book* of 1543/4 (see illustration 6) in a manner similar to rhetoricians who used figures to illustrate their spoken
words.[111]

Although the spiritualist plays were quite unusual, Axel's actors presented the most original performance at the Ghent festival, and perhaps
one of the most unusual of the religious plays composed during the
reign of Charles V. Spurning all theological answers, including the Catholic solution of hope in the mercy of God based on good works and the
merits of Christ, and the Lutheran proclamation of justification by faith
alone, the playwright contends that only a 'rested conscience' provides
complete trust. What is most remarkable is that the author does not seek
to explain the process of obtaining such perfect inner peace in any fashion consistent with even spiritualism. The character Diverse Opinion
(*Diversche Opynye*) presents in turn the whole range of theological
answers to the question of where to find true comfort; neither reliance
upon faith, nor hope, mercy, love, the sacrifice of Christ, nor even good
works provide complete solace in the hour of death.[112] Instead, based on
the promises of God, inner serenity simply wells up within the
believer.[113] Clinching the argument is a painted depiction of Christ crucified between the two thieves, while Scriptural Understanding (*Schriftuerlic Verstandt*) explains to the audience that when the one criminal
asked Christ to remember him in his kingdom, the Lord,

Knowing his conscience
To be pure and at peace, said as his advice:
Today you will be with me in paradise.[114]

Among other things, what this play illustrates is the independence of mind that Dutch urbanites could maintain even when peer and governmental pressure was applied in the direction of intellectual conformity.

Perhaps the most theologically unorthodox performance at the Ghent competition was provided by the Deinze chamber. Although J.B. Drewes doubts that any rhetoricians would have been bold enough to publicly present Anabaptist convictions on the Ghent stage,[115] the Deinze play contains tenets which, when taken together, strongly suggest influence from one of several Anabaptist quarters. Supporting this conjecture is the Deinze playwright's condemnation of human or 'self wisdom' as well as good works, and his affirmation that the truly pious ones, elected by the Holy Spirit, recognize Christ as head of their church (*gemeente*) in spite of persecution and derision.[116] Moreover, the author mentions the belief in the salvation of the whole world in a fashion similar to Melchior Hoffman's idea of the ultimate restoration of all creatures at the last trumpet.[117] Deinze's rhetoricians may not have been members of an Anabaptist conventicle, but they seem to have found some of Hoffman's ideas attractive.

Some sympathetic leanings toward Anabaptists may also have been displayed by Kortrijk's rhetoricians. In his introduction to the Kortrijk text, B.H. Erné comments on an interesting series of events. During the year before the Ghent competition thirty-two religious dissenters, including many Anabaptists, were arrested in Kortrijk and ten of them executed.[118] Then, during the earlier refrain competition, Kortrijk's contribution evidenced much sympathy for the difficult position of the persecuted Anabaptists. In these refrains the poet (whom Erné identifies as the playwright of the Kortrijk *spel van zinne*) writes that once people are united with Christ in faith through the Holy Spirit then they can resist the devil and slay the Whore of Babylon. The worst fools are those who reject the leading of the Holy Spirit, following instead the 'worldly wisdom' and the flesh (as 'the world's fleshly children'). Then the poet writes: 'Purify your hands from the blood of the innocent,' evidently a rejection of the persecution of religious dissenters and a possible reference to the executions of the year before.[119] Although the play of the Kortrijk rhetoricians is much more cautious than the earlier refrains in its criticism of religious persecution, its rejection of worldly wisdom and advocacy of discovering the secrets of the Scriptures through the Spirit's inner light are seen in the writings of spiritualist Anabaptists of the late 1530s.[120] Certainly many of Ghent's residents were not unfamiliar with these concepts, and would have very easily caught the full meaning of the playwright's nuanced presentation of them.

During this rhetorician competition, there was a variety of reform perspectives presented, ranging from traditional Catholic dogma, to a domineering Lutheran presence, to an odd assortment of compromising, spiritualistic, and idiosyncratic works. What was missing, however, was any play strongly defending Catholic drama and rites against the assaults of the reformers. That none of the supposedly orthodox Ghent plays directly repudiated reform precepts reinforces the conception on the part of the inquisitor that this competition merely provided reform-minded rhetoricians with a platform for the spread of heresy, and not just of the Lutheran variety.[121] Furthermore, even lay Catholic playwrights made frequent and knowledgeable use of the Scriptures and chided the religious estate for failing to live up to biblical standards or for conducting themselves in a less than exemplary fashion. In other words, all of the performances criticized the religious status quo to some degree and emphasized the importance of lay people for its improvement.

The Impact of the Ghent Performances

What were the ramifications of the rhetoricians' support of reform during the Ghent competition? Did the chambers of rhetoric contribute in any way to the increase in political or social discontent leading up to the rebellion? Given the state of mind of many of Ghent's citizens in 1539, with the city's economic difficulties, social conflict, religious disquiet, and political frustration, it is fair to say that the rhetorician's largely reform-minded plays had some effect on the populace. In spite of the several hints that we have provided here regarding a close connection between rhetorician drama and popular unrest, we must again remind ourselves that none of the plays presented during the competition openly or, as best as can be determined, covertly, advocated rebellion against the emperor. While he correctly points out that Richard Clough's remarks that the rhetorician contest was one of the principal causes of the revolt is stylistic exaggeration, Johan Decavele also concludes that the contest did contribute to the increase in political, social, and religious tensions within the city.[122] The question, then, is not one of open advocacy of revolt on the part of rhetoricians, for if surviving plays are any indication, most rhetoricians supported their civic leaders.[123] Vernacular drama, however, was not merely performed from the stage to the audience. A play's observers could reinterpret or alter the message of a dramatic performance to fit their life experiences, while the thespians and playwrights would play to the needs and expectations of their audiences in order to increase the popularity of their public presentations.[124] At the very least, then, Ghent's population saw in the rhetorician critique of Catholic tradition and open advocacy of reform or evangelical ideas an example of opposition to traditional authorities. Recent research on the German Reformation has similarly concluded that it was Luther's example of rebellion against the pope, more than his sophisticated theology, that grasped the imagination of the 'common people,' contributing to the outbreak of the Peasants' War of 1525.[125] During the Ghent competition the adoption of reform precepts was lived out in the safe confines of stage drama, so that the spectators could imagine how reform ideas might be incorporated into their lives. In this sense propagandistic drama had effects similar to the experimental inversion of carnival.

Ghent Rhetoricians after 1539

Ghentenaars were soon to experience a very negative consequence as a result of their social experiment. In January 1540 news that Charles V was marching to his birth city struck terror into many hearts; according to one chronicler, the mere sight of soldiers in the neighbourhood caused countryfolk to flee with few possessions into the city.[126] Shortly before Charles V arrived in the city proper on 14 February 1540, its representatives travelled to Dendermonde to meet with the emperor. Whether or not they saw significance in the fact that the meeting took place during carnival is a matter of speculation. Ghent's representatives included the gentlemen of the law and the deacons of the guilds, the weavers, the four shooters' guilds, and the four chambers of rhetoric. Each of these organizations was also to procure a 'torch of six pounds' – a wax torch usually on a staff with the organization's symbols – and to ensure that their representatives were prepared for the arrival of the emperor.[127] When the emperor arrived with an armed force on the first Saturday of Lent, he reasserted control over the city government –

symbolized by the republication of the terms of the Treaty of Cadzand[128] – and removed most of the city's remaining rights.

In order to restore the proper submissiveness to their native prince,
Charles V terrified Ghent's inhabitants with a sombre and impressive
military procession, which included several hundred mounted knights
and thousands of German *landsknechten* (mercenary foot soldiers). Also
prominent were representatives of the entire social hierarchy under
Charles, including high ecclesiastical and secular princes from all of
the emperor's domains. As one contemporary pro-Charles observer
noted, the populace was duly humbled:

> The Emperor, entering his city of Ghent in such company, with such
> might and on such a footing, greatly astounded and frightened the inhab-
> itants. There was much reason for it, for this was not an Entry which gave
> them much pleasure but one of fear and sadness. The Entries which His
> Majesty had made before had not been made with such might and force
> but were all friendliness and pleasantness. Nevertheless the Ghenters per-
> formed their duties in the usual fashion ... [and] went with all reverence
> and humility to greet the Emperor as their count ... welcoming His Maj-
> esty into his city of Ghent and presenting him with its keys.[129]

Surely Charles realized the significance in the timing of his actions, for
the battle between the excess of carnival and the deprivation of Lent
was a long-standing one in both popular and official culture.[130] If so,
his sombrely ritualistic actions restoring the traditional social-political
order can be viewed as a Lenten reinversion of the carnival 'world-
turned-upside-down,' which was Ghent's brief experiment with a populist guild government. Whether intentional or not, Charles's timing
helped reinforce the notion in the minds of Ghent's populace that their
revolt had been little more than a carnivalesque excess. It was now
time for Lenten realities.

Actions taken by the emperor suggest that he believed the rhetorician contest had greatly contributed to the popular unrest in the city.
First, he forbade Ghentenaars from holding any celebratory gatherings
within the city, an order which seems to have been in force for the following two years.[131] Specifically disallowed by the restored old guard
magistracy was the procession of the remains of St Lieven (27 June),
which, it appears, had caused so much disturbance leading up to the
revolt.[132] All other processions and shooter's competitions (*pape-
gaeyen*), an anonymous chronicler noted, were forbidden 'because of

the time.'[133] That this order also forbade any civic funding of the rhetorician chambers is evident in the lack of any reference to such in the city's *Stadsrekening* of 1539–40.[134] Processions on behalf of Charles V were, of course, continued.[135] In spite of these proscriptions, Ghent's magistrates seem to have restored partial funding to their rhetoricians in the following year.[136] Full support was returned in 1542 in response to several petitions from the chambers which pleaded that they were suffering financially from the lack of government support and from their inability to stage dramatic performances during the preceding two years. They also complained about their having to bear the cost for the torches and other expenses related to the emperor's entry of 1540.[137] Within a few years, Ghent's rhetoricians were again celebrating major events for the city; for example, rejoicing over the Peace of Crépy of 1544 involved the chambers,[138] as did the victory of Charles over the Schmalkaldic League and the capture of the landgrave of Hesse and the duke of Saxony in April 1546. Celebrations in early May for this latter victory included dramatic performances at various places in the city on the part of the four chambers of rhetoric.[139] Needless to say these chambers also contributed immeasurably to the celebrations surrounding the Joyous Entry of the young prince Philip in 1549.[140]

Second, and with much more enduring results, Charles issued more general mandates against the scandalous works of rhetoricians. As early as 6 October 1539, the Chancellor of Brabant, Adolf van der Noot, was writing to Mary of Hungary warning her against the plays' 'evil and abusive doctrines,' which tended to Lutheran opinions.[141] We see this impression confirmed in an unpublished imperial mandate of 10 July 1540, which specifically and in great detail forbade the publication and possession of suspicious rhetorician material, including the nineteen Ghent plays of 1539. Among other works placed on the index of forbidden books were

> certain plays recently printed in our city of Ghent and performed there by the nineteen chambers on the word 'which is the greatest trust for the dying person.' And also many unseemly plays, songs, refrains, and scandalous figures, dangerous and suspect of heresy, contrary to our Christian faith, to the constitution and ordinances of our mother the Holy Church, and to the great dishonour of God Almighty, his blessed mother Mary, and the saints, and to the great danger of the loss of many souls ...[142]

It also ordered the University of Leuven to examine thoroughly any suspicious works and to warn 'all rhetoricians and others' to guard against performing or 'communicating' 'any suspect plays concerning and containing the holy Scriptures, the sacraments and ordinances of the Holy Church or other unseemliness; nor alleging the Scriptures or authors thereof; nor also to sing, sell, or distribute refrains or songs concerning these.'[143] Reinforcing this decree was the published mandate of 22 September 1540, which banned the publication of the nineteen plays, without reference to songs, refrains, or printed figures.

Ghent's magistrates also sought to control more carefully their dramatists' satire. They passed a law on 20 June 1542 which forbade the production of any plays, refrains, songs, 'or any other poetry of rhetoric' without the prior examination and approval of the magistrates of the law.[144] Furthermore, on 31 December 1546, Ghent's rulers further specified the types of performances forbidden, which included not only 'any refrains, songs, ballads, gift speeches,' but also any painted figures, which tended to promote any scandalous or suspicious ideas.[145] According to Decavele, such rigorous censorship led, by the 1550s, to a general decline in rhetorician drama.[146] That the 1542 decree was taken seriously is shown by the case of lord Johan Utenhove, who in that year wrote a decidedly Lutheran play and had it performed at his estate at Roborst, a few miles outside of Ghent, as part of the celebrations surrounding the receiving of his inheritance and title on 2 July 1543. According to Johan Decavele and Dirk Coigneau, this was the direct cause of his flight from his homeland in 1544 and forced exile the following year.[147] Typically condemning the various practices of popular religious devotion, Utenhove goes beyond Erasmus's satire in rejecting all good works in salvation and categorizing such as sinful in themselves; only Christ's blood, he insists, is the true 'indulgence' (aflaet).[148] The papacy and priests who taught Unlearned Folk (Ongheleert Volck) to pay, through the toil and sweat of his brow, for indulgences as a means of salvation, are now regarded as 'false dragons' and 'devil's clerics' who have deceived him for so long.[149] True faith, he is informed, comes only by grace through hearing the Word of God preached, and once saved by faith alone he will perform good works for his neighbour.[150] After receiving such faith, he will become a member of the 'elected race,' a kingly priesthood which can interpret the Scriptures better than the learned clergy.[151] Given the play's Lutheran content and similarity to the Lutheran plays of the 1539 Ghent competition,[152] it is no wonder that the Court of Flanders would seek out the perpetrators of this illegal performance. They did not catch Utenhove, who remained a fugitive until his death in 1566, but they conducted a massive search for suspects and 'secret assemblies'; one of those caught in the dragnet was Gillis Joyeulx, a member of a reform circle of Oudenaarde, who in the court records was identified as the author of this play 'full of heresy' (he apparently helped Utenhove write the work).[153] The performance of openly Lutheran drama was a dangerous act indeed after 1539.

Also of importance for our understanding of the experience of Ghent's rhetoricians after the contest is a surviving Ghent play entitled *A play about the Father Who Sent the People to Work in the Vineyard*, which, while undated and anonymous, was evidently composed and performed in Ghent during Charles V's reign.[154] This becomes quite obvious in the conclusion of the work, where Humility (*Ootmoedicheyt*) turns to the audience and says:

> We commend to you all the highest generation,
> Above all, our native prince, the Imperial grain:
> May God always stand him in good stead,
> In order to rule his lands in excellent peace.[155]

To which Graciousness (*Ghenadicheyt*) adds, 'God also guard the noble city of Ghent, and also those who are far from us or around us.'[156] The question arises, then, whether this play was performed before or after the 1539 competition. Unfortunately, nowhere in the play is there any reference to that infamous event. This lacuna might suggest that the work was composed before the contest, or that it was merely a result of prudence on the part of the unknown playwright. An analysis of its contents might help clarify this issue of the historical context of the play.

The play itself begins with two characters, Inflated Spirit (*Opgheblasen Gheest*) and Murmuring (*Murmatie*), speculating over what has caused the odour of roasting flesh. Much heavy oppression has afflicted the city because ordinary laypeople, such as cobblers and chimney sweeps, have had the temerity not only to read the Scriptures for themselves, but to preach the gospel in the city's streets and alleys. While at first reading critical of lay evangelicals, Inflated Spirit and Murmuring's comments, spoken as they were by evil characters, should be interpreted as careful if comic praise of lay preaching of the gospel. Moreover, these Vices criticize reform activity only on the part of lower artisans such as cobblers.[157] Nowhere do they criticize the taking up of reform on the part of the more respectable citizenry from which rhetoricians drew their membership and greatest support.

Central to the play is Jesus' parable of the vintner (Matt. 20) who hires a number of labourers to work in his garden, paying them all an equal wage in spite of their different hours of work. In this dramatic version of the parable, the vintner goes to the market in search of labourers, 'whether lay or clergy.'[158] His offer is accepted by four characters, two Vices, who boast of their virtuous works and complain about their wages and two Virtues, who rely solely on the grace of the Father (*Vader*) and illustrate the importance of humility. Doubt is expressed that Father will find anyone willing to take up his offer, for such work is forbidden to the people, because of 'the ban,' a possible reference to the religious placards.[159] The two grateful workers then argue with the two ungrateful ones over the relative merit of works in entering the kingdom of the Father. In this discussion the playwright clearly presents an evangelical perspective, emphasizing the centrality of grace and the rejection of good works in salvation, the sinfulness of the individual, and the deliverance of the sinner through the death of Christ. In the course of the debate Conceited in Virtues (*Verwaent in duechden*) and Envious Spirit (*Afionstick gheest*) sound like the much maligned Pharisees of the gospels, especially when Conceited 'thanks God that he is not like other people,' and Envious takes pride in his fasting two days a week, both echoing the prayer of the self-righteous Pharisee of Luke 18:11–12. In contrast Humble Heart (*Ootmoedich herte*) takes the position of the publican, pleading for God to graciously receive him as a poor sinful creature.[160] Graciousness (*Ghenadicheyt*) continues that the law brings no one to salvation,[161] nor can works make anyone perfect. And while the Vices continue to rely on traditionally efficacious works such as fasting, walking barefoot, and going on pilgrimages 'where one can purchase indulgences,'[162] Graciousness will 'rejoice only in the cross, in the bitter death and love of Christ.' To love God and one's neighbour, this fulfils all works.

Further confirming the evangelical direction of this play is the playwright's affirmation that Christ alone is the mediator and advocate between God and humanity.[163] Finally, the solution presented to the audience is for people to 'hear graciously the gospel / being chosen they work thankfully as before / and abide until the end in perfect faith.'[164] The play therefore contains all of the theological elements of the evangelical circle in Ghent in the late 1530s and 1540s. As noted above, these evangelicals, most of whom came from a variety of crafts, met in secret to study the Bible and rejected, in particular, traditional salvific works involving purgatory, fasting and prayers, indulgences, saints, the pope, and the Mass. The execution of one of their major leaders, Martin Hueriblocq, in May 1545, may have provided our playwright with the context for his opening prologue, especially with his references to burning flesh (Hueriblocq was burnt at the stake). Moreover, the play's lack of reference to any specifically Anabaptist tenets (which dominated popular reform in the 1530s), or to events in 1539, can be explained by its removal by several years from those earlier events. If our supposition is sound, then this play promotes a late form of evangelical message while at the same time mildly criticizing imperial persecution of religious reformers and praying for the safety of the emperor. Written perhaps only a few years after the suppression of the 1539 revolt, the carefully composed *A Play of the Father* provides us with an example of how Ghent's rhetoricians were able to continue promoting religious reform without raising the ire of the imperial representatives.

With their impressive procession-like entrances, their vivid visual displays, serious and comical dramatic presentations, and the ribald satire of their fools, rhetoricians put on a remarkable display for Ghentenaars that in many respects was similar to the carnivalesque activities which the magistrates had had so much difficulty controlling. Although formally approved and arranged by the city's elite, the *rederijker* contest of 1539, performed as it was in the midst of social and political turmoil, ecclesiastical dissatisfaction, ritualistic satire and inversion, and theological confusion, could only have contributed to the events of the late summer and fall. Even if this contribution was only one of providing an example of lay folk opposing traditional religious norms, it would have been enough to warrant the imperial government's attempts to censor further rhetorician performances. Having witnessed on stage a variety of theological and reform options, the population of Ghent could very well have thought that the old notion of a clerical stranglehold over theological orthodoxy was passé. It is not inconceivable that the Ghent performances assisted some of the populace to reconsider the role of the secular authorities as well.

7

Rhetoricians and Reform after the Ghent Competition, 1539–56

The Ghent competition must be seen as the culmination of pro-reform drama in the Low Countries of Charles V. During this twelve-day event, Ghent's residents and visitors witnessed on the stage the presentation of a wide range of reform programs, but nothing substantial to contradict those ideas. The authorities of course could not tolerate such flagrant disregard of the religious placards and city magistrates throughout the Low Countries were ordered more vigorously to censor their rhetoricians.[1] That the attempted suppression only partially worked says as much about the determination of the Netherlands' *rederijkers* as it does about the weaknesses of Charles V's proto-Inquisition. Twenty-six separate plays, mostly in manuscript, that can be safely dated to the period between the Ghent contest and the acclamation of Philip II as titular head of the Low Countries have been preserved.[2] Fifteen of these focus on religious themes and provide a limited window onto the response of rhetoricians to the attempted suppression of their reformist propaganda and to the ongoing religious controversies in the 1540s and 1550s. An examination of these dramatic works will show that while rhetoricians became more subtle in advocating reform ideas, using a variety of means to soften the rougher edges of their reform propaganda, they continued to express now familiar themes, such as a reform anticlericalism and an assertion of lay responsibility for religious leadership, as well as an increasing emphasis on iconoclastic sentiment and a growing influence from the ideas of south-German and Swiss reformers, such as John Calvin. They also continued to search for means to create a compromise solution to the religious conflicts dividing their society and destroying the civic unity so important to the middle and upper classes of the urban Low

Countries. In all of this, blame for the bloody persecution of religious dissenters was laid at the feet of the higher authorities. The result was a build up of pressure for reform and an end to the heresy placards which would explode in organized iconoclastic riots in 1566 and an open revolt, leading eventually to the division of the Low Countries and the independence of the Dutch Republic.

An Orthodox Catholic Play

Excluding plays that were composed in the late fifteenth or early sixteenth century and copied or performed during the Reformation,[3] only one of the fifteen religious plays, *The Play of Saint Trudo*, represents anything close to a pronounced defence of orthodox Catholicism. However, this work is not typical of rhetorician plays from the sixteenth century, for it came from the quill of a clergyman, Christiaen Fastraets, Dominican preacher of Leuven, and it is not known if Fastraets was in fact a member of a rhetorician chamber. Furthermore, the play focuses on the life of a medieval saint, something that not even Everaert had done. Hence, *The Play of Saint Trudo* is more typical of medieval drama in both style and subject matter. Given that Fastraets was a Dominican from Leuven, the centre of Catholic orthodoxy and opposition to the Reformation,[4] it is quite conceivable that he had turned his hand to the writing of vernacular drama as a means of counteracting the unorthodox reform ideas which rhetoricians were promulgating from the stage. If so, then this work can be viewed as an example of anti-Reformation, perhaps even anti-rhetorician, propaganda.

This long play, which was to be performed in two parts over successive years, covers the life and career of the seventh-century St Trudo, from his baptism to his death. Throughout, the diabolical characters (Lucifer and his minions Baalberith and Leviathan) plot with each other over how they might be able to thwart God's plans for the boy, by turning him to sin or making him despised by the clergy.[5] At every turn the power of the priest and sacraments over the devil highlights one of the Catholic approaches to counteracting the advances of the Reformation. Of course the Vices are frustrated at every turn, beginning with the exorcism and baptism of the future saint, through which The Pastor (*Die Pastoor*) affirms, 'he may escape the devil's clutches.'[6] The rest of the saint's life is told in similar fashion as he grows in virtues, becomes a priest, returns to his homeland to teach the gospel, defeats idolatry, and establishes a monastery, all the while confounding the demons. Throughout, the church hierarchy, priestly estate, and the sacraments are praised, while the sacrament of holy orders is played out in great detail;[7] moreover, in one scene God (*God die Vader*) makes it very clear that he works through the church structure and bishops to fulfil his wishes.[8]

What is most striking about this work is the lack of internal evidence suggesting this play was composed during the height of Reformation controversy. It seems that Fastraets has instead faithfully retold the medieval legend with little modernization. Although at one point St Trudo is warned to preach against heresy, there is no attempt to make reference to contemporary varieties. Even so, the play could have been a useful tool of Catholic counterpropaganda, especially in its strong affirmation that the orthodox sacraments have power against the devil. This approach was frequently used in the later sixteenth and early seventeenth centuries by Catholic polemicists and exorcists, the latter of whom conducted showpiece exorcisms in order to prove the validity of the Catholic rites against Protestant innovations. According to Robin Briggs, this methodology became a speciality of the religious orders because the faithful viewed the religious as the 'spiritual athletes of the early modern world,' whose learning and holiness particularly fitted them for this battle against demonic forces.[9] In other words, Fastraets may have intended his play, with its detailed description of an exorcism and its battle between demonic Vices and the heroic saint, as a polemical defence of orthodoxy. That he made no explicit reference to the Protestants, however, is puzzling, unless he was hoping not to offend any reform-minded people in the audience.

A Rhetorician History of the Early Reformation

In spite of imperial attempts to discourage rhetoricians from using the stage to proselytize on behalf of religious reform, anticlerical plays continued to be performed after the Ghent competition. This is certainly the case with *The Tree of the Scriptures*, which was first performed on 1 August 1539, in Middelburg, Zeeland, and then disseminated in print,[10] and later performed in the city of Antwerp in 1542 by one of the city's unauthorized chambers.[11] This very simple and obviously popular play recounts in allegorical fashion the history of the Reformation in the Low Countries. The script begins with a kneeling Medicine of the Soul (*De Medecijn der Sielen*, an allegorical representation of Jesus), who thanks God for 'hiding your teaching from the learned / and giving understanding to the ignorant.' Each Especially (*Elck Bijsonder*, a nun in one version and a man in the other) is a normally devout but vacillating character who is easily swayed by the charms and wine of Human Teaching (*Menschelycke Leeringhe*). Although she has been delivered from sin by his sacrifice, she is warned by Medicine that false prophets will seek to deceive her through their sophistic teaching and, failing that, they will persecute her, 'for they burn those who are contrary to them, or they exile them from the land, or exterminate them as they condemned me.' In spite of Medicine's admonition and her abhorence of idolatry and simony,[12] Each Especially is deceived by the Vice's offer of costly clothes and good works such as letters of indulgences, the sacraments (including multiple Masses), and all the external trappings of late medieval religion. Human Teaching, noting with glee that his monastic servants pursue wealth rather than poverty, rejoices that while his work had come under potentially disastrous suspicion twenty years before, thanks to his friend Lucifer he is able to return simple folk such as Each Especially to the hypocrisy of his teaching:

> And whoever could not manage with my action,
> Runs out of poverty into a convent;
> They endure voluntary poverty away from the world.
> Do you not think this is a good condition?
> And those who know the Cross brothers well,
> I will teach to chase after good benefices.
> Yes, twenty years ago planting suspicion
> To unseat someone firmly ensconced,
> And through this life full of old malice,
> Lucifer, my friend, fills his kettle.[13]

It is at this moment that Faith (*Ghelooue*) arrives and warns Each Especially of her error. Human Teaching turns angrily to Faith and asks:

> Are you also one of the German doctors?
> In my rage I cause burning and suffocating
> Or beheading as before; you want to disturb my rights,
> Prelateships and choirs, which we enjoy absolutely.
> We learned ones are chosen by God above all treasures
> Or costly ivory and mere fools want to appropriate Scripture.
> Away scabby Moors, we, the shorn, learned ones,
> Take the Scriptures by the ears, it is in our power.[14]

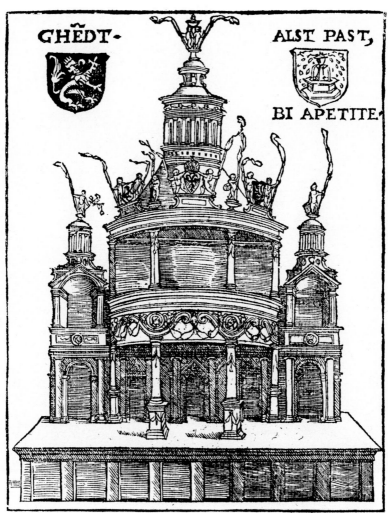

1 An illustration of the Ghent stage. From *Van de sinnespelen die op het land-juweel te Gent van 12–23 Juni 1539 werden opgevoerd* (Ghent: Joos Lambrecht, 1539). Courtesy of the Universiteitsbibliotheek Gent (Res. 1627).

2 Frans Francken II, 'Allegory of Charles V's Abdication.' By permission of the Rijksmuseum Amsterdam.

3 Cornelis Anthonisz (1500/7–1561), 'Banquet of the Civic Guards,' also
known as 'The Braspenny meal.' Inv. Nr.SA7279. © Amsterdams Historisch
Museum. By permission.

Hier beghint een spel van sinne zijnde
menswerdinge Christi volgende Personages

1 · · · Doodende letter ...
2 · · Misbruyck ...
3 · Eygen vernuft ...
4 · · Waenende weten ...
5 · Menich onnosel mensch ...
6 · Simpel Trouwe
7 · Geestelijck begrijp ...
8 · Schriftuerlijcke Zin ...
9 · · Hertneckich
10 · Gabriel ...
11 Maria ...
12 Een aent Cruijs

Doodend letter   Misbruyck
eerst   andere

4 Title-page and list of characters from 'Een spel van sinnen vande menschwerdinge Christo.' By permission of the Society Trou Moet Blijcken, Haarlem.

5 Entry of payment of gifts by the city to the militia guilds and chambers of rhetoric, stadsrekening 1543 (R12), 51r. By permission of the Stadsarchief Antwerpen.

6 'The Fountain of Life' in David Joris, *Twonder-boeck*, 2nd ed. 1551 (Vianen Dirk Mullem 1584). By permission of the University of Amsterdam Library.

Antwerpen,

7 The Antwerp blazon. From *Van de sinnespelen die op het landjuweel te Gent van 12–23 Juni 1539 werden opgevoerd* (Ghent: Joos Lambrecht, 1539). Courtesy of the Universiteitsbibliotheek Gent (Res. 1627).

THE HABSBURG NETHERLANDS

GRONINGEN
Groningen
FRIESLAND
DRENTHE
NORTH HOLLAND
Haarlem
Amsterdam
OVERIJSSEL
Deventer
Leiden
GELDERLAND
The Hague
UTRECHT
SOUTH HOLLAND
Utrecht
Delft
Gouda
Dordrecht
Nijmegen
ZEELAND
's Hertogenbosch
Middelburg
BRABANT
Antwerp
Leffinge
Bruges
Axel
Nieuwpoort
Kaprijke
Mechelen
FLANDERS
Ghent
Leuven
Lo
St Winoksbergen
Deinze
Brussels
LIEGE
Ypres
Oudenaarde
Tienen
Menen
Kortrijk
Edingen
LIMBURG
Mesen
NAMUR
Nieuwkerke
ARTOIS
HANAULT
CAMBRESIS
LUXEMBURG

0 10 20   40   60 Miles

8 The Hapsburg Netherlands.

Chiding Each Especially for the ease with which she was turned away from her redeemer, Faith then threatens the false prophets – led by the Antichrist and the blood-gorged Whore of Babylon – with apocalyptic judgment:

> Through embellished sermons you get to the peoples' goods.
> O Antichrist, what are you doing in the temple of God?
> You regard yourself as God, probing the peoples' kidneys.
> O whore of Babylon! Full of blood so you gab,
> The witnesses of the word [cf. Rev. 11] you have executed.
> The scriptures flow full by your sinful governing.[15]

Each Especially returns to her faith and the scene of the crucified Medicine of the Soul concludes the play.

The most interesting feature of this uncomplicated work is Human Teaching's remarks that twenty years before there had been suspicion of his activities. This brings the reader back to the beginning of the Reformation in the Netherlands around 1519. With Each Especially's initial faithfulness to Medicine of the Soul, then her easy deception and the reinstatement of the old superstitions, and finally her return to the true faith, we see the unknown playwright's rendition of the history of the Reformation. The initial success of the German doctor's teaching was countered by a heavy persecution which terrified many into returning outwardly to the Catholic religion. Clearly the dramatist hoped that reform fervour could be restored by a renewed proclamation of the gospel, such as successfully rescued Each Especially from the entrapments of the Catholic clergy.

In contrast to the continuing use of the stage on the part of Lutheran (or Lutheran-minded) rhetoricians,[16] only *Saint Trudo*, of the surviving fifteen religious plays dating to the sixteen years after the Ghent competition, can be described as promoting Catholic orthodoxy. The others advance some measure of reform, whether in a direction of Lutheranism, or early Calvinism, or spiritualism (whether Protestant or Catholic), the last of which now accounting for one quarter of all the scripts. Whether the domination of the surviving evidence by reform-minded rhetoricians was a result of orthodox Catholic playwrights avoiding religious controversy altogether by directing their efforts to secular matters or classical themes, or more a matter of the chance survival of manuscripts, is a moot point. What is immediately evident from the existing plays is that many rhetoricians continued to risk raising the ire of the authorities by espousing reform ideologies.

Moderate Lutheran Drama

An example of moderate Lutheran drama from this period is the afore-mentioned *An Allegorical Play on How Many Men Seek the House of Peace*, by the Amsterdam city messenger and rhetorician Jan Thoenisz.[17] As noted above, the emphasis in this play is on the Scriptures as the sole source of religious instruction, the futility of relying on one's works for salvation, and the necessity of turning in faith to Christ for salvation. Morningtime notes:

> Take that cross there and do not cling
> To a cross of wood or stone
> But to the pure, crucified Christ
> Who alone has delivered us with his blood.[18]

Many Men is rewarded with 'certain faith' and a 'pure conscience,'[19] a distinctively Lutheran benefit of justification by faith. This play there-fore illustrates the ongoing support for Luther's reform program in the Low Countries, but is presented in a subtle fashion.

While most of the later plays are like *Many Men* in their careful pres-entation rather than the often blatant pre-Ghent reform drama, any proclamation of Lutheran or Calvinist teaching was extremely danger-ous in this period, as one of Antwerp's factors, Frans Fraet, discovered to his dismay. Writing first for The Marigold chamber and then for The Gillyflower, Fraet used Antwerp's drama groups to spread reform ideas throughout Antwerp. He also used his press. In 1551 he received permission from the city to establish his independent book-printing business and the following year he was made a member of St Luke's guild. A mere five years later he appeared before the city council charged with publishing heretical works and was beheaded on 3 Janu-ary 1558.[20] Unlike many printers of unorthodox material, we possess something which Fraet himself composed which confirms that he was an advocate of religious reform. According to E. Hofman, Fraet was something of a transitional figure who added the recently introduced notions of Calvinism to the older ideas of Luther[21] and Fraet's surviv-ing play, *A Present from Godt Loondt, Grammerchijs, Besolos Manos*, evi-dences clear influence of Luther's writings as well as confirming the

Inquisitor's assessment of Fraet's reform perspective,[22] although it must be noted that Fraet was executed for printing heretical works, not for any of his rhetorician activity. As noted earlier (see above, chapter 3), this simple play presents very clearly Luther's doctrine of *sola fide*, as well as condemning, in apocalyptic terms, the persecution of believers. Obviously the attempted suppression of reform drama had caused this playwright to call down the wrath of God upon the oppressors, much along the same lines as Anabaptists had done nearly twenty years before and in terms similar to those used by the Calvinists to great effect. If rhetorician drama is anything to go by, it appears that between the time of the Anabaptist missionizing of the 1530s and the Calvinist hedge preaching of the 1550s and 1560s, there was a continuous line of apocalyptic denunciation used by opponents of the Catholic hierarchy. Certainly the ongoing persecution of religious reformers was a major reason for this frequent appeal to apocalyptic rhetoric on the part of different reform groups. Perhaps another reason for the success of Calvinist reformers was their ability, by using the same eschatological vocabulary as the earlier reform groups, to tap into a groundswell of desire for vengeance against the authorities on the part of those who had lost family or associates to persecution.

Another Lutheran play from Antwerp is Van den Berghe's *The Voluptuous Man*,[23] which like Fraet's piece reveals a preoccupation with Lutheran theology and eschatological judgment. In one passage Van den Berghe refers to the covenant made between God and man: 'If man is doomed everlasting from birth / where then is your covenant of great worth?'[24] a point which suggests that by 1551 Van den Berghe had become acquainted with Calvinist teaching. Also present in this play is a very sophisticated form of anticlericalism. One of the Vices, Bad Faith, explains that he is present at most church councils to distort the gospel for his cause, to introduce bogus laws, and to ruin the church. As a result church leaders have become backbiters and fight against the truth. Against the defence, propounded by Anna Bijns among others, that 'even priests are human,' Van den Berghe argues that the church will fall if the pillars are weak, thus attacking the scholastic notion of *ex opere operato*, that the ecclesiastical means of grace will work on their own account in spite of the human failings of the priest who consecrates them.[25] Even though the preacher who proclaims the gospel in this play is in the costume of a priest and preaches from the Vulgate, the message he declares is clearly reform-minded. Perhaps putting his reform message in the mouth of an orthodox looking character kept Van den Berghe from sharing the fate of Fraet.[26]

Spiritualistic Plays

Another means of avoiding official censure was to spiritualize or internalize reformist notions or to subsume criticism of external ecclesiastical abuses under an overriding emphasis on inner renewal and mystical contemplation. This had, after all, been the emphasis of the *Devotio Moderna*, one which seems to have permeated Netherlandic society by 1500. It should therefore come as no surprise that after two decades of persecution many reform-minded Netherlanders turned to this approach when presenting reform ideas. From the evidence already noted it appears in fact that there was an ongoing tradition of spiritualistic rhetorician drama throughout the decades of the 1520s and 1530s which continued into the last years of Charles V's reign.

Three clearly spiritualistic plays can be dated to the 1540s and 1550s. One of these is the undated *Human Spirit Deceived by the Flesh, the World, and the Devil*.[27] While there is nothing unorthodox about this play by Clodius Presbiter, its very strong flesh/spirit dichotomy, apocalyptic imagery, and satire directed against both 'clerics and peasants' who have been trapped in the snares of Flesh,[28] is much more reminiscent of the writings of spiritualists such as David Joris than of Tridentine Catholicism.[29] The central action of this work is the salvation of Human Spirit, who is rescued only by The Love of God and Fear of Punishment, who urge him to contemplate spiritual things or receive the wrath of God.[30] Yet, given the extreme contrast between the flesh and the spirit and the allures of the former, Human Spirit finds cold comfort in this admonition; further persuasion is required.[31] To convince him, the two Virtues display apocalyptic images and instruct him on the true path to spiritual health, which does not lead through ceremonies, which are mere fleshly works reminiscent of those in which the biblical Pharisees boasted (as do The World's current French, Italian, and Spanish followers),[32] but to a constant struggle against the flesh and a life lived clinging to the Spirit of God, for 'the flesh cannot sin without the consent of the human spirit.'[33] Human Spirit is provided the medicine of 'loathing of sin' in the form of seven pills to assist him purge his system of the flesh and the seven deadly sins. There is, however, no attempt to relate these pills to the seven sacraments, something that a strictly Catholic playwright would surely have done. The play concludes with another *tableau vivant*, this time of the risen Christ standing over a model of the earth from which peer Devil and The Flesh and out of which Christ draws 'a naked living soul,' illustrating how he has delivered the 'spiritual soul' from the world's snare.[34]

In an intriguing fashion this work turns inward the apocalyptic battle (which had been such a preoccupation among reformers of all camps, most especially the Anabaptist) so that it takes place within each person's inner being as the struggle between the flesh and the spirit. This play's intense spirit/flesh dichotomy and the spiritualizing of eschatological events were major features of the later writings of David Joris and those within his circle. So too was Presbiter's comment that the flesh could not sin without the assent of the individual's spirit, which in a slightly different form provided the basis for Joris's idiosyncratic view of the devil.[35] While there is no evidence of strictly Lutheran teaching, the author of this play has clearly depreciated the traditional ecclesiastical ceremony and means of grace and highlighted the interior spiritual meaning of religious devotion. It seems likely that Claudius Presbiter was familiar with the writings of apocalyptic spiritualists, such as Joris, Hendrik Niclaes, and Matthias Wier (1521–60), and incorporated some of their tenets into an broadly defined reformist or Catholic framework.[36]

Two further spiritualistic plays have survived from other quarters. *The Mother and Children of Zebedee*, performed in an unknown city on Trinity Day (8 June) 1544, is an allegorical biblical play based on the story in Matthew 20 of the mother of the disciples John and James, who sought to bring her sons' ambition to the attention of Jesus.[37] When Jesus takes the stage with two or three other apostles, he is describing to them his forthcoming suffering and death and lamenting the external devotionalism and idolatry of his contemporaries. At this poignant moment The Mother presents Jesus with her request, but he uses this opportunity to castigate self-agrandizement, which was inspired by 'fleshly understanding' and 'ignorant desires.' These two Vices then rejoice that many of their followers continue to 'run to church to pray with the crowd' but leave it thinking they have done enough merely by visiting the sanctuary.[38] Their comments are not the final word, for two Virtues elaborate on the words spoken by Christ, emphasizing the otherworldliness of Christ's kingdom and the need to take up the cross in imitation of Jesus. They also place special blame on The Mother, who because she shared the 'weakness of women,' was therefore more susceptible to the inspiration of the devil, a belief that lay at the heart of the witch stereotype.[39]

In its central theme this biblical-allegorical play is a plea for an increased level of spiritual depth among the residents of the Low Countries. Decrying the demise of true faith and love and castigating the lamentable personal ambition of church leaders, the play condemns the hypocrisy inherent in a religion based on external trappings and superstition and instead promotes individual, heartfelt devotion established on a personal appropriation of the passion of Christ. We see in this and similar plays an attempt to create a spiritual lay folk who would be better equipped to lead the church than the professional clergy who had evidently failed.

Also along spiritualist lines is *An Allegorical Mayplay about Human Frailty*, composed by a Jacob Awijts of Thoolen and performed in the chamber room of Amsterdam's In Fiery Love (*In liefde vierich*) in May 1551.[40] Human Frailty (*Menschelycke broosheit*), who seeks 'the profit of the soul which pleases God,'[41] falls into the amorous clutches of the whore The World's Pleasure (*SWerrelts ghenuechte*). Despite her affectionate words, World's Pleasure's ultimate goal is to murder her lover's body and soul[42] through seven other prostitutes, the seven deadly sins.[43] True Preacher (*Vraye predicacie*), attired as a priest, arrives to find Human Frailty in deep despair, bemoaning his condition:

> How shall I leave World's Pleasure?
> I see bishops, legates, abbots, prelates
> Noble and common estate
> Following her everywhere, inside and out.[44]

True Preacher warns Human Frailty that his soul is in mortal danger, something he would be aware of had he attended church and listened to the learned sermons and 'opinions of the high doctors' expounding on their glosses.[45] To this Human Frailty and Lascivious Deception (*Wulpsche doolinghe*) respond that the clergy themselves, so little regarded these days, preach one thing but live another.[46] In the light of such a negative evaluation of the clergy on the part of the common people, all that Human Frailty gains from the preaching of True Preacher is an even deeper depression over his sinful state. This condition is worsened by the comments of two further characters, Needful Business (*Oorboorlijck comenscap*) and Shelter from Harm (*Bescut voir scaede*), whose function in the play is to drive home to Human Frailty the desperation of his condition. They are followed by Inward Motion (*Inwendich berueren*) and Natural Awareness (*Natuerlijck beseffen*), who persuade Human Frailty to abandon his sinful preoccupations for charity. They believe that they will succeed where True Preacher failed because they have special power from their mother, Grace.[47] This power is described as the love of the Son and the will of the Father, transmitted by the Holy Spirit and water.[48] Citing from Romans, the Virtues convince Human Frailty to plead in terror for the grace of God. At this a scene of Christ on the cross suddenly appears, Human Frailty finds salvation, and joins 'those who live in the faith working charity.'[49] To support him in his Christian life the two Virtues provide him with two servants, 'good will' and 'loathing of sin.'

Like the other spiritualistic plays described here the theology of this work could fit either a Reformed or a Catholic perspective, although the emphasis on grace, the citations from Romans, reference to the Holy Spirit, and water baptism, and lack of any defence of the sacramental system (especially after 1540) might suggest a Protestant position. In addition, the work reinforces the popular belief that the religion of spiritually minded laypeople was far superior to that of the professional clergy whose reputation as mediators of piety had long been in dispute. Awijts brings home this point by having the clerical representative, True Preacher, fail in his attempts to convert the erring Human Frailty, while the two spiritual Virtues are able to succeed.[50] And although the author makes it very clear that Frailty's salvation is only through faith in Christ, he also underscores that his deliverance was for a social end, for the performance of works of charity. What this play and others from the late 1540s and 1550s clearly show is that rhetoricians had become quite cautious when presenting plays on religious themes. Undoubtedly *Human Frailty* would have found an appreciative audience among moderates of both Protestant and Catholic camps, although zealots on either side would hardly have been satisfied with the playwright's desire not to take an obvious side on the specific religious disputes. Who would have found the performance most satisfying would have been those of a spiritualistic persuasion who believed that disputes over mere externals were fruitless and that what truly mattered was the maintenance of religious peace and inculcation of spiritual values and practices among the populace.

Plays of Compromise

Along these lines even reform-minded playwrights could reveal a desire to modify Luther's overweening emphasis on faith. Such may have been the case with the Amsterdam play *Concerning our Dear Lord's Charity*, already described above (chapter 4),[51] especially with its emphasis on faith, hope, and love as central components of salvation. Such scripts from the 1540s and early 1550s reflect the approach of reform-minded Dutch urbanites, who were concerned not only with avoiding persecution, but perhaps even more importantly, with ensuring that the evangelical message would increase the level of individual Christian morality and communal charity. The strong emphasis on justification by faith being followed by a life of Christian charity may reflect the increasing influence of the Swiss–south German Reformed tradition, especially John Calvin's reform program which, according to the influential study by Bernd Moeller, was better suited to the urban environment than was Luther's.[52] At the same time, urbanites of the Low Countries, with their strong tradition of antimaterial devotionalism inherited from the *Devotio Moderna*, Erasmian humanism, spiritualism, and Anabaptism, had already developed an affinity for a communal reformation well before the advent of Calvinism in the mid to late 1540s.[53] In other words, the accent on urban communal reform, said to be the hallmark of the Swiss Reformed tradition, was as much a home-grown product in the Netherlands as an import from French Calvinist preachers.

In several of the plays examined so far we have noticed not only a tendency to avoid the most controversial theological points in dispute but a considerable level of intellectual independence from either Catholic or Lutheran orthodoxy. It may also be the case that the Low Countries' proclivity for communal reform made some urbanites of the region much more willing to accommodate themselves on the most divisive doctrinal issues for the sake of preserving the unity and peace of their communities. We see this concern for civic unity in many *rederijker* scripts, such as the 1543 *The Long-suffering Man*, the work of a Jan Valcke, about whom nothing is known except that he was obviously deeply immersed in the Scriptures.[54] He also evidently desired to combine the Reformed emphasis on justification by faith and Christ as the sole mediator with a fairly traditional concept of the sacraments and church. Even so, the function of the religious characters, Minister of God (*Dienaer Godts*) and Priest of the Lord (*Priester des Heeren*), according to the Long-suffering Man (*Duerlijdende Man*), is to

Teach us the word of God ... to teach us the truth, I suppose,
For Christ commanded them to feed my lambs

And keep my sheep ...
And do not live by bread alone, listen great and small,
But by all the fine words which comes out of God's mouth,[55]

reflecting the strong desire on the part of urbanites across Europe for a biblically literate, preaching clergy. In this work there appears a subtle distinction between the Priest and the Minister, for the former holds in his hands a book called 'the old truth' (*haude waerheyt*) while the latter has in his possession a book called 'the Word' (*dWoort*), possibly the Old and New Testaments respectively. If deeper meaning can be read into these props, it is possible that this playwright was suggesting that while the priesthood possessed some of the truth, their function as preachers of the word had been supplanted by the Reformed ministers of the gospel. In any event, both Minister and Priest proclaim the gospel as generally understood by the Reformed; Priest cites the example of Abraham as interpreted by St Paul to emphasis that the 'righteous will live by faith.'[56] They also explain, both in words and figures, how the Old Testament prophecies were fulfilled by Christ, showing, among other things, that he is greater than Solomon and that because Jesus shares his flesh and blood with the participants in the Holy Sacrament, his table is far superior to that of the Israelite king. At the same time, the playwright nowhere refers to the particularly orthodox Catholic aspects of the Mass, such as the priest's role or transubstantiation. Instead, he emphasizes that there is no other mediator but Christ. This play therefore can be viewed as an attempted compromise, the point of which, Priest reminds his 'brothers and sisters,' is that they will be prudent in their decisions so that 'this city might remain always together in unity.'[57]

Early Reformed Drama

We have already noticed in several plays hints of influence from Swiss Reformed circles. Further evidence of Calvinistic influence and of a revival of a concerted critique of Charles V's religious policies is found in two biblical plays dating to the last years of the 1540s and the first of the 1550s. Not surprisingly, like Jan Thoenisz's possibly earlier play *St John's Beheading*, these works, *The Predestined Blind*, by Adriaen Jacopsz, a painter of Briel,[58] and the anonymous *The Conversion of Paul*,[59] implicitly compare the Habsburg and papal representatives to Herod's court and the Sanhedrin. The first of these uses the story of Christ's healing of the one born blind to present in unmistakable fashion the central message of Calvinist reformers: predestination, the Protestant concept of law and grace, salvation by faith in Christ, a rejection of works in salvation, but with a strong emphasis on love as a result of justification.[60] Certain elements of this perspective are clearly presented in the prologue where the unnamed characters glorify the providence and majesty of God, who has 'made us friends,' and then they turn to the audience to ask the 'gentlemen gathered here' to take their interpretation of Luke 18 as 'spiritual food for the soul' and not to follow the leading of 'evil hearts' who cannot grasp the meaning of this passage but instead remain with the 'old meaning' to their damnation. The characters hope instead that their viewers will heed the 'good spirit's' light which overcomes the darkness.[61] If so, they conclude, God's Word will overcome the bloodthirst of the Babylonian whore and the world will witness the 'evangelical victory' and the punishment of those who have 'opposed the truth.'[62]

At this apocalyptic warning Predestined Blindman (*Ghepredestineerde blindeman*) presents his suspicion that his wife, Previous Multitude (*Voorgaende menichte*), is responsible for his miserable poverty. Previous Multitude of course protests that she is a most faithful guide, 'for all estates follow me.' Who else could her husband follow? 'The predestined,' he responds, 'whose small number' alone are on the true path.[63] Ah, Previous Multitude counters, up to now everyone has followed her, both 'poor and rich, religious and secular,' altogether an innumerable multitude.[64] Her mate, however, is determined to leave her odious company, although he fears that under his own power he will fall into the canal because physical blindness is not his only obstacle, for 'the heart is blind from the inside.'[65] 'On whom will you place your trust then?' Previous Multitude inquires. 'On that certain light / which drives away all our darkness / whose clarity is written inside our heart,' is his optimistic response.[66] His mate remains sceptical, for 'new teachings' merely result in confusion.[67]

A Reformed perspective is clear from the two Virtues who next appear, Law of Scriptures (*Wet der Schriftueren*), whose function is to produce fear, and Law of Grace (*Wet der Ghenaden*), who brings a message of joy. Both of them, however, emphasize to the audience that salvation is only by grace, for the law provides only knowledge of sin, not power to fulfil it.[68] After a pause Christ and several of the disciples arrive, with Christ affirming that he had chosen them 'in eternal love'; whoever believes will be saved.[69] The Virtues interpret how Christ has fulfilled the law and emphasize that only through faith alone will a person become righteous[70] and be delivered from the world, which 'persists in its own superstition' in contrast to believers 'who stand in the pure trust.'[71]

Jesus and his disciples soon arrive at the spot where Predestined Blindman cries out for grace and Jesus heals him, telling him several times that 'your faith has healed you.'[72] Not only has Predestined Blindman received divine grace, but now he feels Christ's love welling up within his heart.[73] A good thing too, for his wife takes it upon herself to convince him to stay with her instead of 'following the light.' 'Are you so easily bewitched [that you will] follow the people who teach only falsehood?' she queries.[74] 'These people are ignorant; follow instead the teachings of the learned,' she pleads. To no avail, for Predestined Blindman is determined to follow these simple teachers, for it is the learned ones who have murdered the defenders of the truth.[75] For him, the Word of God is sufficient, for God's Spirit works in the simple ones. His choice is confirmed by Law and Grace, who ask him what his name is; he responds now, 'The Predestined,' who was regarded by the world as an idiot but has now received grace.[76] Now that he has been saved by faith alone, he must diligently perform acts of neighbourly love, not out of obligation nor as a wage, but as a natural outworking of salvation.[77] At this the Virtues rehearse again the central message of the play, that salvation is by grace through faith alone; all those who 'dare to buy works should be ashamed.'[78] The play concludes with the Virtues' warnings against the lies of the Devil and his son the Antichrist, for those not saved will be judged with the Antichrist, cast into the eternal fire.[79] This play's strong emphasis on predestination, its contrast between relying on faith and trusting in the old superstition, and its message that a life of charity and righteousness must follow salvation, all mark it as the work of a Calvinist or Reformed playwright. He is also a pronounced critic of religious persecution on the part of the secular authorities and warns those who so oppose the truth that they will meet with apocalyptic judgment for their efforts.

The conversion of St Paul on the road to Damascus provided Reformed playwrights of mid-century Netherlands with another wonderful opportunity to castigate their rulers for their harsh policies with respect to religious heterodoxy; at least two dramatic versions of this story have survived. According to G. Jo. Steenbergen, one of these, *The Conversion of Paul*, was composed for Vilvoorde's Marigold chamber shortly after Charles V's renewal of his antiheresy mandate on 29 April

1550, and is an implicit critique of the emperor's policies.[80] This is made crystal clear in the play's prologue, when two burghers complain to each other that they are forbidden even to mention the name of Christ.[81] They console themselves with Jesus' warning that his followers will be persecuted as he had been and that those who maintain the truth have been oppressed since the beginning of the world. 'What should they do when persecution comes to them?' First Burgher (*Eerste borger*) inquires of his mate. 'We must suffer / and not depart from the word of the Lord,' Second Burgher (*Tweede borger*) replies, for we must rely solely on the strength of the Lord during the tribulation. This persecution, First Burgher affirms, is the work of 'this nation,' a phrase which could have been interpreted by sixteenth-century viewers as having specific reference to the Spanish overlords of the Low Countries.[82] At this the two Vices spring upon the stage, Hypocritical Heart (*Ypocrytich herte*) and Zealous Labour (*Fortsich labeur*), complaining to each other that people are still preoccupied with this Jesus of Nazareth, whose teachings have not only hindered the work of these devils, but have 'bewitched so many persons.' Their only recourse is to 'persecute them wherever they live,'[83] killing, banning, or 'bringing them to the bench of suffering,' the notorious executioner's bench used frequently in sixteenth-century trials against heretics.[84] The reasons elicited by the Vices justifying these extreme measures likewise had a contemporary significance for the play's audience. First, the message of Jesus has captivated the common folk: 'It is all Jesus before and Jesus after,' complains Hypocritical heart, 'be they peasant or tenant, all are his.'[85] For this reason, the Vices continue, we had Steven executed:

Our authorities did not do that without reason,
For he rebuked the bishops as his enemies
And he said, 'The most high God does not rest in any lands,
Nor in temples made by hands of men.'[86]

The Vices therefore decide to fly to 'our religious lords' to encourage them to persecute 'and bring to harm' all who confess the name of Jesus and to appoint Saul the head of this movement of suppression.[87]

The play then continues with the biblical account of the conversion of Saul. Again, the description of Saul and his plans for persecution would have had a contemporary significance for the play's original audience. For example, his purpose is to 'maintain in honour our excellent religious estate,' while Saul himself is described as a 'doctor in the law,' which could refer to the study of both rabbinical and canon law.[88] His leaders are a Pharisee (*Phariseus*) and a Bishop (*Biscop*); in the course of their dialogue it becomes obvious that these characters also represent the playwright's contemporary clergy and pope respectively. For example, Pharisee calls his religious superior, 'Oh lord bishop, prelate, highest lord, / Regent over our pharisaical estate.'[89] The Vices rejoice over this situation, asserting that Christ had been slain because he had acted against 'imperial law.'[90]

After his conversion, Saul prays for forgiveness for persecuting the Lord's elect and pledges to proclaim the living word of Christ 'in houses, in churches,' without 'fearing either lay or clergy.'[91] When Saul requests baptism, Ananias is jubilant, for this means that God's grace was already growing in the new convert, and he could be baptized as a 'sign that you are covenanted with God.'[92] Naturally the Vices are aghast at this development and lament the potential damage to their prelates 'with all their false notions.'[93] However, instead of giving up they decide to try to empower their 'learned clerics' with 'all their bulls' to persecute Saul, so that he will 'sing the same song as Jesus' for daring to turn the people from their errors and lessen the clergy's profit.[94] The scene then shifts to Saul preaching to the believers, encouraging them to remain steadfast in this persecution, for Christ said that they would be persecuted as he was. In this monologue the playwright highlights those of Paul's teachings which were central features of the evangelical camps, especially the Reformed: Christ as the sole deliverer; predestination; and rejection of idolatry.

> He [Christ] is the truth and no other;
> In his mouth was never found deceit;
> He has chosen us from pure love –
> ...
> Flee all errors,
> Shun idolatry, as it stands written,
> Pray to God alone, whatever happens to you,
> For he is the way, the truth, and the life.
> He is the *Prince* who can forgive sin,
> He is truly humility of heart,
> He is our sole risen advocate
> For the human family into eternity clear.[95]

The play concludes with an epilogue calling upon the audience to turn like Saul to Christ and away from persecuting the Word of God. Overall it is impossible in this work to mistake the Pharisees for anything other than the Catholic priesthood who have promoted Charles V's proto-Inquisition. Moreover, the audience is told that Jesus Christ was executed because he had broken the 'keysers wet' and preached that God alone is the supreme regent. That the author writes from a Calvinist perspective is clear from, among other things, the description of baptism as a sign of a covenant with God. Also confirming Calvinist influence is the high concern for the honour of God and a strong emphasis on divine election. On top of his criticism of religious persecution and the clerical estate, the playwright also condemns the veneration of religious images.

In other words, we see in this and other reformed plays from mid-century the ideological elements which came together to form the rationalization for the Dutch revolt, beginning with the iconoclastic storms of 1566: an assertive Calvinism, an increasingly open condemnation of the Habsburg's religious placards, and a strong iconoclastic and anticlerical sentiment. Certainly the number of blatantly Calvinistic plays continued to increase, especially once the battle against Spain had begun.[96] Throughout the period of the early Reformation in the Low Countries, apocalyptic denunciation remained a popular tool of propaganda, and it seems that the failed Anabaptist experiments with establishing the eschatological kingdom did not deter later reformers from likewise appealing to the fear of apocalyptic judgment. It should be obvious, therefore, that the rhetoricians of the Netherlands of Charles V played major roles in the spread of discontent and of a nascent revolutionary ideology which only lacked the heavy-handed policies of Charles's son Philip II to become a justification for actual revolt. All the same, the surviving plays composed during the reign of Charles V reveal that they thought very highly of their native prince. It is to this subject that we now turn.

8

War, Peace, and the Imperial Majesty in Rhetorician Drama, 1519–56

It is now evident that chambers of rhetoric offered interested burghers a forum in which to meet with their fellows and to express their thoughts on the social, political and religious controversies of their day. Like the related militia or 'shooters' guilds, the chambers seem also to have provided opportunities for socially and politically ambitious men to catch the attention of city fathers and perhaps, with a good measure of fortune, move a little closer to the inner corridors of civic politics. In return, rhetoricians performed valuable celebratory and propagandistic services for their civic authorities, whether dominated by guilds or patrician elites. Although, as we have seen, rhetoricians of the sixteenth century became notorious for their presentations of heterodox religious ideas and anticlerical sentiment, they continued to defend the rights and needs of their urban communities on more secular issues. As a result, rhetoricians came to view themselves not only as instructors of the people, but as prophets to the higher authorities as well. In the surviving manuscripts, the emphasis in their religious drama was to castigate the ecclesiastical authorities, promote a reshaped version of Christianity for sophisticated, literate urbanites, usually within a broadly defined Lutheran or Reformed perspective, and promote religious change with a minimal disturbance of social and economic life. They also took it upon themselves to chastise their secular authorities for disturbing the delicate social tranquillity by their participation in the persecution of religious dissent, and for their ruinous warfare. As with Erasmus, it appears many rhetoricians' reading of the gospel led them to see peace as an essential part of the Christian message.

The Habsburg-Valois Wars and the Netherlands

During the decades of Charles V's reign, Netherlanders experienced the debilitating effects of the Spanish-French wars, and not always at a distance. Although the major battles in the Habsburg-Valois conflict were fought in Italy and elsewhere, several times invading forces reached as far as Holland and Brabant, as did those of France's local ally, the Duchy of Guelders, which occupied The Hague in 1528, extorting from its citizens the immense sum of 28,000£ Fl., and besieged Antwerp in 1542.[1] While major peace treaties were signed in 1526 (the Peace of Madrid), 1529 (the 'Ladies' Peace' of Cambrai), and 1538 (the Armistice of Nice), it was not until the Peace of Crépy in 1544 that Francis I finally agreed to give up Naples and support Charles against the Turks and Protestants, while the emperor promised to return Burgundy and marry a Habsburg princess to the French king's second son. Even this peace proved elusive, in part because of the premature death of the Valois prince. No longer distracted by his campaigns against Francis I, Charles was able to turn his military energy against the Protestant German princes and the Turks. War between the Empire and France (now ruled by Henri II) broke out again in 1552 and lasted – with a brief rest in 1556 – until the signing of the Treaty of Cateau-Cambresis in April 1559, four years after the abdication of the exhausted Charles V. In 1555 he had handed over governance of the provinces of the Low Countries to Philip II and in the following year he abdicated his throne in favour of his son and the imperial title to his brother Ferdinand (for an allegorical depiction of Charles V's abdication that has some of the characteristics of a *tableau vivant*, see illustration 2).[2]

In this context of military conflict it should come as no surprise that rhetoricians composed plays on the theme of war. From the dramas of the Bruges factor Cornelis Everaert in the 1520s and 1530s through a handful of anonymous works composed during the 1540s and the early 1550s to the play performed by an Antwerp chamber for King Philip II in 1556, rhetoricians lamented the disastrous impact of warfare on living conditions, trade, and business and led the joyous festivities celebrating every peace treaty. Here they reflected the attitudes of most residents of the Low Countries, which James D. Tracy has called 'a realm made for peace' but which bore an unequal burden of the costs of war.[3]

Erasmus and Peace

Rhetoricians were not the only ones in the Low Countries to speak out against war. Undoubtedly the most important literary opponent to the Habsburg-Valois wars was the prominent Dutch humanist Desiderius Erasmus of Rotterdam. Erasmus's advice in 1516 to the young Prince Charles (later Charles V) in *The Instruction of a Christian Prince* (*Institutio principis christiani*) illustrates his attitude toward war. According to Richard L. DeMolen, Erasmus sought to inculcate in the young ruler a passion for peace, reminding him that the 'function of power ... is not to extend the "boundaries of one's realm, but to enrich it." War, above all, is to be avoided, except as a last resort.'[4]

Although Erasmus evidently found support for his pacifist position in the works of Cicero,[5] the central elements of his peace position were formulated from the gospels. As seen in his *Complaint of Peace* (*Querela Pacis*) of 1517, the heart of Erasmus's critique of war was his strong affirmation that Christ's message was essentially one of love, peace, and unity.[6] That Christian princes used any pretext to begin wars against fellow believers suggested to Erasmus that for rulers Christian virtues were merely a cover for naked personal ambition and the devilish pursuit of power. Erasmus therefore condemned the hypocritical justification for war by which European rulers rationalized their ambitions. He wrote:

> Let us look at the last ten years. What land or what sea did not witness warfare? What region was not soaked with Christian blood? What river was not dyed with human blood? The cruelty of Christians surpasses that of heathens and beasts. The Jews' wars were against strangers and at God's command. Christians should war against vice. Yet they ally themselves with vice to war against men. All pretense aside, ambitions, anger, and the desire for plunder are at the base of Christian wars. The Jewish wars were against foreigners, yet Christians have allied themselves with the Turks to war with fellow Christians.[7]

The hypocrisy also of soldiers receiving the sacrament – for Erasmus the principal symbol of Christian unity – and then rushing out to slaughter their fellows was too much for him to accept.[8] So too were the terrible consequences of military campaigns on civilian population and property. Speaking in the first person in the *Querela Pacis*, Peace cautions that the result of humanity's rejection of her can only be 'calamity upon calamity.'[9] She then warns rulers to

> consider the ruin of cities, the destruction of thoroughfares, the desolation of fields, and the insidious annihilation of churches. Seriously consider this: these are the fruits of war. If you are repulsed at the thought of bringing into your country wicked and filthy mercenaries whom you must support at the expense of your own people and at a great loss to yourself personally, then consider this as the price of war.[10]

Therefore, when the Emperor Maximilian started his campaign to reconquer the Duchy of Guelders in the second decade of the sixteenth century, Erasmus responded, 'You wish to reconquer some part of your dominion? What has that to do with the welfare of your people?'[11] Instead, Erasmus argued for a permanent peace with France and a nonviolent solution to the Guelders conflict. Only such a resolution could avoid the ravages of war, often conducted by the mercenaries against those they had ostensibly been hired to defend.[12]

The widespread popularity of Erasmus's writings makes them an important source for our interpretation of rhetorician sentiment relating to war and peace.[13] Certainly those residents of the Low Countries with even a modicum of humanistic education would have been introduced to the central pietistic and pacifistic ideas of Europe's most famous scholar. While perhaps influenced to a certain extent by the pacifism of Erasmus, it becomes clear from the surviving rhetorician plays that the *rederijker*'s antiwar sentiment evolved also out of their very practical business concerns.[14] Instead of theoretical or biblical issues, the closure of trade routes and ports, the destruction of supplies and capital, and the increase in artisanal unemployment receive the most prominent attention in these popular dramas.

That many of these plays were performed publicly and in front of visiting dignitaries confirms the conclusion that rhetorician drama, like processions and *tableaux vivants*, provided Dutch commoners with a means of communicating their political and economic concerns to their often distant rulers. What George Kernodle has noted about a prince's brief encounter with the *tableaux vivants* surely relates to the lengthier stage productions of the rhetoricians: 'For that moment a historical picture or an allegorical group impressed him with the ancient glory of the city, with its genuine loyalty, and with its hopes for the future clemency, as well as the future glory, of the ruler.'[15] The several visits of

Charles V to the various cities of the Low Countries (especially those of 1515 and 1549) were opportunities for the residents of those communities to make their voices heard as well as to celebrate their sovereign.[16] The resulting displays could be used to bring the special needs of the burghers to the mind of the ruler.[17]

One of the best documented of Charles V's visits was his entry into Bruges in 1515 as part of his tour of the Netherlands to receive the homage of his subjects now that he had come of age as their archduke. Recorded by the court's official historian, Remi du Puys (and profusely illustrated with scenes of the *tableaux*), eleven of the twenty-seven pageants that highlighted this royal entry were financed by the city and planned by several of Bruges's rhetoricians.[18] These rhetoricians presented in remarkably coherent fashion (if not always accurately) the history of the foundation, rise, and decline of Bruges, 'coupled with a firm indication that their only hope for the future must reside in Charles himself.'[19] Their point was made primarily by having each pageant compare a significant incident in the history of Bruges with a parallel biblical, or occasionally classical, incident, which had the accumulative effect of depicting the citizens of Bruges as the children of Israel and Charles as their messiah, or as Moses, who could lead them out of their financial wilderness, a wilderness created in part by the silting up of the Zwyn, the city port's waterway. Throughout the displays the decline of the once resplendent maiden of Bruges is blamed on the attempts of Merchandise and Business to depart her walls, and while Law and Religion struggle valiantly to keep them within, only a powerful prince could fully stop their flight.[20] Whether or not Charles was convinced by this display is a moot point; the city fathers clearly believed that such festivities could influence royal policy and they therefore invested heavily in them and in their rhetoricians.

War and Peace in the Plays of Cornelis Everaert

Rhetoricians were at the forefront of most princely visit activities and composed and performed plays to celebrate these and the several peace treaties signed during the reign of Charles V. For example, Cornelis Everaert produced at least eight scripts relating to the theme of war and peace during the 1520s and 1530s.

These reveal two major aspects of Everaert's dramatic presentations relating to warfare. First, he naturally takes sides in the conflict. Reading the plays he composed to celebrate Charles V's victory over

Francis I at Pavia in 1525 – a victory which saw the French king captured – one is immediately struck by the patriotic praise for the emperor's achievement. Both *High Wind and Sweet Rain* and *The Aragonese* rejoice over the emperor's victory and blame Francis I for starting the conflict by mistreating the imperial ambassadors and invading the imperial domains without just cause.[21] In the first play, the two leading characters are High Wind (*Hooghen Wynt*), the French king, and Sweet Rain (*Zoeten Reyn*), the emperor. The former is a blustery, pompous, and ambitious ruler who boasts that he will display his might by destroying castles, homes, and churches, and shaking the earth with his power.[22] But Sweet Rain arrives and asks about High Wind, 'Who is this man who thinks he is the lord of lords?' In the face of Charles V's purity, humility, and strength of character, the French overlord does not stand a chance.[23] With the French forces now in retreat, Reasonable Understanding (*Redelicke Verstannesse*, a noblewoman) affirms that Charles, 'noble of spirit from his birth until now,' will continue to rule his lands 'in accord, with wise counsel and prudence, and in peace, love, and unity.'[24]

It is also interesting to note that in both plays Charles is favourably compared to the Israelite King David by means of painted figures; in *High Wind* David, carrying the head of Goliath, is seen entering Jerusalem to the great rejoicing of Israelites,[25] while in *Aragonese* he is taking the crown away from the Ammonites.[26] Given this biblical comparison, it is not surprising that the emperor's victory is credited to God. According to Many People (*Menichte van Volcke*) in *Aragonese*, the emperor had proved his devotion to God and hence sealed his victory, because he had called for daily processions and Masses to that end.[27] It is furthermore hoped that the Holy Spirit will enlighten secular princes so that they will be able to rule their domains in peace and submit to the virtuous rule of their emperor.[28] Thus in these works Everaert reflects what Frances Yates has called a revival of the imperial ideal, a 'late manifestation of the Monarch, the potential Lord of the World, in the person of the Emperor Charles V,' during the century 'in which a new Europe, with its great states built up on principles of realistic statecraft and infused with national patriotism, was in process of formation.'[29] Although the rising nation states had made the imperial ideal a phantom one, in popular imagination the hope that Charles could still exert his overlordship over the lesser kings and bring in a new age of peace seems to have reached a climax after the Battle of Pavia.[30]

The second side to Everaert's drama consists in his not allowing this patriotic sentiment to lessen his deep concern over war's grievous damage to the Low Countries. At the beginning of *High Wind*, the merchant Any (*Eenich*) and the artisan Many (*Menich*) rejoice that with Charles V's victory, they can both return to their normal work routines, although with two such powerful and ambitious lords, 'our peace will not long endure.'[31] However, by the end of the play these two characters, encouraged by the advice of Reasonable Understanding, hope that if Francis I allows Charles V to maintain a long enduring peace, 'merchandizing will increase abundantly' to all corners of the earth.[32]

A clearer explication of the practical effects of warfare is seen in Everaert's *Willing Labour and People of Trade*, composed to celebrate the Peace of Madrid of 24 January 1526 (which saw Francis I's release from his nearly fatal captivity) and performed on the 'Burg' at Bruges exactly one month later.[33] In this work a peasant and artisan search for peace and business, but are forced to live with Tumultuous Times (*Den Beroerlicken Tyt*), an armoured soldier, and hence both are impoverished. If warfare is a divine chastisement, the punishment – robbery, murder, arson, rape, the starvation of the innocent, and the impoverishment of the rich – far exceed their sins.[34] Tumultuous counters with the benefit 'for our noble youth' of seeing the 'courageous spectacle' of armies bedecked in armour and marching under glorious banners; who could object to that?[35] 'Four estates of people,' the aggrieved respond, 'the merchant, the farmer, ... the seaman, and in many places, People of Trade.'[36] Peace, not war, benefits these folk, for peace brings unity, furthers merchandizing and trade, and allows fishers and farmers to produce the necessities of life.

After the Peace of Madrid and the plans for the marriage of Charles V's sister, Eleanor of Habsburg, to Francis I (this marriage may be the reason behind Everaert's very muted critique of the French Crown in this play), Everaert turns to a theoretical discussion of war reminiscent of the arguments of Erasmus, especially in his affirmation that this treaty had been made by the peacemaker, Christ, who brought peace between 'God the Father and the human race,' sealing that treaty with his blood.[37] Furthermore, the playwright reiterates the importance of peace, noting that God 'heeds a peaceful heart'; that 'without God's peace it is all worthless,' but 'where there is peace, there is God'; and finally that 'peace has opened heaven's gates' through the seal of Christ's five wounds.[38] The image of Christ as the great peacemaker is illustrated in this play by a figure of Christ crucified on an olive tree, the ultimate symbol of peace.[39]

These Christological arguments on behalf of peace, when added to the references from Cicero, are reflective of the ideas of Erasmus noted above. Everaert adds a new element, however, when he – in the person of People of Trade – compares Eleanor of Habsburg's willingness to act as the agent of the peace treaty between Charles V and Francis I with the humble compliance of Mary, who willingly became the vehicle for the peacemaker's entry into the world.[40] To seal the treaty 'with women's love' and marriage assured its permanence, just as the peace between humanity and God had been ensured by the participation of a woman.[41] Everaert here has combined his high praise for Eleanor as mediator between her brother and her husband with the ongoing late medieval devotion to Mary and the Christocentric pacifism of Erasmus.

Everaert reiterates these points in the plays which he composed before and after the Peace of Cambrai of 1529,[42] such as the farces *Poor Community and Tribulation* (performed sometime before the 'Ladies' Peace') and *Poor in the Chest* (performed on the first Sunday of August 1529, immediately prior to the treaty), which voice the increasing frustration experienced by the average burghers of Bruges in the face of the ongoing hostilities (see above, chapter 5).[43] A similar solution to the difficulties experienced by the common folk during the Habsburg-Valois wars is depicted in *Great Labour and Sober Growth,* performed on 24 April 1530, in celebration of the Peace of Cambrai. In this play, Great Labour (*Groot Labuer*), a carpenter, and Sober Growth (*Sober Wasdom*), a peddler, complain that even though they work hard at their crafts, the war has brought impoverishment, while soldiers, camp followers, and misers have all prospered. Although the soldier, The Time is Now (*Den Tyt van Nv*), advises them to adopt the same deceitful practices which are making some rich at the expense of others, Prudence of Wisdom (*Beleedt van Wysheden*) persuades them that the only godly path for the suffering artisans is to endure patiently in the face of hardships beyond their control. They should especially keep their suffering private – advice no doubt appreciated by Bruges's city fathers concerned with the potentially rebellious dissatisfaction of their artisans and labourers.[44]

Everaert's last known dated play was *The Play of Peace*, composed to celebrate the Armistice of Nice, the terms of which were to last ten years.[45] All of his major points are by now quite familiar: the treaty between the rulers is praised while Francis I is blamed for having restarted the conflict by spurning the advice of Eleanor of Habsburg; credit for bringing the two rulers to terms is given at various points to the Holy Spirit, who 'rules the hearts of kings,'[46] to Christ, the ultimate peacemaker, and to the pope, who acted as mediator at the behest of the emperor.[47] The play's figure portrays Abigail bringing peace between King David and Nabal, a biblical figure, in the playwright's mind, of Eleanor's bringing peace between Charles V and Francis I:

> This is as a comparison in view of peace.
> For just as Abigail had mollified David's wrath,
> So Leonora has brought peace
> Between her husband and her brother
> By her virtue.[48]

Finally, the play concludes with the hope that with this peace between the two Christian rulers, there would be a united front against the Turks.

To this point Everaert's plays have concentrated on the value of peace for the residents of Flanders. But in one script, Everaert concentrates on the conditions brought about by warfare to a degree not seen in his other works, or in most plays of other rhetoricians for that matter. This undated work, *The Play of the War*, was performed at a feast of the Bruges chamber, Holy Spirit, and most likely was composed between treaties, probably at the height of local military actions.[49] Here Everaert condemns the glorification of war and those who support it, not only the soldiers, but also the priests and female camp followers, although Everaert is careful to note that The Rhetoric (*De Rethorycke*) is not among the company, for warriors find her boring.[50] Although it is obvious that camp followers take advantage of war to line their pockets, the play's actors make it clear that ordinary townspeople, such as artisans, merchants, and innkeepers have also learned to profit unfairly from war. Innkeepers water the beer while master craftsmen underpay their journeymen and with higher prices rob the people of their 'goods and treasure.'[51] Merchants are no better, for, practising the adage that 'bad food follows war,' they take advantage of war crises to mix poor grains with the good and to sell bad milk and beer, all to keep the poor folk (*scaemel volc*) under their feet.[52] The profiteering of rentiers, landowners, and other holders of feudal dues and monopolies is only more sophisticated.[53]

At this rather pessimistic point in the play, two new characters, Faithful (*Trauwe*) and Love (*Liefde*) – a monk and a nun respectively – take the stage, crying, 'Prosperity, prosperity, where are you?' They condemn all who profit by war and deplore the decrease in good works and church services; even the learned chaplains who support warfare 'pursue the devil's commands,' just like Judas, who sold Christ for thirty pieces of silver, or Cain, who slew his brother Abel.[54] Lay people who join soldiers' camps do so to fill their bellies with wine and food, but are merely the blind following the blind. If only warriors would turn their attention to the real threat against Europe, the Turks, instead of slaying 'the inhabitants of our lord's duchy.'[55] End of Time (*Hende des Tyts*) then blows a trumpet announcing that he is Death, the servant of the imperial majesty, who 'will repay each according to his service, without deceit or fraud, for he is no respecter of persons.'[56] Pulling the curtain cord End of Time reveals the figure of God on the cross, and commands the audience to 'see your emperor who was wounded for your sins ... pray for grace.'[57] To assist this process, Love, 'dressed like Mary,' and Faithful, now appearing as St John, stand under the cross, encouraging the play's observers to turn from their sinful lives and seek mercy from God, before 'Death grips them all.'[58] While the concluding moral is traditional – to turn from war and greed to the cross of peace – this play stands as an articulate testimony of the ubiquitous effects of war and how they have destroyed the Christian unity, civic cohesiveness, and prosperity which, in Everaert's opinion, should instead define the communal life of Flanders's urban centres.

What is perhaps most interesting is Everaert's description of the crucified Christ as 'your emperor.' This image must surely have helped to reinforce in people's minds the image of Charles V as a type of Christ and to infuse patriotic loyalty with religious devotion. Everaert was not alone at this point, for, as noted above, he was able to tap into a long history of prophetic notions surrounding the Last World Emperor. Because his estates included both German and Burgundian territories, Charles V could pose as heir to the prophecies surrounding both the German 'third Frederick' and the French 'second Charlemagne.' In these roles he would subjugate unruly European kings, such as Francis I, chastise the church (seemingly fulfilled in the Sack of Rome by Spanish troops in 1527), defeat the Turks, and bring in a golden age of peace. These predictions were taken seriously by learned and lay folk alike.[59] Humanists added to these prophecies their description of Charles as a new Caesar Augustus, with the result that the emperor was widely regarded as a new divinity. Ottavia Niccoli's description of the popular Italian prophetic tradition relates just as well to the Low Countries:

As is evident, these predictions were suffused with propaganda and with adulatory intent, in particular where Charles V was concerned. The imperial fortunes were associated with the fortunes of all those (and only those) who accepted alliance with the emperor and fell in with his aims; when all was said and done, Charles was the sole fixed point of reference in peace or for a just war and the center of a cosmos that was harmonious and content because it revolved around him.[60]

Murderous Work

Although Everaert's works provide the clearest dramatic explication of prophetic imperial perceptions and of an Erasmian-like pacifism, other rhetoricians composed and performed plays relating to war during the period of the Habsburg-Valois campaigns. The unfortunately anonymous *A Play to Perform in Times of War with Murderous Work* provides one of the most eloquent pleas for the end of warfare and its injurious effects on the populace.[61] Although we have already looked at this work (chapter 4 above), its importance to the theme of this chapter requires that we give it more than a passing glance.

The principal Vices are the heavily armed Murderous Work and his wife, Man-Crushing Teeth (red as blood is her beauty), whose multitudinous weapons, which 'spare neither men nor women,'[62] have victimized the farmer, Unblamed, his wife, The Harmed, and their infant, Innocence. Acting as a sibyl is Power of Endurance (*Cracht van ghedooghen*), who explains that their miserable plight is ultimately a plague from God and that all who bear 'God's plagues' with an ill will are not worthy to be his children. Unblamed, however, appeals that he is not aware of any crime which they have committed to merit God's chastisement. Indeed, Harmed affirms, they have had scarcely a moment to say a Pater Noster, having had to flee their home without their possessions.[63] They do not know where to go, for 'sick trade [*crancke neeringe*] is everywhere.' Their support groups are gone: Harmed's mother has died from sorrow and her friends lay beaten in the fields; Unblamed's father has lost his mind; both husband and wife are so full of mourning that 'death comes and hails us.'[64] Power of Endurance interjects that she has been sent from God to teach them patience in suffering, for they are in some respects like a saint who, while not deserving a martyr's death, suffers patiently for eternal rewards.[65] Hearing that they must endure patiently, Harmed pleads for 'Mary's son who tasted the death of a martyr' to abide with them, while Unblamed asks Power if she has any news of peace which might sustain them. In response, the pilgrims Peace and Justice arrive, bringing unhappy news: because of the plagues of the world, God has removed wisdom and prudence from the land. As a result, 'corruption and war are now so great' that both Peace and Justice must flee their noble land and cities.[66] Because 'Peace always makes the bed upon which Justice rests' (there is no justice without peace), both must leave.[67] The result of their departure, of course, is the loss of the world's prosperity. Peace can only hope that God, 'the emperor of the eternal glorious hosts' will 'let us soon return together.'[68]

Peace and Justice then depart and a model of the earth takes centre stage. Rejoicing in the flight of Justice and Peace is the Devil, who speaks and dances inside the globe. To one side Unblamed and Harmed watch this bizarre scene. Unblamed's startled response – 'I say the devil is in the world' – illustrates very well the playwright's belief that the horrible social conditions which during times of war dominate the Low Countries prove that the 'devil rules the world.'[69] Springing out of the model, the Devil confirms this belief, announcing that 'at this time I rule,' along with his children. Distressed at this news, even Power of Endurance is at a loss, for she cries out, 'Lord God, what is to blame that the world is plagued by these?'[70] Unblamed and Harmed plead with Power for some consolation, 'for while we are innocent of this matter ... we are burned, dishonoured, and enslaved' more even than beasts. Again Power responds that the sins of the people have brought the curse of war upon them, and while Unblamed and Harmed might not be personally responsible, 'the good must suffer on account of the evil,' which directs the world 'by the devil's advice.'[71] When Harmed continues to plead the innocence of her rural family, Power asks her if she really thinks that only urbanites commit sins. Is it not instead the case that some sins, such as quarrelling, fighting, scolding, lying, cursing, and drunkenness, are committed in the countryside? Why is it that farmers are not content with receiving wages for their hard labour and on Sundays 'being feasted with God's Word?'[72] Instead they should be careful not to stray from the right path nor dispute with God, but bow under his hand; like good subjects bear the will of the Lord, 'for where there is no sin, there is no plague.'[73] With these words Unblamed and Harmed are convinced that they too have angered God and are not completely innocent of this punishment.

Even Power of Endurance admits that with the lack of improvement in the moral life of the people, their pain will only increase. Turning to the audience, Unblamed pleads with them to turn to a 'mournful condition' (*beweende bedinghe*), calling tearfully in trust upon the grace of God, for only then could the devil be driven out.[74] Kneeling, the trio prays to the prince of angels for him to deliver peace 'before all is lost' and to grant the country's rulers the wisdom to end this war by driving out Murderous Work and Crushing Teeth – 'plucking out prosperity's enemies from our eyes' – and finally ending the carnage which has impoverished most and created many widows.[75] While the answer of this play to the problem of warfare is rather traditional, it illustrates the generally pacifist attitude of many of the Low Countries' rhetoricians during the Habsburg-Valois wars. Not only did war impede the trade and business that formed the basis of the Netherlands' prosperity, but it devastated the countryside and destroyed the social fabric and spiritual and moral values of the people. Furthermore, blaming warfare on the sins of innocent inhabitants was certainly a useful strategy for rhetoricians seeking to cultivate support from civic leaders concerned about the potentially dangerous level of resentment on the part of suffering citizens and labourers. At the same time, rhetoricians were able to vent much of this hostility by also redirecting immediate responsibility for the war devastation to the higher rulers, especially the French Crown.

Later Rhetorician Plays on War

Unlike the undated *Murderous Work* and the plays of Everaert, most surviving rhetorician drama composed during the 1540s and 1550s is much more careful in its critique of the actions of rulers. The turning point seems to have come with the events in Ghent in 1539, which altered the extent to which rhetoricians could publicly express a criticism of political policies. Perhaps because they were composed after 1540, the other surviving play scripts examined here are less forthright in their condemnation of warfare and more effusive in their praise of the Netherlands's hereditary ruler. The mere possibility of imperial representatives being present at public performances meant that rhetorician dramatists composed their works under the shadow of the imperial Inquisition. Moreover, it seems that rhetoricians also wished to recultivate Charles V's imperial favour and to prove that they were his faithful subjects, in spite of their widely known hostility to his religious policies. Five post-1540 plays will suffice as examples of these trends.

The first of these is *A play about the Father Who Sent the People to Work in the Vineyard,* which, as argued above, was evidently composed and performed in Ghent during Charles V's reign (for a fuller discussion, see above, chapter 6).[76] At the end of the play, two characters, Humility (*Ootmoedicheyt*) and Graciousness (*Ghenadicheyt*), directly address the audience, turning to unabashed praise of Charles V, 'our native prince,' begging God to preserve his reign so he might 'rule his lands in excellent peace'[77] and, more to the point, that God will protect 'the noble city of Ghent.'[78] Quite possibly, then, this play was written shortly after Charles V's suppression of the revolt of 1539. It seeks to mollify the emperor, placing the blame for the uprising on the lower artisanal orders of the city and reaffirming the rhetoricians' loyalty. On the other hand there seems an underlying resentment of the imperial repression of the gospel.

These points are confirmed in the first of Cornelis van Ghistele's two versions of the classical story of *Aeneas and Dido*, performed in Antwerp by The Marigold chamber in 1551.[79] In this work's prologue Van Ghistele suggests the rhetorical arts were inspired by the Holy Spirit and that supported by the Scriptures, rhetoric opposes errors and brings praise to God and the emperor. The playwright then uses this mythical story of the fall of Troy and the founding of Rome especially to honour Charles V, 'who has ruled the Roman empire for many years.' Particularly praiseworthy is the emperor's ability, like Aeneas,' to produce fear and obedience in the heathen. But, Rhetorical Spirit and Poetical Mind continue, Charles V has added to this characteristic the wisdom of Solomon, the humility of Joseph, and the righteousness of David. In contrast, when Mars rules the land tyranny and evil have free reign, to the detriment of cities such as Antwerp where, under the normal conditions of the imperial reign, brotherly love, peace, and unity mark the life of the community, for both its 'Dutch and Walloon' residents.[80] It is also evident that the play's references to the siege of Troy are intended to further the playwright's praise of the courage shown by Antwerpenaars during its recent trials, including, no doubt, the siege of 1542 and Antwerp's requirement to pay a large proportion of Charles V's war debts.

Providing a most conservative perspective during difficult times is the short *spel van zinnen, The Clew of Poverty* (i.e., poverty as a ball of yarn), apparently composed in the southern Netherlands by a Jacob Jans, most likely prior to 1550, and then copied and preserved by a Haarlem playwright.[81] The play centres on the plight of the simple cobbler Poor Companion (*Pover Geselle*), who discovers that his poverty, symbolized by the ball of yarn, has grown so large that he could never finish it. In the course of this play, responsibility for poverty is placed not at the feet of rulers or those controlling the local economy (who are not even referred to once); instead poverty is a result of laziness and poor household management on the part of individuals, a message which surely provided comfort to the authorities.

The year after The Marigold performed their praise of the emperor in Antwerp, rhetoricians in Holland's oldest city, Dordrecht, issued a call for a rhetorician contest on the question of 'Who is to be regarded as the most victorious and mighty person in history, who has won cities and castles, but whose works have endured and not been destroyed?'[82] Apparently only the White Columbines (*Witte Acoleyen*) of Leiden answered the summons, presenting to the Fountain (*Fonteynisten*) of Dordrecht a simple satire which ultimately proclaims Charles V as their answer. That this play lacks any significant criticism of imperial policy or anything more satirical than a gentle anticlericalism is a result of Leiden's rhetoricians heeding the dangers inherent in expressing such disapproval. For example, Answer (*Antwoort*), representing *White Columbines*, warns the other characters that their response to the assigned topic must be:

> Embellished with reason, without blame
> Free of indignation of the emperor's placards
> Leaving in peace spiritual and secular estates.[83]

Here the emperor is compared favourably with Jupiter, Hercules, and Jason; Jupiter as a symbol of the 'coat of arms of the imperial majesty / whose power defends us all'[84] and upon which 'trade and prosperity depend.'[85] Hercules, as seen in the pillars, represents the strength and triumphs of the emperor by which he is 'always increasing his empire.'[86] Finally, with the Golden Fleece acting as a concrete symbol uniting the mythical character with the contemporary ruler (Charles V prominently wore the chain of the Order of the Golden Fleece), Peace explains how Jason portrays the emperor's pious wisdom and justice with which he rules his kingdom.[87]

To this point, Leiden's rhetoricians used their considerable knowledge of the ancient classics to heap praise upon their victorious ruler. They however conclude with an even more important analogy: the three elements of the imperial coat of arms relate also to the three persons of the divine Trinity, for Charles V's victories have come only through God's omnipotent power and faithful covenant. As illustrated by the columns, the emperor 'is firmly fixed in God'; he is 'like a lamb,' a meek judge, symbolized by the fleece which he wears. Moreover, God the Father is likened to the imperial columns, the Son to the Golden Fleece, and the Holy Spirit to the wings of the imperial eagle. The last provides divine teaching which is Charles's sole foundation, while his desire is 'only the honour of God.'[88] It seems that especially with the complete absence of any reference to traditional religious authorities, Charles V has united in himself both religious and secular functions as God's regent on earth. As with the prophetic traditions – where the emperor was to bring renewal to the church and triumph to the empire – Charles could only benefit from this transference of religious sentiment to his person.[89]

Was this the tendency of rhetoricians to praise their hereditary prince without a practical goal, or did they so enthusiastically flatter the imperial majesty to gain a better hearing for their more practical requests? It is with this question that we can return to the subject of war and peace. Although residents of the Low Countries at times viewed their native-born emperor with great fondness, they were becoming increasingly frustrated by his excessive taxation at their expense and his harsh religious policies. It can therefore be argued that Everaert and his fellow rhetorician playwrights were extremely effusive in their praise of Charles V in these plays because they wished to gain his attention. Once they had won a favourable hearing, then they could present to the authorities their rather severe criticism about the damage caused by the numerous needless wars.

Rhetoricians and Philip II

This supposition is seen quite clearly in the last play to be considered here, a play composed, in fact, not for Charles V, but for his son, Philip II, who in 1556 had just mounted the thrones of Spain and the Netherlands. At the beginning of the new year (18–23 January 1556), Philip II conducted his royal entry into Antwerp, during which the city's three official chambers performed several different plays to the delight of the dignitaries. While none of these original scripts has survived, we have the description of the performances as recorded by the deacon of The Gillyflower. According to this source, one of the chamber's plays was performed before the royal entourage at the king's residence in St

Michael's Abbey. While it was rendered in Flemish, Philip II had it translated into Spanish.[90] Moreover, The Gillyflower's play 'for the Old Crossbow Guild' was a work 'on the Peace,' entitled *Whole Man* and composed by Jan van den Berghe, which emphasized that 'peace establishes joy, but dispute hinders honour, virtue, and prosperity.'[91]

The surviving (and later published) play performed publicly by The Gillyflower for the city one month later (23 February) was therefore part of the ongoing celebrations surrounding the crowning of the new ruler and the current (and short-lived) truce in the military conflict. Most likely this was the same work previously performed before the king. Composed by Peeter de Herpener, *For King Philip our Gracious Sovereign Lord* has several dozen separate characters, each representing a specific social estate or guild of Antwerp and appearing – most passing by the audience on play-wagons – only briefly to recount their pleasure at the truce,[92] for now 'the house of trade is open again.'[93] The truce has been sent by 'God himself,' who has the hearts of princes in his hands, and the thousands who have been impoverished by the god Mars can now eat 'from all manner of tables.' Now that Mars and his henchmen are banished, the sea is safe for the precious herring fishery; merchants can return to the travel which is essential for their business, 'by which the common man shall profit'; artisans can look forward to both work and paydays, by which they can cover their rent and debts; and farmers can praise God that the pillaging of their hard won produce is now over.[94]

Although the war-induced suffering of ordinary people is now over, they are still chided for their lack of faith in the providence of God, for when faced with difficult times one should deny oneself and submit to the will of God.[95] All are happy to return to work, including those labourers, such as street workers, dock workers, carriers, packers, grain measurers, peat carriers, and the like whose livelihood depended most directly on the importation of goods, all of whom benefit from the restoration of the merchant trade.[96] The benefits trickle through all segments of Antwerp's population, so that All Joyful Artistic Spirits (*Alle vrolijcke constige gheesten*) can announce the return to the enjoyment of music, rhetoric, and archery competitions. Those responsible for the supervision of the poor can 'now sleep until noon each day,' having far fewer impoverished to care for.[97]

The play finally concludes with the maiden Gillyflower riding The Gillyflower's wagon and singing a song which not only reiterates the main points of this performance, but summarizes well the attitudes of rhetoricians toward peace and warfare. God has sent the truce into 'our prince's land,' making Mars terribly weak. In time of peace weapons of war become useless and the status of knights and mercenaries is considerably reduced in favour of those whose labours truly provide the prosperity of the land: merchants and artisans. Farmers no longer have to flee approaching armies and 'each man can now win his bread.'[98] Because labourers can now be gainfully employed, no longer will their wives be forced to earn the household income by spinning; not only was it humiliating for a sixteenth-century husband to rely on the income of his wife, but the cloth industry provided notoriously unreliable employment.[99] Finally, the end of warfare has allowed the restoration of culture; as Gillyflower intones, 'peace awakens rhetoric.'[100]

Philip II's installation as ruler of the Low Countries in 1556 marked a new stage in the history of the region. While Antwerp's rhetoricians were premature in their peace celebrations of that year, the signing of the Treaty of Cateau-Cambresis in 1559 finally brought an end to the wars between France and Spain. Netherlanders, however, were not to see the long-term benefits of peace as they and their rhetoricians had hoped. Indeed, as Herbert H. Rowan has noted, 'Even though the Low Countries played the key role, militarily and financially, in bringing the long Habsburg war against France to a triumphant close in 1559, it seemed to the Netherlanders that the benefits went to Spain while the burdens were left to them.'[101] Residents of the Netherlands, in fact, were to experience even worse conflict and devastation with the start of their eighty-year revolt against Spain beginning in the late 1560s. The Duke of Alba's oppressive regime (1567–73), which witnessed the trial of some 10,000 dissenters by the Council of Troubles as well as the horrendous slaughter of Haarlem's garrison in July 1573, provided a rallying cry for resistance against the Spanish overlord and a stirring theme for rhetorician war propaganda. Now the Spanish soldiers and their leader fulfilled the roles of Mars and his cohorts, who, like the French who had earlier played the parts, are threatened with a severe judgment.[102]

Obviously the prosperity of the Low Countries now required a war that the rebels hoped would win both political independence and economic self-determination. Earlier rhetoricians had praised their sovereign Charles V because they saw their military and financial security intimately intertwined with the peace and stability a powerful and divinely chosen emperor could maintain. They were therefore willing to preserve their devotion to their native prince while at the same time criticize his wars with France, which so hindered their anticipated affluence. However, rhetoricians did express considerable antipathy toward the emperor's religious policies and anti-heresy mandates, conflicts which would play critical roles in the beginnings of the Revolt, as Calvinists turned to the Netherlands's nobility to forge an alliance against their Spanish king. With their considerable support of a modified Reformation message (or at the very least lack of open opposition to it), rhetoricians, perhaps inadvertently, assisted the Netherlandic people to criticize their higher authorities. Although this process began with and was explicitly aimed at the ecclesiastical hierarchy, it helped train audiences across the Low Countries to reflect critically on the whole structure of authority, based as it was on the medieval understanding of secular rulers receiving their crowns at least in part at the behest of the pope or higher clergy. It seems that with Charles V's abdication and the failure of the imperial hopes and prophecies, Netherlanders became much more willing to consider other options which might lead them to their 'golden age.' Ironically, the course which they set upon directed them away from the Erasmian style pacifism of their earlier performances, perhaps illustrating that their anti-war propaganda from the start had been less one of biblical principles and more a matter of pragmatic business and social concerns.

Conclusion

Without a doubt in early modern Netherlands drama was serious business, and rhetoricians knew it. They were well aware of the potential impact of even their light-hearted farces in a period fraught with religious conflict, social tension, and political instability. Furthermore, they aimed openly to disturb the religious establishment but hoped to do so without social upheaval. On this point they shared the naivety of Martin Luther, who believed that the ramifications of his new conception of salvation and rejection of the Roman Catholic hierarchy could be contained within strictly spiritual boundaries. The German peasants, urban journeymen, and Anabaptists, among others, were to prove him wrong. Such naivety aside, it is clear from the plays examined in this study that rhetoricians had another trait in common with the German reformer – the conviction that they were illumined by the Spirit of God to interpret the Word of God to their contemporaries. This belief, developed during the fifteenth century, went hand in glove with the growing desire on the part of lay people to experience spiritual life and communion with the divine in a more immediate fashion, and was reflected in the tremendous rise of a whole host of popular religious practices. These ranged from the traditional pilgrimages, veneration of saints and their relics, purchase of indulgences, and the like, to newer developments, such as the creation of new unofficial religious orders like the Brethren of the Common Life, the establishment of lay confraternities, the funding of city preacherships, the increasing demand for the Bible in the vernacular, and, of course, the establishment of the chambers of rhetoric to promote good religious instruction as well as love of literature and drama. Along with these 'positive' aspects of popular devotion there was heard a rising chorus of cries for reform of the clergy and institutional church. Given the crises faced by the institutional church in the late Middle Ages, including its failure to stop the Black Death and the scandal surrounding the Avignon Papacy and Papal Schism, such criticism is expected of the 'intelligentsia'; what is clear from studies of popular religion in the fourteenth and fifteenth centuries is that many ordinary people also blamed the clergy for the failings of the church and immense social problems of their day. Thus the late medieval popular religious scene reflects both the 'positive' side of increased religious interest and the 'negative' aspect of anticlericalism. Above all, at least as far as the rhetoricians were concerned, was the demand on the part of urbanites for a more sophisticated and literate form of religious practice, and it is this hunger in particular that the plays and poetry of the chambers of rhetoric fed. As the sophistication of the *rederijkers'* literary activities grew, so did their self-esteem and sense of mission.

Prior to the Reformation, this hunger seems to have been at least partially satiated by drama that supported orthodox theology and religious activities. Civic leaders enthusiastically supported the chambers, and while some of the clerical hierarchy were nervous about the anticlerical tendencies of lay organizations which dabbled in the dissemination of religious knowledge, rhetoricians received widespread approval. Their early drama showed few signs of the controversies they would provoke in the sixteenth century. Based on their written works, fifteenth-century rhetoricians were certainly devout, but hateful of the hypocrisy of those religious leaders who did not live up to the rising expectations of Netherlandic urbanites. With the entry of Martin Luther's ideas and those of other reformers into the Low Countries by 1519, rhetoricians in large numbers construed their self-image as religious instructors to mean that they were as skilled and divinely inspired as orthodox priests and Protestant reformers to interpret the gospel and shape its application to the circumstances of their urban communities. Thus, even Catholic playwrights (apart from clerical authors) constructed their plays in ways that defended a traditional understanding of salvation and sacramental faith without unduly alienating reform-minded members of an audience. This could be done by virtually ignoring contentious theological issues, and/or by so highlighting a criticism of clerical abuses that reform-minded viewers could still appreciate the play. Cornelis Everaert provides a remarkable case in point, for in most of his religious plays he defended the essentials of Catholic orthodoxy while at the same time criticizing materialistic piety and clerical abuses, not surprising given his Erasmian approach to religion. It seems he too eventually sided with the reformers, if he was indeed the author of Bruges's contribution to the 1539 competition.

However, many rhetoricians composed and performed blatantly Lutheran or reformed drama during this dangerous era, revealing quite clearly the strength of support for the ideas of the mainstream reformers during the 1520s and 1530s. Luther's theology of salvation by faith alone, his priesthood of all believers and concomitant rejection of the traditional clerical elite, and his emphasis on lay people reading the Bible on their own, struck responsive chords within the urban environs of the Netherlands. Eventually many of the Netherland's reformers would side with the south German and Swiss Reformed on the contentious issues of the Lord's Supper, iconoclasm, and communal ethics, but judging from the plays examined in this study, there was no clear or sharp break between Lutheran reform and the later Calvinist. In fact, the evidence presented here reveals a strong tendency to eclecticism, to selecting reform ideas or interpretations from a variety of sources to fit into the religious culture of the Low Countries. Many rhetorician factors refused to adhere strictly to a Lutheran or Reformed orthodoxy, preferring instead to find some means to adjust the imported reform ideas of Luther to fit the unique situation of the Low Countries, or to find a compromise between Catholicism and Lutheranism, approaches quite evident in the 1539 Ghent competition.[1] In this they often sought to assuage the fears of civic leaders who were understandably concerned about the social and political impact of reform ideas in their urban centres during the reign of emperor Charles V. This helps explain the civic support received by Antwerp's rhetoricians despite their quite strong advocation of a Lutheran approach to salvation. Judging from the play that The Gillyflower performed at Ghent in 1539, this chamber maintained civic approval by using this pro-Luther play to counteract the more radical and socially dangerous opinions of Pruystinck. On the other hand, Amsterdam's rhetoricians took a more hard-nosed approach to reform, flirting briefly with more radical and Anabaptist ideas, and they suffered the consequences. Even better, of course, was to compose drama that was equivocal or enigmatical in its presentation of reform ideas, using words and phrases that at face value implied adherence to Catholic orthodoxy but which when interpreted in the context of the plot as a whole or of allusions to Scriptural references preferred by Protestants, not to mention the ad-lib asides and gestures no longer available to us, became reformist and anticlerical messages. Even though many among the audiences of public performances would not have been literate, we must not underestimate their ability to follow sophisticated and nuanced presentations of ideas, nor should we forget the importance of the visual aspects of these performances, given the widespread acquaintance with religious art and interpretation of imagery. Early modern urban audiences had also become inured, so to speak, to the presentation of rather long and often allegorical sermons, although the clamour for preachers who would preach the simple gospel in a straightforward fashion is indicative of their frustration with older sermonic models.[2]

Another approach to presenting reformist ideas without unduly attracting the ire of ecclesiastical authorities or the attention of Charles V's agents was found in spiritualism. Emphasizing the inner significance of religious beliefs and practices often to the depreciation of external observance, spiritualism could find an outward home in either Catholicism or Protestantism, and sometimes both. If precise dogma was inconsequential for salvation or membership in the divinely chosen elect, then a playwright could advocate a path to salvation that shunned the divisiveness and damage of doctrinal disputes or arguments over specific cultic practices; instead, salvation was found in the correct inner disposition of the believer and adherence to a spiritual church. In spiritualism, then, many playwrights believed they had found a means to ending the religious impasse and ensuring peace and tranquillity for their communities and businesses, while at the same time pushing for a renewal of spiritual life and a greater participation in it on the part of lay people. The popularity of this approach is attested to by a number of the plays discussed in this book, as well as by a wide range of other sources, and is revealed in the developments in the intellectual and religious life of the Netherlands later in the sixteenth century and the next, such as the rise of the Remonstrants and the Collegiant movement.[3] Over the course of the next several decades, as the Netherlands embarked on its fateful wars against Spain, rhetoricians continued to compose plays from this perspective, although whether spiritualism contributed to or blunted criticism against the policies of the higher rulers remains to be seen.[4]

This desire for a peaceful transition to a reformed religion is seen perhaps clearest of all in the plays composed on the theme of peace and warfare. During the period under study, rhetoricians not surprisingly were quite strongly on the side of peace, although they also avoided directly blaming their hereditary ruler for the many conflicts which disrupted their businesses and emptied their purses. The fact that Charles was a native Ghentenaar certainly helped them to envision their ruler as a prince who embodied justice, one who, at least compared to the French monarch, was divinely chosen. Yet that allegiance did not absolve the emperor entirely from blame for the economic and political turmoil of his reign; a number of rhetoricians chided him, indirectly of course, for the frequent debasement of currency and especially for his insistence that the oppressive religious placards be rigorously enforced and that religious dissidents be persecuted. These issues in particular, prominent in several Calvinist or reform-minded plays from the last decade or so of Charles V's reign, helped unite the diverse elements of political and religious dissidence within his realm. Judging from a number of plays written and performed after the ascension of Philip II to the Spanish and Netherlandic thrones, it appears that many rhetoricians joined the forces of discontent and used the stage to promulgate opinions openly critical of the oppressive measures taken by their overlord, especially the renewal of the heresy placards and excessive suppression of the iconoclasm of 1566.[5] And while an increasing number of playwrights also turned to classical themes (a trend which had begun by 1550 in Antwerp), leading to the golden age of Renaissance drama in the Low Countries,[6] during the second half of the sixteenth century the stage remained a central locus of reform propaganda.

Even so, rhetoricians, speaking as they were for literate urban males, adapted reform ideas to suit their specific concerns. Only rarely did they advocate radical change that would upset the relative social stability of their communes, a stability that was essential both for the performance of their literary craft and for the prosperous pursuit of their craft or merchant businesses. Therefore, in almost every play examined here, compromises were made to soften the edge of reform rhetoric. In this climate, political peace, economic growth, and religious tolerance ranked at least as high as the call for religious change. Very few rhetoricians were clergy, and thus most had a vested interest in maintaining the social and economic health of their cities, while at the same time promoting some religious change. Luther and Calvin may have regarded these accommodations to civic reality a betrayal of the gospel message, but to urbanites of the Low Countries, there was great appeal in devising a reformation that suited the needs of their world, rather than that of the German princes or the magistracy of the south German/Swiss cities. This explains why rhetoricians could provoke the ire of the later Calvinist ministers, for once again their drama sought to promote a degree of religious tolerance and adjustment to social and economic realities in the face of Reform demands for religious conformity.

Can we say that rhetorician drama was popular enough to play a significant role in making the Reformation more acceptable to the Low Countries' populace or in the emergence of an atmosphere receptive to resistance against the policies of their hereditary prince? Certainly these plays provide us with sources reflective of the attitudes of sixteenth-century literate urbanites, but were they effective as propaganda, as a means of shaping the beliefs and practices of the people who witnessed and read them? Judging from this study's material, the answer is a qualified yes. During the 1530s in both Amsterdam and Ghent rhetorician performances were linked in the minds of the authorities, justifiably or not, to popular unrest and ritual protest. Even without these obvious examples, rhetoricians were perceived by both the common citizenry and the patriciate as valued members of their communities and their drama was regarded with a greater sense of appreciation and seriousness than was that of wandering acting troupes. Civic leaders certainly believed them to be very useful in both mollifying the frustration of the lower orders of the community and presenting the commune's needs to the higher rulers. When rhetoricians stepped over the line in their enthusiastic endorsement of religious reform, city fathers proved to be extremely forgiving of their dramatists' waywardness, largely because they realized the importance of controlling dramatic presentations in their cities. It must be remembered that while the Reformation message(s) has been remembered largely as one disseminated by print, the vast majority of the populace of Europe, including the Low Countries, was illiterate or only partially literate. Oral and visual means of communication, therefore, were still central to the mobilization of popular support for any particular issue. The urban communes of the Low Countries may have been exceptional in the level of literacy of their populations, but most people still depended on others to read for and to them. Drama, therefore, with its visual splendour and comedic turns, was potentially one of the most captivating of means to propagate ideas, at least in the hands of a competent playwright and skilful chamber. Thus, the advocacy of a wide range of religious reform action on the part of many of the Low Countries' rhetoricians, and the relative silence of orthodox rhetoricians so lamented by Anna Bijns, sent an important message to Dutch urbanites that the Reformation was socially desirable and promoted by respectable citizens. Undoubtedly, it eased the transition from discussing reform ideas in the taverns to witnessing them acted out on stage and finally to adopting them in real life.

Appendix
List of Plays Composed
1515–1556

LEGEND:

Hum.# = reference number for Hummelen, *Repertorium* (who provides there the location of manuscripts, printed editions, etc.).
Type: **SvZ** = Spel van zinne; **TP** = table or dinner play; **E** = Esbattement (comedy); **K** = Kluchten (farce).

Date: ?+ = uncertain date, but most likely composed between 1515 and 1556, therefore included in calculations.
?- = uncertain date, not included in calculations but referred to in text.

Subject categories: **RC** = Orthodox Roman Catholic; **E** = Erasmian Catholic; **L** = Lutheran; **R** = Reform-minded; **C** = Calvinist; **Sp** = Spiritualist; **A** = Anabaptist; **O** = Other Religious (specified in text); **NR** = Secular theme.
Religious sub-themes: **/ac** = anticlerical sentiment; **/icon** = iconoclastic sentiment; **/ap** = antipersecution; **/m** = defence of Mary; **/p** = defence of priesthood/papacy; **/sac** = defence of seven sacraments.
Secular sub-themes: **/w** = war and peace; **/e** = economics and society; **/c** = comedy, cuckolding, etc.; **/cl** = classical; **/r** = defence of rhetorician craft.

APPENDIX

Hum.#	Short Title /Type	Author/Place	Date/Decade	Subject	Page # in Text
1 B 5	De Vigelie / **E**	C. Everaert / Bruges	1526	**E/c**	114
1 B 6	Hooghen Wynt ende Zoeten Reyn / **SvZ**	C. Everaert / Bruges	1525	**NR/w/e**	109, 188–9
1 B 8	Aragoenoysen / **SvZ**	C. Everaert / Bruges	1525	**NR/w**	188
1 B 9	Scaemel Ghemeente ende Trybulacie / **E**	C. Everaert / Bruges	1520–8	**NR/w/e**	109, 190
1 B 10	Wellecomme van den Predicaren / **SvZ**	C. Everaert / Bruges	1523	**RC/p**	108
1 B 11	Stout ende Onbescaemt / **E**	C. Everaert / Bruges	1527	**NR/c/ac**	269n22
1 B 12	Ghewillich Labuer ende Volc van Neerynghe / **SvZ**	C. Everaert / Bruges	1526	**NR/w/e**	189–90
1 B 13	De Dryakelprouver / **E**	C. Everaert / Bruges	1528	**NR/c**	269n22
1 B 14	Tspel van den Crych / **SvZ**	C. Everaert / Bruges	<1533	**NR/w**	191–2
1 B 15	Boerdelic Pleghen ende Ghenoughelic voortstel / **TP**	C. Everaert / Bruges	1526	**NR/r**	269n15
1 B 16	Tspel van Donghelycke Munte / **SvZ**	C. Everaert / Bruges	1530	**RC/e**	110–12
1 B 17	Groot Labuer ende Sober Wasdom / **SvZ**	C. Everaert / Bruges	1530	**NR/w/e**	112, 190
1 B 18	Aerm inde Buerse / **E**	C. Everaert / Veurne	1529	**NR/e**	110, 190
1 B 19	Tspel van Maria Gheleken byden Throon van Saloman / **SvZ**	C. Everaert / Veurne	1529	**RC/m**	115–16
1 B 20	Visscher / **K**	C. Everaert / Bruges	?-	**NR/c**	269n22
1 B 21	Maria Ghecompareirt byden Scepe / **SvZ**	C. Everaert / Bruges	1530	**RC/m**	115
1 B 22	Sinte Pieter Ghecompareert byder Duue / **SvZ**	C. Everaert / Veurne	1531	**RC/p**	115

APPENDIX – Continued

Hum.#	Short Title /Type	Author/Place	Date/Decade	Subject	Page # in Text
1 B 23	Maria Ghecompareert byde Stede van Jherusalem / **SvZ**	C. Everaert and Gillis vanden Houchuse / Bruges	1527	**RC/m**	115–16
1 B 26	Hoedeken van Marye / **TP**	C. Everaert / Bruges	1530	**RC/m**	115
1 B 27	De Nyeuwe Priestere / **SvZ**	C. Everaert / Bruges	1520–33	**RC/p**	114–15
1 B 28	Ghemeene Neerrynghe / **SvZ**	C. Everaert / Bruges	c.1529–30	**NR/e**	112–14
1 B 29	De Zeven Bloetsturtynghen / **E**	C. Everaert / Bruges	1530	**RC**	117
1 B 32	De Berch / **TP**	C. Everaert / Bruges	1526–38 ?+	**RC/sac**	117
1 B 33	De Wynghaert / **SvZ**	C. Everaert / Bruges	1533	**RC/p/sac**	118–19
1 B 34	Jubile / **TP**	C. Everaert / Bruges	1534	**RC/p**	114
1 B 35	Nichte / **E**	C. Everaert / Bruges	?-	**NR/c**	269n22
1 B 36	Pays / **SvZ**	C. Everaert / Bruges	1538	**NR/w**	190–1
1 D 1	Moortdadich Werck en Manhatighe Tanden / **SvZ**	Amsterdam	c.1540–51	**E, NR/w**	81, 193–5
1 D 2	Ons Lieven Heeren Minnevaer / **SvZ**	Amsterdam	c.1540–52	**R/e**	94–5, 176
1 D 3	Sint Jans Onthoofdinghe / **SvZ Biblical**	Jan Thoenisz / Amsterdam	c.1532? <1552	**R/ap**	81, 91–2, 131
1 D 4	Mennich Mensch Suect Thuijs van Vreeden / **SvZ**	Jan Thoenisz / Amsterdam	c.1532–53	**R or E/ac**	93–4, 170
1 D 5	sMenschen Sin en Verganckelijcke Schoonheit / **E**	Leiden	1546	**NR/r**	27–8

APPENDIX – Continued

Hum.#	Short Title /Type	Author/Place	Date/Decade	Subject	Page # in Text
1 D 6	De Ghepredestineerde Blinde / **SvZ Biblical**	Adriaen Jacopsz / Briel	c.1540–52	**C/ap**	177–9
1 D 7	Musijcke ende Rhetorijcke / **SvZ**	C. van Ghistele? / Antwerp?	<1553	**NR/r**	28–9
1 D 8	Naaman prinche van Syrien / **SvZ Biblical**	–	<1553 ?-	**RC**	232n42, 268n12, 303n4
1 D 9	Menschelycke Broosheit / **SvZ**	Jacob Awijts / Thoolen	1551	**E-Sp/ac**	81, 174–5
1 D 10	Een present van Godt Loondt / **TP Gift**	Frans Fraet / Antwerp	<1553	**L/ap**	74, 170–1
1 D 11	Mars en Venus / **SvZ Classical**	Smeecken / Antwerp	<1551	**NR/cl**	76
1 D 12a	Eneas en Dido 1 / **SvZ Classical**	C. van Ghistele / Antwerp	1551	**NR/cl/r/w**	76–7, 196
1 D 12b	Eneas en Dido 2 / **SvZ Classical**	C. van Ghistele / Antwerp	1552	**NR/cl/r**	76–8
1 D 13	Charon de helsche schippere / **SvZ Classical**	Antwerp?	<1551 ?+	**NR/cl**	76
1 D 14	Narcissus ende Echo	Colijn Keyart	<1552	**NR/cl**	256n133
1 D 15	Wie Voirmaels waeren de victorioste / **E**	Leiden	1552	**NR/w/ac**	197–8
1 G 1 /3A1	Dwerck der Apostolen cap.3, 4 en 5 / **SvZ Biblical**	–	<1539	**L/ac/ap**	131–3
1 G 5	De Vader die het Volck Sant / **SvZ**	Ghent	1540–56	**R/ap**	162–4, 196
1 I 1	Siecke Stadt / **SvZ**	Amsterdam	1535–8	**L/ac/ap/e**	81, 89–91, 130
1 I 2	Cristenkercke / **SvZ**	Reynier Pouwelsz / Utrecht	<1539	**L**	121–5

APPENDIX – Continued

Hum.#	Short Title /Type	Author/Place	Date/Decade	Subject	Page # in Text
1 K 2	De Bekeeringe Pauli / **SvZ Biblical**	Vilvoorde?	c.1550	**C/ac/ap/icon**	179–82
1 OA 6	De Wellustige Mensch / **SvZ**	Jan van den Berghe / Antwerp	<1551 ?+	**L/ac**	72–3, 171–2
1 OB 2	De Menschwerdinge Christi / **SvZ**	Reynier vanden Putte	1534	**RC/m/sac**	119–21
1 OB 10	Lazarus Doot / **Biblical**	Amsterdam	1530–8	**R/ap**	81, 92–3, 131, 133
1 OB 11	Piramus en Thisbe / **SvZ Classical**	Goosens ten Berch / Amsterdam	<1518 ?-	**NR/RC/cl**	80, 95–6, 255n130
1 OG 2 / 2 O4	TCloen van Armoe / **SvZ**	Jacob Jans	<1550	**NR/e**	196–7
1 OG 17	Hanneken Leckertant / **E**	Jan van den Berghe / Antwerp	1541	**NR/c**	72
1 OI 16 / 3A2	Die Menichfuldicheit des Bedrochs / **TP**	–	<1539	**Sp/ac**	125–7
1 Y 1	De Moedere ende Kinderen Zebedei / **SvZ Biblical**	Zoutleeuw?	1544	**Sp/icon**	173–4
1 Y 2	De Duerlijdende Man / **SvZ**	Jan Valcke	1543	**R**	176–7
2 O 1	sMenschen Gheest van tVleesch Verleyt / **SvZ**	Clodius Presbiter	c.1550	**Sp/RC**	75, 172–3
2 O 3	Tspel van Sinte Trudo / **SvZ?**	Christianen Fastraets / Leuven	1538–59 ?+	**RC/sac**	166–7
2 O 6	Naboth / **SvZ Biblical**	Jacob Jacobsz / Amsterdam	<1553	**R/ap**	81, 94
2 O 29	Plaijerwater / **K**	Antwerp	1500–25 ?-	**RC/ac**	268n12

APPENDIX – Continued

Hum.#	Short Title /Type	Author/Place	Date/Decade	Subject	Page # in Text
3 A 3 / 1G2	Den Boom der Schriftueren van vi personagien / **SvZ**	Middelburg	1539	**L/ac**	71, 167–70
	Ghent 1539 plays (all **SvZ***): Leffinge*				
3 B 1	Bruges	Leffinge	1539	RC	148–9
3 B 2	Meesen	Bruges	1539	L	150–3
3 B 3	Ieper	Mesen	1539	L	150–1
3 B 4	Nieuwkerke	Ypres	1539	L	150
3 B 5	Nieuwpoort	Nieuwkerke	1539	L	150
3 B 6	Tielt	Nieuwpoort	1539	L	150
3 B 7	Antwerpen	Tielt	1539	R(L/E)	153
3 B 8	Aksel	Jan van den Berghe/ Antwerp	1539	L	68–71, 149
3 B 9	Tienen	Axel	1539	O	155–6
3 B 10	Meenene	Tienen	1539	RC/ac[1]	148–9
3 B 11	Brussels	Menen	1539	**Sp/ap**	153–5
3 B 12	Caperijcke	Gijsbrecht Mercx? / Brussels	1539	L	150–2
3 B 13	Audenaarde	Kaprijke	1539	RC	148–9
3 B 14	Loo	Oudenaarde	1539	Sp	153–4
3 B 15	Kortrijk	Lo	1539	**L/ac**	150–1
3 B 16		Kortrijk	1539	**Sp/A**	153–7

APPENDIX – Concluded

Hum.#	Short Title /Type	Author/Place	Date/Decade	Subject	Page # in Text
3 B 17	Edingen	Edingen	1539	L/icon	150–1
3 B 18	Winoks-Bergen	Sint-Winoksbergen	1539	R(L/E)	153
3 B 19	Deynze	Deinze	1539	O/A/ac/ap	156
4 O 6	Spel voer den Coninck Philippus	Pieter de Herpener / Antwerp	1556	NR/w/e	199–200
4 O 8	Prochiaen, Coster en Wever / TP	Brabant?	1538–40	L/ac/icon	127–31
4 O 9	Een seer schoon spel van zinnen ghemaeckt by mijn Heer Johan Wtenhove	Johan Utenhove / Roborst	1542	L/ac	161–2

1. Anticlericalism directed only against monks.

Notes

Introduction

1 For summaries of the literature, see notes 2, 3, and 4 below. In 1987 Peter Burke announced that it 'is high time for a social history of language, a social history of speech, a social history of communication.' See Burke, 'Introduction,' in Burke and Porter, *The Social History of Language*, esp. 1.

2 For the popular Reformation, see Peter Blickle, 'The Popular Reformation,' in Brady Jr, Oberman, and Tracy, *Handbook of European History 1400–1600*, II, 161–92; and Peter Burke et al., 'Popular Religion,' in *The Oxford Encyclopedia of the Reformation*, ed. Hillerbrand, III, 295–316.

3 See esp. Scribner, *For the Sake of Simple Folk*. For the printing press and popular propaganda, see Chrisman, *Lay Culture, Learned Culture* and most recently her *Conflicting Visions of Reform*.

4 See Scribner, 'Oral Culture and the Diffusion of Reformation Ideas,' in *Popular Culture and Popular Movements in Reformation Germany*, 49–69.

5 For examples, see Ginzburg, *The Cheese and the Worms* and *The Night Battles*.

6 Kieckhefer, 'The Specific Rationality of Medieval Magic,' esp. 832–5. He argues that 'the distinction between "popular" and "elite" cultures can usefully be subordinated to a more nuanced and fluid distinction between "common tradition" and various specialized traditions; once this basic distinction is established, it becomes possible to see diverse "high" and "low" cultures as forms of specialized culture related in complex and shifting ways to common culture.' See also his *Magic in the Middle Ages*, 56–7. For general discussions of popular culture, see Burke, *Popular Culture in Early Modern Europe* and Spierenburg, *De verbroken betovering*. For the Netherlands, see Van Deursen, *Plain Lives in a Golden Age* and Boekhorst, Burke, and Frijhoff, *Cultuur en maatschappij in Nederland 1500–1850*.

7 Parente, Jr, 'Drama,' esp. 4.
8 The richest area of study so far has been England; see, for example, James, 'Ritual, Drama and Social Body in the Late Medieval English Town,' Bryant, *Tudor Drama and Religious Controversy*, Bristol, *Carnival and Theater*, Gibson, *The Theater of Devotion*, Walker, *Plays of Persuasion*, White, *Theatre and Reformation*, Crockett, *The Play of Paradox*, Blasting, 'The German *Bruderschaften* as Producers of Late Medieval Vernacular Religious Drama.' For the Germanic lands, see Jackson, 'Drama and Dialogue in the Service of the Reformation.' For the impact of humanistic Latin drama, see Parente, Jr, *Religious Drama and the Humanist Tradition*.
9 See Van Duyse, *De rederijkkamers in Nederland*. The most recent survey in English of Dutch literature and the rhetoricians' place within it is Schenkeveld, *Dutch Literature in the Age of Rembrandt*.
10 See, for example, Van Deursen, *Plain Lives in a Golden Age*, 150.
11 For the refrains, see esp., Coigneau, 'Beschouwingen over de refreinen in het zotte uit de bundel van Jan van Styevoort' and his *Refreinen in het zotte bij de rederijkers*. The famous sixteenth-century rhetorician Matthijs de Castelein wrote a manual of proper rhetorician style, *De Const van Rhetoriken* (Ghent, 1555). See Iansen, *Verkenningen in Matthijs Casteleins Const van Rhetoriken*, and Coigneau, 'Matthijs de Castelein (1485?–1550).'
12 The importance of ritual to people of the late medieval Low Countries has been discussed by Huizinga in *The Autumn of the Middle Ages*.
13 Scribner, 'Ritual and Reformation,' 143–4.
14 For exceptions, see Van Dis, *Reformatorische rederykersspelen uit de eerst helft van de zestiende eeuw*; Verduin, 'The Chambers of Rhetoric and Anabaptist Origins in the Low Countries'; Drewes, 'Het interpreteren van godsdienstige spelen van zinne'; Erné and Van Dis, *De Gentse spelen van 1539*; Waite, 'Popular Drama and Radical Religion'; Waite, 'Vernacular Drama and the Early Urban Reformation'; Waite, 'Reformers on Stage: Rhetorician Drama and Reformation Propaganda in the Netherlands of Charles V, 1519–1556'; and Waterschoot, 'De rederijkerskamers en de doorbraak van de reformatie in de Zuidelijk Nederlanden.'
15 Many examples which relate to the geographical and chronological focus of this volume will be cited below; see also E. Verheyden, *De Vilvoordse koninklijke rederijkerskamer De Goudbloem*; G. Van Keirsbilck, 'Letterkundig leven te Kaprijke in de vijftiende en zestiende eeuw'; and van den Sluijs, 'Enkele kanttekeningen met betrekking tot de Bossche rederijkerskamers.'
16 See Smits-Veldt, *Het Nederlandse renaissancetoneel*.
17 For this last theme, see esp. Degroote, *Oude klanken, nieuwe accenten*.
18 Schenkeveld-van der Dussen et al., *Nederlandse literatuur, een geschiedenis*; and Erenstein et al., *Een theatergeschiedenis der Nederlanden*.

19 For currency in the Low Countries, see Tracy, *A Financial Revolution in the Habsburg Netherlands*, 30 and 40; see also 'Appendix 1: The Coinages of Renaissance Europe, ca. 1500,' in Brady, Jr, Oberman, and Tracy, *Handbook of European History*, II, 683–90.

1: Civic Culture and Religious Reform in the Netherlands

1 Several excellent studies have appeared lately for the English theatre; for examples, see Wickham, 'The Staging of Saint Plays in England,' James, 'Ritual, Drama and Social Body,' Bristol, *Carnival and Theater*, Walker, *Plays of Persuasion*, Gibson, *The Theater of Devotion*, and White, *Theatre and Reformation*. See also the discussion by Glynne Wickham, 'Introduction: Trends in International Drama Research,' in Simon, *The Theatre of Medieval Europe*, 1–20, as well as the other contributions to this volume on English drama, esp. those by David Staines, 'The English Mystery Cycles' (80–96), David Bevington, 'Castles in the Air: The Morality Plays' (97–116), Alexandra F. Johnston, '"All the world was a stage": Records of Early English Drama' (117–29), and Stanley J. Kahrl, 'The Staging of Medieval English Plays' (130–48). For overviews of other regions also in Simon, *The Theatre of Medieval Europe*, see Alan E. Knight, 'France' (151–68), Sandro Sticca, 'Italy: Liturgy and Christocentric Spirituality' (169–88), Ronald E. Surtz, 'Spain: Catalan and Castilian Drama' (189–206), and Hansjürgen Linke, 'Germany and German-speaking Central Europe' (207–24).

2 For recent examples, see Van Autenboer, *Volksfeesten en rederijkers te Mechelen (1400–1600)*, Beyaert, *Opkomst en bloei van de Gentse rederijkerskamer Marien Theeren*, Van Boheemen and Van der Heijden, *De Delftse rederijkers, wy rapen gheneucht, De Westlandse rederijkerskamers in de 16e en 17e eeuw*, and Ramakers, *Spelen en figuren*.

3 Antwerp was chosen over its Flemish counterparts, Bruges and Ghent, despite the fact that the rhetoricians of the latter two cities could boast of an older and even more glorious history of rhetorician activity. However, socially and economically Antwerp was in the first half of the sixteenth century just reaching the apex of its glory, whereas the stars of both Bruges and Ghent had clearly waned. Therefore, while the Flemish cities' rhetoricians might have the antecedence in terms of history, Antwerp's dramatists were performing in what was clearly the most important and vibrant city in the Low Countries by the start of the sixteenth century.

4 See Van der Laan, 'De regering van Amsterdam in de 16de eeuw,' esp. 9–11.

5 Alfons Bause, 'Het historisch gebeuren,' in Couvreur et al., *Antwerpen*, 21–37, esp. 24.

6 Jan van Roey, 'De bevolking,' in Couvreur et al., *Antwerpen*, esp. 96–9 where

he estimates the city's population in 1496 at 47,000 and in 1567 at between 87,000 and 90,000. Based on a study of house and street construction in the city, Wilfrid Brulez concludes that the years between 1542 and 1560 witnessed the most dynamic growth ('De handel,' in Couvreur et al., *Antwerpen*, esp. 112–14); for the most recent discussion of Antwerp's population, see Marnef, *Antwerp in the Age of Reformation*, 5. Basic information on the history of Antwerp is also taken from Prims, *Geschiedenis van Antwerpen*, esp. vol. V.

7 Lesger, 'Tussen stagnatie en expansie,' 45–62, esp. 45.
8 See Etienne Scholliers, 'De lagere klassen. Een kwantitatieve benadering van levensstandaard in levenswijze Antwerpen in de XVI^{de} eeuw,' in Couvreur et al., *Antwerpen*, 161–80.
9 This discussion is based on Vanroelen, 'Het stadsbestuur,' in Couvreur et al., *Antwerpen*, 45–52.
10 Ibid., 51–2.
11 Brady, Jr, 'Patricians, Nobles, Merchants' and *Ruling Class, Regime, and Reformation at Strasbourg, 1520–1555.*
12 Brulez, 'De handel,' 112.
13 H. Soly, 'Economische vernieuwing,' 521; for the cost of living in Antwerp, see also Prims, *Geschiedenis van Antwerpen*, V, 194–6.
14 Soly, 'Economische vernieuwing,' 535.
15 Prims, *Geschiedenis van Antwerpen*, V, 269–72.
16 For the number of Antwerp merchants and artisans who moved to Amsterdam between 1585 and 1589, see the tables in J.G. Van Dillen, ed., *Bronnen tot de geschiedenis*, xxxiv–liv. Prior to that decade, shipping merchants of Antwerp and Amsterdam had frequently been at loggerheads. For an example of such conflict from 1547, see Dillen, *Bronnen tot de geschiedenis* I, 180 (no. 320).
17 B.J.M. Speet, 'Een stad raakt verstopt ... Ruimtelijke ontwikkelingen in Amsterdam in De Roever and Bakker, de 16e eeuw,' in *Woelige tijden*, 31–44, esp. 31–2.
18 This discussion is based on Lesger, 'Tussen stagnatie en expansie,' here p. 50.
19 Ibid., 50–7.
20 Ibid., 57.
21 Ibid., 58.
22 This discussion is based on Van der Laan, 'De regering van Amsterdam in de 16de eeuw,' esp. 13–19.
23 Ibid., 14–15.
24 Ibid., 20.

25 Burke, *Venice and Amsterdam*.

26 Burke (*Venice and Amsterdam*, 65) notes that while Venetian nobles maintained unusually frugal standards compared to their social equals elsewhere, this 'ideal of personal frugality coexisted with an emphasis on public splendour, for the honour of the family or the honour of the state.' Further on (84) Burke remarks, 'Despite their ideal of personal frugality, Venetian patricians were believers in "magnificence".' For the importance of public display, the family, and traditional aristocratic values among the nobility of the Netherlands, see Van Nierop, *Van ridders tot regenten* and Marshall, *The Dutch Gentry, 1500–1650*.

27 Burke, *Venice and Amsterdam*, 66. Unlike the extravagant robes of the Venetian nobles, for example, Amsterdam regents wore the plain black coats of businessmen. Many did, however, allow themselves luxuries such as pleasure houses in the country or sumptuous wedding feasts.

28 Brady, Jr, 'Patricians, Nobles, Merchants,' 38–45. Brady calls these processes the 'feudalization of the urban merchants' and the 'embourgeoisement of the nobility.'

29 Burke discovered, however, quite a few members living off interest income as *rentiers* by the seventeenth century.

30 See also Vanroelen 'Het stadsbestuur,' 51; Marnef, *Antwerp in the Age of Reformation*, 14–17.

31 See the list in Prims, *Geschiedenis van Antwerpen*, V, 129–32. The list does not always indicate title and the actual percentage is probably higher. It is interesting to note that some members of the Van Liers and Van Berchems, including the lord of Berchem, Cornelius van Lier, and the lady of Schilde, Anna van Etten (widow of Jan van Berchem), became patrons of the notorious heretic David Joris. Waite, 'The Dutch Nobility and Anabaptism, 1535–1545.'

32 This breaks down to 15 of 39 burgermasters and 32 of 170 *schepenen*. Another 10 per cent of *burgermeesters* and 11.8 per cent of aldermen were masters.

33 The figures are 27 of 32 mayors (plus five masters) and 66 of 267 aldermen (and a further 60 *meesteren*). For Antwerp's government, see Vanroelen, 'Het stadsbestuur,' 38–52.

34 Van Nierop, *Van ridders tot regenten*, 39, 57–62.

35 See also D'Ailly, *Zeven eeuw Amsterdam* and Van Gelder, *Amsterdam. The Golden Age, 1275–1795*. For a list of burgermasters and aldermen, see Wagenaar, *Amsterdam* III, 298–357.

36 Brugmans, *Geschiedenis van Amsterdam*, 217.

37 From the respective cities' *stadsrekeningen*: Amsterdam – Amsterdam GA,

Archief Burgemeester, mcf 6258 (Stadsrekeningen 1536–45) and Antwerp –
Antwerp SA, Rekenkamer van Antwerpen, Stadsrekeningen, R9 – 1537.
Antwerp in this year funded the performances of the city's singers and
musicians during feasts, financed several processions, and sponsored ban-
quets in honour of the peace concluded between the emperor and France,
as well as providing 12£ Fl. 8 stuivers to the city's three official chambers of
rhetoric. Amsterdam, on the other hand, restricted its much more limited
amount to the musicians and processions. For the finances of Antwerp, see
Masure, *De stadsfinances van Antwerpen, 1531–1571,* for Amsterdam and
Holland, see Tracy, *A Financial Revolution.*

38 Income was 39,594£ Fl. Expressed in relation to income, Antwerp spent .5
per cent of its income on religious and cultural festivities.

39 In that year Antwerp received 99,319£ Fl. and spent 96,280£ Fl.

40 In 1537 the surplus was only 36£ Fl., but by 1540 it was a hefty 3,000£ Fl.
and it remained approximately at that level through the decade.

41 For recent major studies, see Decavele, *De dageraad van de reformatie in
Vlaanderen (1520–1565),* and his 'Vroege reformatorische bedrijvigheid in de
grote Nederlandse steden; Trapman, 'Delenus en de Bijbel' and 'Ioannes
Sartorius'; and Ten Boom, *De reformatie in Rotterdam, 1530–1585,* esp. 76–98.
For the Anabaptists, see Mellink, 'Antwerpen als anabaptisten-centrum tot
±1550' and *De wederdopers in de Noordelijke Nederlanden;* Waite, *David Joris
and Dutch Anabaptism, 1524–1543.* For the early Calvinists, see esp. Crew,
Calvinist Preaching and Iconoclasm in the Netherlands, 1544–1569. For an excellent overview, see Duke, 'The Netherlands'; Tracy, *Holland under Habsburg
Rule, 1506–1566,* esp. 147–75. I am indebted to Dr Trapman for sending me
offprints of his articles.

42 Duke, *Reformation and Revolt,* 7.

43 See Hyma, *The Christian Renaissance* and Post, *The Modern Devotion;* see also
Oberman, *Luther: Man between God and the Devil,* 96–9, and especially
Weiler, 'Recent Historiography on the Modern Devotion: Some Debated
Questions.' I am indebted to Prof. Gerrit Gerrits of Acadia University for
this last reference.

44 Van Engen, ed. and trans., *Devotio Moderna: Basic Writings,* 10.

45 Duke, *Reformation and Revolt,* 20; for Hoen, see also Williams, *The Radical
Reformation,* 107–8. For sacramental piety in the late medieval Netherlands,
see Caspers, *De eucharistische vroomheid,* who argues that the popular devotion shown the elevated host did not necessarily reflect a strictly materialistic form of piety; instead, he suggests it could often lead to an
internalization of religious practice. See also Webber, 'Varieties of Popular
Piety Suggested by Netherlandic *Vita Christi* Prayer Cycles.'

46 Decavele, *De dageraad*, vi. Decavele sees this development as a result of the growing prosperity of this increasingly important segment of the population: 'een nijvere middenstandsklasse werd door de economische groei en de welvaart geconditioneerd voor een versnelde geestelijke emancipatie' ('an industrious middle class was conditioned by the economic growth and prosperity for an accelerated religious emancipation').

47 See esp. John van Engen, 'Late Medieval Anticlericalism: The Case of the New Devout,' in Dykema and Oberman, *Anticlericalism in Late Medieval and Early Modern Europe*, 19–52.

48 See the various essays in Dykema and Oberman, *Anticlericalism in Late Medieval and Early Modern Europe*, esp. Peter Blickle, 'Antiklerikalismus um den Vierwaldstättersee 1300–1500: Von der Kritik der Macht der Kirche' (115–32), Bob Scribner, 'Anticlericalism and the Cities' (147–66), and James D. Tracy, 'Elements of Anticlerical Sentiment in the Province of Holland under Charles V' (257–70).

49 Decavele, *De dageraad*, vi.

50 IJsewijn, 'The Coming of Humanism to the Low Countries,' esp. 200.

51 Streitman, 'The Low Countries,' esp. 77. There is also little doubt that by providing lodging for students and encouraging literacy, morality, and hard work among them, the Brothers and Sisters of the Common Life helped create a general atmosphere favourable to educational reform. At the same time James K. Cameron is undoubtedly correct when he argues that in most respects such support was more a matter of the Brothers and Sisters reacting positively to the initiatives of humanistic rectors of the city schools, and thereby helping 'to put into effect what was being advocated by others' (see Cameron, 'Humanism in the Low Countries,' esp. 139). Later humanists such as Rudolf Agricola of Groningen (1444–85) and Erasmus of Rotterdam (not to mention the German reformer Martin Luther) had early contacts with residences run by the Brothers and Sisters, although one must not make too much of childhood association with such a residence. See Strietman, 'The Low Countries,' 78, and Veldman, *Maartin van Heemskirck and Dutch Humanism in the Sixteenth Century.*

52 IJsewijn, 'The Coming of Humanism,' 223–4.

53 Ibid., 229–30, 261.

54 Strietman, 'The Low Countries,' 77–8. She notes in particular that Agricola's *De inventione dialectica* 'integrated elements present in the teaching of the schools of the Devotio Moderna, such as their *ora et labora* ethic and their emphasis on the moral values which one could glean from a reading of the Ancients, into his own strong plea for a classical education which shaped characters, moulded morals and provided insight and knowledge

in life and letters.' One should not assume, however, that Italian humanism was secular, but that its overarching emphasis was the study of *bonae litterae* for their own sake, even though many Italian humanists were also deeply concerned about church reform.

55 For a recent comprehensive biography, see Augustijn, *Erasmus: His Life, Works, and Influence.*

56 As cited by IJsewijn, 'The Coming of Humanism,' 224.

57 Cameron, 'Humanism in the Low Countries,' 143.

58 See the essays in Mostert and Demyttenaere, *De betovering van het midde-leeuwse christendom.* It must be remembered that despite this humanistic critique, late medieval religious devotion was not always materialistic or 'superstitious'; see Caspers, *De eucharistische vroomheid* and Brandenbarg, *Heilig familieleven.*

59 See Duke, *Reformation and Revolt*, 1, 4.

60 Duke, 'The Netherlands,' 142–4.

61 *CDIN*, IV, 265, 416–17; for the razing of the Antwerp house, see ibid., IV, 209, 415. See also Duke, *Reformation and Revolt*, 29–31.

62 See esp. Duke, *Reformation and Revolt*, 71, esp. n. 1.

63 Both Alastair Duke and I have described this transition in leadership of the early reform movement: Duke, *Reformation and Revolt*, 72–3, 85–7 and Waite, *David Joris*, 28–34. For a good description of the conventicles, see Duke, 'The Netherlands,' 148–53; for reform conventicles in England, see Martin, *Religious Radicals in Tudor England*, esp. 13–39.

64 Duke, 'The Netherlands,' 154.

65 Scribner, *For the Sake of Simple Folk.*

66 See Isaak, 'The Struggle for the Evangelical Town.' Responsibility for the symbolic interpretation of the Lord's Supper, which came ultimately to influence Ulrich Zwingli of Zurich, has been laid at the feet of the Dutch lawyer Cornelius Hoen, although now it is believed that the Wittenberg professor Andreas Bodenstein von Karlstadt was more likely responsible for the popular dissemination of sacramentarianism. See Duke, *Reformation and Revolt*, 20–2.

67 See especially Augustijn, 'Anabaptism in the Netherlands: Another Look.'

68 *CDIN*, V, 170.

69 *CDIN*, V, 349–50; see also Waite, *David Joris*, 52–5, and 'Een ketter en zijn stad.'

70 Duke, *Reformation and Revolt*, 10–11. According to A. den Hollander, over eighty Dutch editions of the Bible appeared between 1522 and 1545 (*De Nederlandse Bijbelvertalingen 1522–1545 / Dutch Translations of the Bible 1522–1545*, 17–26).

71 Duke, *Reformation and Revolt*, 47.

72 Ibid., 59.

73 See especially the experience of Joris, detailed in Waite, *David Joris*, 55–66, and *The Anabaptist Writings of David Joris*. For a good discussion of the rise of Anabaptism in the context of the earlier reform movements see Hamilton, 'The Development of Dutch Anabaptism in the Light of the European Magisterial and Radical Reformation.'

74 Melchior Hoffman, *Das XII Capitel des propheten Danielis aussgelegt*, as cited by Deppermann, *Melchior Hoffman: Social Unrest and Apocalyptic Visions in the Age of Reformation.*   .

75 Obbe Philips, 'A Confession,' in Williams and Mergal, *Spiritual and Anabaptist Writers*, 206–25, esp. 208.

76 See esp. Mellink, *Amsterdam en de wederdopers*.

77 Philips, 'A Confession,' 211.

78 For brief discussions in English of Hoffman's career, see Deppermann, 'Melchior Hoffman' and Packull, 'Hoffman (Hofman), Melchior.' Packull has discovered evidence that Hoffman may have been released from prison instead, in 'Melchior Hoffman – A Recanted Anabaptist in Schwäbisch-Hall?'

79 See Deppermann, 'Melchior Hoffman,' and Waite, *David Joris*, 28–46. For studies on Münster and Dutch Anabaptism, see Stayer, 'Was Dr. Kuehler's Conception of Early Dutch Anabaptism Historically Sound?'; Mellink, 'The Beginnings of Dutch Anabaptism in the Light of Recent Research'; and most recently, Klötzer, *Die Täuferherrschaft von Münster.*

80 For Oldeklooster, see Stayer, 'Oldeklooster and Menno' and Zijlstra, 'Blesdijk's verslag van de bezetting van Oldeklooster.'

81 For several years after the Münster debacle, Joris attempted to reunite the covenanter movement under his charismatic leadership, but by the time of his move to Basel in 1544 he had largely given up the attempt. See Waite, *David Joris*.

81 See also Jansma, 'Crime in the Netherlands in the Sixteenth Century' and Waite, 'From Apocalyptic Crusaders to Anabaptist Terrorists.'

83 They did, however, form a considerable minority or occasionally majority of the population of some regions or towns. See Van Deursen, *Plain Lives in a Golden Age*, esp. 304–18; for an example of a Mennonite town, see Visser, *Dat Rijp is moet eens door eygen rijpheydt vallen.*

84 Tracy, *Holland under Habsburg Rule*, 170.

85 Ibid., 172.

86 For the former, see *DAN*, esp. vol. I: *Friesland en Groningen (1530–1550)* (Leiden, 1975), vol. II: *Amsterdam, 1536–1578* (Leiden, 1980), and vol. VII: *Friesland (1551–1601) and Groningen (1538–1601)* (completed by Samme

Zijlstra, (Leiden, 1995); for the latter, see S. Cramer, ed., *Het Offer des Heeren*, in *BRN*, II; also Van Braght, *The Bloody Theatre or Martyr's Mirror*.

87 For the trials of the Davidites, especially Joris's major lieutenant, Jorien Ketel, in Deventer, see Waite, *David Joris*, 155–7; for those of Pruystinck and his followers in Antwerp (who were compromised by the testimony of Ketel), see Julius Friederichs, *De secte der Loïsten of Antwerpsche Libertijnen (1525–1545)*.

88 Duke, *Reformation and Revolt*, 71.

89 For a fascinating discussion of Nicodemism throughout Europe, see Zagorin, *Ways of Lying*.

90 Crew, *Calvinist Preaching*, 51–2; Duke, *Reformation and Revolt*, 277–8.

91 Crew, *Calvinist Preaching*, 53.

92 The first Calvinist congregation in Antwerp was established in 1555; see Marnef, *Antwerp in the Age of Reformation*, 61–72.

93 Duke, *Reformation and Revolt*, 279. See also Marnef, *Antwerp in the Age of Reformation*, 72–87; 171–210. The intense competition faced by Calvinists from the Anabaptists is also taken seriously by Marnef. Moreover, Dutch reformers continued to look to the writings of Luther, Melanchthon, and Bullinger, as well as the Reformed superintendent of East Friesland, John à Lasco. The works of a number of native Dutch writers were also thrown into the intellectual pot, not only those within the evangelical camps but also the controversial publications of spiritualists such as Joris and Hendrik Niclaes, founder of the House of Love. See Kaplan, '"Remnants of the Papal Yoke": Apathy and Opposition in the Dutch Reformation.' See also Samme Zijlstra, '"Tgeloove is vrij": De tolerantiediscussie in de Noordelijke Nederlanden tussen 1520 en 1795,' in Gijswijt-Hofstra, *Een schijn van verdraagzaamheid*, 41–67 and Waite, 'The Longevity of Spiritualistic Anabaptism: The Literary Legacy of David Joris.'

2: Rhetoricians and Urban Culture

1 Willems, 'Oorkonden van rederykkamers: 1. Pryskaerte van de rederykkamer der stad Hulst,' 12.

2 For example, see the Calvinist ministers' response as cited by Van Deursen, *Plain Lives in a Golden Age*, 152.

3 Van Es, *Een esbattement van sMenschen Sin en Verganckelijcke Schoonheit*, esp. 7–21, where he discusses the play's date and context. There is now an English translation of this play by Potter and Streitman, 'Man's Desire and Fleeting Beauty: A Sixteenth-Century Comedy.' Citations from this play here, including its title and character names, will follow the translation of Potter and Streitman.

4 Potter and Streitman, 'Man's Desire and Fleeting Beauty,' 41.

5 Ibid., 43–4.

6 'Esbatement van musijcke ende rhetorijcke welcke conste de beste es ende is
   lanck achthondert en lvi regelen,' Brussels KB 21654 (Hummelen, Repertorium van het rederijerskamers, number 1 D 7. Hereafter Hum.). The author
   is unstated, but the surviving manuscript was copied in 1553. A later parallel text is Hum. 1 P 2, 'Een spel tegen de verachters van rethorijcke en ter
   contrarie van haer aerdicheijt mitsgaders den lof van de soete musijcke en
   wije van beijden toecomt de meeste waerdicheijt dit salmen u verthoonen
   met vaerdicheijt oock de nutticheijt beijder consten verclaren en wije eerst
   haer oprichters en voorstanders waren.' Included within 'Esbatement van
   musijcke' is a presentation of Cicero's main points on the development of
   rhetorical skills: 1. *inventio*, finding the material; 2. *dispositio*, setting the nar-
   ration; 3. *elocutio*, putting words together artfully; and 4. *tropus figura
   schema*, decorating and polishing the result. The play therefore seems
   intended as a training vehicle for young rhetoricians-in-training, a point
   confirmed by the several references to 'youth' in the play, including one
   comment by an allegorical character that since youth cannot easily understand subtle ideas, he will put it simply 'for these young clerics' (fol. 14r).

7 Ibid., 4r:

> GHEESTS: Rhetorica allen wysen behueuelijc
> ouerreyniger conste en was noyt bekent
> wiens lof rijst tot aen dat firmament
> excellent is sy bouen allen die meeste
> Want sy is dochter van den heyligen gheeste
> In allen foreeste prys waerdich der crone.

8 Many Evil Hearts (*mennich quaet herte*) says at one point, ('sietmen niet
   rhetorijcke naect lopen upter straten ghemeene als sinte anthonis swynken,'
   ('Does one not commonly see rhetoric running naked upon the streets like
   St Anthony's swine?') which may simply be a reference to the public performances of rhetoricians, although it is tempting to see it as a more specific
   allusion, such as to the infamous 1535 *naaktlopers* of Amsterdam, among
   whose number was a rhetorician (see below, chapter 4).

9 'Musijcke ende rhetorijcke,' fol. 9v:

> Der Sinnen beradere gheen suethet van sange herpen ofte luyten
> mögen vermuyten rhetoricaes officie
> haer grote waerde en stercke condicie
> is met repetitie vrolijc wesens oorspronck
> Regele des leuens alder döchden tronck
> oudt ende jonck verlichtende vöchlijck
> dats haer natuere.

10 Ibid., fol. 12v.
11 Ibid., fol. 17r:

> WYSE BELEDINGE up dese fonteyne muet ghy syn stichtende
> al uwe hope ende hier in spegelen
> met tbuecxken vanden voirgaende regelen
> eer dat ghy intreedt rhetorycken foreest
> Want dese fonteyne is de heylige gheest
> van wien alle consten mildelijc vluyen.

The play's description of the fountain is reminiscent of the 'Fountain of Life' which graced David Joris's *The Wonder Book* (see illustration 6).

12 For a brief overview, see Streitman 'The Netherlands' and Nijsten, 'Feasts and Public Spectacle,' as well as Muir, 'Playing God in Medieval Europe,' Hüsken, 'Politics and Drama,' and see also Roose 'Lof van Retorica.' For the Burgundian Netherlands, see Nicholas, *Medieval Flanders* and Prevenier and Blockmans, *The Burgundian Netherlands*. For the now classic discussion of culture in the Burgundian territories, see Huizinga, *The Autumn of the Middle Ages*.

13 As elsewhere, the urban elites by and large also dominated guild leadership, so that even if guilds were represented on city councils, the interests of the ordinary artisans were not always well served. For an example of this process, see Brady, Jr, *Ruling Class, Regime, and Reformation at Strasbourg*. For an excellent overview of urban society in early modern Europe, see Friedrichs, *The Early Modern City, 1450–1750*.

14 A good introduction is Prevenier and Blockmans, *Burgundian Netherlands*.

15 See especially Pleij, *Het Gilde van de Blauwe Schuit* and most recently his 'Inleiding: op belofte van profijt,' in Pleij et al., *Op belofte van profijt*, 8–51, as well as the other essays in this volume.

16 Pleij, *Het Literaire leven in de middeleeuwen*, 67–8.

17 Most examples of late-medieval and renaissance art served a functional purpose, whether as a memorial of the patron, an encouragement of morality, a heightening of religious devotion, or as a warning against civic disobedience. As noted by Michael Baxandall for Renaissance Italy, 'in the fifteenth century painting was still too important to be left to the painters' (Baxandall, *Painting and Experience in Fifteenth-Century Italy*, 3).

18 Scribner, 'Ritual and Reformation,' 125.

19 See esp. Ramakers, *Spelen en figuren*, 93–166. According to G. Kalff, by the end of the century several independent drama societies had been established in order to produce the increasingly complex carnival plays, often performed on wagons. As an example he refers to the situation of Oudenburch, near Bruges, where in 1406 the local priest was assisted by 'the

clerics of the church and other fellows (*ghesellen*) performed the play' (Kalff, *Geschiedenis der Nederlandsche letterkunde*, II, 77–8). For the early religious drama in the Low Countries, see also W.N.M. Hüsken, '1391–1392. In Dendermonde wordt tijdens de Paasdagen een verrijzenisspel gespeeld. Kerkelijk drama in de volkstaal,' in Erenstein et al., *Een theatergeschiedenis der Nederlanden*, 24–9. For an example of the institutional similarities between *rederijkerskamers* and confraternities in the Low Countries, see Van der Meersch, 'Kronyk der rederykkamers van Audenaerde.' For confraternities and drama, see also Blasting, 'The German *Bruderschaften*.' See also the rest of the essays in this volume of *Renaissance and Reformation / Renaissance et Réforme* (25 [1989]), especially Dieterich, 'Confraternities and Lay Leadership in Sixteenth-Century Liège,' Douglas, 'Midsummer in Salisbury,' and Roberts, 'Cornelis Buys the Elder's *Seven Works of Mercy*.' For civic communities and drama in general, see Knight, 'Drama and Society in Late Medieval Flanders and Picardy' and James, 'Ritual, Drama and Social Body.' See also the comments of Rothkrug, 'Holy Shrines, Religious Dissonance and Satan in the Origins of the German Reformation.'

20 Kalff, *Geschiedenis der Nederlandsche letterkunde* II, 79–80, and Ramakers, *Spelen en figuren*, 5–42. For the rhetoricians and religious plays and processions, see also Nijsten, 'Feasts and Public Spectacle,' esp. 115–21.

21 H. de Keyser, 'Het ontstaan en de werkzaamheden van de Brusselse rederijkerskamers tussen 1400 en 1500,' esp. 65. It is possible that this was the oldest chamber in Brabant.

22 Antonis van Elslander identified 185 chambers as in existence by the end of the sixteenth century (in 127 different communities); see his 'Lijst van Nederlandse rederijkerskamers uit de XVe en XVIe eeuw.'

23 Haeserijn, 'Oorspronck der cameren van rethorijcke,' esp. 39.

24 Ibid., 31. The fifteen men chosen were bound 'inden goddelijcken dienst ende in die edel conste van Rethorijcken' ('in the divine worship and in the noble art of rhetoric') for life, or for as long as they lived in Ghent.

25 'Iegelyck sal hem vermyden eenige spelen lieckens ofte Refereynen te componeeren oft pronuncieren tegen het Catholieck Geloof nog eennige andere onbehoorlycke lasteringen oft schimpen, waer toe den Prince van de Personagiën ende den Facteur toesicht sullen nemen die niet en sullen toe laeten datter jet int minste gemaeckt, gescreven oft gepubliceert en worde ten sy dat't selfte sy gevisiteert by de ordenarise visitateurs ende toegelaeten' (Van der Straelen, *Geschiedenis der Antwerpsche rederijkkamers*, 5).

26 Based on the level of fines, it appears to have been a worse offence to create

a disturbance among the 'brotherhood' (*confrerie*), for each such occurrence netted twenty stuivers and continuation of such disruption led to dismissal from the chamber. What is perhaps even more telling is the punishment exacted to a member who had actually slandered, publicly or secretly, fellow rhetoricians or other chambers of rhetoric; this extremely serious offence merited a severe fine of ten guilders and expulsion from The Gillyflower. 'Niemant tzy Facteur of Componisten sal mogen maken op eenige persoonen schimpen oft lasteringen noch op eenige Cambers van Retorycken in geender manieren tzy in heymelyck often openbaer' (ibid., 7).

27 See in particular Pleij, 'Geladen vermaak.' See also Kernodle, *From Art to Theatre*. Kernodle (52) remarks of a ruler gazing on a *tableau vivant*: 'For that moment a historical picture or an allegorical group impressed him with the ancient glory of the city, with its genuine loyalty, and with its hopes for the future clemency, as well as the future glory, of the ruler.'

28 This is one suggestion for the obscure origin of the Delft chamber, The Sweet Name of Jesus, later known by its motto, 'Wy rapen gheneucht' ('we glean pleasure'); see Van Boheemen and Van der Heijden, *De Delftse rederijkers*, 21. For militia competitions and drama, see Dirk Coigneau, '1 februari 1404. De Mechelse voetboogschutters schrijven een wedstrijd uit. Stedelijke toneelwedstrijden in de vijftiende en zestiende eeuw,' in Erenstein, *Een theatergeschiedenis der Nederlanden*, 30–5.

29 Vandecasteele, 'De Haagse rederijkerskamer "Met Ghenuchten" in 1494,' esp. 126 and 139.

30 Van Boeckel and Van Boeckel, 'Landjuwelen en haagspelen in de XVᵉ en de XVIᵉ eeuw,' 6: 'ende oick om eendrachfigheid, vrintscap ende minne tusschen de ... steden en vryheden te voedene, vermeerderene ende tonderhoudene.' In the fourteenth and fifteenth centuries militia guilds, whether the original archers,' crossbowmen's, or halberds' guilds or the later marksmen or 'shooters' guilds (*schuttersgilden*), competed not only in marksmanship, but also in costumes, music, and drama. It was in the militia competitions that the term *Landjuwelen* originated, a term later applied to certain major competitions of rhetoricians

31 Haeserijn, 'Oorspronck der cameren van rethorijcke.'

32 Meijer, *Literature of the Low Countries*, 49–50, remarks: 'Interested in unification as they were, they [i.e., the Burgundians] realized that these Chambers of Rhetoric could play a part in their policies. They therefore approved wholeheartedly of the literary festivals which the Chambers organized and which, in days of little inter-provincial traffic, drew large crowds from various parts of the country.' Ghent was the capital city of Flanders. In their

account books (*stadsrekeningen*), the Oudenaarde magistrates justified the financing of the Oudenaarde *rederijkers'* trip to the 1539 Ghent competition in these words: 'ter eeren deser stede [i.e., Oudenaarde] Ende omme de stede van ghendt als hoift stadt vanden Landen van Vlaenderen te eerne' ('to honour this city and in order to honour the city of Ghent as head city of the Lands of Flanders'). See Waterschoot, 'De Oudenaardse rederijkers te Gent in 1539,' 19. That the statutes of the Burgundian head chamber were renewed by Philip's Habsburg successors Emperor Maximilian I and Archduke Charles (later Emperor Charles V) in 1512 lends weight to this interpretation of the political motivation for the establishment of *Jesus with the Balsam Flower.*

33 Prevenier and Blockmans, *Burgundian Netherlands,* 10.
34 For general discussions of the chambers, see Worp, *Drama en Tooneel,* and Kalff, *Geschiedenis der Nederlandsche Letterkunde,* II–III. For studies in English, see Meijer, *Literature of the Low Countries,* Knight, 'Drama and Society,' Gibson, 'Artists and Rederijkers in the Age of Bruegel,' Hummelen, 'Types and Methods of the Dutch Rhetoricians' Theatre,' Van Dijk et al., 'A Survey of Dutch drama Before the Renaissance,' and Strietman, 'Teach Yourself Art: The Literary Guilds in the Low Countries.'
35 They were often used for serious political events. See W.N.M. Hüsken, '1 augustus 1541. De klucht *Tielebuys* van Willem Vrancx wordt als welkomstspel gespeeld op het landjuweel van Diest. De kluchtentraditie in de Nederlanden,' in Erenstein, *Een theatergeschiedenis der Nederlanden,* 106–11. For some examples, see Van Vloten, *Het Nederlandsche kluchtspel van de 14ᵉ to de 18ᵉ eeuw,* Lyna and Van Eegham, *De sotslach: Klucht uit ca. 1550,* Van der Laan, *Uit het Archief der Pellicanisten,* Mak, *Vier excellente kluchten,* and the following editions by C. Kruyskamp: 'De klucht van Koster Johannes,' 'Het esbatement vant Gelt,' and 'Het spel van het Cloen van Armoe.' For an example of a sixteenth-century farce translated into English, see Van Dijk et al., 'Plaijerwater: A Sixteenth-century Farce with an English Translation.'
36 The best study of the dinner play is Pikhaus, *Het tafelspel bij de rederijkers.* For examples, see also Willems, 'Tafelspelen' and Lammerns-Pikhaus, 'Het tafelspel van een man en een wachter.'
37 See esp. Ramakers, *Spelen en figuren.*
38 See esp. Pleij, 'Van keikoppen en droge jonkers.' See also chapter 6 below.
39 For these competitions, especially those of Brabant, called '*landjuweels,*' see Steenbergen, *Het landjuweel van de rederijkers.*
40 See Paul de Keyser, 'De Prinsen, de Koningen en de Keizers bij de rederijkers.'
41 See Puts, 'Geschiedenis van de Antwerpse rederijkerskamer De Goud-

bloem,' esp. 10–11. A handwritten copy of the original is in Antwerp, SA
PK2902, Van Grimbergen, St. Lucasgilde en rederykkamers.

42 For an example, see the biblical play about Naaman, edited by Hummelen
and Schmidt, *Naaman, Prinche van Sijrien. Een rederijkersspel uit de zestiende
eeuw.* The contents of this play, copied by the Amsterdam rhetorician Reyer
Gheurtz around 1553, do not make any reference to the religious controversies of the Reformation, and so it was likely composed just prior to the Reformation.

43 Noted by Van Boheemen and Van der Heijden, *De Westlandse rederijkerskamers,* 16.

44 For a detailed analysis of these charters, see Ramakers, *Spelen en figuren,* 93–
121; see also Dirk Coigneau, '9 December 1448. De statuten van rederijkerskamer De Fonteine worden officieel erkend door de stad Gent. Rechten en
plicthen van spelende gezellen,' in Erenstein, *Een theatergeschiedenis der
Nederlanden,* 50–5. Chamber ordinances from other southern Netherlandic
cities are very similar in tone and content to The Gillyflower's. For example, on 17 August 1482, the Lord of Hasselt in Limbourg, Willem de Corte,
formally issued the letter of foundation of the Hasselt chamber of rhetoric,
The Red Rose (*De Roode Roos*), under the patronage of St Kathleen (*St.
Kathelinen*), the patron saint of rhetoric. This chamber was instituted for the
benefit of 'diverse good men andyouth of our domain' to promote among
them 'good will, great affection, affectionate desires, joy (*jonst*) and friendly
accord,' as well as to the support and increase of the 'noble art of rhetoric.'
The result was to be an affectionate brotherhood that would bring greater
honour to God and St Kathelinen. Hasselt's smaller chamber was to be
governed only by one deacon and two jurors (*ghezwoerne*); presumably the
Lord of Hasselt was to be the permanent patron or prince. Entrance and
yearly fees were more modest than for Antwerp's The Gillyflower, reflecting the difference in size and prosperity of the two communities. See
Willems, 'Oorkonden van rederykkamers,' 418–23. See also the ordinance
uniting Veere's two chambers into Sending Pupils (*Missus scholieren*) in
1530, in Kops, *Schets eener geschiedenisse der rederijkeren,* appendix B, 331–8,
and the 1494 charter of The Hague's With Delight, in Vandecasteele, 'De
Haagse rederijkerskamer,' esp. 129–33.

45 'Ordonnantie gemaeckt tot conservatie ende onderhoudinge van de Gulde
van de Violieren gevoecht by de Gulde van Sinte Lucas int' Jaer XIII^c
LXXX,' in Van der Straelen, *Geschiedenis der Antwerpsche,* 2–10.

46 See also De Keyser, 'Bijdrage tot de blazoenkunde van de rederijkerskamers.'

47 Likewise, the election of the deacons and elders was to occur one month

prior to St Luke's Day, as was that of the *Busmeesters*, who managed the chamber's poor box for the benefit of any members who had fallen upon hard times. The deacon was responsible for the ordinary finances of the chamber and ensuring that all members had paid their fees and expenses before completion of his term. Unlike the case with most rhetorician societies, The Gillyflower's deacons performed double duty, for they were also St Luke's deacons. Within one month of election, the deacons were to check the chamber's financial accounts.

48 'Niemant en sal mogen aengenomen woirden in deser gulde, dan met gemeynen advyse van den Hooftman, Prince, Dekens, en Ouders die den eedt doen sullen op der voorscreven gulde camer ende elders niet' ('No one shall be received into this guild except with the common consent of the captain, prince, deacons, and elders, and he shall give the oath in the aforementioned guild chamber, and nowhere else') (Van der Straelen, *Geschiedenis der Antwerpsche rederijkkamers*, 3).

49 Haeserijn, 'Oorspronck der cameren,' 39: 'Zoo eyst dat wij . vut der macht . ende auctoriteyt ons ghenadichs conijncx voornoumt tghetal van desen onsen voors' medebroeders oud ende jonc . los ontheffen ende bevrijdt stellen . van allen gulden broederscepen ende ghezelscepen . Om daer af nemmermeer te dienene.'

50 'De persoonen die in andere eeden syn, aengenomen woirdende in dese Gulde als vrypersoonen oft liefhebbers, en sullen niet gehouden syn eenen anderen eedt te doen oft oock in eenige subjectien, breuken, noch eenige officie te bedienen, dan sullen gestaen met hun incomgelt ende jaercosten dies en sullen sy oock niet gerekent woirden in den nomber van de gepriviligierde der selve Gulde' ('The persons who are [bound] by another oath, being received into this guild as associates or amateurs, shall not be held to give another oath or to serve in any subject, service, or any office, then shall they keep their pledge with their fees and yearly costs and they shall not be reckoned among the number of the privileged of the same guild'). (Van der Straelen, *Geschiedenis der Antwerpsche rederijkkamers*, 3).

51 If the deacon was informed in advance that a member could not attend for reasons of illness or absence from the city, only two guilders were due.

52 'Item alsser publicque vergaderingen op de camer syn, en sal niemant mogen aldaer spreken van coopmanschappen, weddingen lotteryen, noch oock spelen met caertspel in teerlingen, noch oock onbehoorlyck gerucht maecken alsser eennich spel geproeft oft gespeelt wort op de pene van sesse stuyvers' (Van der Straelen, *Geschiedenis der Antwerpsche rederijkkamers*, 7).

53 'De Personagien sullen gehouden wesen, te spelen alsulcken rollen, as hun

lieder gegeuen sullen worden by den Prince van de Personagien ende Facteur sonder eennighe contradictie.' The fine for disobeying this injunction
was two guilders. Before leaving the city, guild members were required to
ensure that all of their debts had first been paid, presumably in case the
traveller fell to one of the many hazards of the road. In such a case the guild
would organize and publicize the funeral among the members, whose
attendance was required. Those who missed the service would be fined ten
stuivers (more for the leaders) and the family tipped the messenger twenty
stuivers. If a member on his deathbed desired a guild burial, the messenger
would bring the request to the family, who would then supply fifteen guilders for the service, plus the usual tip to the messenger (Van der Straelen,
Geschiedenis der Antwerpsche rederijkkamers, 8).

54 Kops, *Schets eener geschiedenisse der rederijkeren*, 334.
55 Van Autenboer, *Volksfeesten en redeijkers*; see also his 'Organisties en
   stedelijke cultuurformen 15de en 16de eeuw.'
56 Davis, 'Strikes and Salvation at Lyon,' in her *Society and Culture in Early
   Modern France*, 1–16; for the various levels of literacy among artisans, see
   also her 'Printing and the People,' ibid., 189–226, esp. 209–11.
57 Gibson, 'Artists and Rederijkers,' 426–6.
58 Veere's charter of 1530 specified in fact that: 'Item no one of the society will
   bring other persons into the chamber during a meeting, except by consent
   of deacons and the members gathered there, nor also any women, being
   honourable wives or maidens, who also perform in plays, upon the correction of the deacons and common members.' ('Item nyemant van den
   geselscape en sal andere parsoen bringen in de Camere als zij vergadert
   zijn, dan bij Consente van Dekens ende der gesellen daer int zijnde, noch
   eeneghe Vrouwen ten waeren eerbaer Vrouwen oft maeghdekens, die mede
   in spelen speelden, op gecorrigeert te zijn van Dekens en gemeen gesellen.')
   Kops, *Schets eener geschiedenisie der redeijkeren*, 334. For some evidence that
   some chambers allowed a few women members, see Willems, 'Oorkonden
   van rederykkamers,' 421; Van Autenboer, *Volksfeesten en rederijkers*, 162;
   Vandecasteele, 'De Haagse rederijkerskamer,' 135 and 141 (for rhetorician
   confraternities); and Prevenier and Blockmans, *Burgundian Netherlands*,
   305.
59 This is the conclusion of Van Autenboer, *Volksfeesten en rederijkers*, 162. For a
   preliminary discussion of the depiction of women and gender relations in
   rhetorician plays, see Gastelaars, *Ic sal u smiten op uwen tant*; for the theme
   of love, see Coigneau, 'Liefde en lichaamsbeleving op het rederijkerstoneel,' and Van Gijsen, *Liefde, kosmos en verbeelding mens- en wereldbeeld in
   Colijn van Rijssels Spiegel der Minnen*. The subject of the depiction of women

and marriage in rhetorician plays is a vast one deserving of its own monograph. There will be no attempt to deal with the subject here.

60 See Van Autenboer, 'Organisaties en stedelijke cultuurvormen,' 148. For the classic discussion of the differences between popular and elite cultures, see Burke, *Popular Culture in Early Modern Europe*.

61 See Sterck, 'Onder Amsterdamsche humanisten,' 296, and Pleij, 'De laatmiddeleeuwse rederijkersliteratuur als vroeg-humanistische overtuigingskunst.'

62 As cited by Beuken, *Die Eerste Bliscap van Maria en Die Sevenste Bliscap van Onser Vrouwen*, 7. The dominance of religious subject matter in fifteenth- and sixteenth-century painting is true even for the relatively 'secular' society of Italy; Peter Burke notes: 'A sample study suggests that the proportion of Italian paintings that were secular in subject rose from about 5 per cent in the 1420s to about 20 per cent in the 1520s. In this case, "secularization" only means that the minority of secular pictures grew somewhat larger' (Burke, *The Italian Renaissance*, 23).

63 'Wat de meeste mistery ofte gratie was die Godt verleent of geordoneert heeft tot de mensche salicheyt?' (Torfs, *Feestalbum van Antwerpen*, 24). On this competition, see Vandecasteele, 'Het Antwerpse rederijkersfeest van 1496: een onderzoek der bronnen.'

64 Other reports had it as 'door de ontfanckenisse der menscherlijcker naturen in Maria' (Van der Straelen, *Geschiedenis der Antwerpsche rederijkkamers*, 13–17, and Bertrijn, *Chronijck der stad Antwerpen*, 58).

65 See Ramakers, *Spelen en figuren*, 27–42.

66 See Spies, '"Op de questye ...": Over de structuur van 16e-eeuwse zinnespelen.'

67 Forster, 'Literary Relations between the Low Countries, England and Germany, 1400–1624,' esp. 16; the most recent and balanced treatment of cross-channel dramatic and literary influences is Johnston, 'The Continental Connection: A Reconsideration.' It still seems evident that *Elckerlijc* was reworked into English as *Everyman*. For relations between the Low Countries and England, see also Barron and Saul, *England and the Low Countries in the Late Middle Ages*, esp. Barron, 'Introduction: England and the Low Countries c. 1400,' 1–28; Sutton and Visser-Fuchs, 'Choosing a Book in Late Fifteenth-century England and Burgundy,' 61–98; and Johnston, 'Traders and Playmakers: English Guildsmen and the Low Countries.'

68 For English mystery plays, see Happé, *English Mystery Plays: A Selection* and Cawley, *Everyman and Medieval Miracle Plays*. For the many French plays, see Muir, 'The Saint Play in Medieval France,' in Davidson, *The Saint Play in Medieval Europe*, 123–80; and Knight, 'France,' in Simon, *The Theatre*

of Medieval Europe, 151–68. For Europe as a whole, see Muir, *The Biblical Drama of Medieval Europe*. For the Low Countries, see Hummelen, 'The Biblical Plays of the Rhetoricians and the Pageants of Oudenaarde and Lille.' Unlike the case for England and France, however, no Dutch mystery play cycles have survived, suggesting that the massive productions of the entire history of salvation which were put on in many English towns – often taking several days to perform – were not a familiar sight in the Netherlands. For Corpus Christi and rhetoricians, see Ramakers, *Spelen en figuren*.

69 For the first two, see the edition and comments by Beuken, *Die eerste bliscap*; for the last, Hoebeke, *Het spel van de V vroede ende van de V dwaeze maegden*. For other late-medieval Dutch plays, see Van der Heijden, *Hoort wat men u spelen zal*.

70 Ramakers, '5 mei 1448. Begin van de traditie van de jaarlijkse opvoering van een van de zeven *Bliscappen* in Brussel. Toneel en processies in de late middeleeuwen,' in Erenstein, *Een theatergeschiedenis der Nederlanden*, 42–9. In 1485, in fact, the actors performed this work twice, once for the people of Brussels and the other for a meeting of the States General (Beuken, *Die eerste bliscap*, 11–12). Performances of the seven joys, along with those on the seven woes of Mary, were typically performed during her feast days, perhaps on processional wagons. Again Beuken notes that on 19 February 1448, Brussels's magistrates ordered the performance of *The First Joy of Mary* to take place at two in the afternoon on the day of the procession in honour of the Virgin in the city's lower market (*nedermerct*). The following year the dramatists would perform *The Second Joy of Mary* and continue in this manner until the seven joys had been portrayed. Then they would return to the first.

71 See also Rubin, *Corpus Christi. The Eucharist in Late Medieval Culture*, esp. 286–7. For saint plays in Europe, see, among others, Wickham, 'The Staging of Saint Plays in England,' and the essays in Davidson, *The Saint Play in Medieval Europe*.

72 Beuken, *Mariken van Nieumeghan*; see also Van Dijk, 'Mariken van Nieumeghen'; Raftery, *Mary of Nemmegen*; Decker and Walsh, *Mariken van Nieumeghen: A Bilingual Edition*; Coigneau, *Mariken van Nieumeghen*; Herman Pleij, 'Omstreeks 1515. De Antwerpse drukker Willem Vorsterman brengt een slordige druk uit van de *Mariken van Nieumeghen*. Drukpers en toneel,' in Erenstein, *Een theatergeschiednis der Nederlanden*, 86–91. Witchcraft was regarded as the most heinous of crimes, as a *crimen exceptum*. For witchcraft beliefs and prosecution in the Low Countries, see Gijswijt-Hofstra and Frijhoff, *Witchcraft in the Netherlands from the Fourteenth to the Twentieth Century*. For the devil in rhetorician drama, see Herman Pleij,

'24 juni 1500. Spectaculaire duivelscènes domineren de opvoering van het mirakelspel *Vanden heilighen sacramente vander Nyeuwervaert* in Breda. De duivel in het middeleeuwse drama en op het toneel,' in Erenstein, *Een theatergeschiedenis der Nederlanden*, 64–9.

73 See, for example, Waterschoot, *Het esbatement van den Appelboom*. Note also Meertens, 'Het esbatement van de Appelboom. Een volksvertelsel omgewerkt tot esbatement.'

74 R.A. Potter, 'Morality Play and *Spel van Sinne*: What are the Connections?' esp. 10. For English moralities, see Fifield, 'Methods and Modes: The Application of Genre Theory to Descriptions of Moral Plays.'

75 Hummelen, 'The Dramatic Structure of the Dutch Morality,' 17; see also his *De Sinnekens in het Rederijkersdrama* as well as Spies, '"Op de questye ..."'

76 Hoebeke, *Het spel van de V vrode ende van de V dwaeze maegden*, 14.

77 In this way, the *sinnekens* had come to represent a 'spiritualized' or internalized devil, in some respects similar to the spiritualization of the devil in the hands of David Joris. See Waite, '"Man is a Devil to Himself": David Joris and the Rise of a Sceptical Tradition towards the Devil in the Early Modern Netherlands, 1540–1600.'

78 Hummelen, 'The Dramatic Structure,' 17.

79 There is a parallel to this in the function of the Vices in Tudor drama, where, as Paul White and others note, 'laughter evoked by the Vices in Tudor homiletic drama is a means of implicating and involving the audience in the very experience of temptation and corruption the protagonist undergoes' (White, *Theatre and Reformation*, 85).

80 Scharpé, 'De Rovere's spel van Quiconque vult salvus esse,' esp. 155; Hum.1B1. For more on De Rovere and his literary corpus, see Oosterman, 'Anthonis de Roovere. Het werk: overlevering, toeschrijving en plaatsbepaling' and Westgeest, 'Zeven verborgen Marialoven van Anthonis de Roovere.'

81 Part of the argument, naturally, involves the typical accusation that the Jews were the killers of Christ (interestingly, De Roovere has Heathen making the charge, to which Christian assents). Jew responds by affirming that his people still fervently await the coming of the Messiah, and that Christians 'lept too early.' For example, when he first appears, Half Zot Half Vroet remarks to the audience:

Wat sallic hier vut mercken
Die Half Sot Half Vroet gheheeten bin?
Sy staen en cabbelen recht meer noch min
Al waerent harync kutseghen ter maerdt.
Wat gheist elc vuust loock onghespaert.

Godt zal den ongheluckeghen scenden.
Heyden en Jeuden zynt anders dan blenden?
Sy staen hier en stryden omde meesterye! (Scharpé, 'De Rovere's spel,'
    161, ll. 143–5).
Jew responds that the Christians 'te vrouch ontsprongen' ('lept too early')
(ibid., 162, l.164); at this the fool jumps in and expostulates to the audience,
'ende ghy slaept te langghe ghy Jeude jonghen. / Dus es hu beyden al
verlooren' ('and you slept too long you Jewish youth / thus it is all lost to
both of you') (ibid., 162, ll. 165–6).

82   Dat zy van Xpristus de naeme voeren
    Ende niet meer vp zyn lachter en roeren.
    Want zy laten onslieden wuenen met vreden
    Daer Xpristus zyn passie heift gheleden
    Maer selue slaen zy elc andren doot
    Als wulfuen de scapen (ibid., 178, ll. 460–5).

83   Dies muecht ghy hu wel scaemen claer
    Ghy wouckeraers wisselaers die talder tyt
    Blyft jn openbaer sonden vermalendyt
    Ghy vervooppers ghy groote fynanchieren
    Die ghemeenen weluaert doet faylgieren
    Met vutwendegher aercheyt openbare!
    Godt roupt hu zo menichwaerf binden jaere
    Met predicacien met zoeten vermaene,
    Hoe meent ghy toordeel Gods tontghaene
    Ende ghy hu openbaer leuen quaet
    Met sinte Matheeus nit of en ghaet?
    Ghelooft ghy wel dats wonder groot (ibid., 180, ll. 519–30).

84 Ibid., 184–5.

85 Ibid., 190–3.

86 *Elckerlijc*, translated by Barnouw as *The Mirror of Salvation, A Moral Play of
    Everyman c1490* (1971). Several editions of the original Dutch edition have
    been produced: Vos, *Den spieghel der salicheit van Elckerlijc* (1925); Van
    Mierlo, *Elckerlijc. Nieuwe bijdragen met ge-emendeerde uitgave* (1949); and
    Endepols, *Den Spyeghel der Salicheyt van Elckerlijc* (1955). For the priority of
    Elckerlijc over *Everyman*, see the comments by Barnouw, *Mirror of Salvation*,
    xvi. According to Barnouw, the work was first performed at an Antwerp
    landjuweel in the last decade of the fifteenth century; he suggests the 1496
    Antwerp competition referred to above. If this is the correct historical con-
    text for the first performance of *Everyman*, then it was composed in
    response to the contest's question: 'What is the greatest mystery or grace
    ordained by God for the blessedness of humanity?'

87 Death brings the summons to Everyman, whose attempts to bribe the messenger are quickly spurned in terms which must have been familiar to an audience still preoccupied with the 'dance of death.' Death responds:

I spare neither count, duke, nor king.
Nor pope, as God commandeth me.
If I with bribes could tempted be,
All the world's wealth would be mine in the end.
All must with me contend,
And none from me obtains a stay (Barnouw, *Mirror of Salvation*, 5).

For the dance of death in Burgundian art and literature, see Huizinga, *The Autumn of the Middle Ages*; also Grijp, Tamboer, and Hoek, *De dodendans in de kunsten*; and the late medieval 'ars moriendi,' edited by Geus et al., *Een scone leeringe om salich te sterven*.

88 Barnouw, *Mirror of Salvation,* 35–6, ll. 676–86, 696–703, 708–12.

89 Ibid., 37, ll. 730–2.

3: The Chambers of Rhetoric in Antwerp

1 For studies of literature and drama in Antwerp during the sixteenth century, see Van Ertborn, *Geschiedkundige aenteekeningen aengaende de Ste Lucas Gilde*; Donnet, *Het jonstich versaen der Violieren*; Prims, 'Cultuurwaaden en cultuurtekorten te Antwerpen in de eerste helft van de XVIe eeuw'; Lode Roose, 'De letterkunde,' in Couvreur et al., *Antwerpen in de XVI^{de} Eeuw*, 321–48; Puts, 'Geschiedenis van de Antwerpse rederijkerskamer'; Keersmaekers, 'De rederijkerskamers te Antwerpen'; and Marnef, *Antwerp in the Age of Reformation*, 29–33.

2 All extant volumes of the Antwerp Treasurer's books (Antwerp SA Stadsrekeningen, R7–13) from 1530 to 1550 refer several times to funds provided to these three chambers. Surviving volumes cover the years 1530–1, 1536–8, 1542–3, and 1549–50. For sources relating to all three, see Van der Straelen, *Geschiedenis der Antwerpsche rederijkerskamers*. See also Keersmaekers, 'De Rederijkerskamers te Antwerpen,' and Puts, 'Geschiedenis van de Antwerpse rederijkerskamer,' esp. 5–15.

3 Van der Straelen, *Jaerboek der St. Lucas gilde*, 1, cites a document which suggests the guild was in existence already in 1382.

4 'Dit jaer wonnen onse guldebruers dland juweel te Lovene, ij silveren scalen voir den hoochsten prys, daer Heer Jan de Buysenere, Ridder, als prince was. Doen wort onser camer geordineert de Violier bloeme metten woorde: Wt jonsten versaemt.' Rombouts and Van Lerius, *De liggeren en andere historische archieven der Antwerpsche Sint Lucas gilde*, I, 31. See also Van der Straelen, *Jaerboek der St. Lucas gilde*, 24.

5 Van der Straelen, *Jaerboek der St. Lucas gilde*, 35.

6 Van der Straelen, *Geschiedenis der Antwerpsche rederijkkamers*, 10. As Alan Knight has noted, the considerable financial support provided by civic magistrates for rhetorician contests shows that 'these were not casual cultural exchanges' (Knight, 'Drama and Society,' 380).

7 As detailed below, in 1510 the two societies became embroiled in a dispute over which chamber was the oldest and most preeminent. For whatever reason, the city council resolved the issue in The Gillyflower's favour. See Van der Straelen, *Geschiedenis der Antwerpsche rederijkkamers*, 19.

8 For its part The Gillyflower performed several plays for the triumphal entrance of Emperor Frederick III, his son Maximilian (newly installed king of the Romans), and Duke Philip the Fair in 1486; see Rombouts and Van Lerius, *De liggeren*, I, 39. Not to be outdone, on 30 August 1490, The Marigold participated in a major competition at Lier, involving eleven other chambers; see Van der Straelen, *Geschiedenis der Antwerpsche rederijkkamers*, 112.

9 As cited by Van der Straelen, *Geschiedenis der Antwerpsche rederijkkamers*, 11–12: 'Om de Rethorike te onderhouden ter eere en luyster dezer stad, aen elke derzelve twee gezelschappen is vergund, alle jaeren druy ponden grooten Brabants, voor soo lange sy de Rethoriken zullen oeffenen, en dat tot medehulp van hun camerhueren en ander lasten.' See also Puts, 'Geschiedenis van de Antwerpse rederijkerskamer,' 12. Later, The Gillyflower received 6£ Brabants per annum.

10 Two years earlier The Gillyflower put on a refrain festival in honour of St Jerome and won top prize in the refrain competition in Mechelen, performing there 'a beautiful, glorious play of the Avaricious Belly' (*Gieregen Buyc*). They won top prize of three lovely tin pots for a comedy (*esbatement*) performed in Brussels. In 1492 The Gillyflower's leaders won first prize for best entrance at Lier and performed both an unnamed *spel van zinne* and a comedy van de Asen in Leuven; see Rombouts and van Lerius, *De liggeren*, I, 43–5.

11 'Daer wy in incomen hadden eene heerlyke burch van Antwerpen op ten waghen, daer Sinte Lucas op was conterfeytende Maryen.' See Rombouts and Van Lerius, *De liggeren*, I, 47; also Van der Straelen, *Geschiedenis der Antwerpsche rederijkkamers*, 13. That same year saw The Gillyflower's members come away with several prizes at a contest in Brussels, including top award for the most glorious entrance; an unspecified prize for a comedy 'Of the Kettlemaker' (*van de Ketelere*); a first place award of a silver image of Mary for a prologue; and a prize to the chamber's fool, Laureys van Ypersele, who won in the category of 'best actor'; see Rombouts and Van Lerius, *De liggeren*, I, 47, and Bertrijn, *Chronijck der stod Antwerpen*, 56.

12 The participants were described as 'helmets' (*helmen*). Rombouts and Van Lerius, *De liggeren*, I, 49; Van Grimbergen, Antwerp SA PK2902, 'St. Lucas-gilde en rederykkamers,' fol. 2r.

13 See also Roose, 'De letterkunde,' 323: 'Zoals elders hebben de Antwerpse kamers zich niet alleen met de beoefening der dichtkunst, in de opvoering van toneelstukken onledig gehouden, maar hebben zij zich met de organisatie van andere publieke plechtigheden en vermaken, processies en "incomsten" in het byzonder ingelaten.'

14 Rombouts and Van Lerius, *De liggeren*, I, 51.

15 Van der Straelen, *Geschiedenis der Antwerpsche rederijkkamers*, 12–17. See also Vandecasteele, 'Het Antwerpse rederijkersfeest,' 149–76. This competition was a major undertaking, involving the delivery by messenger of the competition's card during Lent inviting all interested chambers to join the competition slated for St John's Day (25 June). The question, 'What is the greatest mystery or grace ordained by God for the blessedness of humanity?' and the listed prizes (amounting to a total of thirty-six Flemish marks of silver) aroused enough interest that twenty-eight chambers from nineteen communities, from as far away as Amsterdam, arrived by land or water. As hosts, The Gillyflower's members had to oversee all of the preparations, including construction of the stage and housing and fêting of their guests. The city funded most of the preparations, for such a gathering had considerable potential to boost the reputation of the host community.

16 Rombouts and Van Lerius, *De liggeren*, I, 56. The following year The Gilly-flower was awarded six pitchers (*stoopen*) of wine for their performance of a play performed in the Lombardstraat honouring the triumph of the king of Portugal (ibid., 57).

17 Rombouts and Van Lerius, *De liggeren* I, 59. See also ibid., 65 (1506); in 1513 after The Gillyflower's visit to Mechelen in May, The Peony came to Antwerp to perform 'triumphen speelen,' to the great pleasure of the magistrates of both cities, 'welc sy beyde wel beweesen in 't d'minlyc bescincken ende feesteringhe tot byde steeden ghedaen' (ibid., 80); Roose, 'De letterkunde,' 323, notes that the exchange had begun in 1487.

18 Rombouts and Van Lerius, *De liggeren*, I, 63.

19 For example, The Marigold performed in the chamber of The Growing Tree on 9 August 1506, where they were honoured with wine. They are known to have returned the following year (Van der Straelen, *Geschiedenis der Antwerpsche rederijkkamers*, 112).

20 Rombouts and Van Lerius, *De liggeren*, I, 72. On top of this event and the usual exchange with The Peony, The Gillyflower also performed a play called *The Smith of Cambrai* (*den smit van Cambron*), described by St Luke's deacon as long, rich, and beautiful to behold.

21 Ibid., I, 74; Van der Straelen, *Geschiedenis der Antwerpsche rederijkkamers*, 19. A copy of the original letter is in Antwerp SA PK4622, 'Gilden tegen Vener. Kap tegen Violier.,' a bundle of miscellaneous letters relating to disputes among and between the rhetoricians and civic guard.

22 Van der Straelen, *Geschiedenis der Antwerpsche rederijkkamers*, 19.

23 Bertrijn, *Chronijck der stad Antwerpen*, 64. Another source suggests they were mostly satin workers; see Keersmaekers, 'De rederijkerskamers te Antwerpen,' 173–85.

24 Handwritten notes in Van der Straelen, 'Jaerboek der St. Lucas,' Antwerp SA PK2910; Bertrijn, *Chronijck der stad Antwerpen*, 83.

25 Bertrijn, *Chronijck der stad Antwerpen*, 64–5; Van der Straelen, *Geschiedenis der Antwerpsche rederijkkamers*, 139. Seven years after its formal establishment The Olive Branch funded a late-morning Friday mass on the chamber's Holy Cross altar in the Borcht church, in remembrance of two deceased patrons, Simon van den Bogaerde and Elisabeth Skeysers. Van der Straelen, *Geschiedenis der Antwerpsche rederijkkamers*, 140.

26 Van der Straelen, *Geschiedenis der Antwerpsche rederijkkamers*, 20, 113; Rombouts and Van Lerius, *De liggeren*, I, 83; and Puts, 'Geschiedenis van de Antwerpse,' 9–10.

27 Van der Straelen, *Geschiedenis der Antwerpsche rederijkkamers*, 170.

28 Another, called 'De Bloeme' or 'Camere vande Damastbloeme,' appears from the testimony of Jacob van Middeldonck to have been established around 1540 (see below).

29 Included were members readily identified from the St Luke's guildbook, the city's *stadsrekeningen*, or the citizen books (*poorterij*) of Antwerp. Two of these, Gommaer, a *Grootwerker* who joined The Gillyflower in 1550 (Rombouts and Van Lerius, *De liggeren*, I, 173), and Gommaer van Nerenbroer, identified in the *stadsrekening* of 1550/51 (Antwerp SA R 14, fol. 486r) as the chamber's deacon, may instead have been the same person. Not included in this figure were most of the artists who participated in the organization of the Antwerp *Landjuweel* of 1561, for there is no evidence that they were members of Antwerp's chambers prior to 1556 (Gibson, 'Artists and Rederijkers,' 431–2). Also excluded from the calculations are the unspecified number of unnamed cabinetmakers described as The Olive Branch's charter members in 1510, although it would not be unusual if some of these were still members by 1515.

30 Rombouts and Van Lerius, *De liggeren*, I, 191.

31 Hofman, 'De Antwerpse drukker Frans Fraeten' and Pikhaus, *Het tafelspel*, 444–5.

32 Most information about these rhetoricians was garnered from the city's citizenship books in Antwerp SA – Stad Antwerpen, Poortersboeken, 1464–

1533, and Stad Antwerpen, Antwerpse Poortersboeken, 1533–1608, as well as from Rombouts and Van Lerius, *De liggeren*, Van der Straelen, *Geschiedenis der Antwerpsche rederijkkamers*, Gibson, 'Artists and Rederijkers,' and the other literature. Although some information was discovered in the *stadsrekeningen*, no attempt was made to conduct a systematic search in these volumes for information on specific rhetoricians.

33 For example, for Lent 1518 The Gillyflower performed, 'at great expense,' the *Play of the Defiled* ('*t spel van de Masscharon*), following that with participation in a contest at Leuven (Rombouts and Van Lerius, *De liggeren*, I, 91). Then, the following year this chamber performed a play on 'Amyca, or the Maker of Flowers' ('*t spel van Amyca, oft de Makere der bloemen*), an apparently enjoyable play requiring two days to perform (ibid., I, 94: 'Dit jaer deden dese Regerders, voerscreven spelen 't spel van Amyca, oft de Makere der bloemen, welc zeer wel ghespeelt wort, behaghelyc om hooren, twee daghen na een duerende.')

34 Rombouts and Van Lerius, *De liggeren*, I, 94.

35 Aegidius, *Hypotheses sive Argumenta Spectaculorum, quae Sereniss.*

36 Cited in Torfs, *Feestalbum van Antwerpen*, 16 and 21: 'Op Zondag na O.L. Vrouween Hemelvaertsdag heb ik den grooten Ommegang te Antwerpen gezien, toen de geheele stad vergaderd was, van alle handwerke en standen, eeniegelyk naer zynen staet op het kostelykste gekleed ... In dezen Ommegang waren zeer vele vrolyke dingen gemaekt en met groote kosten toebereid, want men ziet er vele wagens, spelen, schepen en ander klugtwerk. Daer ander was de orde in schaer der Propheten, vervolgens het Nieuw Testament, also de Groetenis des Engels, de Drie Koningen op groote kemels en op andere zeldzame wonderdieren rydende en zeer aerdig uitgerust, ook de vlugt naer Egypte, zeer stichtelyk etc.'

37 Van der Straelen, *Geschiedenis der Antwerpsche rederijkkamers*, 20, where it is noted that in 1522 (the deacon of St Luke's records it as 1521) the chamber paid 34£ Fl. 6st toward the feast of the previous year and in 1523 paid 15£ Fl. 12st for a total of 49£ Fl. Rombouts and Van Lerius, *De liggeren*, I, 99: 'Item, dit jaer hebben dese Regherders voerscreven betaelt van de costen die ghedaen waren in 't jaer voerleden aen de persongie op ten Couwenberch, xxxiiij £ ende vj myten.' Rombouts and Lerius, *De liggeren*, I, 101: (1522): 'Dit jaar so hebben dese Regerders voerscreven oeck noch van den costen ghedaen in de incomst van den keysere op ten Couwenberch betaelt dat daer af noch t'achter was, betaelt xliiij £ xij sc. viij den.'

38 In the 1521 visit both The Gillyflower and The Olive Branch competed, receiving gifts of wine for their efforts. At the 1541 competition, The Gillyflower won first prize for the farce *Hanneken Leckertant*.

39 In 1542 the city paid eighteen stuivers to the 'guilds of rhetoric in order

to honour the folk who came from St Truyen' (Antwerp SA R 11, fol. 55v).

40 Handwritten notes in Van der Straelen, *Jaerboek der St. Lucas*, Antwerp SA PK2910; Rombouts and Van Lerius, *De liggeren*, I, 106: 'Item in dit selve jaer haelden de guldebruers van onser Gulden metten Deken den mey, in den mey, d'welc noyt derghelyck bynnen Antwerpen ghesien en was, daer de guldebruers groote eer en prys af hadden van den heeren van der Wet ende van de ghemeyn lieden, van welcke triumphe lange memorie af weusen sal. Meester Peeter Gielys die ha d'ordenanse ghegeven.'

41 Van der Straelen, *Jaerboek der St. Lucas*, 40. The guild, in fact, had been for several years struggling to balance its books; in 1526, for example, its deacons had been granted permission to send a letter to any guild members who were delinquent in the payment of their dues (Rombouts and Van Lerius, *De liggeren*, I, 108).

42 Van der Straelen, *Jaerboek der St. Lucas*, 171.

43 Van der Straelen, *Geschiedenis der Antwerpsche rederijkkamers*, 20.

44 'Om de noodige bekostingen te vinden tot de spelen van Rhetorica, Esbattementen oft Klucht spelen en andere noodzakelykheden' (Van der Straelen, *Jaerboek der St. Lucas*, 56).

45 For example, on 11 March 1530, The Olive Branch received eight pitchers or bottles of wine (Antwerp SA R 7, fol. 82v) for a separate occasion and then, along with The Marigold, received its annual award of 8st. for the feast day, as well as the usual 3£ Fl. for the rental of the chamber (fols. 85r, 107v). The Gillyflower also received 3£ Fl., while in this year The Marigold received 6£ Fl. In 1532 the treasurer recorded three separate gifts of wine to The Olive Branch, two for performances and another for their feast day (Antwerp SA R 8, fols. 85v, 87v). It seems to have been more normal, however, for each of the three chambers to receive an equal amount for their yearly feast and hall rental (Antwerp SA R 9, fols. 92v, 112v).

46 The Gillyflower's participation in June 1529 in a contest at Leuven garnered its members two first prizes and a second prize, certainly to their minds just recompense for their considerable expenses of over 37£ Fl. (Rombouts and Van Lerius, *De liggeren*, I, 113; Van der Straelen, *Geschiedenis der Antwerpsche rederijkkamers*, 20).

47 Van der Straelen, *Geschiedenis der Antwerpsche rederijkkamers*, 114.

48 'Item, de Regerders hebben doen spelen 't spel van den coninc van Aragon, dat zeer wel gespeelt wort' (Rombouts and Van Lerius, *De liggeren*, I, 113). Presumably the rhetoricians also participated in the following month's procession, which was conducted to end the devastating outbreak of the notorious 'sweating sickness' which, according to Antwerp's chroniclers, killed

hundreds of people each day (as summarized by the eighteenth-century Antwerp chronicler Geraard Bertrijn [1648–1722], *Chronijck der stad Antwerpen*, 253–4). If nothing else, such ceremonial action helped at least briefly to take the population's mind off the horrible decimation, if not to provide them with a sense of being able to do something about it.

49 'Ende in dit jaer soe vierde men op de Mart ende voor de scilders camer tryumphelick, om den pays tusschen Carolus, de Keyserlicke Magesteit, ende Franciscus de coninck van Vranckericke ghemaeckt te Agamorte' (Rombouts and Van Lerius, *De liggeren*, vol. 1, 133; Van der Straelen, *Geschiedenis der Antwerpsche rederijkkamers*, 21). The banquet for the city's craft and ceremonial guilds and rhetoricians was sponsored by the city and cost its treasury 15£ Fl. (Antwerp SA R 10, 1538, fol. 132v).

50 'Item ter zaken vanden pyse tusschen de K Ma. ende den Co. van Vranck-ryck heeft men alhier geviert ende zekere genuechen bedreuen ende heeft-men navolghen den publicatie daer aff gedaen gegeven zekere prisz zo van hamelen also van wyn den gherne die scoonste geviert hadde zo vanden gulden also vanden rethoryke ende ambachten ende heeftmen betaelen ter zake vande hamelen ende elcke hamel tot 6st vry ende den wyn is ... 14£ 15st 6d' (Antwerp SA R 10, 1538, fol. 132v).

51 'In dit jaer soe quam ons een tydinge van een heerlycke feeste van rethoriken, opghestelt van de Fonteynisten binnen Ghent, daer wy seer tryumphelick ons intre deden met veel scoenen fygueren, personagyen, etc. ende met veel heeren, cooeplyeden ende guldebruers seer costelyck, ende wy hadden daer af prys, iij coppen iiij merc; en van 't blasoen dat wy voor theuneel presenterden hadden wy een scoen sielveren fonteyne weghende iij onsen. Ende wy speelden daer een seer goet spel, daer wy af hadden den hooghen en meesten prys, vier sielveren cannen, tel samen ix merc. Ende den factuer, voor synnen persoen, j silveren cop van iiij onsen. Ende onsen sot ha voor synen prys een silveren scimme van iiij onsen' (Rombouts and Van Lerius, *De liggeren*, I, 136). For its part, the city was still paying off the debt incurred by The Gillyflower for its participation in Ghent; in 1542 The Gillyflower's deacon recorded that 'Dese Regerders hebben betaelt van de oncosten gedaen in 'tjaer van xve en xxxix, tot der feesten van rethoriken te Ghent, vj £ v sc' (Rombouts and Lerius, *De liggeren*, I, 143).

52 As summarized by Bertrijn, *Chronijck der stad Antwerpen*, 83; under 24 August 1539, he notes, 'doen werden tot Antwerpen opgehangen die prijsen op de Melckmeert, voor die kinderen om te battementen ende deurde tot den 31 Augustij; doen trocken die kinderen op die Torffbrugge, daer die van de Cammerstraete hadden den prijs van 't battementen ende van't schoonste incomen.' ('There were offered upon the milk market in

Antwerp the prizes for the children to perform entertainments and this
went on until August 31; then the children marched up to the Turf bridge,
where those from the Chamber Street won the prizes for the entertainment
of the loveliest entrance.') Then he records, 'Hieraner, op den 29 september,
hinghen die van de Cammerstraete eenen prijs op van battementen, refer-
ijnen, singhen ende vieren, waervan die van de Lombaereveste hadden het
2^e battement ende het schoonste incomen' ('Hereafter, on September 29,
those of the Chamber Street offered up a prize for entertainments, refrains,
songs and decorations, whereof those of the Lombard Wall won the 2nd
entertainment and the loveliest entrance.')

53 Van der Straelen, *Geschiedenis der Antwerpsche rederijkkamers*, 22.
54 Van der Straelen, *Album der St. Lukas gilde*, 16. The wars included those
   between the Empire and France and between the Empire and the province
   of Guelders, the latter led by Duke William of Cleves.
55 Bertrijn, *Chronijck der stad Antwerpen*, 82–3.
56 For this contest, see Dirk Coigneau, 'Maer die steden apaert'; and W. Waterschoot, '3 augustus 1561. De veertien aan het landjuweel deelnemende rederijkerskamers houden een schitterende inkomst in Antwerpen. De
   organisatie van een landjuweel,' in Erenstein, *Een theatergeschiedenis der
   Nederlanden*, 120–5.
57 'Ende in't selve jaer so hadden dese Regerders een seer tryumphelycke
   vieringe voor de schilders camere, om de comst van den keysere Carolus,
   den xiijst dach in mey' (Rombouts and Van Lerius, *De liggeren*, I, 141).
58 'Ende als de gulden vander Rethorijcken des stadt te weten de goubloeme/
   de violien ende den oyftack Inde vasterie lestleden gespeelt hebben hun
   spelen van sinnen dan heeftmen voer myn heer ende andere goede mannen
   comen hooren de voirsc[reven] spelen opt stadt huys gepidteert het banquet ende daer af betaelt 4£ 9st 6d' (Antwerp SA R 11 [1542], fol. 58v).
59 Antwerp SA R 11 (1542), fol. 87v. The city also paid for torches for this
   event, to be placed 'opter stadt huys int Conninckfeesten ende camer van
   Rethorycken ende elder,' to a cost of 14£ Fl. 14st (ibid.).
60 'Dese Regeerders hebben doen spelen het spel van den Wellustigen Mens-
   sche, dat zeer wel gespeelt wert, dat gemaekt hadd M. Jan van den Berghe,
   alias van Diest, factuer van onser caemere' (Rombouts and Van Lerius, *De
   liggeren*, I, 178).
61 Van der Straelen, *Geschiedenis der Antwerpsche rederijkkamers*, 115.
62 Unfortunately the *stadsrekening* of 1549/50 were destroyed by a fire later in
   the century. There are, however, several important documents describing
   the expenses and preparations specifically for this event in Antwerp SA
   PK1627. There is also a cursory summary of revenue and expenses for the
   city in Antwerp SA R 1788, Rekening van Jan de Meyere, rentmeester, 1549

(12 Mei–31 Jan.); transcribed as 'De rekening der stad Antwerpen van het jaer 1549–1550,' *AA*, old series, I, 17–104.

63 Seven other guilds paid 100£ Fl. or more (Rekening van Jan de Meyere, fol. 71r).

64 Antwerp SA PK1627, loose parchment, '1549, Inkomst van Philippus prins van Spagnien – Contributien der Ambachten tot het verhalen der onkosten gereken op die Bleyde Inkomst.' This figure is taken from the totals on the left side of the page, which appear to list actual receipts. According to the figures on the right side, 1,512£ Fl., 10 stuivers had originally been allocated from the guilds.

65 Antwerp SA PK4622, bundle of letters, Gilden tegen Vener. Kap tegen Violier, in a loose page beginning 'ander zaken geport.'

66 In Antwerp SA PK4622, letter beginning 'Aen mynen heeren Borgheren ende Schepenen ...'

67 In Antwerp SA PK4622, fol. 2r–v: 'Zullen mogen nomineren vier gequalificeerde persoonen burgeren/ poorteren ende Inwoonders onser voirss. stadt nae huere qualiteyt totten dienst vanden gulden bequaem zynde/ tzn datse waren In eenige bruerscappen oft gulden gheen schutters zynde oft nyet/ ende de selue presenteren den burgermren. en scepenen onser voirss. stadt/ Om den eenen vanden voirgez. vier gequalificierde persoonen te kiesen/ nemen ende tordinerene totter voirss. gulden/ De welcke gehouden sal wesen den voirgez. dienst aen te nemen ende accepteren/ ende doen den behoerlycken eedt soemen gewoenlyck Is van doen nyet tegenstaende dat hy ware In eenige andere gulden oft bruerscappen/ Te wetene vanden bruerscappe oft gulde vanden heyligen Sacramente van onswer Lieuer vrouwe/ van sinte Barbelen vanden gulden der Rethorycken/ oft eenige andere/ gheen gulde van schutterye wesende.'

68 See Antwerp SA PK81, Blyde Incompsten, 1260–1637, esp. fol. 68v, 20 Sept. 1552, letter from Mary of Hungary. The Old Footbow (*Oude Voetboog*) was increased by twenty to eighty; the Young Footbow (*Jonge Voetboog*), the Old Handbow (*Oude Handboog*), and Young Handbow (*Jonge Handboog*) were all ordered to add twenty to their membership lists to a total of sixty each; the Pikemen (*Kolveniers*) remained at 100; while the Halberds guild (*Hellebardiers*) went up to 120 (Prims, *Geschiedenis der Antwerpsche rederijkkamers*, V, 93).

69 Puts 'Geschiedenis van de Antwerpse rederijkerskamer,' 15–16.

70 In Antwerp SA PK4622, bound manuscript, 'Memorien Privilegum en Vonnisse voor de Cameren van Rethorijcken *De Goudbloeme* en den Olyfftack wegens het bevreyden uytter Schuttereye, van 75 bruderen hunner Camere, nyet ontfanckbaer; gewezen Anno 1555, 1558 en 1559.'

71 Handwritten notes contained within the Antwerp SA copy of Van der

Straelen, *Geschiedenis der Antwerpsche rederijkkamers*, Antwerp SA Bib. 136.

72 For a recent discussion of her, see Joldersma, 'Anna Bijns,' esp. 93–119. See also Roose, *Anna Bijns*.

73 Pleij, *'T is al vrouwenwerk*, esp. 112–13; also Herman Pleij, '1512: Antwerpse maagd wint aanmoedigingsprijs op Brussels rederijkersfeest,' in *Nederlandse literatuur*, ed. Schenkeveld-van der Dussen et al., 126–30.

74 There have been attempts to attribute some plays to her; see Lievens, *Tghevecht van Minnen naar de Antwerpse Postinkunabel van 1516*, although Kristiaan P.G. Aercke, among others, has found these attempts unconvincing (see note 75 below).

75 Aercke, 'Germanic Sappho'; see also Roose, *Anna Bijns*, 150–2.

76 Aercke, 'Germanic Sappho,' 367.

77 See esp. the 1542 refrain, 'Yet, When Compared, Martin Rossom Comes Out Best,' excerpted in Aercke, 'Germanic Sappho,' 384–6; a modern edition of the original, 'Nog schijnt Merten van Rossom de beste van tween,' is in Pleij, *'Tis al vrouwenwerk*, 59–63. For other contemporary accounts of Rossum's assault, see *Een nieuwe zekere ende Warachtighe tijdinghe vanden Tyrannighen Wolf Merten van Rossem* and *Een schone triumphante Godlijcke victorie gheschiet voer dye stadt van Lueuen tegen mertten van Rossom met zijnen adherenten den tweden dach Augusti 1542*.

78 'tZijn aardse duivels, die de mensen kwellen,' in Pleij, *'Tis al vrouwenwerk*, 41–5, esp. 41:
Een vertwijfeld ketter, arger dan een Jode,
Verloochend monk, recht Antichrists bode,
En alle-t volksken van zijnder partijen
Verleiden de mensen in spijte van Gode.
'tWaar wel van node, dat men ze vlode
Als draken, serpenten, venijnige prijen ...

79 'Dit zijn de mirakelen die Luther doet,' in ibid., 45–9, esp. 49:
Schrifture wordt in de taveerne gelezen,
In d'een hand d'evangelie, in d'ander den pot.
'tZijn al dronken zot-oren; nochtans van dezen
Worden geleerde predikanten bespot.

80 Aercke, 'Germanic Sappho,' 371.

81 Ibid., 370.

82 Ibid., 368–9.

83 'If sin be virtue, then Lutherans are saints,' transl. Joldersma, 'Anna Bijns,' 122.

84 Joldersma, 'Anna Bijns,' 123–6.

85 Aercke, 'Germanic Sappho,' 378–9.

86 Joldersma, 'Anna Bijns,' 110.

87 The most careful discussion of the religious controversy as expressed in the Ghent plays is Drewes, 'Interpretatie van de Gentse spelen van 1539.' By his careful and detailed analysis of the idiom and theology of these plays, Drewes has shown that most of them were particularly dependent upon Luther's thought. See also Drewes, 'Het interpreteren van godsdienstige spelen.' For the texts, see the critical edition by Erné and Van Dis, *De Gentse spelen*. See also the sources drawn from the Ghent *stadsrekeningen* in ibid., 50, and below, chapter 6.

88 Steenbergen, 'Het spel der Violieren op het Gentse "Landjuweel,"' affirms that the play is directed against the teachings of Pruystinck. See also Roose, *Anna Bijns*, esp. 8–11. For sources on Pruystinck, see Friederichs, *De secte der Loïsten*.

89 'Eyn brieff D. Martini Luther An die Christem zu Antorff,' in Friederichs, *De Secte der Loïsten*, 4–7.

90 Friederichs, *De secte der Loïsten*, 8–9.

91 'Uittreksel uit het Antwerpsch chronykje,' in Friederichs, *De secte der Loïsten*, 9: 'Anno 1526, den 26 February, wert alhier een stellagie gemaeckt, daer op waren den Cancelier, Raetsheeren ende Borgemeesteren, den Marcgrave ende de Schepenen van Antwerpen, aldaer dn Opper Prochiaen een sermoen begonste ende in het preecken quamen der tien persoonen op, daer twee vrouwen onder waren, elck met een kerse, ende een droech een tortse, ende corts liet hy het preeken, mits het groot gerucht van het volck, ende corts quamp de processie generael over de mert, aldaer de schutters int hernasch stonden, van het Stadhuys tot aen de Breederystrate toe, ende de rest van de ambachten waren op heur cameren, ende oock van de gulden, oock int harnas sommighe. Ende de groote clock luyden, ende doen tHeylich Sacrament quam, soo dede men hunlieden som een mantelthien aen, op deen stont tHeylich Sacrament, op dander Luyter met veel duvelen, ende op sommighe boecken, ende alsoo volchden sy tHeylich Sacrament in de kercke; ende van daer gingen sy weder op tStadhuys, ende men dede hunlien haer mantelthiens aff, ende elck ginck thuys, ende men verberden hunlieden bocken.' For an earlier example of a public recantation of a heretic as a dramatic performance, see Knight, 'Drama and Society,' 384–6.

92 See also Cohn, *The Pursuit of the Millennium*, 170.

93 Eighteen Anabaptists who were executed at this time were not so fortunate (Génard, 'Personen te Antwerpen in de XVI eeuw voor het "feit van religie" gerechtelijk vervolgd,' series 13, 12–15).

94 See Friederichs, *De secte der Loïsten*, 23ff; De Hullu, *Bescheiden betreffende de*

hervorming in Overijsel, esp. 308; Waite, *David Joris*, 155; Waite, 'The Dutch Nobility and Anabaptism.'

95 He enters the stage accompanied by Self Reliance (Eyghen Betrauwen) and Human Assistance (tsmenschen bystant), and laments:

O vreezelick ghepeyns met zorghen belayen,
Waer zal ic my drayen,
Wat zal my ter noodt nu commen in stayen,
Nu ic moet gaen mayen mijns levens vruchten?
Wie zal my toch vanden vremden weder payen
En wel berayen,
Op dat mijn droevigh herte wat moght verfrayen?
Huere wilt verspayen, ghy doet my verzuchten.
Tgepeys doet my duchten duer staervens geruchten,
Ic en cans niet vluchten, dies therte moet beven.
Dus willic my totter Redene begheven,
Daer ic al mijn leven totten dagh van heden
Eerlick naer hebbe gheleift.'
[Oh fearful misery, burdened with cares,
Where to shall I turn,
What will now come to help me in my need
Now that I must go to harvest my life's fruit?
Who shall put my mind at ease from the strangers
And give good advice,
That might beautify my mournful heart somewhat?
The hour [of death] delays for a bit, you ask me.
This reassurance brings me dread through death's report,
I cannot flee, at this the heart must tremble.
Thus I will give myself over to Reason
Where I, all my life to this present day have honourably lived.
'Antwerpen,' Erné and Van Dis, *De Gentse spelen*, 278, ll. 24–36 (Hum.3 B 8).

96 DE WET: Wilt eerst maercken
Op datter staet: daer en es niemant rechtvaerdigh.
Ia niet eenen, noch verstandigh, maer onwaerdigh.
Ooc zo en es daer niemant die naer God vraeght;
Al zijn zy af gheweken, haer zelven behaeght
En tzamen onnut worden, zo datter niemant
En es die daer goet doet, ooc niet eene, want
Huer kele es een open graf dwelc tvuul ontluuct,
En tot bedrogh hebben zy haer tonghe ghebruuct,
Tfenijn der slanghen onder haer lippen ghetast ... (ibid., 281, ll. 88–97).

97   EYGHEN BETRAUWEN: Zydy droncken?
Gheift God den mensche dan een wet, tes onrecht
Als hyze niet hauwen en can. (ibid., 282, ll. 126–8).
98 Ibid., 282, ll. 178–9.
99   VERCONDGHER DES WOORDTS: O Mensche, zwijght toch stille.
Ic ben ghezonden om de ghene alleene
Dier huer zonden bekennen, tzy groot of cleene,
Te troostene; dus zijt u tot my keerende
En verhuecht u.
STAERVENDE MENSCHE: Wildy my ooc zijn leerende,
Ghelijc deis twee nu doen, die my verdomt hebben?
Wie zydy dan?
VERCONDYGHER DES WOORDTS: Wildy my ooc ghenomt hebben?
Ic ben de Vercondygher des Vreids met Gods woort,
Dwelc u belooft es dryvuldigh in accoort
Inden paradyze, tot een verlossijnghe
Des menschen die verdomt was (ibid., 285, ll. 197–209).
100   VERCONDYGHER DES WOORDTS: Der Evangelyen en valt noyt te spade.
Maer scheet dus de ghenade met wyzen rade:
Devangelye en wet zijn beede tzamen
Gods woordt, maer zy hebben verscheeden namen.
De wet verdomt en devangelye vergheift,
Dus elc een zonderlijnghe officye heift,
Al eyst tzamen gheschreven in eenen bouck,
Tzy int oude oft nieuwe (ibid., 290, ll. 306–13).
101   VERCONDYGHER DES WOORDTS: De zone Gods hijngh ghediffameirt te
schanden,
Ghewont duer zijn voeten, zyde en handen.
Dus heift Christus gheleden uwe qwalen
Ende ghedraghen uwe smerten zonder falen (ibid., 292, ll. 350–3).
102   VERCONDYGHER DES WOORDTS: Zondigh zuldy ooc blyven al u leven
lanck;
Maer die ghelooft, dezen es God niet tellende
Voor zondigh, want God is u Christum stellende
Tot wijsheyt, helikheyt ende gherechtigheyt (ibid., 295, ll. 426–9).
For the presentation of Luther's doctrines in other dramatic performances,
see Parente Jr., *Religious Drama and the Humanist Tradition*, 78–82.
103   VERCONDYGHER DES WOORDTS: Rust u zelven noch, en wilt een weynigh
zwyghen.
Hy es begraven, den derden dagh verrezen

Inden zelven staet; zo moet ghy ooc wezen,
Want die ghedoopt zijt in Christo Iesu goet,
Hebt Christum anghedaen en zijt zeer zoet
Leden zijns lichaems en ghebeenten staerck.
Dus zijn de gheloovyghe in swaerelts paerck
Tzamen met Christo ghecruust gheweist rijckelic,
Ghestorven en begraven autentijckelic,
Ende ooc met hem verrezen, want al dat hy es
Zijt ghy ooc; dus ziet hoe Christus vry es
Levende ende ooc over al triumpheirt. ('Antwerpen,' Erné and Van Dis,
   De Gentse spelen, 296, ll. 434–45).

The figure is described in the margin at l. 442: ' Figuere. Hier zalmen
tooghen de figuere daer Christus, verrezen zijnde triumpheirt over tser-
pent en de doot.'

104   VERCONDYGHER DES WOORDTS: Dit es de figuere van u bruloft cleedt
Tot eenen rocke daer ghy u mede bedect,
Ende den nieuwen mensche die ghy antrect,
Die naer Gods beilt es gheschepen onstaervelic;
Zo dat ghy met Christo nu zijt aervelic
Trijcke der hemelen, daer Christus in eeren
Gheclommen es met hem, om ws vrueghs vermeeren,
De ghevanghenesse ghevanghen leydende,
En es aldaer uwe plaetze bereydende
Ende ooc zittende tzijns vaders rechter handt (ibid., ll. 449–58).

The reference to putting on Christ like a cloak is evidently taken from
Luther's doctrine. See also chapter 6 below.

105   STAERVENDE MENSCHE: Zeght my, ic moet vraghen, want zeer goet
propoost es:
Eyst my, zondyghe mensche, naer de schriftuere
Niet ghenough, dat God wt bermhertigheyt puere,
Naer zijns zelfs beloften, niet en heift ghespaert
Zynen zone, maer voor ons ghegheven vermaert?
Die ons gheboren es in swets vulbrijnghen,
Ghepassijt, ghestorven, boven alle dijnghen
Verrezen; heift zonde, doot, duvel verwonnen.
Zoo God den mensche dat heift willen ionnen,
En zijn in Christo ghestorven onghestoort,
Met hem begraven, verrezen, en noch voort
Gheestelic met hem ten hemel ghevaren? (ibid., 299, ll. 500–11).

106   VERCONDYGHER DES WOORDTS: Nu wilt deze solucye wel bewaren,

Want de helyghe apostolysche kaercke
Gheloovende belijdt (elc hier op maercke)
Des vleeschs verryzenesse heel lichamelic.
En Iob zeght ooc: Ic weet dat ic beqwamelic
Zal verryzen inden wtersten daghe,
Ende in mijn vleesch tot mynen behaghe
God zien; en Paulus willet ooc bedien,
Dat ghy ten wtersten daghe eerst zult zien
De doot gheheel te nieten met hueren strale.
Dus es tvleesch verryzen, tot mynen verhale,
Des menschen troost meest, want en caem dat niet,
Zo waert van Christo al te vergheifs gheschiet
Dat hy ghedaen heift, en smenschen troost waer wte (ibid., ll. 512–25).

107 VERCONDYGHER DES WOORDTS: Ziet, dus zalt commen inde laeste mynute,
Dwelc God Ezechiel heift ghetooght gheheel.
En Christus zal hier gheven het oordeel
Over levende en doode: dus verblijdt nu,
Dat hy oordeel gheven zal die daer bevrijdt u.
En alsdan zuldy eewigh zonder zwaerheyt
Met Christo, u hooft, ghebruucken inder waerheyt
Al dat hy heift en es, met God dryvuldigh (ibid., 300, ll. 526–33).
The direction for the illustration is found at l. 531: 'Figuere. Hier
tooghtmen de verryzenesse des vleeschs.'

108 See the discussion in Erné and Van Dis, *De Gentse spelen*, 26–30, and below, chapters 5 to 7. Unfortunately we do not know very much about Van den Berghe himself, except that he had followed J. Casus as factor of The Gilly-flower in 1537. In 1543 he is listed as factor of The Book (*Het Boek*) at Brussels, but is mentioned in 1551 and 1556 as factor of The Gillyflower again (Kruyskamp, *Dichten en spelen van Jan van den Berghe*, xi–xii).

109 Gérard, 'Personen te Antwerpen,' series 8, 360.

110 'Den Boom der Scriftueren,' in Snellaert, 'Drie spelen van zinne uit den tijd der reformatie.'

111 His trial record is found in Génard, 'Personen te Antwerpen,' series 7, 464 and 467, and series 8, 347–62. See also his 'Ordonnantien van het Antwerpsch magistraat, rakende de godsdienstige geschillen der XVIe eeuw.' The play will be discussed in chapter 7 below.

112 This new wave of arrests also included the prominent printer, Jacob van Liesvelt.

113 Génard, 'Personen te Antwerpen,' series 8, 364–75.

114 In February 1560, the city fathers found it necessary, because of the mis-

conduct of the *pap-gilden*, to outlaw their meetings. In 1563 the *pap-gilden* 'Leliken' hence petitioned to become an official chamber, 'hebbende de Rethorica van over meer als dertig jaren altijd met eer en deugd geoeffende' (Straelen, *Geschiedenis der Antwerpsche rederijkkamers*, 170).

115 *Hanneken Leckertant*, in Kruyskamp, *Dichten en spelen van Jan van den Berghe*, 63–88 (Hum. 1 OG 17). At the conclusion (88) is found the following: 'Is gespeelt bij die Violieren van Antwerpen indie feeste der Lelijen in Diest a° 1541 en hebben den oppersten prijs gehadt. Fecit Jan vanden Berge.' Quite interesting are the comments made by The First and The Second in the opening prologue, who tell the members of the audience not only to relax and enjoy the play, but also 'to guard your bundles from the pickpocket's art.' 'Stand still a bit longer,' these characters command their viewers, 'both poor and rich,' to watch this play (64, ll. 29–35). See also Vorrink, *Hanneken Leckertant*.

116 Van der Straelen, *Geschiedenis der Antwerpsche rederijkkamers*, 23. There are two modern editions of this play: the first is a criticial edition in Kruyskamp, *Dichten en spelen van Jan van den Berghe*, 91–144 (Hum. 1 OA 6); the second is an English translation by King, 'The Voluptuous Man.' This play will receive more detailed attention in chapter 7 below. Also extant is Van den Berghe's 'Het Leenhof der Gilden,' an extended refrain published in 1564, although it must have been written well before van den Berghe's death in 1559 in Brussels. This work satirizes Antwerp through the creation of a fictitious community reminiscent of Antwerp and its environs (see Kruyskamp, *Dichten en spelen van Jan van den Berghe*, 3–36).

117 King, 'The Voluptuous Man,' 69, ll. 205–16. Later Carnal Lust comments, 'Priest too are 'uman,' to which Bad Faith responds, 'That's a good one, neighbour! / But the church will fall if the pillars are weak' (70, ll. 248–50).

118 Ibid., 70, ll. 241–2.

119 Den Hollander, *De Nederlandse Bijbelvertalingen*, 17–26.

120 King, 'The Voluptuous Man,' 70, ll. 243–50.

121 See Edwards, Jr, *Luther's Last Battles*, and especially Oberman, 'Teufelsdreck.'

122 Een present van Godt loondt, Grammerchijs, Besolos manos, Brussels, KB, II 367 (Hum. 1 D 10). That it was composed for this chamber is indicated by the phrase 'wij semple goudtbluemkens hier presented' at the end of the manuscript.

123 The play is evidently based on Luther's hymn ('Een feste Burg') 'A Mighty Fortress.' At one point Grammerchijs calls Christ 'een vaste borcht' (ibid., fol. 6v).

124 Ibid., fol. 7r.

125 Roose, *Anna Bijns*, 26. He was at the time factor of The Gillyflower (see Hofman, 'De Antwerpse drukker').

126 'sMenschen Gheest van tVleesch verleyt,' in De Vooys and Mak, 'Een verloren vastenspel van sinnen uit de XVI^{de} eeuw' (Hum. 2 O 1). See also De Vooys, 'Een Antwerps sinnespel van Smenschen Gheest door De Clodius.'

127   Want mijn devotie nu vervlooten is
         doer uwe vleesselijcke quellinghe
         en weet ick hier teghen gheen rebellinghe
         daer en helpt aflaet noch processie an (ibid., 617, ll. 256–9).

128 'Menichfuldich lof Christe gheschie u weerdich alleene verlosser myn' (ibid., 648, ll. 810–11).

129 That spiritualism was a popular option among Antwerp rhetoricians is seen in a refrain composed in 1566, the year of the iconoclastic storms. The poet suggested that none of the religious camps, including the Anabaptist, Lutheran, Calvinist, Zwinglian, and Catholic, had the monopoly on truth. In Kalff, 'Eenige 16de eeuwische onuitgegeven gedichten van Coornhert, Spiegel en Anderen.' For the influence of spiritualism in the Netherlands, see Bergsma, *Aggaeus van Albada (c.1525–1587)*; Samme Zijlstra, '"Tgeloove is vrij"' and Wiebe Bergsma, '"Uyt Christelijcken yver en ter eeren Godes." Wederdopers en verdraagzaamheid,' in Gijswijt-Hofstra, *Een schijn van verdraagzaamheid.*, 41–68 and 69–84 respectively; and Kaplan, 'Remnants of the Papal Yoke.'

130 Classical plays and stories had long provided the material for Latin school dramas of humanistic teachers. There is, however, little evidence of classical penetration into Dutch vernacular drama prior to the 1540s and 1550s, although there is an apparent exception in *Piramus and Thisbe*, possibly performed ca. 1518, which uses the story of the two ancient lovers as an allegory of Christ's sacrifice. See below, chapter 4. Matthijs de Castelein also composed a version of this story: *Pyramus ende Thisbe. Schoon retorike amoureus bequame es dit barblijke voor sulcken eersame* before 1550. For Latin school drama, see Parente, Jr, *Religious Drama and the Humanist Tradition.*

131 De Vreese, ed., *Een spel van sinne van Charon, de helsche schippere (1551)*; the original is in Ghent Universiteitsbibliotheek 900 (Hum. 1 D 13). De Vreese suggests that in this case an earlier Flemish version of the play was reworked into the Brabant dialect by Reyer Gheurtz of Antwerp. For later plays of this genre, see B.H. Erné, ed. *Twee zestiende-eeuwsche spelen van de hel* (Groningen, 1934).

132 Smeecken, *Mars en Venus*, Brussels KB II 368 (Hum. 1 D 11).

133 Cornelis van Ghistele, *Eneas en Dido* (1, 1551), Brussels KB II 369 (Hum. 1 D 12a); Cornelis van Ghistele, *Eneas en Dido* (2, 1552), Brussels KB II 369

(Hum. 1 D 12b). From elsewhere in the southern Netherlands there appeared also Colijn Keyaert's version of *Narcissus and Echo*, Van Narcissus ende Echo, ghemaect byden amorösen Colijn ende is lanck in dicht 2193 regulen, Ghent Universiteitsbibliotheek 900 (Hum. 1 D 14).

134 De Vreese, *Een spel van sinne van Charon*, 46–7, esp. ll. 663–70; 691–2.

135 Van Ghistele, *Eneas en Dido* (1), fol. 2r: 'ghevluydt uyt sheylighen gheests monde.'

136 Ibid., fols. 2v–3r.

137 Ibid., fols. 3r–4r.

138 ONWEETENDT: Way wech ghy van hier mit u visevaesen
     Condy anders niet praesen dan (soot is ghebleecken)
     Ydes poeterije ghij soudt spreecken
     Vander scriftueren daer soudt nijpen [?]
     ONGHELEERDT: Ja en der menschen ghebreecken begrijpen
     Gheestelijck weerlijck tsy van wat persoonen
     EEN STATELIJCK MAN: Men sal gheen sotten (seydtmen) half werck thoonen
     Ghy spreeckt beyde onwysselijck tsaemen
     Alsulcke woorden möghdy u wel scaemen
     Tschyndt dat tot argheydt u sinnen gheneeghen sijn
     In schimp en begrijp luttel döghden gheleeghen sijn
     Mit schimp en en begrijp salmen niemandt vruedt maecken
     Maer men seydt mit medicijnen de suet smaecken
     Daer sal men die siecke crancken mee laeven (ibid. [2], fol. 39v).

139 Ibid., fol. 40r.

140 Ibid., fols. 40v–1r.

141 Ibid., fols. 41r–v.

142 In the early 1560s Willem van Haecht, factor of The Gillyflower, wrote and had performed a series of Lutheran plays based on the Acts of the Apostles. See Steenbergen, 'De apostelspelen van Willem van Haecht' and Ramakers, 'Maer en beroemt u niet!'

4: Amsterdam Rhetoricians and the Reformation

1 See Van Elslander, 'Lijst van Nederlandse rederijkerskamers,' 32.

2 The actual date of the founding of this chamber is a matter of some contention. See Ellerbroek-Fortuin, *Amsterdamse rederijkkersspelen*, 24–5.

3 Amsterdam GA 5023 Groot-Memoriaal I (Mfc 8), fol. 276r. Discussed in Ter Gouw, *Geschiedenis van Amsterdam*, IV, 29, and Ellerbroek-Fortuin, *Amsterdamse rederijkkersspelen*, 24.

4 'Hier begint een spel van sinnen van de historie van Piramus en Thisbe

ghenaempt de Sinnelijcke Genegentheijt,' Haarlem, Archief, 'Trou Moet Blijcken' (hereafter TMB) B, fols. 141v–9r (Hum. 1 OB 10); edited by Kalff, *Trou Moet Blycken*, 29–53. The chamber's motto is found in the last line, 'Van ons Egelantierkens, die noch eerst groeyen.' For the dating of the play, see Ellerbroek-Fortuin, *Amsterdamse rederijkkersspelen*, 138–9. See also De Vooys, 'Twee rederijkerssepelen van Pyramus en Thisbe' and Van Es, *Een esbattement van sMenschen Sin en Verganckelijcke Schoonheit*. See below for the summary of the contents.

5 Cited in Blaauw and Van Toorn, 'De zin van het spel, rederijkers in moeilijke tijden,' esp. 83.

6 Ellerbroek-Fortuin, *Amsterdamse rederijkkersspelen*, 25–6. For the critical edition of the play, see Grondijs, *Een spul van sinnen van den Siecke Stadt*; Hum. 1 I 1. The motto of Eglantine, 'In liefde bloijende,' is discovered in l. 73: 'maer stelde v altijt in lieft bloijende'; that of the other chamber, in l. 1260: 'dat duer hem die daer is in liefden vierich.'

7 'Een spel van sinnen van Lazarus doot ende hoe dat Christus hem opweckte,' Haarlem Archief TMB, B, fols. 126v–49r (Hum. 1 OB 10). See also Ellerbroek-Fortuin, *Amsterdamse rederijkkersspelen*, 133–8.

8 'Van sint Jans onthoofdinghe ghemaect tot Amsterdam en is lanck in ghedichte 667 reghelen,' in Brussels KB, 21650 (Hum. 1 D 3). The motto is found on fol. 16r. For the dating of this work, see Ellerbroek-Fortuin, *Amsterdamse rederijkkersspelen*, 161–2, who notes that there is a mention in the 1532 Amsterdam *thesauriersrekening* of a Jan Thönisz listed as one of the five 'rodbearers'; also Van Bemmel ('Toneel in Arnhem van 1500 tot 1565,' esp. 131) postulates that this might be the play performed in Arnhem, Guelders, in 1534, which the city treasurer described as 'Yst gespuelt van die onthoeffdenysse Sint Jan Baptyste.'

9 'Naboth,' Brussels KB II 130. (Hum. 2 06) The hand is extremely difficult.

10 Amsterdam GA, Thesaurus Rekening, 1559, fol. 63v: 'die Rethorizijns In Liefde bloyende een ton engels biers mitten excijs ende een vette weer' worth 9, 18s; 'die Rethorijzijns in L. vuerich, een ton engels biers mit excijs ende een ham' worth 8f, 18s. Quoted in Ter Gouw, *Geschiedenis van Amsterdam*, IV, 506.

11 'Een Meijspel van sinnen van Menschelijcke Broosheit, de met sWerlts Genuechte triumpheert inden Ghemeijnen Beijaert.' Brussels KB, 21659 (Hum. 1 D 9). It is not known whether the Amsterdam or Thoolen chamber performed this work. See Ellerbroek-Fortuin, *Amsterdamse rederijkkersspelen*, 147–53.

12 The Amsterdam *stadsrekeningen* are available on microfilm in Amsterdam GA, Archief Burgemeester, mcf 6257–60 – stadsrekeningen (6257 – 1531–6;

6258 – 1536–45; 6259 – 1545–51; 6260 – 1551–7). Unfortunately the volume for 1536 has not survived. For the importance of *stadsrekeningen* for our knowledge of chamber activities, see Van Boheemen and Van der Heijden, *De Delftse rederijkers*, 8, and Van Bemmel, 'Toneel in Arnhem.'

13 Kernodle, *From Art to Theatre*, 59.

14 Written by Mr Peter Woots, rector of the New Side School.

15 Amsterdam GA, Archief Burgemeester, mcf 6259, Stadsrekening 1549. Council discussions regarding the arrival of the future king of Holland are included in Van Iterson and Van der Laan, *Resoluties van de vroedschap van Amsterdam, 1490–1550*, 90.

16 *CDIN*, IV, 239.

17 Ibid., V, 172: 'roerende seckere spelen voirden stadthuys ende binnen ander huysen aldair gespeelt by sommighen rethoryckers tot confuys, derisie ende bespottinghe vande sacramenten der heyliger kercke ende andere goiden jnstitucien.'

18 At the time Hoffman was in prison in Strasbourg and hence no longer in direct control over his followers.

19 Waite, 'The Anabaptist Movement in Amsterdam and the Netherlands, 1531–1535,' 262–4, and Mellink, *Amsterdam en de wederdopers*, 42. A figure of 5,000 would have included nearly one-third of all residents of the city. The actual number was probably much lower.

20 Apparently before the radical events of the spring of 1534 and 1535 Anabaptists were allowed to proselytize virtually unmolested in the city. See the 'Memorie vant ghundt ... van de lutherije ende anababtisterije met tgundt dairaen cleeft, januari 1536,' *DAN*, V, 252–3.

21 Goertz, *Die Täufer. Geschichte und Deutung*, 23; see also the splendid collection of essays in Dykema and Oberman, *Anticlericalism in Late Medieval and Early Modern Europe*.

22 'Instructie voer meester Abel van Coulster, raidt ordinarys in den Hove van Hollant ... 17 februari 1534,' *DAN*, V, 21. The Court dated the performance to mid-January, although we know it occurred a couple weeks earlier. See also Boomgaard, *Misdaad en straf in Amsterdam*, 113, and W.N.M. Hüsken, '31 december 1533. In Amsterdam worden negen rederijkers veroordeeld tot een bedevaart naar Rome vanwege de opvoering van een esbattement dat spot met de geestelijkheid. Rederijkers en censuur aan de vooravond van de Opstand,' in Erenstein, *Een theatergeschiedenis der Nederlanden*, 92–7.

23 The commentary is *Das XII Capitel des propheten Danielis aussgelegt* (Stockholm: The Royal Press, 1526). It is described in Deppermann, *Melchior Hoffman*, 63–84. Hoffman made much of the chapter's references to periods of

1290 and 1335 days in his own calculations of the time of Christ's return, which he confidently dated to 1533.

24 *DAN*, V, 15. The letter is dated 14 February 1534.

25 Amsterdam GA, Archief Burgemeester, Mfc 446, *Keurboek* D, fol. 277r; included in *DAN*, V, 10–11.

26 See I.H. van Eeghen, 'De inquisitie in Amsterdam,' in De Roever and Bakker, *Woelige tijden*, 73–81.

27 *DAN*, V, 15–16.

28 Ibid., 43. The picture depicted 'eenighen gemaelden duvelkens mit verscheyden cappen becleet, visschende ghelt, kasen ende andere goeden.'

29 The question of whether or not Jacobsz can be counted among the members of this rhetorician group cannot be answered, but that he provided both a stage and painted backdrop seems to suggest so. The use of painted scenes or figures was a common feature of *rederijker* performances; for example, each of the 1539 Ghent competition plays contains descriptions of several of them which were to be interpreted by the actors during the performance.

30 'Memorie van tgunt dat mijn heere die grave van Hoochstraeten ... den Xen octobris anno etc. XXXIII om darticulen daerinne verclairt te beantwoirden,' *DAN*, V, 49.

31 Ibid., 50. One of the numbers of the Halberds did admit to having said something like this in the church, but he denied having brought his weapon with him.

32 Ibid., 51.

33 For information on the radical Anabaptists in Amsterdam, see Mellink, *Amsterdam en de Wederdoopers*. Historically there were close ties between the marksmen's guilds and the chambers of rhetoric. See Sterck, 'Onder Amsterdamsche humanisten,' 296. See also his *Onder Amsterdamsche humanisten* and Kölker, *Alardus Aemstelredamus en Cornelius Crocus*.

34 'Antwoorde gedaen bij den schout ... in een memorie henluyden bij mogenden, eedelen ende waelgeboeren heere mijnen heere de grave van Hoochstraeten ... XXXIIII,' *DAN*, V, 56. Mellink, *DAN*, V, 56, n. 161, notes that Van Assendelft had reported on 11 November 1534, that he had received a copy of the '*batement*' from Amsterdam.

35 *DAN*, V, 59. It is not inconceivable that something like a preliminary version of the anonymous 'Spul van Sinnen van den Siecke Stadt' was performed in this instance.

36 'Memorie vant ghundt dat uuft diversche informstien tot Amsterdam ...' *DAN*, V, 256. See also Sterck, 'Onder Amsterdamsche humanisten,' 295–6.

37 Ter Gouw, *Geschiedenis van Amsterdam*, IV, 244. The other eight rhetoricians were Claes Mollenz, Willem Gommertz, Willem Henricxz, Jan Wouterz,

Claes Janssz (glasspainter), Ysbrant Cornelisz (woolcarder), Dirk Remenscz and Peter Henricxz. The other six male *naaktloopers* were Gheryt Ghijsen, alias Gheryt van Wou from Benscop; Mr. Adriaen Anthoenis Focxen; Steven van Oudewater; Steven Janssen, armourer from Den Berch; Dirck Janssen, glassmaker; and Claes van Venloo. Five unnamed women also participated, although one escaped capture (*DAN*, V, 113). In court the defendants continued to refuse clothing insisting that 'they had been sent from God in order to proclaim the naked truth.' Hendrikszoon had encouraged the others to burn their weapons and clothing as a sign of the coming fiery vengeance which God alone would enact on the godless. 'Brief van Gerrit van Assendelft aan stadhouder, 25 februari 1535,' in *DAN*, V, 110–11. See also the 'Buyck over de naaktlopers, februari 1535,' *DAN*, V, 114–16.

38　*DAN*, V, 145. For more on the Anabaptist rhetorician activities, see Waite, 'Popular Drama and Radical Religion.'

39　Deelen was appointed to his post by the city magistrates in 1533. *DAN*, V, 145 n. 348.

40　Ibid., 145: 'Seyt dat hij de slotele van der rethorijckerscamere dyckwils heeft gehadt. Seyt dat up sonnendaechsavonts tot hem gecomen es Henrick Goedtbeleet, begerende van hem dat hij den slotele voers. Haelen zoude van meester Wouter, zeggende dat hij begeerde op de rethorijckerscamer te wesen omme daer wat te zien, ende desen naevolgende heeft hij die spreect de slotele geeyscht van meester Wouter op manendage lestleden nae middage, die hem de slotele voors. gegeven heeft, ende heeft hij die spreect dezelve slotele gelevert Henrick voors., die daerup wachte, sonder dat Henrick hem zeyde wat hij mitten voors. Slotele wilde doen, dan zoude hem die spreect die weder leveren ... Seyt dat Henrick hem die spreect geseyt heeft dat hij die spreect zoude zeggen totten voors. Meester Wouter dat zijn tassche gescoort was ende hij daeruuyt wat hadde verloeren.'

41　Claes Semmenz confessed on 12 July 1535 that Frederycxz had frequented Deelen's house and that Wouter's wife had told him that on the evening of the revolt her husband had handed over the keys to the *rederijkerscamer*, because Frans 'had forgotten his bundle in the same chamber' (ibid., 221).

42　The chamber regulations of the Antwerp De Violieren indicate that audiences at performances and meals in the chamber room itself were somewhat restricted: point 24 affirms that guests to chamber meals must be approved by the prince or deacon and a fee paid; point 25 orders the *Cnape* (doorman and messenger) to close the doors to the chamber at the hour of the performance so that no one could enter after the beginning of the show (Van der Straelen, *Geschiedenis der Antwerpsche rederijkkamers*, 6).

43　According to witnesses, on the evening of the revolt Frederycxz, armed and

wearing a partial suit of armour, had gone through the city hall district telling residents that the noise was merely a squabble between the priests and
the watch over some decorations and that they should stay inside and
bring in their lanterns. The accounts are summarized by the authorities
during Frederycxz's sentencing (*DAN*, V, 202).

44 Ibid., 145. A price was placed on Mathijs's head on 2 March of that year.
The accusation was confirmed by one Luduwe Coockebackers, among
others. Coockebackers confessed under oath that about a month before the
revolt (hence April 1535), he had seen a certain Mathijs conversing with
Mr Wouter inside the latter's home and one time Wouter had given his
hand to Mathijs and had said, 'My dear man, conduct yourself well.' At this
the other said, 'I will certainly do so' (ibid., 215). He furthermore remarked
that the aforementioned Mathijs was well known to Goossen Jansz Recalff
and Heyman van Aemstel Jacobsz, the two new burgermasters of the city
(ibid., 216). See also the testimony of Claes Semmenz (ibid., 220–1).

45 'Memorie vant ghundt dat uuyt diversche informatien tot Amsterdam,'
ibid., 257: 'There were arrested two suspected persons from the school,
namely Mr Wouter, hired to teach Greek, and Mr Jan Certorius, [hired] to
teach Latin. Their disciples daily said many blasphemies and taught [from]
suspect books and the later treasons were committed by the principal ones
among them.'

46 See the Ordinance of the Antwerp De Violieren, numbers 12 and 13, in Van
der Straelen, *Geschiedenis der Antwerpsche rederijkkamers*, 3. If Deelen was a
deacon and Frederycxz a member of the chamber, then the question of the
loaning of the keys becomes less of a puzzle.

47 See Van Itterson and Van der Laan, *Resoluties van de vroedschap van Amsterdam*, 13, and D'Ailly, *Zeven eeuw Amsterdam*, I, 180.

48 The evidence for this public celebration comes from the city's account book
of 1537 in a section regarding other expenses relating to the revolt of the
Anabaptists. Amsterdam GA, Mfc 6258, Stadsrekening, 1537, fol. 57v. References to this procession end in the stadsrekening of 1542, when Amsterdam
residents were preoccupied with preparations for the defence of the city
against Maarten van Rossum.

49 The Latin plays written by the humanist Catholic schoolmaster, Cornelius
Crocus, and performed by his students received some support. See Sterck,
'Onder Amsterdamsche humanisten,' 89. For Crocus, see Parente, Jr, *Reli-
gious Drama and the Humanist Tradition*, 32–5. See also the play composed by
another Dutch humanist, Gulielmus Grapheus in Atkinson, *Acolastvs: A
Latin Play of the Sixteenth Century by Gulielmus Grapheus*.

50 For example, note the actions of Emperor Charles V after he arrived to

restore order in the city of Ghent after its aborted tax revolt. See the anonymous account excerpted and translated in Rowen, *The Low Countries in
Early Modern Times* esp. 23–5. The emperor entered first, followed by thousands of his troops, ecclesiastical princes, and members of the aristocracy.
The city was duly humbled.

51 Crocus's *Comoedia Joseph* was performed by his students in June or July of
1535 on the Dam (the central square) on the occasion of a feast in honour of
the plundering of Tunis by Charles V in 1534. Although this Latin school
play was not a chamber performance, the incident confirms the close relationship between feast and drama in Amsterdam at this time (Sterck,
'Onder Amsterdamsche humanisten,' 286).

52 'Amsterdamse kroniek over gerucht van aanslag, maart 1534,' *DAN*, V, 23:
'Ende hoer meening die was dat sij, terwijl dat die processie soude omgaen,
een oploop in der stat soude maken ende dat sij aldereerst al den monniken
ende al den priesteren souden dootslaen ende dat sij dat heylighe sacrament souden mit voeten vertreden ende dat sij dan voort al den gemeent
uuyt die stede souden yaghen ende dat sij dan in hoer goet souden gaen sit-
ten.' The procession referred to was in remembrance of the late medieval
'Miracle of Amsterdam,' which celebrated the survival of the communion
wafer after it had been vomited from a dying man and thrown into the fire.
The site of the miracle, housed in a chapel, was until the Eighty Years War a
popular place of pilgrimage and Anabaptists from the surrounding districts could therefore have slipped unnoticed into the city. The authorities
were warned of the plans and took the necessary defensive precautions.
The festival fell on the Wednesday after St Gregory's Day, hence 18 March.

53 See the fascinating study by James, 'Ritual, Drama and Social Body' and the
review article by Bossy 'Holiness and Society.' The concept of the late medieval urban community as a 'sacred society' comes from Moeller, *Imperial
Cities and the Reformation*, 46.

54 Grondijs, *Siecke Stadt*, xxi, suggests that the play originated sometime
around or before 1538; Brands, 'Reynier Pouwelsz, Tspel van de Cristenkercke en een spul van sinnen van den Siecke Stadt,' 205, and Ellerbroek-
Fortuin, *Amsterdamse rederijkkersspelen*, 25–6, find good evidence to place
its date of composition between 1535 and 1536; Sterck, 'Onder Amsterdamsche humanisten,' 286–93, argues that it was composed around the
time of the Anabaptist revolt and furthermore contends that it is from the
same period as the Latin play *Comoedia Joseph*, composed by the Amsterdam humanist schoolmaster, Cornelius Crocus, which was written shortly
before the Anabaptist revolt and performed shortly thereafter.

55 Grondijs, *Siecke Stadt*, 10–11, ll. 267–72:

Maer die officiere
Ist seer diere bij eede belast,
Dat alle suspecte van hem moesten sijn angetast,
Om te leggen vast hoort mijn motijue.
En sou hij dan sulcke niet brengen van lijue,
Sijn geblijue waer niet, maer mosten vlien.
Maer sij willen het heerken sijn ouer die lien.
Dit wij dus gaeren sien om die minste vrede
Te hebben in die stadt.

56 Ibid., 10, ll. 258–9. HYP.: 'Wij verdempen immers die Gemeent niet.' TYR.:
   'Niet: plaegen die schutters en ghilden gheen ouerluij te kiesen?'

57 Ibid., xxvii–xxviii. Several years later, the dispute between wealthy but
   powerless Amsterdam merchants and the ruling patriciate broke out again,
   and the complaints of the former were set out in a petition to the regent in
   Brussels in 1564. The closed family government in Amsterdam, obstacles
   impeding trade, and the slow enforcement of justice were prominent
   among their complaints. The magistracy responded that it was necessary to
   restrict membership in the ruling elite so as to ensure that the spectre of
   heresy dominating the city's administration would not reappear. See Kistemaker and Van Gelder, *Amsterdam*, 44.

58 Grondijs, *Siecke Stadt*, 46, ll. 1287–95:
   Waer om veriaechdij van mijn, respondeert al gelijcke,
   Die edele rethorijcke en die lustige musijcke,
   Die welcke soe autentijcke mijn doen assistentie,
   In elcx presentie laet reden doch blijcken?
   Waer om moetense wijcken want haer soete eloquentie
   En constige inventie brachten mijn tot excellentie
   Van volcoemen credentie van Godts woorden vercooren.
   Tanhooren bracht mijn tot magnificentie.
   Maer doer donconstige gaet die conste verlooren.
   Earlier, Hypocrisy noted gleefully that So Many (representing rich Catholic
   Amsterdamers) regarded all rhetoric as weeds:
   Want sij houwense voor dooren alle rethoresijnen.
   ...
   Want sij sienter die lieuer hooren der vorscen gesanck
   Dan der rethorijcken geclanck dus ist beeter gesweegen (ibid., 24, ll. 649,
       652–3).

59 Community warns,
   'Die Heer sal die pest bij v laeten dueren al.
   Mit grilling, coortse, hittige brant, verstaet tenemael mijn

Sal die Heer v visiteeren al sijdij groot van getal.

Den hemel bouen v sal weesen als den metael fijn,

Die aert onder v ijser, dus suldij haest cael sijn,

Want die Heer sal v van v vianden laeten slaen (ibid., 19, ll. 500–5).

Such apocalyptic foreboding was a major characteristic of the Anabaptist community in Amsterdam between 1533 and 1535. Its use here, therefore, would have resounded loudly among Amsterdam audiences.

60 See esp. 'Siecke Stadt,' 22, ll. 588f and 602f.

61 Ibid., 44, ll. 1214–15, 1220.

62 Ibid., 44, ll. 1234–50.

63 Ibid., 45, l. 1279.

64 Ibid., 48, l. 1350.

65 Ibid., 48–9, ll. 1361–9:

Al souwene noch soe seer fulminieren,

V gheestelicken int eerste buijten weegen sijn getorden.

Ansiet nv hoese gaen en vp die preecstoel stieren,

Soe dat sij die scaepkens behooren te sijn, sijn woluen geworden

En leggen v die Gemeenten hals onverdraechlicke borden,

Diese selfs mit den vinger niet an willen rijnen eenpaer.

Dese sijnt die die uwen tot tweedracht dus porden.

Christus sant di sijnen als scaepkens in mits der woluen, voorwaer,

Haer niet meer beuelende dan te preecken teuangelijom claer.

66 Ibid., 12, ll. 293–8.

67 Van Sint Jans Onthoofdinghe, fols. 2v and 4r.

68 Ibid., fols. 6r and 14r.

69 Here, as in medieval literature, the misogynist sentiment against ruling women is counterbalanced by the high praise for 'the most pure virgin Mary' (ibid., fol. 15v). There is no mention, however, of Mary's role as mediatrix. The play could therefore be Lutheran.

70 Ibid., fol. 10v:

DEERSTE HEER: Wie soude Möghen haeten die suete practijcke

Van snaerspel en rhetorijcke vol van delicicie

DANDER HEER: Ken gheloof datter iemant is so plomp van condicie

De tot sulcken expercicie sou draeghen wangonste

So eedel is de const

DE DERDE HEER: Sy heeft seker myn ionste

Maer mennich ghefronste houdtse beneepen

So datse van elckerlijck niet word begreepen.

71 'Een spel van sinnen van Lazarus doot.' Blaauw and Van Toorn, 'De zin van het spel,' 84, suggest that the play came from the same period as *Sick*

City, but they provide no further analysis. Ellerbroek-Fortuin, *Amster-damse rederykersspelen,* 133–8, Kalff, *Trou Moet Blycken,* xiv, and also Kalff, *Geshiedenis der Nederlandsche,* III, 22–3 suggest ca. 1530. Certainly *Lazarus's Death* is strongly tainted with heresy, and was probably composed before 1538.

72 'Een spel van sinnen van Lazarus doot,' 133v:
> Die aen mijn sijn gelooff can geuen
> Al waer hij doot die sulcke oock leuen sal
> Tgelooff doet leuen wie dat can beseuen
> En derft niemmermeer voor steruen beuen
> Gelooff dij dit martha hier int aertschen dal
> Ghij verlost u zielen vuijt allen misval.

73 Ibid., 136v:
> Loopt al voor den duyvel den met den anderen
> Hem wil mij met die ketters dingen moegen niet
> Maer tot ons geleerden wil ick mijn spoeijen siet
> Vertellende hoe Jesus doet dusdanigen dingen noch
> Daer mede verscheijen ick.

74 Ibid., fol. 136r. From the context it appears that the central meaning of this comment is a condemnation of religious persecution of Christians by the state. Yet it could very well carry an ulterior, antisemitic meaning, since it was believed that Jews were thirsty for the blood of Christian children. See Hsia, *The Myth of Ritual Murder: Jews and Magic in Reformation Germany.*

75 'Een spel van sinnen van Lazarus doot,' fol. 138r.

76 Ibid., fol. 138v. It reads in part,
> Ketterijen van desen Jhesus gespreijt werdt te menigenn spacijen
> En noch daegelijcke oneerlijcke hem self gedregen quaet
> So dat met sijn doctrijnen sorgende al ons landste bewegen stat
> So dat donnoselen vallen in criemenele misdaden
> ...
> En wij verbannen se met hem al sijn partijen
> So datse niet meer sullen gaen opentlijcken
> Binnen onsen landen heerlijckheden ofte rijcken
> Op goet en lijff van Justijcien.

The date of issue is 10 March, which may be an intentional reference to one of Charles V's placards.

77 Ibid., fol. 139r.

78 'Een spel van sinnen hue Mennich mensch suect Thuys van Vreeden,' Brussels KB, 21651 (Hum. 1 D 4). See Ellerbroek-Fortuin, *Amsterdamse rederijkkersspelen,* 164–9.

79 'Een spel van sinnen hue Mennich mensch,' suect Thuys van Vreeden
   fol. 3r. He is singing:
   'So Paulus heeft beleeden
   duss wil ick voort nae Christijs woort
   Ghaen suecken thuys van vreeden.

80 Ibid., fol. 11v: 'Werpt af die Wercken der duysternis tuwer vroomen, / die
   Waepenen des lichts duet aen met lusten.'

81 Ibid., fol. 12r:
   MENNICH MENSCHEN: Wie is de avont
   MORGHENSTOND: Valsche predecanten
   Godts aduersanten diet volck verdullen
   En dör valsche predicacie hör kisten vullen.

82 Ibid., fol. 14r:
   MORGHENSTONT: 'Warachtich gheloof gheeft der sonder penitente
   Dan coomt een puer consciencie wilt dit onthouwen
   Ghy muet uwen heer vwen godt betrouwen
   Sonder ennich verflouwen met der liefden branders
   En ghij sult crijghen vreede ...

83 Ibid., fols. 15r–v:
   MORGHENSTONT: Neemt daer dat cruys en wilten u aenhouwen
   Niet aen dat cruys van hout ofte steene
   Maer aenden ghecruysten Christum reene
   De ons alleene met syn bluet verlast heeft.
   Again, the play affirms that Christ was born of a pure Virgin (fol. 16v), a
   doctrine affirmed by most reformers as well as Catholics.

84 At one point, Appetite accuses Hypocrisy of being of the 'sect of Luther'
   (ibid., fol. 10v). Putting satirical words into the mouths of evil allegorical
   characters was a humorous means to praise the subject.

85 Ellerbroek-Fortuin, *Amsterdamse rederijkkersspelen*, 124–5.

86 *Naboth*, fols. 12v–13v (see n. 9 above); Ellerbroek-Fortuin, *Amsterdamse rederijkkersspelen*, 127–32.

87 'Van ons Lieven Heeren Minnevaer,' Brussels KB, 21649 (Hum. 1 D 2). See
   Ellerbroek-Fortuin, *Amsterdamse rederijkkersspelen*, 139–47.

88 True Love leaves her husband in his simplicity. To the audience she remarks
   that Little Trust will not find his Lord in church, 'for he is at the right hand
   of the Father' ('Van ons lieven heeren minnevaer,' fol. 3v).

89 The author has some things to say about the special sins of merchants:
   PASTOOR: Peyst hue de ghierige gesellen
   De om deertsche guet haer siel in peryckel stellen
   Uyt sijn om haren euen naesten te bedriegen

In haer comescap sy mennige logen liegen
Men hoortse uytvliegen alst geluyt der trompetten (ibid., fol. 8v).
90 Haarlem Archief TMB, B, 'Van de Historie van Piramus en Thisbe' (see
n. 4), 49, ll. 545–8:
Die nae den vleesche leeft, sal sterven
Niet alleen lichamelijck maar naer der zielen mede;
En men preeckt ons mede daegelijckx ter stede,
Dat minne boven al andere deuchden gaet.
91 Ibid., 49, ll. 573–80.
92   POET: Bij die fonteijnne, somen daer aff maeckt mensije,
Salmen die heijlige wonden verstaen,
Die Christus vuijt leffden heeft ontfaen,
Om ons daer onse salicheijt aen nam dbeginnen,
Daer die sacramenten in sijn bevaen
Aen den boom des cruijcen voor ons vuijt minnen,
Waerbij men den moerboom mach versinnen (ibid., 51, ll. 588–94).
93   Dits origo pecatij, waer bij was gebroocken
Die volmaeckte natuer in "smenschen betegenheijt
En al heeft den mensch van goodtspassije de vercregenheijt,
Dat bloet der erffsonde moeter in blijven,
Tot meerder verdiensten is die gelegenheijt,
Also ons veel doctoren dat beschrijven" (ibid., 51, ll. 604–9).
94 Ibid., 52–53. In ll. 650–1, Poetelijck Geest describes Christ's 'buijt der can-
tijcken' as 'Marije, daer ick die kercke bij verclaere.'
95 This had been Luther's original hope.
96 '[T]ot alle lichtvaerdigheyt ende ydelheyt (die meestendeel zijn de mater-
unt vande voorsz. Camer-spelen) worden gedeverteert' (Noordkerke,
Handvesten, I, 117).

5: Anticlerical Drama and the Reform Controversies in the Low Countries, 1519–38

1 Van Dis, *Reformatorische rederijkersspelen*.
2 Ellerbroek-Fortuin, *Amsterdamse rederijkkersspelen*; Erné and Van Dis, *De
Gentse spelen*; Grondijs, *Een spul van sinnen van den Siecke Stadt*, and
Decavele, *De dageraad*, who suggests that the chambers contributed to the
desire on the part of Flanders's growing middle class for religious emancipation. See also Decavele, 'Jan Utenhove en de opvoering van het zinnespel
te Roborst in 1543,' esp. 101–2, where he provides additional examples of
rhetoricians persecuted for reform activities, including a woman, who in

1552 was suspected of heresy because her husband was 'vande rhetoric-quen, handelende mits dien de scrifture,' thereby falling into heresy. See most recently, Waterschoot, 'De rederijkerskamers en de doorbraak van de reformatie in de Zuidelijke Nederlanden.' A popular treatment is Ranke, *Rederijkers in de branding.*

3 See Brands, *Tspel van de Cristenkercke* and his 'Reynier Pouwelsz Tspel,' 203–8.

4 Van Gelder, *Erasmus* and Degroote, 'Erasmus en de rederijkers van de XVIe eeuw.'

5 For the literature, see above, chapter 1.

6 Spruyt, 'Listrius *lutherizans,*' esp. 747.

7 For Joris and Nicodemism, see Waite, *David Joris;* for Niclaes, see Hamilton, *The Family of Love.* Even some normally separatist Mennonites adopted the practice in the urban context; around 1545 Menno Simons wrote to some of his supporters in Amsterdam castigating them for practising Nicodemism (see Horst, 'Menno Simons: The New Man in Community,' esp. 203–4).

8 Among other things, Drewes analysed the use of Scriptural references in the plays and discovered that seemingly benign references were often based on Lutheran translations of the Scriptures and supportive of Luther-an or general reformation doctrines (Drewes, 'Het interpreteren van gods-dienstige spelen' and 'Interpretatie van de Gentse spelen'). See also Decavele, *De dageraad,* I, 193–230. For Lutheran drama in Latin, see Parente Jr, *Religious Drama and the Humanist Tradition.*

9 See especially Dykema and Oberman, *Anticlericalism in Late Medieval and Early Modern Europe,* esp. John van Engen, 'Late Medieval Anticlericalism: The Case of the New Devout,' 19–52, and Tracy, 'Elements of Anticlerical Sentiment in the Province of Holland under Charles V,' 257–69.

10 See, for example, Van Deursen, *Plain Lives in a Golden Age,* 150–2, and Smail, 'Predestination and the Ethos of Disinheritance in Sixteenth-Century Cal-vinist Theater.'

11 See Waite, *David Joris,* and Eire, *War Against the Idols,* 234–75. Drewes's dis-cussion of Anabaptism does not fully recognize the rich diversity of ideas and practices among the various Anabaptist groups, nor does he clearly distinguish the specific teachings of Melchior Hoffman from those of Swiss or German Anabaptism. One of the unique elements of Dutch Anabaptism was its propensity to Nicodemism.

12 The appendix lists eighty-four plays examined in this study. Five of these – Hum. 1 B 20 (Everaert's Visscher), Hum. 1 B 35 (Everaert's Nichte), Hum. 2 O 29 (Plaijerwater, performed in Antwerp between 1500 and 1525), Hum. 1 OB 11 (Goosens ten Berch's Piramus and Thisbe), and Hum. 1 D 8 (the

anonymous Naaman prinche van Syrien) were most likely composed prior to 1519 and therefore excluded from the statistical analysis here, but included in the general discussion for illustrative purposes.

13 Of these secular plays, twelve were by Everaert. Some of these plays did refer to religious reform.

14 Drewes, 'Interpretatie van de Gentse spelen,' 271, lists several key epithets used principally by Lutherans and other reforming rhetoricians to display their disgust at the priesthood. These include 'dromen' (dreams), 'fabelen' (fables, as proclaimed by 'sophists'), 'hypocrieten' (hypocrites – priests), 'jaarmarkt' (annual fair), and 'kramerij' (small wares; priests as hired servants), 'mensengeboden' (human commands, such as fasts), 'misknecht' (bad steward), 'papist,' 'sielvermoorder' (murder of souls), 'sofist' (those who combine pagan philosophy with theology, including Humanists such as Erasmus), 'swermer' (bee swarm), and 'werkheilige' (works righteousness).

15 Boerdelic Pleghen ende Ghenoughelic Voorstel, in Muller and Scharpé, Spelen van Cornelis Everaert, 234–42 (Hum. 1 B 15). Further on Everaert, see Willems, 'Cornelis Everaert, Tooneeldichter van Brugge'; Van Dale, 'Een spel van zinne van Cornelis Everaert'; Muller, Cornelis Everaert's spelen als spiegel van de maatschappelijke toestanden zijns tijds; and most recently Hüsken, 'Cornelis Everaert en de Troon van Salomon.'

16 For more on drama in Bruges during this era, see the studies by Hüsken, 'Kroniek van het toneel in Bruges (1468–1556),' and 'Politics and Drama,' in Knight, The Stage as Mirror, 165–87.

17 Nicholas, Medieval Flanders, 357–89; see also Prevenier and Blockmans, The Burgundian Netherlands, esp. 374–87.

18 Nicholas, Medieval Flanders, 390–1.

19 Ibid., 371, notes that in 1449 there were some 4,000 poor receiving peat from the city, of a population of ca. 35,000.

20 Wellecomme van der Predicaren, in Muller and Scharpé, Spelen van Cornelis Everaert, 145–65 (Hum. 1 B 10). For a discussion of the literary structure of Everaert's plays, see Spies, '"Op de questye ..."', esp. 145–8.

21 Wellecomme van den Predicaren, 149, ll. 79–91. His greeting of the Dominicans as the learned in contrast to the rhetoricians, who were 'simple men' and of 'little doctrine,' moreover, has the flavour of sarcasm.

22 There are also several purely comical plays, such as Stout ende Onbescaemt (1527; Hum. 1 B 11) and Visscher (Hum. 1 B 20), which tell the well-known story of the cuckolded husband; Nichte (Hum. 1 B 35), an undated work which relates a 'taming of the shrew' and abusive husband story; and De Dryakelprouver (Hum. 1 B 13), which satirizes wandering quacks.

23 *Tspel van den Hooghen Wynt ende den Zoeten Reyn*, in Muller and Scharpé, *Spelen van Cornelis Everaert*, 87–102, esp. 98 (Hum. 1 B 6).

24 *Scamel Ghemeente ende Trybulacie*, ibid., esp. 140, ll. 207–12 (Hum. 1 B 9):

    Ghy hebt te vele te onderhoudene.

    Den edelen staet ende gheestelicke prelaten

    Tscaemel volc aerm van staten

    Leven by hu hier vp der eerden.

    Volcxskin van dues aes van cleender weerden

    Moeten by hu ooc somtyts ghevoet zyn.

25 Ibid., 144, ll. 333–4: 'Al mach deen een habyt meer dan dander cleeden / Wy moeten al tsaemen ter eerden keeren.'

26 *Aerm inde Buerse*, in ibid., 285–96 (Hum. 1 B 18).

27 *Tspel van Donghelycke Munte*, in ibid., 245–62 (Hum. 1 B 16), esp. 247, ll. 90–103:

    MENICHTE VAN VOLCKE: Neerrynghe den coopman volcht bedwanc.

    Want daer de munte ten hoochsten loopt

    Den coopmaan alderande waere coopt

    Omden pennync ten hoochsten te begheuene.

    DEN DAGHELICXSCHEN SNAETERE [a woman selling apples]:

    Den coopman weet tweesins proffyt te beleuene

    Daer de munte hooghe ghaet jnt openbaere.

    Tdeene an tghelt tdander ande waere

    Dus volcht hy tvoordeel van proffytte.

    SULC RETHORISIEN: By dien zoo wortmen de neerrynghe quytte.

    Want zou volcht de munte ter hoochster reyngnacie.

    Dus daer de munte staet ter neirster valuwacie

    Daer moet de vtynghe van coopmanscepe minderen.

The result is that many are forced to sell their business to their neighbours.

28 Ibid., 253, ll. 300–31:

    AERBEY: Menichte van Volcke met herten met zinne

    Ghy behoort my Aerbeyder dach ende nacht

    Ghehuldich te zyne met al uwe cracht.

    Want an hu Menichte van Volcke cleen ende groot

    Moetic Scaemel Aerbeyder winnen myn broot.

    Gheen renten dan wercken jc en weet.

    Ende alst twerc faelgiert zo moetic ghereedt

    Wyf ende kyndren met honghereghen doluere

    Vut nootsakelicheden zenden voor hu duere

    Om by hu te ghecryghene der benauten ontset.

...

DAGHEL: So ghy ghaet ghevoert
Tscynt dat al hu zinnen naer den thoy staen.
Sulc Scaemel Aerbeyder wil alzo moy ghaen
Als eenich poorter ofte eenich rentier.
Ooc ghelaet hy hem coragieus ende fier
Als of hy machtich waere ende rycke.
Maer wanneer hy valt by siecten ter tycke
Of dat hy neerrynghe moet deruen een jaer
Aermoede dwynt hem ter stont zo naer
Et sitter al vooren habytten en cleeren.
AERBEY: Jc zoude gheerne als ander ghaen met eeren
Hoe wel Menichte van Volcke my dies versmaet waen.
DAGHEL: Ghy muecht wel eerlic naer uwen staet ghaen.
Better waere by hu eenen pennync vermostelic
Dan te ghaene bouen uwen staet costelic.

29 *Groot Labuer ende Sober Wasdom*, in ibid., 264–82 (Hum. 1 B 17), esp. 277,
ll. 495–6.
30 Ibid., 282, l. 637: 'Hout lyden secreit jnt herte verboorghen.'
31 *Ghemeene Neerrynghe*, in ibid., 438–50 (Hum. 1 B 28), esp. 440, ll. 29–30:
'Want Elckerlyc die alle dync an my versochte / En begheert nv wullen
lynen noch douck.'
32 GHEMEENE NEERRYNGHE, 442, ll. 101–8; in the words of Sulc Scaemel:
Elckerlyc die ghelt heift mach nv proffyt doen.
Alle dync crycht hy te zynder begheerrynghe.
Want Sulc Scaemel van dyveersscher neerrynghe
Heuet nv sober naer myn ghevoel
Mids dat hy met Alle Dync my vp den stoel
Allomme achter volcht hier ende daer
Daer jc selue plochte te reysene naer
Jn allen feesten wyt ende zyt.
33 Ibid., 442, ll. 304–10:
Ten ghelieue van Neerrynghe jn allen houcken
Jn allen dynghen heift willen zoucken
Nyeuwicheyt tot der tyt van noch
Daer Elckerlyc meestdeel jn vynt bedroch
By dat Elckerlyc seght ende zo hy claecht
Hier by wort Neerrynghe verjaecht
Vut allen dynghen wat et zy.
34 Ibid., 449, l. 373: 'Elckerlyc moest hem beteren zoude Neerynghe commen.'

35 See Ladurie, *Carnival in Romans,* esp 1–34, 289–704.

36 *De Vigelie,* in Muller and Scharpé, *Spelen van Cornelis Everaert,* 77–86 (Hum. 1 B 5).

37 *Jubile,* in ibid., 522–30 (Hum. 1 B 34).

38 *De Nyeuwe Priestere,* in ibid., 422–37 (Hum. 1 B 27).

39 Ibid., 430, ll. 259–75. See also 434, ll. 439–44, where Twyffelic Zin refers to Luther's teaching that the priests did not have such divine power:

> Waer zytge au ghy Luters vul van malicie?
> Scaemt hu dat ghy hu seluen vermiet
> Te segghene dat ghy tmisterye tsecreit
> Tgoddelic officie zoudt vermeughen te doene
> Ghelyc als den priester.

40 Ibid., 427, ll. 162–3: 'Den priesterlicken staet van hem [i.e., Christ] vercoren wiert / Bouen der hyghelen staet jnt hemelsche pleyn.'

41 Ibid., 426, ll. 141–5 (the character Nyeuwe Testament is speaking of God's creative power):

> Schelycx heift hyse ten avenaele gheleert
> Dat wyn broodt zullen worden verkeert
> Duer de cracht zyns woords tallen termyne
> Jnde specie zyns helichs lichaeme dyvyne
> Vulmaect ghelyc hem Maria ontfync.

42 Ibid., 427, ll. 170–2:

> Dat elc priester tusschen zyn handen edelic
> Godt ende meinsche bloet ende vleesch
> Consacreren mach naer zynen heesch.

43 Ibid., 429, ll. 229–30: 'Dan den priester jn Christus gheconsacreirt. / Wee hem diese bespotten zottinnen en zots.'

44 Ibid., 428, ll. 215–7: 'Gheen keyser hoe excellent / Conync herthoghe hoe hooghe gheacht Die vp deerde ghegheuen es sulcke macht.'

45 Ibid., 431, ll. 323–5:
'Menich pries zeer lettele kent / De eereweerdicheyt excellencie ende prys Die hem Godt gheift.'

46 Ibid., 432, ll. 329–35:

> Constantinus seght al wilde mesdoen
> Een priester eeneghe sonde openbaer
> Ende jct zaghe met myn ooghen claer
> Jc zoude tzynder eeren myn mantel vut trecken
> Ende hem veil lieuer daer mede decken
> Dant hyement zaghe binden eerdsche wiele.
> NYEUWE: Tsyn de bewaerders van smeinschens siele.

47 Ibid., 434–5, ll. 411–38.
48 *Sinte Pieter Ghecompareert byder Duue*, in ibid., 343–59 (Hum. 1 B 22). See also *Visscher*, 319, l. 11.
49 Mayer, 'Cornelis Everaert's *Maria Hoedeken*: A Critique of Popular Piety in Late Medieval Bruges.' An abbreviated version of this paper was presented to the Sixteenth Century Studies Conference in Toronto, 25 October 1998.
50 *Tspel van Maria gheleken byden Throon van Saloman*, in Muller and Scharpé, *Spelen van Cornelis Everaert*, 297–316 (Hum. 1 B 19), esp. 300, ll. 43–6, where Fyguerlicke Prysynghe, a matron of the old law, says:

> Nochtans machse wel worden ghecompareirt daer
> Eeneghe fygueren thuerder weerdicheyt strecken
> Om dat men den volcke zoude verwecken
> Ter deuocien tot Godt ende thueren dienste net.

51 Ibid., 301, ll. 95–8:

> RETHORYCKELICKE VERJOLYSYNGHE: Maria es den throon die onbesmit zy
> Daer Christus onsen Salomon te zyne luste
> Neghen maenden jn nam divyne ruste
> Om meinsche te wordene duer Adams mesdaet quaet.

52 Ibid., 302, ll. 121–8:

> FYGUERLICKE: Godt den zuene heift zynder moeder serteyn
> Schelycx verghift met zuuerheden perfect
> So dat huer zuuerheyt jnden hemel strect
> Naest de goddelicke zuuerheyt vut ghelesen milde.
> RETHORYCKELICKE: Christus die van Maria gheboren wesen wilde
> Jnden hemel hebbende eenen vader ontsteruelic
> Onbesmit ende zuuere zo moest hy verweruelic
> Jnder eerden een zuuer moeder vynden.

Later in the play (ibid., 312–13, ll. 523–5), Scriftuerlicke remarks of the Holy Spirit: 'Teerste ghewerck dat hy vermochte / Jn huer te blusschene der sonden spaercke / Huere helich makenende.' God had to make Mary eternally sinless, Fyguerlicke points out (ll. 535–8), for:

> Hadde Maria ghesondicht te eeneghen stonden ziet
> Christus en hadde niet jc darfs my berommen
> Jn huer ghebenendyt lichaeme willen commen
> So Sapiencie primo ons ghescal biet.

53 Ibid., 304, ll. 198–205:

> FYGUERLICKE: De tweesten trap beteekent scamelheyt
> Die elcke vrauwe naer Ambrosius woort
> Met allen rechten te hebbene behoort.
> Want scamelheyt es de slotel van alder reynicheyt.

RETHORYCKELICKE: Scaemelheyt doet scuwen alle vyleynicheyt.

Want maechden behooren zo scamel te leuene

Datse jn smans spraecke behooren te beuene

Hoedanich dat hy zyn woorden voert.

54 Ibid., 306, ll. 265–88.

55 Ibid., 308, ll. 338–43:

SCRIFTUERLICKE BEWYSYNGHE: Maria was ooc sachtmoedich gheestelic.

Want wanneer datter eeneghe questye resen

Tusschen de apostelen zou heifse bewesen

Sachtmoedich te wesene voor eene lesse.

Dus was Maria der appostelen meestresse

Want zou heifse jnt ghelooue versterct gheleert.

56 Ibid., 308, ll. 351: 'Die vercoren was te zyne net ghepeerelt / Coneghinne shemels ende vrauwe der weerelt.'

57 Ibid., 315, ll. 631–8:

RETHORYCKELICKE: Dus zyt ghy naer zeden

De rechte middel dits trechte slodt.

SCRIFTUERLICKE: Dat bouen huer es dats alleene Godt.

Beneden zyn wy meinschen jn deerdsche weeden.

Dus es Maria als middel van beeden

Tusschen Godt ende ons aerme creathueren.

JONSTICH BEGHEERREN: Dies wy huer anroupen talder hueren

Als aduocate om stroostens ghescieden.

For a fuller examination of this play and its sources, see Hüsken, 'Cornelis Everaert en de troon van Salomon,' who argues that Everaert's intricate imagery was inspired more by works of art than by literary works. For a confirmation of the importance of visual imagery to popular piety, see Webber, 'Varieties of Popular Piety Suggested by Netherlandic *Vita Christi* Prayer Cycles,' esp. 216–17.

58 *Maria Ghecompareert byde Stede van Jherusalem*, in Muller and Scharpé, *Spelen van Cornelis Everaert*, 362–76 (Hum. 1 B 23).

59 Yet he could also tell husbands and wives not to enquire too thoroughly after each other's sins but instead to be at peace with each other; *Visscher*, 326, ll. 282–90.

60 His several plays condemning war and its devastating effects on the lives of Flemish people undoubtedly also owed something to the pacifist writings of Erasmus. See below, chapter 8.

61 *Zeuen Bloetsturtynghen*, in Muller and Scharpé, *Spelen van Cornelis Everaert*, 453–61 (Hum. 1 B 29), esp. 453, ll. 1–4.

62 Ibid., 459–60, ll. 245–62.

63 *De Berch*, in ibid., 488–95 (Hum. 1 B 32), 491. The pilgrim Duechdelic Voort-stel tells Lustich van Herten that he has been to Rome, at which Lustich asks him if he has returned with relics; Duechdelic says yes, he has brought back 'de ghelyckenesse van eenen berghe.' Erasmus was also a vigorous opponent of the devotion to relics.

64 *De Berch*, 494, ll. 200–12.

65 These are the conclusions of Mayer, 'Cornelis Everaert's *Maria Hoedeken*,' 31–46.

66 Erné and Van Dis, *De Gentse Spelen*, 91–2. Erné bases his conclusion on a stylistic comparison of the Ghent play with Everaert's known works, the last of which was composed in 1538. Given Everaert's status as a play-wright in Bruges, it seems quite likely that he would have composed the 1539 work as well.

67 There is a secular play from 1538, *Pays*, which celebrates the Peace of Nice but this work makes no reference to the religious controversies.

68 *De Wynghaert*, in Muller and Scharpé, *Spelen van Cornelis Everaert*, 498–520 (Hum. 1 B 33), esp. the prologue, 499, ll. 19–27:
Sheeren beuel es elc wilter vp mercken
Tsy leecke of clercken
Dat wy sullen wercken
Jn zyns wynghaerts heerscepye.
Dats thelich ghelooue der kerstene kercken
Dat jn eeneghe percken
Men ziet bezwercken
Met de Lazerussche sonde der ketterye
Vul heresye.

69 Ibid., 516, ll. 624–31:
DUECHDELIC VERMAEN: Den wynghaert der kercken heift jn bewaeren
Voorghaende Bewys elc gheestelic prelaet
Met Vroom Labuer den edelen staet
Mids Ghewillich Volghen den ghemeene volcke.
VROOM LABUER: Wy drye staeten onder shemels reene wolcke
Gods wynghaert ons ghelooue dheleghe kercke
Synse sculdich te bescermenne by onsen ghewercke
Van alderhande quaede heresye.

70 Ibid., 513, ll. 530–3:
Soo slachtense die vander ketterye ghedeert zyn
Half groene half drooghe jn Gods leerynghe.
Quaelic can mense doen ofkeerynghe
Van huerlieder quaeder opynye vermetelic.

71 Ibid., 508, ll. 315–18:

Den wynghaert daer my den zin vp acht
Aldus duer groeyen vul ketterien
Ende bouen dien
Vulder onvruchtbaereghe ranken ghescacht.

72 Drewes, 'Het interpreteren van godsdienstige spelen,' 14–15 and 59–61.

73 For a more detailed examination of Anabaptism and rhetoricians, see Waite, 'Popular Drama and Radical Religion.'

74 'De Menschwerdinge Christo,' Haarlem Archief TMB, B, fols. 15r–34v (Hum. 1 OB 2). It has been transcribed and edited by Voolstra, 'Een spel van sinnen van de menswerdinge Christo,' and briefly summarized by De Vooys, 'Rederijkersspelen in het archief,' 176–8. Nissen, *De Katholieke polemiek tegen de Dopers*, 135–9, suggests that because Van den Putte was likely trained in the Franciscan tradition, his defence of the Virgin is particularly strong.

75 Voolstra, 'Een spel van sinnen,' 62: Doodende letter is a woman dressed like a wandering procuress (*coppelersse*) with a book in her hand; Misbruyck is her husband with an inkhorn on his side and a roll in his hand.

76 Voolstra, 'Een spel van sinnen van de mensweidinge Christo,' 63, where Killing Letter says to her colleague:

Ick can immers dit blat lesen
Ter schoolen gehouden van desen sophisten
Cont ghij oock schrijven.

See also ibid., 67. Catholic authorities frequently complained that allowing untrained laypeople to read the Scriptures led automatically to heresy.

77 Ibid., 65: 'Ja, soudij en ghij doet meer quaets alleene / ter werrelt dan al de tovernaers tsaemen / soudij dan vrij blijven.' They are also under the inspiration of Lucifer (ibid., 66–7).

78 Ibid., 73: 'Compt heylighe geest, wilt ghij ons leeren / van den gelove die oprecht manieren.'

79 Ibid., 74–5. The playwright thereby condemns Lutheran and Zwinglian views, as well as those of the Anabaptists.

80 Ibid., 76–7. They describe the Anabaptist position on separation from the world in the following terms:

VERNUFT: Wil u wijff en ghij niet, sij mach u laeten blijven
Het is een bevel van gods vinger beschreven
Bekent u dootsondich, heydens sneven
En versaeckt dat u Antichrist heeft gedaen over 't hooft
WAENENDE: Als ghij u van u heydens weesen hebt berooft
Sullen wij u in 't recht gelooff onderwijsen
En daernae doopen nae die rechte ghijsen
Want 't gelooff moet voorgaen, dit's ons bescheyt (ibid., 77).

81 Ibid., 79.
82 Ibid., 80:

> SCHRIFTU: Daer staet geschreven: allen menschen en geesten niet en
>   gelooft
> Maer proefftse, dit is des heeren gebodt
> SEMPEL: Sij seyden opentlijck datse quamen van godt
> Om ons te vercondigen het godlijck bevel
> GEESTEL: Waenende weten en eygen vernuft ken ick wel
> Elck is een schalcken sayer bijsondere
> ONNOS: Wadt sij sijn off niet, ick hoor van hun wondere
> Van bidden, van vasten, weet ick wadt elck noch doet
>
>   ...
>
> GEESTELIJC: Waer siet men dat simpel en trou door faelgeert
> Dan door de geveynsde hypocrysije
> De seer menigerhande is ten desen tijen
> 'T sijn al teerroeden daer men u meede vangt.

83 Ibid., 93–9. For example, Onnosel exclaims:

> O siele, o mijn siele, ja welcken soetheyt
> Gevoel ick nu in mijnen consientye
> Wech, wanen en vernuft, met u intentye
> Wie ben ick dat ick goods werck sou ondersoecken

To which his wife responds:

> Maryja, Maryjam, wee hem die u vervloecken
> Welcken wonder heeft godt ons uuyt u ghethoont
> Godt en mensch, twee naetueren, eens gepersoont
> Hebdij boven natuere wonderlijcke gebaert (ibid., 97).

84 Ibid., 98–9.
85 In the introduction Misuse tells his cohort that he had come from 'Eemder-lant' where he had fled the 'Gelderman.' Voolstra (ibid., 59–60) proposes that this refers to the plundering of East Frisia by the troops of Karel van Guelder in the winter of 1534 and that therefore the play was composed before the end of this military campaign in March of the same year. Nissen, *De Katholieke polemiek tegen de Dopers*, 137–8, however, argues for a date of composition after the spring of 1534 (but before the fall of Münster at the end of June 1535) because East Frisia is mentioned here as a possible place of refuge. Voolstra's contention, however, seems more convincing. If the play was written after March 1534, surely the author would have ridiculed the attempt of thousands of Melchiorites to reach Münster – the so-called Great Trek – which occurred in that month.
86 See above, chapter 3.
87 *Tspel van de Cristenkercke*, in Brands, *Tspel van de Cristenkercke*, Hum.1 I 2.

The dating of the play is problematic. Brands (xxiii), because he identified the play as orthodox, was forced to conclude that Pouwels had composed it as proof of his orthodoxy after 10 Nov. 1540, the date on which he was mildly punished by Utrecht's magistrates for having bound and sold a forbidden book. Drewes ('Het interpreteren van godsdienstige spelen,' 7–10), however, has shown that the play instead promotes a Lutheran perspective. It most likely was composed before the punishment, and it is known that Pouwels had become a member of Utrecht's rhetorician's chamber by 1534.

88 *Tspel van de Cristenkercke*, ll. 17–21:
> Welck broot, woordt, lichaem, des viants gheboetheyt
> Met scandaliserende scrifts onvroetheyt,
> Ja met verblinde hertnackighe verwoetheyt
> Gharen souden extirperen,
> Mer heer, doer v stercke handt sullen zij falgeeren.

89 Ibid., 4, ll. 79–83:
> Daer is meer een wegh inder scriftuer,
> Mer dese beueynsde clercken maken dese erruer
> Ter werlt duer, zeer zinnich van kuese,
> Want sij maken de scrift een wassen nuese,
> Die buyghende nae haer vreemt opinioen.

90 Ibid., 5, ll. 113–15:
> Soe twoort, soe de wercken,
> Ende tgheuoelen goet hebt van der cristenkercken,
> V submitterende als een ghehoorsaem kint.

91 Ibid., 6–7. At l. 202 Uprecht states that Gharen must 'Van sonden suldij na v macht een aflaet doen,' a phrase which Brands interpreted as doing penance. Drewes, 'Het interpreteren van Godsdienstige spelen,' 7–8, however notes that the phrase actually means to turn from sin to God, and best fits a Lutheran interpretation.

92 *Tspel van de Cristenkercke*, 9, ll. 206–19:
> GHAREN TBEST: Hort meester, wat mijn hert noch seer ontvuecht,
> Van dees, die men heet nieuwe ewangelisten,
> De wercken niet achtende sij gheheel verquisten,
> Als niet behooflick tot onswer salicheyt,
> Mer tgheloof alleen.
> UPRECHT: Laet sulcke wederpalicheyt
> Ende wilt de scriftuer te recht anmercken.
> De wercken alst gheloue verstercken
> Voor den mensch van buijten, vaet wel tbediet,

Mer god alleen tgheloof des herten ansiet,
Inwendich merckende wat den mensch is.
Mer twerck der menschen een vuijtwendich wensch is.
Ten voordele van ons moeter twerck oeck wesen,
Mer twerck der liefden is alleen voor god ghepresen.

93 Ibid., 13–14, ll. 309–16:

VERBLENDE: Wa, baals propheten, dat waren mannen,
Die nv ghebannen zijn vuijt allen houen
Met sophisma. vprecht simpelick ghelouen
Can nv verdouen ons gheleerde sophisten.
Hoe worden verblent onse teologisten,
Logijken, legisten noyt misten nv ketterije subiect.
Hoe wijt argueren, daer en es niet dat strect,
Een ijghelick ons beghect soe laten wijt legghen.

Their father, Judas, moreover, is known to the world by his printed bulls
and books (ibid., 13, ll. 322–3).

94 Ibid., 22, ll. 496–9, where Cristelijcke Kercke describes her as

Die rose van gernaten,
Maecht, moeder eersame,
Enich zijnde, god den gheest wijs van fame,
Den apostelen sant.

95 Ibid., 31, ll. 755–60:

Ghij gheestelijcke, wilt v nv verschijnen.
Vp doet nv der rechter scriftueren scrijnen.
Segt, laet der handen ghewranck.
Ghij exempt al vander valscher doctrijnen
Looft nv den heer, alleen thooft der devijnen,
Nae gheest ende waerheijts bevanck.

96 Ibid., 40–58.

97 Ibid., 61–2, esp, l. 1411:

Verachtende goeds woordt, dat warachtighe sacrament.

98 Ibid., 65, l. 1479, and 66, l. 1515.

99 Ibid., 67, ll. 1534 and 1538.

100 Ibid., 76, ll. 1747–52, where Schriftverlijcke Hoede, speaking to the priests,
remarks:

Der aerden soetheijt was v god ghehingende,
Besmet ghijn, v priesters, na ijdelheijt dringhende,
Van god niet ghewaghen,
V herders, twoort soet met bitterheijt minghende,
V propheten, in baals naem singhende,
Na afgoden iaghen.

He continues,

Want ghij helijam met root bloedighee armen
Vervolghende zijt, met Iesabels karmen,
Raetgheuers tot naboths doot (ll. 1778–80).

101 Ibid., 88–94.

102 For example, in a letter written to the Court of Holland at The Hague in 1534, an unidentified Anabaptist (possibly David Joris) accused the court of reviving the bloody persecution of Antiochus and in terms similar to those of this play called down divine wrath on the authorities; see Waite and Zijlstra, 'Antiochus Revisited.'

103 *Tspel van de Cristenkercke*, 100, ll. 2330–40 (includes Selfs Goetduncken's earlier remarks):

Ende ick bin Selfs goetdunckende wetere,
Ghewonnen van vpgheblasen valsch vermeten
An de oude hoere, mer onversleten,
Ketterije, die gheleijt heeft den eersten steen
Int fondament vander hellen met swaer gheween,
Ande welcke haer leen alle ketters versoecken
Ghecapt, ghescoren, sonder verstandt altijt lesende in boecken
Es doer haer vercloecken bekent gheworden,
Alle opinien zijn doer Scriftuerlijcke hoede verblent gheworden,
Die thans ter werlt noch sterck in vigoor zijn.
In allen consten singt ketterije garen den tenoor fijn.

104 Drewes ('Het interpreteren der Godsdienstige spelen,' 7–13) however, shows that each of the supposedly orthodox passages which Brands uses to prove his argument is better interpreted in a Lutheran context. See Brands, *Tspel van de Cristenkercke*, xxi–xxviii.

105 See William R. Russell, 'Martin Luther's Understanding of the Pope as the Antichrist,' Oberman, *Luther,* and Barnes, *Prophecy and Gnosis*. For an eastern Netherlandic Catholic example from the 1520s, see Frijhoff, 'Het Gelders Antichrist-tractaat (1524) en zijn auteur.'

106 See n. 93 above. Later, Simple Faith defines heretics as:

Alle ketters versoecken
ghecapt, ghescoren, sonder verstandt altijt lesende in boecken
Es doer haer vercloecken bekent gheworden,
Alle opinien zijn doer Scriftuerlijcke hoede verblent gheworden (*Tspel van de Cristenkercke*, 100, ll. 2335–8; see n. 103 above).

107 Brands, *Tspel van de Cristenkercke*, xxi.

108 *Een tafelspel van die menichfuldicheit des bedrochs der werelt,'* in *BRN* I, 369–87. Original in Haarlen Archief TMB, I (Hum. 3 A 2 and Hum. 1 OI 16).

109 Apparently around the same time as this play, it had become popular for wandering clerics claiming to have been on Venusberg to extort money from the gullible, who were terrified by their claims to be able to call up the 'Furious Horde,' those who had died prematurely (Ginzburg, *The Night Battles*, 33–68, esp. 44). Ginzburg (55–6) cites an intriguing example of popular Venusberg beliefs from Swabia, which were noted by a sixteenth-century chronicler under the year 1544: 'Wandering about the Swabian countryside at that time were certain *clerici vagantes* ... They had approached a group of peasants and told them they had been on the Venusberg and had seen extraordinary things there. They claimed knowledge of the past and could foretell the future; they had the power to discover lost objects and possessed charms which protected both men and animals from witches and their crimes; they could even keep hail away.' See also Waite, 'Talking Animals, Preserved Corpses and Venusberg: The Sixteenth-Century Worldview and Popular Conceptions of the Spiritualist David Joris (1501–1556).'

110 *Die Menichfuldicheit*, 375:
   OERSPRONCK DER SONDEN: Ick bin ghecomen wt vrou Venus berge
   Daermen sonder erge, alderley consten handteert
   MENICHFULDICH BEDROCH: Hebdy in vrou Venus berch gelogeert
   Daer worden versiert, veel vremde cueren
   Vertelt ons doch wat.

111 Oerspronck der sonden describes his wares in the following terms:
   Ick heb hier recepten cleynogien en iuweelkens
   Veelderley deelkens, van groter crachten
   Vol vreemder condicien wilt her op acthen
   Sijn groote machten, sullen v sijn bequaeme
   Siet daer isser een (ibid., 376).

112 Ibid., 378–9:
   OERSPRONCK DER SONDEN: Synen naem is Haet en nydicheyt
   Datter werelt heeft geseyt, veel discorden
   Doer nydicheyt ginck Cain synen broder vermoorden
   Doer nydicheyt sijn die Propheten gestouren
   En Christus heefter oock den doot doer verworuen
   Doer nydicheyt, die de Pariseen beleden
   Doen den Heer straften haer giericheden
   En eygen instellen altemaelen
   MENICHFULDICH BEDROCH: Men en vint gheen gebreck onder die
       conuentualen
   Oft onder tgeestelicke volck wilt heir op mercken

OERSPRONCK DER SONDEN: Al die ghene die nae den gheest Gods
   wercken
Sijn gheestelicke clercken, na Gods bekinnen
Waer salmense vinnen?
MENICHFULDICH BEDROCH: Dats goet te versinnen
Alle die den gheest Gods beminnen
Sijn gheestelike menschen in Gods presentie
Wat meyndi dat God vraecht nae enige differentie
Naet scheeren, habyte, oft ander faetsoen.

113 Ibid., 379–80.
114 Ibid., 381–2, esp. 382:
   Ghehuyrde officie doet die schaepen verstroyen
   Wt die rechte schaeps coyen, tot haerder onvromen
   Wanneer sy den wolf van vere sien comen
   Beginnen sy te scromen, en gaen loopen.
115 Ibid., 385:
   MENICHFULDICH BEDROCH: tMoet voer die geleerden wel een groot
      verdriet sijn
   Die met neerstich studeren haer hoofden breecken
   OERSPRONCK DER SONDEN: Maer dat sijn dese plompe leecken
   Die niet en weten te spreecken
   En seggen noch dattet sijn Gods giften
   Diemen ontfanckt van den heyligen gheest ...
116 The play's modern editors, S. Cramer and F. Pijper, suggest that it origi-
   nated in a Mennonite (Doopsgezinden) circle (BRN, I, 371).
117 This procedure was frequently the case with prose works of various Dutch
   reformers, including spiritualists such as Joris, many of whose writings
   were published for the first time after his death (Waite, 'The Longevity of
   Spiritualistic Anabaptism').
118 Prochiaen, Coster en Wever, Van Dis, Reformatorische rederijkersspelen,
   150–221 (Hum. 4 O 8), esp. 152, ll. 65–8:
   En is dit niet een plaghe, een pestilentie,
   Ergher dan pocken, Lelmten oft Enghels sweet,
   Dat tgemeyn volck nu maect sulcken mencie,
   Vander scriftueren, dwelc hem niet en versteet!
119 Ibid., 156, ll. 203–5:
   Siet kint, ghy moet Schriftuere laten varen,
   Want sulcke mensche beschaemt en gerooft hebben
   En blijft bi tgeloove dat u ouders gelooft hebben.
   For a more thorough summary of this play, see Waite, David Joris, 13–16.

120 Priest delivers a list of fifteen accusations against the Lutherans. *Prochiaen, Coster en Wever*, 162, ll. 405–26.

121 Weaver says of Anabaptists, 'Ich houdse even voor Monicken, als ghy zijt/ Vaten superstitieus, kuerieus van wercken,/ Sy bannen, sy schelden, sy blijven wter kercken ...' (ibid., 202, ll. 1883–4). This reference to Anabaptists, instead of to Mennonites, helps date the composition of the work to the 1530s instead of later.

122 Ibid., 181: ll. 1091–8, 1110–11:

> Hoe onderwint ghy u den geest Gods te blasphemeren,
> Dat ghy sPaus heylicheit so groot hebt vercoren?
> Hy is doch even so wel in sonden geboren
> En in sonden ontfangen als ander menschen?
> Wat vragen wy dan na zijn huylen en wenschen,
> Na zijn benedictie oft vermaledien?
> Ic houdse al voor consten van tooverijen,
> Want hy niet dan gelt en soect en wereltlijc eere.
>
> ...
>
> Hy macht door de cracht des grooten Antichrists doen,
> Dwelc hy doch selve is en eewelijck blijft.

If the pope turned from his errors,

> Maer sochte he de rechte Apostolische leere,
> Hoe de menschen moeten op Christum staen,
> So sout hem also Paus Adrianus gaen,
> Die van zijn valsche Apostles wert vergheven (ibid., ll. 1099–1102).

Later the Weaver said, 'So zijt ghy den Antechrist oft Antechrists knecht' (ibid., 193).

123 Ibid., 189, ll. 1401–6:

> Ja, maer tis om uwen leckeren mont te vullen,
> Daerom segdy dat noot is, ghy Canoniken,
> Maer tis recht een spijse voor papen en moniken,
> En niet voor Wevers, Pelsers oft Smeden,
> Die zijn met een stuck kaes wel te vreden,
> En grof broot en water, gelijckende den hane.

124 Ibid., 190. This particular criticism may have reflected the concerns of the merchant class, which was strongly represented in the rhetorician chambers.

125 Ibid., 208. For the popularity of this belief, see Robert Scribner, 'Cosmic Order and Daily Life: Sacred and Secular in Pre-Industrial German Society,' in Scribner, *Popular Culture and Popular Movement*, 1–16.

126 *Prochiaen, Coster en Wever,*' 209, ll. 2135–9.

127 Ibid., 211, ll. 2221–3.

128 Ibid., 220, ll. 2552–5, where Weaver tells Sexton:
> Int sweet dijns aensichts sult ghy eten u broot.
>
> Dats u yerst van noode, dat sult ghy weten,
>
> Want die niet en wilt wercken, die en sal niet eten,
>
> En voort sal u de cracht des Evangeli stercken.

Sexton then agrees to learn the craft of weaving.

129 Ibid., 197–8 ll. 1706, 1716, 1719, 1722–3:
> SEXTON: Gregorius seyt: tzijn der ongeleerden boecken ...
>
> WEVER: Ja, maer God spreect, ghy en sult geen gelyckenisse maken ...
>
> Hoe God alle Godemakers sal verderven ...
>
> Ghi sultse wel leeren, preect haer trechte Gods woort
>
> En leert haer, als der heligen, Christi voetstappen gaen.

This suggests a parallel to what Werner Packull has called the celebration of lay emancipation from the tutelage of clergy in the pamphlet literature in the early German Reformation ('"The Image of the Common Man" in the Early Pamphlets of the Reformation [1520–1525],' esp. 260).

130 See Eire, *War Against the Idols*, and Wandel, *Voracious Idols and Violent Hands*.

131 *CDIN*, V, 349–50: The sheriff of Delft, Jan de Heuter, remarked that Joris had told the 'gemeen volck datse waren upten dwaelwech, mit meer andere scandeluese woirden, tenderende tegen die goide usancien ende loeffelicken onderhoudenisse, dair uuyt seducie heeft oic in dezeluen libellen fameus gescreuen grouelicken tot mispryzinge der beelden in den temple, alsof tselue onbehoorlick ende occasie van misleydinge van den volcke waren, scryuende tot streckenisse van dien dese woorden: "dese valsche ypocryten, monicken ende papen, hebben ons diets gemaect, dattet die ongeleerden haer boucken waren; mair de Gheest des Heeren zeyt, dattet stricken zyn tot vallen van die ongeleerden ende bekoirders van de menschen hair zielen".'

132 For the 1520s, see *CDIN*; for the 1566 incidents, see Crew, *Calvinist Preaching*.

133 Brady, Jr, *Ruling Class, Regime, and Reformation at Strasbourg*, 217–27.

134 *Siecke Stadt*, in Grondijs, *Een spul van sinnen van den Siecke Stadt*. See above, chapter 4.

135 Another example of using biblical drama to condemn religious persecution may come from fifteenth-century England. Gibson (*The Theater of Devotion*, 32), suggests that the East Anglian two-day N-Town Passion play, composed sometime in the third quarter of the fifteenth century, used the story of the high priest Annas to oppose the persecution of suspected Lollards.

136 *Dwerck der Apostolen cap. 3, 4 en 5,* the printed edition of which is in *BRN,* I, 273–366, where the editors suggest (285) that it was in existence by 1539.

137 Ibid., 296:

> Doer den name Jesus hebdijt vercreghen,
> In welcken veruult is met corter verhalicheyt,
> Heel Moyses Wet, tot smenschen salicheyt.

138 Ibid., 302: 'Doert tghelooue in Christum twelck wy v leeren ... Ghelooft ghy in Christo uwer sielen pant / Ghy wort salich, so schriftuere claer, seyt.'

139 Ibid., 324:

> Twoort Gods blyuen wy altijt vermanich
> Gods woort is eewich bouen allen dinghen,
> Twoort en was noyt yemant onderdanich,
> Twoort Gods als God moet bouen dringhen.

140 Ibid., 290:

> Hoe de gheleerde, seer onuersaecht
> Gods woort begheerden te brenghen tondere
> Met verbieden, veruolghen, tsy Gode geclaecht.

Peter also remarks to the gathered crowd (301):

> Ghy hebt den onnoselen gheaccuseert,
> Roepende den dootslagher te behouden tleuen.

141 Ibid., 306:

> SCHOON YPOCRIJT: Maer dese nieuwe predicanten,
> Die als truwanten, ons heeren, onteeren,
> Ende Teuangelie met haren leeren, vermeeren,
> Dus int verseeren, verkeeren, de simpel ghemeente.

142 Ibid., 307.

143 Ibid., 331. Here the Vices describe their wares, including 'all manner of virtues, adorned words, outward appearances, fasts, vigils' and the like.

144 Ibid., 308–9.

145 Ibid., 356–8.

146 Ibid., 312.

147 Ibid., 346.

> PROPHET: Dese Hoere bedriecht de gheheele werelt,
> Doer die beeste verkerelt, wiens hoofden gecroont,
> Met vele dyademen schoone verschoont,
> Als hoochste ghetroont, in swerelts slodt.
> HYPOCRITE: Dese valsche beeste die can het ghebodt,
> Vanden almachtighen Godt, heel tonder vellen,
> Ende zijn gheboden int hoochste stellen,

Als Godt, regerende der menschen conscientien.
PROPHET: Dit is den Babylonischen stoel der pestilencien,
Vol reuerencien, vanden grooten Antechrist,
Thooft der sonden.

148 Ibid., 325–6:

PETRUS: Mijn broders bereedt v als de vayllianden,
Teghen de tanden, der woluen bloetghierich,
Want Gods ghenaden vol soeter playsanden,
Sal onse vyanden, noch maken obedierich.
JACOBUS: Heere die doer Dauid uwen kinde spraecste,
De Coninghen der aerden ende Princen quamen
Grymende, als de nydighe duerblaecste,
Teghen haren Heere en Cristum vol vramen.
JOANNES: Siet Here, nv comen als stekende bramen
Teghen uwen sone, als de gheexalteerde
Herodes, ia Israel ende Pilatus tsamen
Om te doene dat ghy predestineerde.

149 Ibid., 365.
150 *Lazarus Dood*, fols. 136r and 139r. See above, chapter 4.
151 Beemon, 'The Myth of the Spanish Inquisition and the Preconditions of the Dutch Revolt.'

6: Popular Ritual, Social Protest, and the Rhetorician Competition in Ghent, 1539

1 Ladurie, *Carnival in Romans*, argues that 'the Carnival was in fact the climax of a vast regional revolt. It was a rebellion against government and against taxes' (xiv–xv, 35–59).
2 Davis, *Society and Culture*; see also her 'From "Popular Religion" to Religious Cultures' and 'The Sacred and the Body Social in Sixteenth-Century Lyon.'
3 See Scribner, *Popular Culture and Popular Movements*, 'Ritual and Reformation,' *For the Sake of Simple Folk*, and most recently his 'Introduction' in *Popular Religion in Germany and Central Europe, 1400–1800*. See also Zika, 'Hosts, Processions and Pilgrimages.' Many works have appeared on the subject for other regions as well, including England, i.e, Bossy, 'Holiness and Society,' James, 'Ritual, Drama and Social Body,' Slack, *Rebellion, Popular Protest and the Social Order in Early Modern England*, and Bristol, *Carnival and Theater*. For recent examples of the subject for Italy, see, among others, Edward Muir, *Civic Ritual in Renaissance Venice* (Princeton, 1981).

4 Pleij, *Het Gilde van de Blauwe Schuit*; also his 'The Function of Literature in Urban Societies in the Later Middle Ages' and 'Inleiding: Op belofte van profijt,' in Pleij et al., *Op belofte van profijt* 8–51; in the same volume see other essays esp. Rob Resoort, 'De koopman en de verhalende literatuur' (280–301), and P.J.A. Franssen, 'Tekstpresentatie als spiegel van stedelijke mentaliteit (1470–1540)' (302–17). See also the essays in Rooijakkers and Van der Zee, *Religieuze volkscultuur* and Nijsten, *Volkscultuur in de late middeleeuwen*.

5 Pleij, 'Van keikoppen en droge jonkers.' See also the other articles in the special issue of *Volkskundig Bulletin* 15 (Oct. 1989), *Charivari in de Nederlanden: Rituele sancties op deviant gedrag*, ed. Rooijakkers and Romme. I am thankful to Dr Rooijakkers for providing me with a copy of this volume. On this theme, see also Nijsten, *Volkscultuur in de late middeleeuwen*.

6 Pleij, 'Geladen vermaak.'

7 Scribner, *Popular Culture*, 100–1.

8 In her discussion of youth groups in urban France, Davis remarks, 'Not surprisingly, the charivari and carnival license to deride could also be turned against the political authorities, and with the changed social and age composition of the urban Abbeys it sometimes was.' She continues that it 'was not the domestic disorder of the governing families that was criticized, but rather their political misrule' (*Society and Culture*, 117).

9 See the critical edition of the published plays by Erné and Van Dis, *De Gentse spelen*. The Burgundians had selected Ghent's *Fonteine* chamber as the official chamber of the Low Countries.

10 The most important recent study of the revolt is Decavele, *Keizer tussen stropdragers*.

11 Cited in Vandecasteele, 'Letterkundig leven te Gent van 1500 tot 1539,' esp. 56–7.

12 Decavele, *Keizer tussen stropdragers*, 49–50.

13 See ibid., 123–40, the source of this discussion.

14 See ibid., 148, where Johan Dambruyne describes the result of the *calfvel* as a 'climate of cold war' between the emperor and his birth city.

15 See ibid., 141–56.

16 Verheyden, *De hervorming in de Zuidelijke Nederlanden in de XVIe eeuw*, 45–7, esp. 46.

17 Community of goods was practised in Anabaptist Münster in 1534–5, and was an important component of Anabaptist ideology (see Stayer, *The German Peasants' War and Anabaptist Community of Goods*). This development also reflects the growing population of the unemployed and impoverished in the city; in 1535 Ghent's magistrates were forced to radically reform their system

of poor relief (see Decavele, *Keizer tussen stropdragers*, 155; Decavele, *De dag-eraad*, 117–63. Apparently the Poor Chamber of Ghent had in 1545 six to seven thousand poor people on its support list (Decavele, *De dageraad*, 136).

18 Decavele, *Keizer tussen stropdragers*, 115–16.

19 During the reign of Charles V, thirty-nine individuals were executed in Ghent for heresy (ibid., 113). Another prominent member of the reform cir-cle, Jan Utenhove, was banned on 9 May 1545, although he had already fled to Germany (Decavele, *De dageraad*, 81).

20 Verheyden, *De hervorming in de Zuidelijke Nederlanden*, 44–5.

21 Decavele, *De dageraad*, 64, writes, 'Die geest van tolerantie van de christel-ijke humanist, in de latere geschiedschrijving ook wel Cassandrianisme genoemd, heeft in Vlaanderen lange tijd verder doorgewerkt'; and (76), 'In deze erasmiaanse grope toonaangevende figuren leefde sterk de geest van minnelijk overleg, van dogmatisch relativisme en van pacifisme, ook van openheid voor het nieuwe dat zich op Europees plan aan de intelligentsia aanbood.' See also Duke, *Reformation and Revolt*, 45.

22 Decavele, *Keizer tussen stropdragers*, 157–8. This discussion is based on Dam-bruyne's description of the revolt on 157–69.

23 Dambruyne, ibid., 162.

24 Ibid. As part of Pien's examination the questioners shaved off all the hair on his body in their search for the devil's marks, a procedure common dur-ing the later witch trials! Perhaps it was believed that the old civic leaders had made a secret pact not only with Charles V, but also with the devil? For witches and devil's marks, see Levack, *The Witch-hunt in Early Modern Europe*, 51, 237. For witch trials in Flanders, see among others Vanysacker, *Hekserij in Bruges*.

25 Apparently they demanded, 'Geef ons te eten en te drinken; wij mogen niet werken en moeten nochtans leven' and 'Weldra zullen wij uw rijkdom bezitten en gij onze armoede' (Decavele, *Keizer tussen stropdragers*, 171–2).

26 For a more detailed examination of the history of one of these chambers, *Marien Theeren*, see Beyaert, *Opkomst en bloei van de Gentse rederykerskamer Marien Theeren*. A fifth chamber from a nearby community, Sint-Pieters bij Gent, is often included among Ghent's rhetorician societies. For the ordi-nance regulating Ghent's *De Fonteine*, see Coigneau, '9 December 1448,' in Erenenstein, *Ein theater geschiedenis der Nederlander*, 50–5.

27 Vandecasteele, 'Letterkundig leven te Gent.' The following references are transcribed in his footnotes.

28 Ibid., 12–13.

29 Ibid., 23.

30 Ibid., 27.

31 Vandecasteele (ibid., 27 n. 115) discusses the evidence for this contest.

32 Ibid., 28.

33 Beyaert, *Opkomst en bloei van de Gentse rederykerskamer Marien Theeren*, 41. The reasons for such public support are given by the magistrates: first, the chambers had sustained at their own costs their dramatic activities 'in peace and unity'; second, in these chambers were many 'poor fellows' [*scamele ghesellen*]; third, Ghent, as the capital of Flanders, to its own honour frequently hosts the rhetoricians of other cities; fourth, the chambers of other cities were often financially supported by their civic governments; and fifth, the rhetoricians argued that civic support of militia guilds was a precedent for civic support of the drama and literary culture which rhetoricians provided (41–2).

34 Ibid., 42. For *Corpus Christi*, see Rubin, *Corpus Christi: The Eucharist in Late Medieval Culture*, and Ramakers *Spelen en figuren*, 43–166 and 249–350.

35 On 27 February 1537, a wagon play composed by Willem van der Blommen was performed at various spots in the city, deriding the religious estate. In this work three fools – a lawyer, a doctor, and a religious – sang the following song:
    De sotten en synder noch niet al
    Die capproenen draghen.
    Zy gaen ghescoren, al waeren zij mal,
    Al naer ghewin zy vraghen.
    Men siet ze van duere te duere loopen;
    Donnoosele die sij tvel afstroopen,
    Onder haerlieder schijn van deuchden;
    Zy cryghent al, wat baetet gherelt,
    Huusen, Hoven ende daertoe ghelt
    Daer leven zij op met vreuchden (Decavele, *De dageraad*, 196).

36 Vandecasteele, 'Letterkundig leven te Gent,' 22. Although *coninxspelen* (king plays) were normally performed in most cities on Epiphany (6 Jan.), it seems that these performances had been transposed to April and May in Ghent. These plays are not to be confused with the *conincfeesten* (king festival) of the rhetorician guilds, which were festivities honouring their patrons.

37 See Davis, *Society and Culture*, esp. 97–123; Scribner, *Popular Culture and Popular Movements*, 71–101.

38 Vandecasteele ('Letterkundige leven te Gent,' 22) notes that the last mention for one in Mechelen occurred in 1503. Duplessis in *Lille and the Dutch Revolt*, 195–8, notes that Lille's magistrates had once subsidized feast of fools festivities but in 1519 they forbade them, although unapproved festiv-

ities continued into the 1530s. In the 1520s the magistrates acted against Feast of the Holy Innocents activities, this time prohibiting anyone but youths to participate, and finally prohibiting such festivities altogether in the 1550s. There was, according to Duplessis (197–8), a growing fear that youth festivities, games, even communal processions, 'might augment rather than release tension, impair rather than promote civic solidarity, question rather than legitimate religious and secular norms.' Interestingly, Lille remained loyal to both the church and the emperor during the 1550s and 1560s. For civic attempts to control feast of fools activities, see also Herman Pleij, 'Eind juli 1551. Op het zotten feest van Brussel wordt Meester oom als vorst in een massaspel beëidigd. De stedelijke feestviering van bevrijdend ritueel naar gecontroleerd schouwtoneel,' in Erenstein, *Een theatergeschiedenis der Nederlanden*, 112–19.

39 Burke, *Popular Culture*, 199–204; Scribner, *Popular Culture and Popular Movements*, 83; See also Roper, *Oedipus and the Devil*, esp. 'Blood and Codpieces: Masculinity in the Early Modern German Town,' 107–24.

40 Davis, *Society and Culture*, 117–21; Scribner, *Popular Culture and Popular Movements*, 85–6. Youth groups could also act as positive agents for reform, as they did in Florence in the 1490s under Savonarola. Trexler in 'Ritual in Florence,' esp. 250–64, describes how the Dominican preacher Savonarola organized Florence's young boys into a reforming band of somber, pious examples for the whole community.

41 Vandecasteele, 'Letterkundig leven te Gent,' 25–6.

42 De Potter, *Gent, van den oudsten tijd tot heden*, IV, 6–7. From Ghent, Stadsarchief, Register 93-BB, eersten bouck vanden voorgheboden der stede van Ghendt beghinnene int Jaer 1482 (hereafter Ghent SA Reg. BB).

43 Herman Pleij, '24 Februari 1527: Intree te Gent op vastenavond van de zottenkeizer: Het repertoire van de volksfeesten,' in Schenkeveld-Van der Dussen, *Nederlandse literatuur*, 137–42.

44 As Keith P.F. Moxey has noted, the result of such attempted suppression was not quite what church leaders had hoped for, as 'the dramatic festivals associated with the feast of fools at Lille and in several other French cities were divorced from their religious context and became the sole responsibility of secular rhetorical societies' (Moxey, 'Pieter Bruegel and *The Feast of Fools*,' 642).

45 Vandecasteele, 'Letterkundig leven te Gent,' 26–7. Originally 'feast of fools' festivals were put on by the clergy at Christmastime, during which the clerics would elect a choirboy as bishop, parody the Mass, and lead an ass around the church. By the sixteenth century, however, the church had officially ended such clerical horseplay, while lay organizations, craft guilds,

confraternities, or 'fool-societies' (abbeys of misrule) took them over (Davis, *Society and Culture*, 98).

46 'Ende ooc boven al tguent voorscreven, dat hem eren yeghelic, jnt selve vastenavont spel spelende, verdraghe eeneghe langhe messen, hallebaer-den, pansijsers oft eeneghe andere ongheoorloofde wapene te draghene, ten ware van fijnen haute, up de correctie als boven' (Ghent SA Reg. BB, fol. 94r; De Potter, *Gent*, IV, 9).

47 'Ende ommedieswille dat dit voorn. spel uit ghenouchten uute ghestelt es end ooc ommedectelic behoort ghespeelt te zijne, so verbietmen alsboven dat hem niement en vervoordere verdect ofte vermomt te gane jnt voorn. spel, ofte ooc eeneghe persoonen met stroebanden oft anderssins te beleg-ghene oft ommerynghene omme alzo huerlieder vrijen wegh te belettene ende yet te heesschene, zo voorseit es' (Ghent SA Reg. BB, fol.94r; De Potter, *Gent*, IV, 9).

48 The prizes ranged from 2£ Fl. for first and 8s for eighth place. The account reads: 'Omme dat de keyserinne onlancx byder gratien gods gheleghen es van eenen Jonghen Zoene / Daerby hiernaermaelen groote aliamche ende blyscepe des lande commen mach ... zo ghebiedtenen ende laet weten van heere ende wetweghe / datmen in zondaghen naestcommende houde zal processie generale ende ommedraghen thelich sacrament' (Ghent SA Reg. BB, fols. 225v–6r, Actum 23 November 1537). For the *stadsrekeningen* records of rhetorician participation in this celebration, see Vandecasteele, 'Let-terkundig leven te Gent,' 29, esp. notes 126–8. Vandecasteele was appar-ently unaware of the birth of the unfortunate Juan and hence suggested that the celebration may have been for the birth of the princess Juana; she, however, had been born two years earlier. For the imperial family, see Alva-rez, *Charles V: Elected Emperor and Hereditary Ruler*, esp. 111, 114–15, 192.

49 Davis, *Society and Culture*, 108–23. She writes (113) about some sixteenth-century cities which 'continued to see informal groupings such as street gangs of males in their teens who played games and threw stones at neigh-borhood enemies.'

50 Ghent SA Reg. BB, fol. 229v. Actum 8 January 1537 (1538 in modern calen-dar).

51 Ibid., fol. 230r; Vandecasteele, 'Letterkundig leven te Gent,' 29–30n.129. Popular unrest may have been on the increase also because of the frequent visitations of a plague (*haesteghe siecte*) and a rise in the number of poor and vagabonds in the city (see Ghent SA Reg. BB, fols. 220r–1v).

52 Ibid., fol.237r; Vandecasteele, 'Letterkundig leven te Gent,' 30 n. 129.

53 Ghent SA Reg. BB, fols. 238v–9v. Actum 27 June 1538.

54 Ibid., fol. 238r. Actum 28 June 1538.

55 Ibid., fol. 246v. Actum 27 June 1539.

56 Decavele *Keizer tussen Stropdragers*, 138–9.

57 Arnade, 'Secular Charisma, Sacred Power: Rites of Rebellion in the Ghent Entry of 1467,' 72.

58 Ibid. See also B.A.M. Ramakers, '13 April 1458. Blijde inkomst van Filips de Goede in Gent. De theatrale versiering van vorstelijke intochten,' in Erenstein, *Een theatergeschiedenis der Nederlanden*, 56–63.

59 Scribner, *Popular Culture and Popular Movements*, 103–22; Rublack, 'Martin Luther and the Urban Social Experience,' esp. 128–31; Eire, *War against the Idols*.

60 Scribner, *Popular Culture and Popular Movements*, 64.

61 Vandecasteele, 'Letterkundig leven te Gent,' 31. For the contest, see also Brachin, 'La Fête de Rhétorique de Gand (1539).'

62 Described by Vandecasteele, 'Letterkundig leven te Gent,' 36–9. The refrains were published by Joos Lambrecht, who also printed the edition of the plays.

63 Van Elslander, 'Het refreinfeest te Gent in 1539,' esp. 42–3. The poets of Meesen, Tielt, and Loo especially made fun of pilgrimages and saints.

64 Ibid., 50–1.

65 Ibid., 52. Van Elslander (53) argues that the refrains of Kortrijk also display an affinity to early reformation thought, and that kernels of reform precepts are found in the poetic works of Nieuwpoort (in a passage against persecution), Edingen (in a reference to martyrdom), Ypres (with some lines against the veneration of images), and Lo (with its judgment against idolatry).

66 See Vandecasteele, 'Letterkundig leven te Gent,' 40–3. Oudenaarde's council approved an enormous subsidy of 2280£ Fl. 19s 3d for their chamber, while most others spent in the range of several hundred pounds.

67 Ghent SA Reg. BB, fol. 246r. Vandecasteele, 'Letterkundig leven te Gent,' 43 n. 193. For a discussion of the staging of the plays and of their publication, see W.M.W. Hummelen, '31 augustus 1539. De eerste bundel met rederijkersspelen die bij een wedstrijd opgevoerd zijn, komt uit bij Joos Lambrecht Lettersteker te Gent. Spelen van sinne en hun opvoeringspraktijken,' in Erenstein, *Een theatergeschiedenis der Nederlanden*, 92–7.

68 Ghent SA Reg. BB, fol. 246v; Vandecasteele, 'Letterkundig leven te Gent,' 46–7.

69 Ghent SA Reg. BB, fol. 246v.

70 Ibid., fol. 246v. Actum 27 June 1539.

71 Decavele *Keizer tussen stropdragers*, 94–6. The plays were judged to be heretical on 10 June 1540, and Charles V published his edict against them on 22 September 1540, although, as will be noted below, there is extant a manu-

script mandate against reforming rhetoricians dating from July 1540. A quite recent discussion of the Ghent competition is W.M.H. Hummelen, '12–23 Juni 1539: Negentien rederijkerskamers nemen deel aan een wedstrijd te Gent: rederijkersdrama en reformatie,' in Schenkeveld-Van der Dussen, *Nederlandse literatuur*, 142–6.

72 See Drewes, 'Interpretatie van de Gentse spelen,' 242–3, 247, 255–64.

73 *Leffynghe*, in Erné and Van Dis, *De Gentse spelen*, I, 51–91 (Hum. 3 B 1), esp. 72, ll. 334–9, where Leffinge's playwright affirms that the supreme consolation for the dying man is hope, which rests on both the good works of men and the grace of God. For its defence of free will, see ibid., 70, l. 302; for good works, 71, ll. 311–12; and for the necessity of confession and penance, 80, l. 517: 'Bekendt u zonden, beweent u mesdaden.'

74 *Caperijke* in ibid., II, 436–70 (Hum. 3 B 13).

75 Erné and Van Dis, ibid., II, 439, contend that the play promotes the Catholic doctrine of Mary. The evidence, however, is an ambiguous passage where Hope promises to support *Mensch*: 'Tot dat ghy zijt in thuus van uwen vadere / En inde slaepcamere van uwer moedere' (462, ll. 442–3). No explicit mention is made of Mary.

76 *Thienen*, in ibid., II, 341–69 (Hum. 3 B 10). Interestingly, in the prologue the playwright devotes a prayer to the Trinity and a blessing to the emperor, calling him 'Onzen Keyzere met der maeght reene / Van Ghendt, ghevende in voorspoede goet / Metten edelen Bourgoenschen bloede zoet' (347, ll. 47–9).

77 Ibid., 362, ll. 442–5.

78 Ibid., esp. 352, ll. 175–95, where two monks, Schijn van heligheyt and Ydel voortstel, compete with Stærvende mensche for his devotion, who instead orders them to leave.

79 See the list of prizes in Vandecasteele, 'Letterkundig leven te Gent,' 52.

80 *Antwerpen*, Erné and Van Dis, *De Gentse spelen* 290, 306–13. Luther's doctrine of *semper justus et peccator* is also evident. For example, Vercondygher des Woorts proclaims:

Zondigh zuldy ooc blyven al u leven lanck;
Maer die ghelooft, dezen es God met tellende
Voor zondigh, want God is u Christum stellende
Tot wijsheyt, heligheyt ende gherechtigheyt (295, ll. 426–9).

For a more detailed discussion of this play, see chapter 3 above.

81 *Brugghe*, in Erné and Van Dis, *De Gentse spelen*, I, 87–117 (Hum. 3 B 2); *Meesene*, in ibid., 119–47 (Hum. 3 B 3), esp. 138, ll. 355–7; *Ipre*, in ibid., 149–77 (Hum. 3 B 4), esp. 165, ll. 294–9, and 169, ll. 380–97; *Nieuwkerke*, in ibid., 179–205 (Hum. 3 B 5); *Nieuwport*, in ibid., 207–35 (Hum. 3 B 6), esp. 219, ll.

199–204; *Bruessele*, in ibid., II, 399–433 (Hum. 3 B 12); *Loo in Vuerne Ambocht*, in ibid., 506–35 (Hum. 3 B 15); and *Edijnghe*, in ibid., 569–96 (Hum. 3 B 17). For the essentially Lutheran perspective of the Ypres text, see Drewes 'Interpretatie van de Gentse spelen,' 248–51, against Erné and Van Dis, *De Gentse spelen*, I, 151, who argue that it is essentially orthodox. For the Brussels's contribution, see also Brachin, 'De Brusselse kamer "Den Boeck" op het Gentse rederijkersfeest van 1539.'

82 *Edijnghe*, in Erné and Van Dis, *De Gentse spelen*, II, 581, l. 160; 589, l. 343; 591, l. 383; 592, l. 399; 593, l. 422.

83 Erné and Van Dis, *De Gentse spelen*, II, 509; Drewes 'Interpretatie van de Gentse spelen,' 251, 259–66.

84 *Loo in Vuerne Ambocht*, in Erné and Van Dis, *De Gentse spelen*, II, 529–30, ll. 415–31.

85 Ibid., 525, ll. 316–19:

> Ach broeder, an Christo tot u confoort blijft,
> Bekennende naectelic al uwe mesdaden;
> Hy en zal u als tresoor der ghenaden
> Vry niet versmaden.

See also Erné and Van Dis, *De Gentse spelen*, II, 509.

86 *Bruessele*, 424–5, ll. 329–46; *Edijnghe*, 587–9, ll. 310–45; *Ipre*, 169–71, ll. 380–423; and *'Nieuwkerke*, 186, ll. 85–97. Erné and Van Dis, *De Gentse Spelen*, I, 30, suggest that this last play was inspired by the published tract, *Een Troost ende Speigel der Siecken*, written by the Lutheran-minded Willem Gnapheus in 1525.

87 *Bruessele*, 411–12, ll. 40–60.

88 Ibid., 433, ll. 506–10.

89 *Loo in Vuerne Ambocht*, 526–7, ll. 349, 361–80; *Meesene*, 145, ll. 519–25; *Edijnghe*, 575, ll. 6–35. The non-Lutheran Deinze play also rejects the mediation of priests and presents Christ as the eternal mediator (*Deinze*, in Erné and Van Dis, *De Gentse spelen*, II, 624–43, esp. 643, ll. 396–402).

90 *Brugghe*, in Erné and Van Dis *De Gentse spelen*, 107–8, ll. 307–45. This belief was also maintained, in a modified form, by the Meesen rhetoricians, who affirmed that while believers remain sinners, they have a mediator and advocate in Jesus Christ (*Meesene*, ibid., 141, ll. 439–44). Erné (Erné and Van Dis, *De Gentse spelen* I, 91–2) suggests that Everaert was probably the author of the Bruges contribution to the Ghent competition, leading to the possibility that by 1539 Everaert too had adopted a reform perspective.

91 *Bruessele*, ibid., 431, ll. 476–7: 'Liefde: Doet dit nieu onbevlect cleedt, Christum, aene.' For Luther, see *Luther's Works* 25, 265; see also McGrath, *Luther's Theology of the Cross*, 134.

92 The Nieuwpoort author, speaking of the church, wrote:
   Gheen sacramenten helich en administriet,
   Noch bedijnghen, collecten daer gheuzeirt,
   Zy henden al met dien woorde crachtigh;
   Uwen eenighen zone met u levende (230, ll. 496–500).
   Interestingly, the Lo play affirmed that in the Eucharist one eats Christ's
   flesh and blood as a remembrance, in order to become one with him; *Loo in
   Vuerne Ambocht*, 531, ll. 451–67.
93 *Brugghe*, ibid., 94, ll. 26–8:
   TWIJFFELIC ZIN: Eyst niet ghenough datse de gheleerde weten,
   Op dat zy ons waerschuwen van ghebreken
   Daer wy in mesdoen?
94 Ibid., 94, ll. 29–36:
   Hoort Paulum spreken:
   Al datter gheschreven es, verre of naer,
   Es tot onzer leerijnghe gheschreven voorwaer;
   Ende een andere gheift ons verstandt,
   Dat elc magh nemen boucken inde handt
   En lezen, erlezen, waer dat zy gaen,
   Tot dat zyze duer veil lezens verstaen,
   Zo cryghende een vast gheloove expres.
95 Ibid., 99, ll. 132–5:
   'Al dat niet wt gheloove gheschiedt, es zonde.'
   Voort zeght hy tot een ander nacye:
   'Ghy zijt zaligh ghemaeckt duer gracye
   En niet duer u ghewaercken' ...
96 Ibid., 100, ll. 156–62:
   SCHRIFTUERLIC TROOST: Christus es ons van Gode ghemaect gheworden
   Wijsheyt, rechtvaerdigheyt, dit my verhalen greyt,
   Helighheyt en dat meer es, onze zalighheyt.
   Voort een ander troost op ons noch breeder daeckt:
   Wy zijn zaligh zonder ons verdiensten ghemaect;
   Hy es rechtvaerdigh ende maect rechtvaerdigh
   Die in hem ghelooven.
97 Ibid., 103–5.
98 Ibid., 107, ll. 307–15:
   TWIFFELIC ZIN: Zo en esser gheen zonde meer, zoo ghy zeght.
   Waerom heeten wy zondaers? ken cant niet verstaen.
         Gheestelic bewijs.
   Christus heift de zonde te niete ghedaen.

Niet datter gheen zonde es in onslien gheschacht,
Maer he heift de zonde benomen haer cracht,
Datse in ons gheen macht en heift,
Als in yemandt die zonder gheloove leift,
Maer wilt duer zijn eyghen ghewaercken ter nood
Zaligh zijn.

99 *Thielt*, in Erné and Van Dis, *De Gentse spelen* I, 237–69 (Hum. 3 B 7); *Wynox-
    berghe*, in ibid. 598–622 (Hum. 3 B 18), esp. 611, ll. 235–45. On the author-
    ship, see I, 30, where Erné suggests that these plays show the influence of
    Erasmus.
100 *Wynoxberghe*, 615, ll. 345–8.
101 Ibid., 620, ll. 481–2: 'De mens mag geen volledige heilszekerheid
     verwachten / wel op grond van betrouwbare tekenen hopen.'
102 Luther, of course, also affirmed that once justified, believers should live
     virtuous lives.
103 *Meenene*, in Erné and Van Dis, *De Gentse spelen* I, 371–97 (Hum. 3 B 11);
     Audenaerde, in ibid., 471–503 (Hum. 3 B 14), esp. 485, ll. 120–3, 486–7, ll.
     150–66, 501–2, ll. 465–505; *Cortrijcke*, in ibid., 537–68 (Hum. 3 B 16), esp.
     548–9, ll. 75–7, 86–91, 564, ll. 452–64, which emphasize the importance of
     the Holy Spirit in revealing the secrets of God and subjugating the flesh to
     the spirit (566, ll. 504–7). See also Drewes, 'Interpretatie van de Gentse
     spelen,' 253–5, 263–7.
104 *Meenene*, esp. 378–9, ll. 61–8 and ll. 85–90, where Schriftuerlicke Approbacye
     remarks that not even faith working through love is sufficient on its own:
     Maer doude vaders, al zijn zy ghestorven
     Int gheloove met wærcken wter liefden vat,
     Zy en hebben den meesten troost niet ghehadt,
     Want den hemel was voor hemlieden gheloken;
     Al waerby de beloften Gods voorsproken
     Zy niet ontfaen hebben, maer van verre ghezien.
     And while great comfort is found in the death, resurrection, and media-
     tion of Christ (380–2, ll. 120–66), the greatest consolation is in the 'blyde
     roerijnghe des helighs gheest' (383, l. 195).
105 Die daer tuught onzen gheest zonder inderen
     Dat wy zijn Gods wtvercoren kinderen;
     En zijn wy kinderen Gods zonder besmitten,
     Zo moeten wy dan zijn rijcke bezitten ... (ibid., 385, ll. 239–41).
106 Ibid., 388, ll. 305–26.
107 *Audenaerde*, 492, ll. 258–60.
108 *Cortrijcke*, 558, ll. 313–16:

Dwoordt der waerheyt.
Niet duer de wærcken der rechtværdigheyt
Die eenich mensche moght hebben ghedaen,
Maer alleene duer zijn barmhertigh voortgaen,
Welcke barmhertigheyt gheleghen es in Got.

Then Dwoordt adds:

Ghebenedijt es God int hooghste verblyden,
De vader ons heeren Iesu Christi bemint,
Die ons ghebenedijt heift, zoo Paulus ontbint,
In allen benediccyen gheestelic
Tot bin den hemelschen throone feestelic;
Alzoo hy ghehadt heift ons in beminsele
In hem voor des swærels beghinsele,
Om dat why heligh ende onbesmet
Voor hem zouden zijn in de liefde net;
Dies ons hem danckelic ghemaect heift ydone
Alleene by zynen beminden zone ... (559–60, ll. 345–55).

109 Ibid., 548, ll. 73–7, 86–91:

CLAERCKELIC WTEN: God svaders ghehuldigheyt zal zynen gheest
Zenden dien beghaeren ende die onbevreest
Met zijn woordt bezigh zijn, net, bequwame;
Zynen gheest alle Gods secreten eerzame
Duerlustert, zijnder verholentheyt grondt waer ...
GHEESTELICKE VERLICHTIJNGHE: Ghelijc haer wtwerpt in een
schoon riviere
Een fonteyne levende neder ten dale,
In sghelijcx Gods liefde principale,
In zijn secreten gheest besloten blijckelic,
Es eeuwigh vloeyende tot meer ghelijckelic,
Want therte hem meest tooght in dooghe gheprezen.

110 See Waite, *David Joris*, and 'The Dutch Nobility and Anabaptism.'

111 For Joris as an artist, see Boon, 'De Glasschilder David Joris.' Joris also wrote some refrains in rhetorician style; see Waite, 'The Holy Spirit Speaks Dutch.'

112 *Axcele*, Erné and Van Dis, *De Gentse spelen*, 305–39 (Hum. 3 B 9), esp. 311–13 and 316–21, ll. 39–106, 278–303. Of all these good works, Schriftuerlic Verstandt says:

Deze en zullen al den mensche niet troosten,
Ten zy dat hy heift (verstaet al nu dit snel)
Een goe consciencye gherust zeer wel.

En daer die niet en es (heir op zo gloost fijn)
En magh tgheloove daer gheenen troost zijn (ll. 286–90).

113 Ibid., 322–3, ll. 320–63.

114 Ibid., 327, ll. 434–6:
zijn consciencye bekende
Zuver en gherust, zeyde naer zijn advijs:
Heden zult ghy met my zijn int paradijs.

115 Drewes, 'Interpretatie van de Gentse spelen,' 251.

116 *Deynze*, in Erné and Van Dis, *De Gentse spelen*, II, 622–47 (Hum. 3 B 19). The central identification of the church as the suffering body of Christ was also the major interpretation of Dutch Anabaptists. See Melchior Hoffman, 'The Ordinance of God,' in Williams and Mergal, *Spiritual and Anabaptist Writers*, 184–203, and Horst, *Melchior Hoffman. De ordonnantie Gods*. In the Deinze play, Trust of Scriptures remarks:
Want zy [i.e., thieves] int hooft Christo niet en blyven,
Waer an tgheheel lichaem der ghemeenten hanght
Ende hulpe van elc anderen ontfanght ... (*Deynze*, 636, ll. 204–6).
Later, Troost der Schriftueren notes that believers are 'leden zijns lichaems, zijn wy tghemeente / Van zynen vleessche en van zynen ghebeente' (638, ll. 243–4).

117 Troost der Schriftueren, speaking of the final salvation of all, says:
hoe dat Christus niet alleene en es de verzoenijnghe,
Noch vuldoenijnghe onzer zonden alleene,
Maer ooc voor de gheheele wærelt ghemeene,
Op dat zy reene tleven in hem betrapen (*Deynze*, 637, ll. 226–9).
At the last 'trumpet blast,' he continues, everything will be changed and become a new creature (641, ll. 322–3). For Hoffman's ideas, see Deppermann, *Melchior Hoffman*, 185–92, 220–67, and Waite, *David Joris*, 94–103. The play's comparison between David and Christ (*Deynze*, 633, ll. 102 ff) was also prominent in the writings of David Joris, who regarded Jesus Christ as the second David and himself, rather obscurely, as the third.

118 Erné and Van Dis, *De Gentse spelen* II, 541.

119 As cited by Erné and Van Dis, *De Gentse spelen*, II, 540–1, who quote the passage in its context:
Reynicht dijn handen van het onnoozel bloet,
Dijn ooghen ontdoet, maer neen, tlicht niet en vermueght.
Inwendigh zo zijt ghy een vreezelick ghebroet,
Zouckende eyghen spoet; der charitaten dueght
Niet achtende, maer in tonderbrijnghen verhueght
Der waerheyt vrueght; claghelic datt God ghedooght.
See also Elslander, 'Het refreinfeest,' 53.

120 The following excerpt from the Kortrijk play is quite reminiscent of the
    spiritualism of David Joris, who was also preoccupied with the imagery of
    the fountain of living water:
    Ghelijc haer wtwerpt in een schoon riviere
    Een fonteyne levende neder ten dale,
    In sghelijcx Gods liefde principale
    In zijn secreten gheest besloten blijckelic
    Es eeuwigh voloeyende tot meer ghelijckelic
    Want therte hem meets tooght in dooghe gheprezen (*Cortrijke*, Erné and
    Van Dis, *De Gentse spelen* 549, ll. 86–91).
121 Decavele, *Keizer tussen stropdragers*, 94–6.
122 Ibid., 96.
123 Exceptions are found, such as the Amsterdam *Sick City* discussed in
    chapter 4 above.
124 Jackson, 'Drama and Dialogue in the Service of the Reformation,' 121–2.
125 Paul Russell, *Lay Theology in the Reformation*, esp. 213.
126 Ghent SA *Memorieboek* II, 154–5.
127 Ibid., 174. City leaders spared little expense to fête their angry prince: the
    stadsrekening of 1539–40 lists a total of 261£ Fl. 2s 6d spent in gifts for
    Charles (Ghent SA 400, *Register stadsrekeningen* 47, (1539–40, fol. 71r). The
    preparations for this meeting seem parallel to a general procession held 13
    July 1539, in which the representatives of the city government, guilds,
    militia guilds, and rhetoricians proceeded through the streets carrying
    candles while the doormen of the various guilds and societies held torches
    along the sides of the streets (Ghent SA *Memorieboek* II, 126).
128 As a further humiliation, the city was forced to pay for all of the events,
    including the publication of the treaty (Ghent SA Reg. 400 *Stadsrekeningen*
    47 [1539–40], fol. 95v).
129 In Rowen, *The Low Countries*, 24. The anonymous observer was from Lille.
130 Burke, *Popular Culture*, 207–43. See also Arnade, 'Secular Charisma, Sacred
    Power' 86–94, for a similarly crafted ritualistic punishment of rebellious
    Ghentenaars on the part of Charles V's Burgundian ancestor, Charles the
    Bold.
131 Also forbidden were most processions and the shooting contests of the
    militia guilds (14 April 1540, Ghent SA *Memorieboek* II, 184, 215); on 12
    May 1540, Charles ordered that St Baef's Cloister, a source of pride for
    Ghent's religious community, be turned into a military barracks. Its relics
    were solemnly removed to St Baef's Cathedral in the heart of the city.
132 This prohibition apparently did not include the procession of Our Lady of
    St Peters held on 22 August 1540 (Ghent SA *Memorieboek* II, 211).
133 Ibid., 215.

134 Ghent SA Reg. 400, *Stadsrekeningen* 47 (1539–40), esp. the section 'Extra-ordinary Expenses,' fols. 94r–106v, where in the volumes of previous years the regular financial support of the chambers is listed.

135 Such as those in 1541 and 1542, to honour the emperor's success against the Turks (Ghent SA *Memorieboek* II, 219, 221).

136 Ghent SA Reg. 400, *Stadsrekeningen*, 48 (1540–1), fols. 250v, 257r–v.

137 Ibid., 49 (1541–2), fols. 209v, 211v.

138 Ibid., 52 (1544–5), fol. 230v.

139 Ghent SA *Memorieboek* II, 245; Ghent SA Reg. 400, *Stadsrekeningen* 54 (1546–7), fol. 321v, which notes that the *Fonteine* in particular was paid 4£ Fl. for preparing 'in great haste and diligence' a play performed on 3 May in honour of the victory.

140 Ghent SA *Memorieboek*, II, 252–3. At each of the triumphal arches the rhet-oricians acted as various allegorical figures, most of which showed biblical or historical examples of a peaceful transfer of power from a king to his son.

141 Decavele, *De dageraad*, I, 198.

142 Translated from De Groote, 'De overheid en het Gentse rederijkersfeest van 1539,' 108. The reference to scandalous refrains may refer in part to the publication of the 1539 Ghent refrains by Joos Lambrecht, who also printed the plays.

143 Ibid., 109.

144 'Dat niement van nu voorts an en vervoordere vut te stellene, vertooghene ofte vut te ghevene eeneghe spelen, refreynen, liedekins, loven of andere dichten van rethoricquen, of andersins, in eeneghe maniere, anders dan de ghone van heere ende wet weghe ghevisiteert ende gheconsenteert, telcken opde boete van drie ponden parisis ende de correctie van scepe-nen' (Decavele, *De dageraad*, I, 201). A similar enactment was passed in Bruges on 23 June (see also Decavele, 'Jan Utenhove,' 107).

145 'Voorts dat hem niement en vervoordere te makene, dichtene ofte voort te stellene eeneghe refreynen, liedekins, baladen, spraken van presenten noch anderssins, noch eeneghe scilderyen of signeren vut te stellene of conterfaictene, ten scimpe, cleenechede, diffamatie ofte vilonie van yemande, gheestelic ofte weerlic, ofte ooc smakende eeneghe suspecte materien ofte andere fameuze zaken' (Decavele, *De dageraad*, I, 201).

146 Ibid., 203, where Decavele notes that a rhetorician contest approved by the inquisitor, Pieter de Backere, for Ghent for 17 August 1561, was cancelled by Ghent's magistrates out of fear of the spread of strange ideas in the city with the influx of foreigners. See also Decavele, 'Jan Utenhove,' 101–2.

147 Decavele, 'Jan Utenhove,' 107; Coigneau, 'De Evangelische Leeraer.' The

play has recently been edited: De Bruin, 'Een seer schoon spel' (Hum. 4 09); for the manuscript, see also Zieleman, 'Van Venator tot Duircant.' Thanks to Coigneau's excellent summary of the play, we do not need to analyse it in depth here. For Utenhove's reform career, see Decavele, 'Jan Utenhove,' 103–7, and for the investigation into the performance by the authorities, 108–16. Decavele (116) calls the Roborst performance 'an important milestone' for the further development of the Reformation in the Netherlands.

148 Coigneau, 'De Evangelische Leeraer,' 139; For example, when Dienaer Gods asks about these good works, Evangelische Leeraer responds:

Dus, Ongheleert Volck, laet af van sulcke dinghen,
Want Paulus seyt om ons verstercken
Dus: Broeder, wilt doch mercken
Op de ghene die twist en aerghernisse maken
Nevens de leeringhe Gods; voor alle saken
Scheedt u van sulcke verleeders, ziet,
Want de sulcke en dienen Christum niet,
Maer sy dienen haren buyck, seyt de Schriftuere.
Wy zijn ghewasschen in Christus' bloet puere;
Waer sulcke verghevinghe es als wt Gods monde,
Daer en es gheen offerande meer voor de sonde;
Dese aflaet sal eeuwich blijven (De Bruin, 'Een seer schoon spel,' 32–3, ll. 113–24).

149 De Bruin, 'Een seer schoon spel,' 41, ll. 301–19; 73, l. 1048.

150 Coigneau, 'De Evangelische Leeraer,' 140–4; De Bruin, 'Een seer schoon spel,' 72–6.

151 De Bruin, 'Een seer schoon spel,' 84–5, ll. 1302–11. However, Utenhove eventually sided with the Swiss Reformed on the subject of the Lord's Supper, rejecting Luther's belief in the Real Presence of Christ's body in the communion bread.

152 Coigneau, 'De Evangelische Leeraer,' 131–4, where he suggests that Utenhove had probably read the published edition of the plays and that his work shows considerable structural and thematic similarity to the plays of Nieuwkerke and Edingen.

153 Ibid., 120; Decavele ('Jan Utenhove,' 108–10) discusses this investigation as well as Joyeulx and the other actors who participated in the Roborst performance.

154 *Een spel vanden Vader die het Volck sant om inden Wijngaert te Wercken*, Brussels KB (Hum. 1 G 5) II 129, partially edited in Snellaert, 'Drie spelen van zinne,' 335–8. The play is part of a manuscript volume containing Refor-

mation plays and refrains, the earliest dated being the 'Tree of Scriptures' of 1539, and most others dating to the 1550s.

155   OOTMOEDICHEYT: Wy bevelen v allen die hoogste generatie,
Alvoren onsen ingheboren prince, dat keyserlic graen:
Godt die wille hem altijt in staden staen,
Om sijn landen te regierne in payse excellent (Een Spel vanden Vader, fol. 91v; Snellaert, 'Drie spelen van zinne,' 338).

156   GHENADICHEYT: 'Godt wil ooc bewaren d'edel stede van Ghent, / Ende ooc alle die ons verre sijn oft omtrent' (Een Spel vanden Vader, fol. 91v). That the play may have been performed by the Fonteine chamber is suggested by a reference to a 'leuender fonteyne' on fol. 86r.

157   The preaching of these lay folk is compared to swineherding.
MURMATIE: Ja wel, men loopt metter evangelie achter straten siet,
Hou schoelappers, caefvaghers [schoorsteenvegers], sonder twisten.
OPGHEBLASEN GHEEST: Nichte, het werden al evangelisten,
Al en sijnt maer swijnders die achter de verckens loopen (ibid., fol. 81v, Snellaert, 'Drie spelen van zinne,' 337).

158   Een Spel vanden Vader, fol. 82v.

159   Ibid., fol. 83r: 'Sulc volcxken wert int wercken oncoustich [oncouslich] / want tis hemlieden verboden op den ban.'

160   Ibid., fols. 85v–6r.

161   Ibid., fol. 88r: 'Paulus schryft de wet den heeft niemant tot salicheyt bracht.'

162   Ibid., fol. 88r: 'Ende plaetsen besoecken daermen mach aflaten ontfaen.'

163   Ibid., fol. 90r:
OOTMOEDICHEYT: He is ons middelaere by Godt den Vadere;
GHENADICHEYT: sonder desen middelaer en moghen wy tot Godt niet commen;
en voor synen vader so is hy ons advocaet.

164   Ibid., 91r:
OOTMOEDICHEYT: Die evangelische ghenade wel mochten horen
Vercoren synse die sullen wercken als voren
Ende blyuen totten eynde int ghelooue perfect.

7: Rhetoricians and Reform after the Ghent Competition, 1539–56

1   See Decavele, De dageraad, I, 201–3; and his 'Jan Utenhove,' 107; see also chapter 6 above.

2   These figures exclude the Spel voer den Coninck Phillippus, which was performed in 1556 but which will be mentioned below, chapter 8.

3   The play Naaman, prinche van Sijrien (copied by the Amsterdam rhetorician

Reyer Gheurtz in the early 1550s) is a possible example of the enduring
popularity of late-medieval scripts, yet its supposedly orthodox stance is a
mild one, with no hint of polemics. It could, in fact, be performed by a
moderate Protestant as much as by a Catholic. See Hummelen and
Schmidt, *Naaman, prinche van Sijrien*. This work, about the healing of Naaman at the hands of the prophet Elisha (2 Kings 5), contains some fascinating material illustrative of medical knowledge in the sixteenth century.

4 De Jongh, *L'ancienne faculté de théologie de Louvain au premier siècle de son
   existence, 1432–1540*.
5 *Tspel van Sinte Trudo*, in Kalff, *Trou Moet Blycken* (Hum. 2 O 3), esp.
   Lucifer's commission to his minions, 85, ll. 73–80:

   > Dus ziet, dat ghy dit kint aen elcken cant tant
   > En doeghet in sonden duer u wercken hercken.
   > Doet hem schoen vrouwen tallen percken mercken,
   > Dobbelen, vloecken, bannen en maeckten wel fel;
   > Doet hem versmaden allen der kercken clerken
   > En vader en moeder vallen rebel snel;
   > Maeckt, dat gheheel quaet sy allen syn opsten hel,
   > En dat hy van elcken gheacht voer een kockyn syn.

6 Ibid., 89, l. 192: 'Want duer doopsel mach hy duyvels clauwen ontspringen.'
   While the demonic Vices initially scoff at the exorcism held outside the
   church doors, they find themselves in great danger when the priest commands Satan to flee. Once the sacrament is completed, the demons openly
   admit their defeat at the hands of the cleric.
7 Ibid., 173–5.
8 Ibid., 129. During Trudo's consecration, the actors, in accord with late-
   medieval depictions of the Mass, describe an image of the bleeding Jesus as
   a fountain spouting five streams of blood, into which the priest dips the
   cup of the Mass (176, esp. ll. 2483–4 and 2498–2503):

   > DIE DIAKEN: Loff bloedeghe Jesu, aent cruce vloeyende,
   > Als fonteyne met vyff bloedighe stralen!
   >
   > ...
   >
   > MEESTER W: Loff bloedeghe beecken, vuyt handen, vuyt voeten,
   > Met allen aderkens, die daer vuyt springhen!
   > Loff laeffenisse, onser zielen versoeten!
   > Loff voetsele, dwelck ons die preesters bringhen
   > Van deser schoender fonteynen sonderlingen
   > In dat heylich sacrament tallen wercken.

9 Briggs, *Witches and Neighbors*, 202–3. See also, among others, Klaits, *Servants
   of Satan*, 111–19, and Roper, *Oedipus and the Devil*, 172–93.
10 *Den boom der schrifturen, van 6 personnagien, gespeelt den 1 augusto 1539, tot*

Middelborgh in Zeelant. Both a manuscript (Hum. 1 G 2) and a published version (Hum. 3 A 3) are extant; the printed version consulted here is an early edition housed in the City Library of Haarlem. The manuscript version is partially edited by Snellaert, 'Drie spelen van zinne,' 322–35. See also Schotel, *Den Boom der Schriftueren van VI personagien* and Van Mierlo, *'Den Boem der Schriftueren' en het geval Jacob van Middeldonck.* I am thankful to Mr Henk Duyser of the Haarlem Stadsbibliotheek for allowing me access to a copy of the printed edition.

11 See above, chapter 3. In 1546 Jacob van Middeldonck was ordered to complete a pilgrimage to Russemadouwe for 'writing' in 1542 a play called 'Den boom der Scriftueren' which 'smacked of heresy' (see Génard, 'Personen te Antwerpen,' VII, 464 and 467 and VIII, 347–62). At the time of the performance Middeldonck was only fifteen or sixteen years old and belonged to one of the unofficial chambers, De Damastbloeme, which, according to his testimony, consisted of other youths (ibid., VIII, 361).

12 *Den boom der schifturen*, fol. Aii v, where Each Especially says:
Och wie den mensche die afgoden adoreren,
Sy destrueren en souwen geerne mineren
V leuende woort der sielen confoort.

13 Snellaert, 'Drie spelen,' 332:
Ende dier niet mede behelpen en connen met mijnder daet,
Die loopen van groot ghebrec in een couvent;
Ghewillighe aermoede leyden sy absent.
Dincket v niet en van goeden conditien?
Ende die metten Cruysbroers wel sijn bekent,
Die leeric jaghen naer goede beneficien'
Ja twintich iaer te voren legghende suspicien
Om eenen te stekene wt sijnen setel vast,
Ende door dit leuen vol alder malitien,
Lucifer, mijn vrient, wel vol sijnen ketel tast.

14 Ibid., 333:
Sijdy ooc eene vande duytsche doctooren?
In mijnen thooren doen ic branden en versmooren,
Oft onthalsen als vooren ghy wilt mijn rechte verstooren,
Prelaetschepen en chooren die wy helighelic oorbooren.
Why gheleerde sijn van Godt vercooren bouen ander tresooren,
Oft costelicke yvooren en slechte dooren willen schriftuere slooren,
Wech ruyde mooren why gheleerde ghescoren
Nemen schriftuere byden ooren tis in ons macht.

15 Ibid., 334:
Door versierde sermoenen aen tvolcs goet gheraecty.

O Antechristen, inden tempel Godts wat maecty?

V houdy als Godt, ondertastende svolcx nieren.

O hoere van Babel! vol bloets so snaecty,

Die ghetuygen swoorts doedy iusticieren.

De schrift vloeyt vol van v sondich bestieren.

16 See especially the aforementioned play by Johan Utenhove which he composed in 1542 and had performed the following year at his estate outside of Ghent (above, chapter 6). The performance of this work led to his exile and to the arrest of his collaborator, Gillis Joyeulx (Coigneau, 'De Evangelische Leeraer,' 117–20). Utenhove's play was printed in 1570 by Willem Gheylliaert, who in 1556 had moved to Emden and who also printed·Den boom der schriftueren as well as Een spel van sinnen op tderde / tvierde ende tvijfste Capittel van Twerck der Apostolen; ibid., 117–18.

17 Een spel van sinnen hue Mennich mensch suect thuys van vreeden, Brussels KB 21651 (Hum. 1 D 4). For a fuller description, see above, chapter 4. There is no internal evidence regarding the play's date of composition, although it is possible that, like Thoenisz's play on the beheading of St John, it was composed prior to the 1539 Ghent performance.

18 Ibid., fol. 15r–v, where Morningtime remarks:

Neemt daer dat cruys en wilten u aenhouwen

Niet aen dat cruys van hout ofte steene

Maer aenden ghecruysten Christum reene

De ons alleene met syn bluet verlast heeft.

19 Ibid., fol. 14r.

MORNINGTIME: Warachtich gheloof gheeft der sonder penitente

Dan coomt een puer consciencie wilt dit onthouwen

Ghy muet uwen heer vwen godt betrouwen

Sonder ennich verflouwen met der liefden branders

en ghij sult crijghen vreede ...

20 Roose, Anna Bijns, 26; Hofman, 'De Antwerpse drukker Frans Fraeten,' 72–3.

21 Hofman, 'De Antwerpse drukker Frans Fraeten,' 77–8.

22 Een present van Godt loondt, Grammerchijs, besolos manos, Brussels KB II 367 (Hum. 1 D 10). He had also printed a number of Luther's writings. See Hofman, 'De Antwerpse drukker Frans Fraeten,' 77.

23 'De Wellustige Mensch' in Kruyskamp, Dichten en spelen van Jan van den Berghe; see also King, 'The Voluptuous Man.' It was performed in 1551 (Van der Straelen, Geschiedenis der Antwerpsche rederykkamers, 23). Also extant is Van den Berghe's 'Het Leenhof der Gilden,' an extended refrain published in 1564, although it must have been written well before Van den Berghe's death in 1559 in Brussels. See above, chapter 3, n. 116.

24 King, 'The Voluptuous Man,' 103.

25 Ibid., 68–9. Those who argued that the power of the sacraments relied on the personal character of the priest believed they worked *ex opere operantis*.

26 Because the character of the preacher is in his external form a Catholic priest, Kruyskamp argued that the play was orthodox. Given the propensity of Dutch reformers and spiritualists to depreciate externals altogether, it is not surprising that Van den Berghe would seek to disguise his reform message in the external guise of orthodoxy.

27 For the dating of this work, see De Vooys and Mak, 'Een verloren vastenspel van sinnen,' 593–8.

28 Ibid., 602–3.

29 The writings of spiritualists such as Joris and Niclaes found particular appeal among moderate Catholics who were dissatisfied with the rise of the Reformed church to preeminence in the northern Netherlands but who likewise found Tridentine Catholicism too rigid. One of the clearest examples is the career of the former Cistercian monk Herman Herberts, Reformed pastor of Dordrecht and Gouda, who, although he left his Catholic profession, was clearly uncomfortable with several key Reformed dogmas, finding a solution instead in spiritualism. See Kaplan, 'Hubert Duifhuis and the Nature of Dutch Libertinism' and 'Dutch Particularism'; and Waite, 'The Longevity' and 'Man is a Devil.' For Catholicism in the Netherlands after the revolt, see Kooi, 'Popish Impudence.'

30 De Vooys and Mak, 'Een verloren vastenspel van sinnen,' 628–9.

31 Ibid., 629–30, ll. 468–77:
   SMENSCHEN: Myn gheest de weyghert maer tvleesch opiniŭen
   Is swaer lamŭen tis al groot verschil
   Tusschen een die wil en dander niet en wil
   Tvleesch en den gheest gheen ondŭenlycker knoop
   Gheen stercker ghespan gheen ghegrŭyder hoop
   Noyt strick of stroop so vast aen een ghehecht
   Tvleesch uytwendich de gheest inwendich vecht
   Maer de sieghe des vleesch bedwingt den gheest
   Wat dient my dan ontrocken den leest
   Des vleesch daer niet dan verdriet mŭet volghen.

32 Ibid., 638, ll. 599–606:
   WERLT: Bylo ick hebt mennich iaerken wel bescict
   Voortbrengende veel nieuwe tailgekens
   Daer ick mee locke alle myn caelgekens
   Ŭp syn fransz ŭp syn hoofts ŭp syn italiaensch
   Ghebaert ghecapt gheknevelbaert ŭp sijn spaensch
   Syde laken draeghen fluweel ofte samijt

Fransche pareersels minioot ende petijt
Diet can de machs diet niet en can de wils.

33 Ibid., 642–3, ll. 680–701, esp. 690–1: 'Dattet tvleesch niet sondighen can sonder consent / van smenschen gheest totten vleesche ghewent.'

34 Ibid., 648–9, esp. l. 810 and ll. 835–40. Before this scene the Virtues and Human Spirit kneel and proclaim Christ as the 'true merciful medicine' and 'sole deliverer.'

35 See Waite, 'Man is a Devil' and 'David Joris en de opkomst van de sceptische traditie.' Herman Herberts for one argued against his Reformed colleagues that the antichrist was not the pope, but resided in each person's heart (Waite, 'Man is a Devil,' 26). Joris wrote that the devil was powerless without human cooperation. Joris's illustrations in his *magnum opus*, the *Wonder Book*, are quite similar to the painted figures described in Presbiter's script. For Joris's influence, see Waite, *David Joris*.

36 For Matthias Wier, the brother of the surgeon Johan Wier, see Waite, 'Demonic Affliction or Divine Chastisement?' esp. 63.

37 *De Moedere ende Kinderen Zebedei*, Brussels KB 7812 (Hum. 1 Y 1). The phrase 'Jonste voor conste' on fol. 13r may be the slogan of the chamber. One chamber is known to have had this slogan, that of the town of Zoutleeuw. On biblical plays in general, see Hummelen, 'The Biblical Plays of the Rhetoricians.'

38 *De Moedere ende Kinderen Zebedei*, fol. 7r–v: 'En als zij huter kercken comen Dan eyst te zweeren / Alle eeden tis ghenouch hebben zy de keercke ghesien.'

39 Ibid., fol. 9v: 'Den duuele der vrauwen crancheyt kennende.'

40 *Een Mey spel van sinnen van menschelycke broosheit De met swerlts ghenuechte triumpheert inden ghemeynen beyart*, Brussels KB 21659 (Hum. 1 D 9). The information on its performance is included on the title page.

41 Ibid., fol. 3r: 'tProfijt der sielen dwelck Gode behaegt.'

42 Ibid., fol. 5r.

43 Ibid., fol. 6r.

44 Ibid., fol. 6v:
Hue soudich swerlts ghenuechte laeten
Ick sie bisscoppen legaeten abten prelaeten
Eedele ende ghemeyne staeten
Volghense al omme buyten en binnen.

45 Ibid., fol. 7r:
Acharmen iaet
En vreeslycker dan men v seggen of preecken mach
Ghy weet wel tvalt selden binnen der weecken dach
Men duet v in allen kercken sonder hoonen

So weerdelycke sermoonen uyt scrifts bethoonen
En dopinioonen der hoogher doctoren
Hue wij die gloosen dor wrueten dorporen
Verwen coloren verstaetet bysondere
Tcoomt al up een nyt.

46 Ibid., fol. 7r:
MENSCHELYCKE: So gheeuet mij dan wondere
Nae dat sijt vinden en leesen bij clergien
Dat sij daffgryselijckeit so luttel ontsien
Hue veel synder nu onder die predicanten beschraven [beschraeuen]
De dwoort Gods soo sijt preecken beleeuen
Of hen schien cleenen aen tse kerste knoopken
VRAYE: Men vinter al somen duet
WULPSCH: Maer tis tminste hoopken
Sy saeghen ons gheerne gaen wat heeft dat in
Inden hemel maer selue gaense dander pat in
Sy peysen hen liden schaed luttel een cleene wolcke
VRAYE: Dats altijt tseggen van tgemeene volcke
Sonder tolcke crayende vorschen de up den cant springen
Maer dat en sal gheen vruchten int lant bringen ...

47 Ibid., fol. 12r:
NATUERLIJCK: Ick seegt seker gheerne
Al eest vraye predicatie ontvuchten
Içk wilde wel dat wijen bekeeren muchten
Ons modere wees ons die maniere
Hue wijen tue gaen sellen
INWENDICH: Sy is sa guedertiere
Wij sullen verwinnen claer sy sechtet ons.

48 Ibid., fol. 12v.
49 Ibid., fol. 15r: 'Sij woont int ghelooue werckende caritaeten.'
50 It is possible that these characters may have been monks, although there is no accompanying description of their attire that would support such.
51 *Van ons lieven heeren minnevaer*, Brussels KB 21649 (Hum. 1 D 2).
52 Moeller, *Imperial Cities*, 41–115, esp. 89–115.
53 According to Decavele, *De dageraad*, xiv–xv, the influence of Calvinism became apparent in Flanders around 1545–50.
54 *De Duerlijdende Man*, Brussels KB 7812 (Hum. 1 Y 2). The play was to be performed 'met scoone figueren vertooght vp doctaue vanden heleghen sacramente, meerre [March?],' 1543.
55 Ibid., fol. 2r.

56 Ibid., fol. 2v:
   Die Rechtueerdighe zal vut dat ghelooue seuen
   Dits bij Ste Pauwels bescreue in gheen vercleijuen
   Int 1st cappittele totten Romeynen.
57 Ibid., fol. 9v.
58 *De Ghepredestineerde Blinde*, Brussels KB 21653 (Hum. 1 D 6). It was copied
   in 1552 and was probably composed not too long before that date.
59 Steenbergen, *De Bekeeringe Pauli.*
60 For the presentation of the doctrine of predestination in Calvinist drama,
   see Smail, 'Predestination and the Ethos.'
61 *De Ghepredestineerde Blinde*, fol. 2v:
   Der menschen verblintheit vol alder weninghe
   En can niet begrijpen des woorts vereninghe
   Mits dat hij gheleyt is in Duuels tempteringhe
   Dies refuteert hij der gracien verleninghe
   Dör blintheit blyuende bij doude meninghe
   Volghende die mennich te der zielen deringhe
   Maer tlicht dwelck is des gheests begheringhe
   Brengt thans die duysterheit in sulke falinghe.
62 Ibid., fols. 2v–3r, esp. 3r:
   DEEN: De soon der verduemenisse dör synder onvruetheit
   Heeft oyt met aduersantelijcke verwuetheit
   Weder ghestaen des waerheits precioosheit
   Maer godts woordt als tlicht vol alder suetheit
   Om ons te bethoonen die godtlijcke ghuetheit
   Brengt thans in schanden all sijn pompoosheit
   De stanck sijnder grooter argheloosheit
   Heeft godt verdrooten in swerlts naerheit
   Al hebben sijn dienaers dies doloroosheit
   Aensiende die euangelijssche victorioosheit
   Wee de hör oyt stelden teghen die waerheit.
63 Ibid., fol. 5r–v:
   De ghepredestineerden
   Wiens cleyn ghetal verschouen personagen
   Behielden nochtan die rechte passagen
   Dwelck voirgaende mennichte vorwaer gheseyt
   Noyt en bekende.
   Starting at this point in the manuscript the playwright, or copiest, records
   appropriate scriptural references.
64 Ibid., fol. 5v:

Want het volgt my al arm mitten rycken
Gheestelijck waerlijck de in tyden voirgangen waeren
Mits gaders ons onders ouer mennighe langen jaeren
End heeft dese hoop onnuemelijck groot.

65 Ibid., fol. 6r: 'Want thert verblint is van binnen verduysteert.'

66 Ibid., fol. 6r: 'Up dat waerachtich licht / dwelck all onse duysterheden verdrijft / wiens claerheit int herte binnen schrijft.'

67 Ibid., fol. 6v: 'Daer dander nauwelijcx connen houden tlant / de minste valt dicmael in die meeste confusie.'

68 Ibid., fols. 7v–9r.

69 Ibid., fol. 10v: 'In ewigher liefde als liefde vermaert / heb ick v voirsien bemint ende beghaert / Wie dit ghelooft sijn ziel wert salich.'

70 Ibid., fol. 12r: 'Tgeloof alleen o mensselijcke sinnen / streckende tot gode ter hemelscher tinnen.'

71 Ibid., fol. 12v: GHENAED. 'De werlt staet in sijn eyghen supersticien'; WET. 'De gheloouighen staen inden betrouwen reene.'

72 Ibid., fol. 14v: 'V ghelooue heeft v ghesont ghemaect.'

73 Ibid., fol. 15r: 'Dies seg ick v lof sonder cesseeren / v liefde beghint mij te inflammeeren.'

74 Ibid., fol. 15v: 'Sij dij so lichtelijcken betouert verkeert / sij dij dus dwaes dat ghij den gheenen / Wilt volghen de tvolck alle valscheijt leert.'

75 Ibid., fol. 15v:
> WIJF: Siet selue wie hem eert
> De ongheleerde, de noyt kennisse druech
> Maer de gheleerde waer bij de döcht vermeert
> Versmaet hem is dat niet teykens ghenuech
> BLINDE: Ja en dat neem ick princepael tot mijn ghevuech
> Want so de werk oijt was bedacht
> De die waerheit belijden tsy spar of vruech
> Dien hebben de gheleerden ter doot ghebrocht.

76 Grace tells him to proceed on the path of charity, for faith must work itself out in righteousness, in acts of service to one's neighbour, as Paul has written in I Cor. 13 (ibid., fols. 16v–17v).

77 Ibid., fol. 17v:
> Daer dinct mij verstae ick die saecke pleynlijck
> Als dör tgheloof de gheest salich is bekent
> So wert dat gheloof dör tlicham certeynlijck
> Synen brueder wercken der caritaten diligent
> Maer niet om loon.

78 Ibid., fol. 18r: 'Schaemt v de v wercken vercoopen deruen.'

79 Ibid., fol. 19r–v.

80 Steenbergen, *De Bekeeringe Pauli*, 14–19. The other appeared after 1555.

81 Ibid., 40, ll. 1–4:

> O gebuerman, ist niet quaet om verdragen
> Het iammer datmen hier ter weirelt siet
> Vanden genen die den naem *Christi* gewagen?
> Die sietmen iagen en brengen int verdriet.

82 Ibid., 48, ll. 99–104:

> EERSTE BORGER: Wat sullen wij doen
> Als die veruolgers coen vol tirannijen
> Ons comen bestrijen?
> TWEEDE BORGER: Wij moeten ons lijen
> En oock niet vermijen het woort des Heeren.
> EERSTE BORGER: O Heere bewaert ons!
> TWEEDE BORGER: Ons sterckheyt wilt vermeeren,
> Dat wij ons niet en keeren deur tribulatie
> Van uwen naeme.
> EERSTE BORGER: O Heere geeft gratie,
> Tegen dees natie wilt ons bystaen.

83 Ibid., 50, ll. 116–31, esp. Fortsich labeur's comments at ll. 128–9: 'Ick en cant niet beuroeijen / Hoe dat hij betoouert heeft soo veel persoonen,' and Ypocrijtich herte's reply at ll. 130–1: 'Wij sullense veruolgen, ia, waer dat sy woonen, / Soo meugen wy toonen dat tegen onsen wil is.' The Latin term 'extra ordinaris,' which appears at l. 123, 'Dat moeten wij vreken / extra ordinaris,' suggests a sixteenth-century legal context, rather than a first century, and refers to the 'extraordinary' judicial procedures required in trials against heretics.

84 Ibid., 51–3, esp. 53, l. 174: 'Wij sullender noch vele op slydens banck bringen.'

85 Ibid., 52, ll. 154–5: 'Waij, tis al *Jesus* voore en *Jesus* achtere, / Tsij boer oft pachtere aen alle sijen.'

86 Ibid., 52, ll. 158–61:

> YPOCRIJTICH HERTE: Dat en deden ons ouersten sonder reden niet,
> Want hij strafte de biscoppen als syn vyanden
> En hij sprack: 'De hoogste Godt en rust in geen landen,
> Oft in tempelen die met handen van menschen geuracht sijn.'

87 Ibid., 55–6, esp., 55, ll. 198–9: 'Al die synen name belijen moeten wij veruolgen / En brengen ter schanden met groot verseeren.'

88 Ibid., 59, l. 264: 'Om in eeren te houdene onssen geestelijcken staet excellent'; ibid., 61, l. 283; where a servant calls Saul 'den grooten doctoor inde

wet.' Confronting two citizens of Jerusalem who have converted to Christianity, Saul tells them that the Pharisees have decreed that Jesus 'had the devil inside him,' a stock charge brought also against the Anabaptists of the sixteenth century. See Steenbergen, *De Bekeeringe Pauli*, 63, ll. 310–1: 'Ia, en sy sagen wel dat hy hadt den duijuel binnen. / Tis iammer dat volck dus deur hem verdooft is.' See also Waite, 'Between the Devil and the Inquisitor.'

89 Steenbergen, *De Bekeeringe Pauli*, 67, ll. 375–6: 'O heere biscop, prelate, / ouerste heere, / Regent ouer ons phariseeusche statie.' The Bishop, moreover, provides Saul with 'brieuen,' proving his special authority to prosecute heresy, a possible reference to the office of inquisitor.

90 Ibid., 74, ll. 464–5: 'Hij heeft misdaen / Tegen skeysers wet met een valsch wtgeuen!'

91 Ibid., 85–6, ll. 626–45.

92 Ibid., 86, ll. 658–9: 'Dus suldy ontfangen en het sal u wesen / Een teecken dat gij met Godt verbonden sijt.'

93 Ibid., 90, ll. 696–7: 'Waer sullense nu blijuen, onse potestaten / Ende prelaten / met alle haer valsche instellen?'

94 Ibid., 90–3, esp. 92, ll. 723–6:

YPOCRIJTICH HERTTE: Ia, eer hy singt den seluen sanck
Daer *Iesus* me dwanck ons hooge vassalen,
Als dat sy met haer leeringe tvolck doen dwalen,
En deur sulcke talen sou tgroot profijt minderen.

95 Ibid., 94–5, ll. 774–6, 786–9:

Hij is de waerheijt en anders geene;
In synen mont en was noyt bedroch geuonden;
Hy heeft ons vercoren wt liefden reene –
...
Alle dwalinge vliet,
Schout afgoderije soo daer staet geschreuen,
Aenbidt Godt alleene, wat u geschiet,
Want hy is den wech, de waerheijt en tleuen.
Hij is de *Prinse* die de sonden can vergeuen,
Hij is ootmoedich van hertten voorwaer,
Hij is ons eenige advocaet verheuen
Voort menschelyck geslacht inder eeuwicheijt claer.

96 Numerous examples have been edited and published and many others are still in manuscript, such as the collection in the Haarlem *Trou Moet Blijcken* society. For published editions, see, among many others, Heeroma, *Protestantse poëzie der 16de en 17de eeuw*, and Van der Laan, *Noordnederlandse rederijkersspelen*.

8: War, Peace, and the Imperial Majesty in Rhetorician Drama, 1519–56

1 For the impact of the Habsburg-Valois wars on Holland, see Tracy, *Holland Under Habsburg Rule*.

2 See Lovett, *Early Habsburg Spain*, esp. 22–60.

3 Tracy, *Holland under Habsburg Rule*, 50–1. He notes that in 'the larger scheme of dynastic politics, however, decisions that led to war were made in Paris or Valladolid or even in smaller capitals allied with the great powers. The Netherlands were but a pawn or at most a rook in the struggle for hegemony between Habsburg and Valois, which erupted into full-scale war six times between 1515 and 1552.'

4 Cited in DeMolen, *The Spirituality of Erasmus of Rotterdam*, 91.

5 In the first book of *The Duties (De Officiis)*, Cicero commented: 'And so diplomacy in the friendly settlement of controversies is more desirable than courage in settling them on the battlefield; but we must be careful not to take that course merely for the sake of avoiding war rather than for the sake of public expediency. War, however, should be undertaken in such a way as to make it evident that it has no other object than to secure peace' (Cicero, *De Officiis*, trans. by Walter Miller, book I, part xxiii, section 80). In book I, xi, 35, he also affirms, 'The only excuse, therefore, for going to war is that we may live in peace unharmed.' I am indebted to my colleague Prof. James Murray, of the Department of Classics, University of New Brunswick, for his assistance in finding these and other references from Cicero.

6 *The Complaint of Peace* is in Dolan, *The Essential Erasmus*, 177–204. Erasmus wrote, 'But can we say that Christ is of no consequence among men? Why is it that his most cogent doctrine, that of peace, has no effect among men? If nature is inadequate, then why is the more powerful teaching of Christ also ineffective? Why does his urging to mutual benevolence not deter them from the madness of war?' (ibid., 180).

7 Ibid., 188.

8 Ibid., 191.

9 Ibid., 177.

10 Ibid., 198.

11 As cited by Tracy, *The Politics of Erasmus*, 56. The bulk of this discussion on Erasmus's pacifism is based on Tracy and *The Complaint of Peace*.

12 Tracy, *Politics of Erasmus*, 73–4, quotes Josse de Weert, an Antwerp chronicler, who records that on 29 June 1516, 'There were in Antwerp around 500 men-at-arms from Namur who did much damage in the city and in Berchem, for they overpowered and held captive the men, carried off the women, and refused to pay the inns where they were quartered; wherefore

three were slain in Berchem, and many taken prisoner in Antwerp; but they were released the next day, which angered the commons.'

13 That a modern collection of Erasmus's statements on the subject found substantial relevant excerpts from some two dozen of his works composed between 1504 and 1530 illustrates both the importance of the topic for Erasmus and the easy availability of his writings on peace (see Margolin, *Erasme: Guerre et Paix*). Another study lists twelve works of Erasmus on peace which he composed before the *Querela Pacis* of 1517 (see Erasmus, *La Complainte de la Paix*, 19–22). It is, moreover, quite possible that Erasmus's ideas on pacifism were instrumental for the intellectual development of other proponents of pacifism or nonviolence, such as the Anabaptists (see Schrag, 'Erasmian and Grebelian Pacifism: Consistency or Contradiction?'). The question of whether Erasmus's pacifism was absolute or opportunistic, while important, is not an issue here.

14 For the influence of Erasmus on rhetoricians, see Van Gelder, *Erasmus, schilders en rederijkers*, and Degroote, 'Erasmus en de rederijkers.' On the question of the religious disputes, however, Drewes, 'Het interpreteren van godsdienstige spelen,' has shown that the rhetoricians owed much more to Luther's doctrines than to those of Erasmus.

15 Kernodle, *From Art to Theatre*, 52. For rhetoricians and *tableaux vivants* see also Hummelen, 'Het tableau vivant, de "toog," in de toneelspelen van de rederijkers.'

16 According to Tracy, *Holland under Habsburg Rule*, 44, Charles spent a total of fifty-five months in the Netherlands on five different visits, the longest taking place during the years 1520–2, 1531–2, and 1548–50. Kipling ('The Idea of the Civic Triumph,' 79) suggests that these political celebrations were imbued with deep religious meaning, whereby the ruler was depicted as a type of Christ – a 'political saviour' – and the event, a kind of *Corpus Rei Publicae*, as his advent celebrating the communal political bond uniting the ruler and his people. For an account of the 1515 visit, see Du Puys, *La tryumphante Entree de Charles Prince des Espagnes en Bruges 1515*; for the 1549 visit, during which Charles V introduced his son Philip II to his Netherlandic subjects, see *Die Blyde Incomste den Hertochdomme van Brabant*; for the political importance of royal entries in France coterminous with Philip II's, see McFarlane, *The Entry of Henri II into Paris 16 June 1549*, and McGowan, *L'Entrée de Henri II à Rouen 1550*.

17 An earlier example was provided by Bruges's city fathers while seeking the forgiveness of the duke of Burgundy for their rebellion in 1440, who with bared heads and feet, met the duke and presented him with a *tableau vivant* of ancient rulers who had shown clemency to their erring subjects (Kernodle, *From Art to Theatre*, 68–9).

18 The other pageants were under the control of the foreign guilds of the city: two by the Aragonese, three by the Hanseatic League, seven by the Spanish, and four by the Italian.

19 Du Puys, *La tryumphante Entree*, 21.

20 The purpose of the entry was made clear by a verse on the Porte Sainte Croix, where Charles made his entry into the city:

> Charles prince digne de longue vie toute liesse et iubilation
> Pour ta presence est Bruges assouvye, car en toy gist sa consolation
> Las bien est temps que on aye compassion de son declin qui souloit estre chief
> Dhonneur de biens et dexaltation
> Dont plus est dur a supporter son grief (Du Puys, *La tryumphante Entree*, 22).

21 *Aragoenoysen*, Muller and Scharpé, *Spelen van Cornelis Everaert*, 118–30, esp. 122.

22 *Hooghen Wynt ende Zoeten Reyn*, ibid., 87–102. The artisan Many adds the following about Francis I's character:

> Den Vrancxschen conync tes waer ic kent
> Mach men wel den Hooghen Wynt nomen
> Die alomme met foortsen wil duere dromen
> Ghelyc als den wynde onghestichtich (ibid., 95, ll. 232–5).

Zoeten Reyn is translated as 'Sweet Rain' instead of 'Sweet Purity' because the character is described as '*waterachtich,*' and '*regen*' was often spelled '*rein*' or '*reyn*' in the sixteenth century. It appears that Everaert intended the double meaning of Sweet Rain and Sweet Purity to describe the emperor.

23 Ibid., 95. The noble Reasonable Understanding elaborates:

> Hy es den Zoeten Reyn tot elcx confortacien
> Wiens dauweghe duecht ons zal toe vloeyen.
> Al hebben wy gheleden jn zyn vp groeyen
> Byden Hooghen Wynt wat bestoormen
> Hy heift hem nv tonder jnder voormen (ll. 248–52).

24 Ibid., 96, ll. 280–4:

> Ter contrarie Kaerle edele van gheeste
> Van zyn gheboorte tot nv jeghenwoordich
> Heift ghehouden zyn landen accoordich
> Met wysen raede ende voordachticheyt
> In payse jn liefde ende jn eendrachticheyt.

25 Ibid., 100.

26 Ibid., 127. This account is based on II Sam. 10, in which King David enacts vengeance on the Ammonites after the latter had mistreated his officials, whom he had sent to the Ammonites to establish friendly relations with them.

27 *Aragoenoysen*, 126, ll. 258–63:

> Ghelyc Kaerle onsen keyser heift ghedaen
> Om wysselicken voortghanc jn al zyn wercken
> Jeift processie doen draghen jn alle kercken
> Alle weke jn grooter bekente
> Met den heleghen sacramente
> Om alle zyn saken te beleedene wysselic.

In *Hooghen Wynt ende Zoeten Reyn*, 101, ll. 482–4, Reasonable Understanding remarks:

> In dese scoone victorye es beloken
> Dat sichtent Christus doot ghebenendyt
> Ende daer te vooren ter weerelt was vonden.

The procession of the previous Friday, the playwright continues, was held so that God might bring peace to the Christian empire. In *Aragoenoysen*, 120–1, ll. 61–5, the woman Earth comments that the victory of Charles has resulted in a glorious procession through the city of Bruges:

> De Aragoensche nacie
> Om Gode te louene met dancbaerhede
> Hebben gheordoneirt binder Brugscher stede
> Goddelicke diensten solempnelic ende scoone
> Ten loue van Gode.

28 In *Hooghen Wynt ende Zoeten Reyn*, 120–1, ll. 61–5, Many hopes that 'the Holy Spirit will enlighten noble minds for peace for the kingdom' and that:

> Den Heleghen Gheest wilder jn wercken
> Ende verlichten zyn edele zinnen
> Dat kerstenrycke mach pays ghewinnen
> So mueghen wy leuen onghetruert (ibid., ll. 489–92).

In *Aragoenoysen*, 129, l. 396, it is affirmed that the Holy Spirit will bring grace to Charles V and that Francis I should gladly submit to his overlord.

29 Yates, *Astraea: The Imperial Theme in the Sixteenth Century*, 1.

30 Comparisons between biblical figures, such as Moses and David, and Charles V were popularized by the many prophetic works circulating during the first half of the sixteenth century. See Reeves, *The Influence of Prophecy in the Later Middle Ages*. For example, Reeves notes (364–5) that in the second quarter of the century, 'Charles V was clearly the prophetic favourite' who, under the inspiration of the Holy Spirit, would lead Europe into the golden age; he was also 'the new Moses to lead the human race into liberty, the new Caesar to overcome all barbarian tyrannies, the Pastor, like David, to gather all sheep into one fold. He could even be compared with advantage to the Apostles.' For pamphlet accounts of Charles's victories,

see, among many, *Een Nieuwe Verclaringhe* and *Een Warachtighe Keyserlijcke victorie*.

31 *Hooghen Wynt ende Zoeten Reyn*, 92, l. 109.

32 Ibid., 96–7, ll. 292–3.

33 *Ghewillich Labuer ende Volc van Neerrynghe*, Muller and Scharpé, *Spelen van Cornelis Everaert*, 182–96. Obviously Everaert was able to compose this work within a few weeks of hearing of the peace treaty. That it was performed as part of a competition – probably local – is indicated by its winning a prize of some silver plate.

34 Ibid., 185, ll. 65–72:

> GHEWILLICH LABUER: By hu tyt Beroerlic tzyn hu condicien
> Ghebuerter alle quaetheit jc en cant ghehelen.
> VOLC VAN NEERRYNGHE: Roouen moorden
> GHEWILLICH: Branden stelen
> VOLC: Bynden ende coorden
> GHEWILLICH: Sulc byder kelen
> Die onnoosselic steruen by cleene bedrachten.
> VOLC: Maechden vyoleren
> GHEWILLICH: Ende vrauwen vercrachten.
> De rycke van machte ghy ter aermoede brynct.

35 Ibid., 185, ll. 76–81:

> Eist niet melodie voor dedele juechden
> Alsse byden toedoene van myn verwecken
> Tlichaeme met fynen arnassche decken
> Ende dan vut trecken met opene bannieren
> Te velde jn een coragieus versieren?
> Tes edelic te ziene sulc eenen staet vry.

36 Ibid., 185, ll. 84–7.

37 Ibid., 192–3.

38 Ibid., 193, ll. 365–9.

39 Ibid., 194–5.

40 Ibid., 193, ll. 346–51:

> Ende zo Maria by hueren odmoede
> Den leuende Gods zuene heift bejuert
> Huer niet te naer ghesproken zo eist ghebuert
> Met Leonora wien dat heift ghegreyt
> Den Vrancxschen conync die an huer gheleyt
> Heift zyn liefde tes goet te peynsene.

41 Ibid., 193, ll. 352–61:

> Sonder te deynsene.

> Taccoort by desen wort te noeder ghebroken
> An beeden zyden duer thuwelic besproken.
> Want der vrauwen liefde doet jonste rysen.
> PAYS: Ghelyc jc hu te vooren wilde bewysen
> Sichtent dat Godt meinsche wiert tonser noot
> Heift hy tonswaert jonste ghehadt zo groot
> Dat hy lieuer de doot noch eeins zoude steruen
> Dan by zynen toedoene een siele bederuen.
> So vaste houdt hy den pays beseghelt.

42 Most other communities similarly celebrated the Peace of Cambrai. On 16 August 1529, Antwerp's magistrates ordered a feast in honour of the event, enjoining all militia, rhetoric, and artisan guilds to attend the festivities in their best costumes and to render plays and 'costumed performances' (Van der Straelen, *Geschiedenis der Antwerpsche rederijkkamers*, 114). According to the secretary of Antwerp's De Violieren, they had performed in that year a play 'of the King of Aragon' which was very well enacted (Rombouts and Van Lerius, *De liggeren*, I, 113).

43 *Scaemel Ghemeente ende Trybulacie*, Muller and Scharpé, *Spelen van Cornelis Everaert*, 135–44; *Aerm inde Buerse*, in ibid., 285–96. This last title was formulated as a word play on the motto of the Veurne chamber, 'Aerm inde Buerse,' for which chamber the work was composed (Everaert acted also as factor of this *rederijker* group).

44 *Groot Labuer ende Sober Wasdom*, ibid., 264–82. Rhetoricians elsewhere performed plays to celebrate this treaty; Tracy, *Holland under Habsburg Rule*, 66, describes the contents of one from the French town of Amiens: 'While merchants and peasants plead for peace, Mars objects; when the parties appeal to Lady Nobility, she explains that peace is difficult because the nobles are nourished by war. The conclusion is that only God can bring war to an end.'

45 *Tspel vanden Pays*, Muller and Scharpé, *Spelen van Cornelis Everaert*, 544–56 (Hum. 1 B 36). As noted above, it is possible that he composed Bruges's contribution to the 1539 competition in Ghent (see Erné and van Dis, *De Gentse spelen*, 29).

46 *Tspel vanden Pays*, 548, l. 108: 'Die de herten der conynghen regiert.'

47 Ibid., 552.

48 Ibid., 555, ll. 358–62. Cf. I Samuel 25.

49 *Tspel vanden Crych*, Muller and Scharpé, *Spelen van Cornelis Everaert*, 210–31 (Hum. 1 B 14).

50 Ibid., 214, ll. 99–103:
> MENICH: Hadden wy de waghene hier es juuste tvolcxskin
> So mochten wy de lieden een rollekin spelen.

DYVEERS: De Rethorycke zoude hemlieden vervelen.
Men zietse by dien quelen met onlusten.
LUEGHEN: Den crych en volchse niet.

51 Ibid., 217, l. 228.
52 Ibid., 219.
53 Ibid., 220.
54 Ibid., 224, ll. 461–2; and 225, ll. 484–5.
55 I.e., Flanders; ibid., 227, l. 576.
56 Ibid., 229, ll. 634–6.
57 Ibid., 230, ll. 654–6.
58 Ibid., 231, l. 681.
59 Reeves, *The Influence of Prophecy,* 347–72. She remarks (362) that it 'seems that prophecy even penetrated the Imperial electoral chamber in 1519. Some of the speakers in the debate attached great significance to the issue of this election, declaring that the salvation of Europe hung on it, that he who could sustain this office must be of heroic mould and vast strength, and that he must be comparable to an Alexander.'
60 Niccoli, *Prophecy and People in Renaissance Italy,* 184.
61 *Een speel te speelen in tijden van oorloghe,* Brussels KB 21648 (Hum. 1 D 1). De Vooys, 'Amsterdamsch rederijkersleven,' 138, says that this was written for Amsterdam's Eglantine chamber. The manuscript is dated 1551, which is probably the year that it was copied. Interestingly, the opening prologue begins with Vengeful Principle (*Wraeckghierich Voortstel*) and Old Grudge (*Ouwe Wrock*), respectively the father and mother of Mars, recounting a long list of their past achievements. They take credit for the ultimate failure of ancient and biblical figures and for so blinding the Pharisees and the Roman governor Pilate that they willingly persecuted and killed Christ. Then the Vices proudly rehearse how they have successfully changed the course of history of many nations, leading all to their ruin. Each empire, regardless of how rich and powerful it might have been, has fallen into decay and given way to the next: Assyria and Mede to the Persian; the Persian to Alexander the Great; with Alexander's death, the Greek empire splintered and became easy prey to the Romans, who 'domineered over all the world in glory.' In spite of its strength, the Roman empire was soon beset by a variety of enemies, including the Germanic and Frankish tribes, so that only a portion of it remains in the German and Italian lands (the Holy Roman Empire). Moreover, by Vengeful Principle and Old Grudge's influence, 'France remains apostate to the Spanish empire' and Turks, Africans, and Moors, not to mention the English, all seek to strike at the remnants of the Roman empire.

62 *Een speel te speelen in tijden van oorloghe,* fol. 2r. See Ellerbroek-Fortuin, *Amsterdamse rederykersspelen,* 142–7, and De Vooys, 'Amsterdams reder-ijkesleven,' 138. The last line of the play provides Eglantine's motto: 'Dit schencken u de gheestkens van In lieft bluyende.' The two characters list their weapons of war which include daggers, hatchets, swords, fist-hammers (*vuysthamers*), bows, artillery (*bussen*), serpentines (a variety of cannon used in the fifteenth and sixteenth centuries), crossbows, lances, stilettoes (*moortpriemen* – common throughout Europe in the latter part of the sixteenth century), and the like.

63 *Een speel te speelen in tijden van oorloghe,* fol. 4r.

64 Ibid., fol. 4v.

65 Ibid., fol. 5r.

66 Ibid., fol. 6r–v.

67 Ibid., fol. 6v:
  JUSTICE: Waer ick alleen ben sonder payse
  Corruptie verkeert daer ten pallayse
  By cause want wille mach dan regieren.

68 Ibid., fol. 7r.

69 Ibid., fols. 7v–8r, esp. the words of Duuel at fol. 8r, l. 300: 'Ick meen icxse up deese tijt regiere.'

70 Ibid., fol. 9r: 'Heere God wat blaemen / Dat deese die werlt te houwene pleeghen.'

71 Ibid., fol. 9v: 'De guede is lyende om die quaede / de welcke tregiment hebben vruech en spaede / by sduuels raede.'

72 Ibid., fol. 9v. This portion of the play suggests a Protestant or Reformed reli-gious perspective on the part of the playwright.

73 Ibid., fol. 10r: 'Want waerender gheen sonden daer waeren gheen plaeghen.'

74 Ibid., fol. 13r:
  DONBESCULDIGHE: O alle ghy de dit hoorende sijt en siet
  Wildt u tot beweende beedinge keeren
  Troost ruepende aen die ghenaede ons heeren.

75 Ibid., fol. 13v. The entire passage is worthy of citation:
  DONBESCULDIGHE: O heer Sebaoth laet u beweeghen
  Ons karmen ende claghen in deesen noot
  Up dat orlooghe mach sijn ghesleeghen
  De so mennighen heeft ghebrocht ter doot
  Weduwen en Weesen ghemaect tis bloot
  Gherooft ghepluystert veriaegt verdreeven
  Voirvluchtichtich synde ghebreect ons broot
  Alle nootdruft is achter ghebleeven

Verhoord ons aalmöghende god verheeven

Verstoort uyten ooghen Welvaerts vianden

En laet aminnighe pays weder belanden.

76 *Een spel vanden Vader, die het Volck sant om in den wijngaert te wercken,* Brussels KB II 129, partly edited in Snellaert, 'Drie spelen van zinne,' 335–8 (Hum. 1 G 5).

77 Snellaert, 'Drie spelen van zinne,' 337–8:

OOTMOEDICHEYT: Neemt danckelic, mijn heeren, ons simpel collatie.

Isser ieuers misseyt, miswrocht, misdaen,

Wy bevelen v allen die hoogste generatie,

Alvoren onsen ingheboren prince, dat keyserlic graen:

Godt die wille hem altijt in staden staen,

Om sijn landen te regierne in payse excellent.

78 Ibid., 338.

79 The first version is entitled *Eneas en Dido. Imperium sine fine dedi,* Brussels KB II 369 (Hum. I D 12). See above, chapter 3. Ghistele was also prominent in the translation of Greek and Latin drama, such as Cornelis van Ghistele *Een Tragedie/ghenaemt Antigone;* and *Teretius Comedie.* See Grietens, *Antigone van Sophocles.*

80 *Eneas en Dido* (1), fol. 4v.

81 Kruyskamp, 'Het spel van het Cloen van Armoe,' esp. 49. The original survives in two manuscripts, one in the Ghent Universiteitsbibliotheek, 899 (Hum. 2 O 4); the other in the Haarlem Archief Trou Moet Blijcken collection, volume G, fols. 7r–14v (Hum. 1 OG 2).

82 'Wie voirmaels waren de victorioste' (Hum. 1 D 15), in Meertens, 'Een esbatement ter ere van keizer Karel V,' esp. 75–8, where Meertens discusses the contest.

83 Ibid., 90, ll. 260–70. The entire passage reads:

ANTWOORT: Mij is gevraecht inder warachtichede

Wie voirmaels waeren de victorioeste verheven,

Daer noch blijcken de wercken int leven.

O Gepeijs, wilt mij nu gheven / u avijs excellent

En ghij Arguacie hout u niet absent,

Maar thoont u diligent / tselve dör mij te solveren,

Speelwijs tot Rhetoricams eeren

Sonder faelgeren / tot deser spacie,

Verchiert met redene sonder blamacie,

Vrij van indignacie / des Keijsers placaeten

Laetende in vreen gheestlijc en werlijcke staeten (emphasis mine).

84 Ibid., 94, ll. 417–18.

85 Actually spoken by Dander in the prologue; ibid., 82, ll. 7–8.
86 Ibid., 95, l. 458.
87 Ibid., 96, ll. 477–88. The comparison between Charles V and Jason was a natural and fairly common one. For an example dating from Charles's youth, see Degroote, *Jan Smeken's gedicht op de Feesten ter Eere van het Gulden Vlies te Brussel in 1516*. Charles V's device was frequently the object of interpretation, usually affirming that his was an empire extending further than that of the ancient Romans, which had been bounded by the columns of Hercules. According to Yates, *Astraea*, 23, the 'device carried with it also this prophetic implication that the discovery of the new worlds was providentially timed to coincide with the coming of one who should be the *Dominus mundi* in a wider sense than was known to the Romans.'
88 Meertens, 'Een esbatement ter ere van keizer Karel V,' 101.
89 See Reeves, *The Influence of Prophecy*, 366, where one of the prognosticators describes Charles's mission in cosmic terms, to 'orbem invenire, emendare, componere: qua advocatus Ecclesiae illam fovere, erigere, propagare pertinet' ('To find the world, to change it, to set it right, by which a supporter of the Church means: to cherish it, to elevate it, to preserve it'). [My thanks to John Geyssen, Department of Classics, University of New Brunswick, for his assistance in translating this passage]. From Egidio of Viterbo's *Scechina*, published in the second quarter of the sixteenth century.
90 Van der Straelen, *Geschiedenis der Antwerpsche rederijkkamers*, 24; and esp. Rombouts and Van Lerius, *De liggeren*, 189–191. According to the latter source, The Gillyflower had contributed to the festivities also by constructing a punt in front of the city hall with banners depicting the seventeen Netherlandic provinces as well as a scene of Apollo and his Nine Muses displayed in front of their chamber hall.
91 'Vrede sticht vreucht, maer twist, eer, deucht en welvaert belet' (Rombouts and Van Lerius, *De liggeren*, 191). For their efforts, the secretary records, the deacons of The Gillyflower spent 53£ Fl. more than they received.
92 The Gillyflower had a minimum of seventy-five official members.
93 Willems, 'Een Factie oft spel, Voer den Coninck Philippus onsen ghenadigste lantsheere' (Hum. 4 O 6).
94 Ibid., 247.
95 Ibid., 249–50.
96 Ibid., 251–2.
97 Ibid., 254–6.
98 Ibid., 257.

99 Ibid., 255, where Brother Jacob, a 'Peter's Pot Brother,' remarked:
    Wy souwen oock die lacker brocken prijsen
    Veel lackernijen zijn quaey ghewenten
    Maer haer lackernije en is geen seker renten
    Haer voernemen moet dicwils falen
    Dan comen zij tot Peeterspots een broyken halen.
100 Ibid., 257.
101 Rowan, 'The Dutch Revolt: What Kind of Revolution?' 571.
102 For examples, see *Een spel van Sinnen, die sin is: hoe sommich mens al syn goet beroeft is* (1576), in the archives of the Haarlem Society, Trou Moet Blijken, Book C, fols. 1r–18v, and *Een esbatement van 8 personaetgen ende gespeelt van T.M.B. tot haerlem, A° 1579, op Kursdach*, Book C, fols. 19r–24v. Several other scripts in this collection depict the evils of idolatry as well as the heroism of the Dutch and the atrocities of the Spanish during the revolt. For an example of iconoclastic propoganda, see *Een spel van sinnen van de Propheet Eliseus die Naman den Syrier van syn melaetsheyt genas*, Book B, fols. 63r–75v.

Conclusion

1 See also Ramakers, *Spelen en figuren*, 443.
2 For a summary, see Ulrich Nembach et al., 'Preaching and Sermons,' in Hillerbrand, *Oxford Encyclopedia of the Reformation*, 323–32.
3 See Ten Boom, *De reformatie in Rotterdam*, 98–110; see also the studies by Van Slee, *De Rijnsburger Collegianten*, Hylkema, *Reformateurs: Geschiedkundige studiën over de godsdienstige bewegingen uit de nadagen onzer gouden eeuw*, Fix, *Prophecy and Reason*, and Benjamin J. Kaplan, *Calvinists and Libertines*.
4 One of the most prominent writers of verse, drama, and commentary in the second half of the sixteenth century was Dirk Volckertsz Coornhert (1522–90), a prominent spiritualist and advocate of religious toleration; Bonger, *Leven en werk van Dirk Volckertsz Coornhert*. For Mennonites and drama, see esp. Visser, *Broeders in de geest*.
5 See Schenkeveld, *Dutch Literature*, 38–75. For examples of reformist plays performed during the reign of Philip II, see William van Eeghem, *Drie scandaleuse spelen*, Galama, *Twee zestiende-eeuwse spelen van de verlooren zoone door Robert Lawet*, and Van der Laan, *Noordnederlandse rederijkersspelen*.
6 For a review, see Smits-Veldt, *Het Nederlandse renaissancetoneel*.

Bibliography

Primary Sources

Amsterdam Gemeente Archief Amsterdam (GA)
5028: 554 Het Register vanden incomste en belastinge van alle godts huysen en gilden binnen Amsterdam mesgaer ornamente, 1570.
5039–115 Stads Financiën: Overzicht van de inkomsten en uitgaven van de stad over 1534–1536, met totaalcijfers over 1537–1538.
H5 Handvesten en privilegiën, before 1530.
Noordkerke, H. *Handvesten*. 3 vols. Amsterdam, 1748.
  Mayor's Archive (Archief Burgemeester)
5023 Groot-Memoriaal, I (Mfc 8)
Mfc 446 Keurboek, D (1512–37)
Resolutiën Vroedschap, I, to 1565
Mfc 6257–60 Stadsrekeningen
  6257 – 1531–6
  6258 – 1536–45
  6259 – 1545–51
  6260 – 1551–7
Antwerp Stads-archief Antwerpen (SA)
BIB823 *Album der St. Lukas Gilde*. Antwerp, 1855.
BIB1247 Génard, P. *Verhandelingen* III. *Luister der St. Lucasgilde*. Antwerp, 1854.
BIB1495 *Chronycke van Antwerpen sedert het Jaer 1500 tot 1575*. Antwerp, 1843.
BIB3037 Burbere, L. de. Inventaris der nog bestaende Registers en Oorkonden voort komende van de Sint Lukas-Gilde, van de Rederijkkamers, genaemde de olyftak en de Goudblem en van de oude Koninglijke Akademie van Antwerpen, sedert het Jaer 1442 tot in 1796.

PK81 Blyde Incompsten, 1260–1637.

PK101 Seer Oude Geschiedenissen tot Antwerpen Vorgevallen 870 tot 1543. Copied by Vincent Verhoeven, 1583.

PK103 Boeck der Tyden of die Chronike van Nederlant etc. van Adams Tyden totten Jaere 1550.

PK105 Kronyk van Antwerpen, 1500–50.

PK171–3 Sanden, A. van der. Oud Konst Tooneel van Antwerpen. MS. ca. 1769.

PK264 Edicten en Ordonnanten voor de Stadt Antwerpen, 1539–1591.

PK1626 Blijde Inkomsten van 1310–1477 en documenten van 1372–1544.

PK1627 Inhuldiging van's Landsvorsten, I, 15e en 16e Eeuw.

PK1629 Blyde Incompst van Carel V.

PK1644 Ommegangen en Processien, 1302–1765.

PK2902 Grimbergen, V. van. St. Lucasgilde en Rederykkamers.

PK2910 Straelen, J.B. van der. Jaerboek der St. Lucas gilde. Geschiedenis der Antw. Rederijkkamers.

PK3080 Jaerboeken der wijd Oud-Vermaerde en Konst-rijke Gulde van Sinte Lucas binnen de stad Antwerpen; alsmede dry Reden-rijk Camers der selve Stad, te weten: de Violieren, de Goudblom en den Olijftak, 1435–1795.

PK3243 Dilis, E. Rekeningen – Olijftak, Bundel.

PK4622 Gilden tegen Vener. Kap. tegen Violier.

R1788 Rekening van Jan de Meyere, rentmeester, 1549 (12 May–31 Jan.).

Stadsrekeningen

    R7 – 1530
    R8 – 1532
    R9 – 1537
    R10 – 1538
    R11 – 1542
    R12 – 1543
    R13 – 1550
    R14 – 1551
    R15 – 1555.

Stad Antwerpen, Poortersboeken, 1464–1533.

Stad Antwerpen, Antwerpse Poortersboeken, 1533–1609: Vol. 1, Oct. 3, 1533– Mar. 24, 1559. Vol. 2, Mar. 31, 1559–Jan. 29, 1609. Vol. 3, Index.

Viershaarboek, IV. 1544–48.

Brussels Koninklijke Bibliotheek (KB):

Gheurtsz Collection (Verzameling Gheurtsz)

21648 Een speel te speelen in tijden van oorloghe van Moortdadich Werck en Manhatighe Tanden, 1551.

21649 Van Ons Lieven Heeren Minnevaer, by 1552.

21650 Sint Jans Onthoofdinghe, 1552.

21651 Thoenisz, Jan. Mennich Mensch suect Thuijs van Vreeden, 1553.

21652 sMenschen Sin en Verganckelijcke Schoonheit, by 1552 [1546].

21653 Jacopz, Adriaen. De Ghepredestineerde Blinde, by 1552.

21654 Musijcke ende Rhetorijcke, by 1553.

21655 Naaman, 1553.

21659 Menschelijcke Broosheit, 1551.

II 367 Een Present van Godt Loondt, by 1553.

II 368 Mars en Venus, Antwerp, by 1551.

II 369(1) Ghistele, Cornelis van. Eneas en Dido, 1551.

II 369(2) Ghistele, Cornelis van. Eneas en Dido, 1552.

16912–13 Droncke Taverne; Sanct Jooris; Het Verijdelde Huwelijk; De Drie Minners.

Reformation Plays Collection (Verzameling Reformatorische Spelen)

II 129 T'Werck der Apostelen Cap. 3, 4, en 5; Den Boom der Schriftueren; Weereltsche Gheleerde en Godlicke Wijse; Heijmelic Lijden; De Vader die het Volck Sant; Schamel volck en coninck Abuijs

Apostle Play Collection (Verzameling Apostelspel)

21664 DWerck der Apostelen; De Bekeeringe Pauli.

Van der Stoct Collection (Verzameling van der Stoct)

7812 De Moedere ende Kinderen Zebedei; De Duerlijdende Man; Eertsche Meynsche.

II 130 Naboth.

Ghent Universiteitsbibliotheek

899 TCloen van Armoe.

900 Charon.

900 Keyart, Colijn. Narcissus ende Echo.

Ghent Stadsarchief Gent

Register 93 BB, Eersten bouck vanden Voorgheboden der stede van Ghendt beghinnene Int Jaer 1482, 1482–1545.

Register 400 Stadsrekeningen
    47 – 1536–7, 1537–8, 1538–9, 1539–40
    48 – 1541 (10 May 1540–May 10 1541)
    49 – 1542 (1541–2)
    50 – 1543 (1542–3)
    51 – 1544 (1543–4)
    52 – 1545 (1544–5)
    53 – 1546 (1545–6)
    54 – 1547 (1546–7)

55 – 1548 (1547–8)
56 – 1549 (1548–9)
57 – 1550 (1549–50)
63 – 1556 (1555–6).
Memorieboek der Stad Ghent van t J. 1501 tot 1793, vol. 2. Gent, 1854.
The Hague – Koninklijke Bibliotheek (KB)
71 J 27 (oud.N 137) Pietersz, Joris. Wie Voirmaels Waeren de Victoriöste.
72 J 48 Cornelijssz, Lucas. Palmen.
131 G 32 Warde, Merten vanden. Paeijs, Vrede En Een IJegelictsijne.
132 F7 Gommersz Collection (Verzameling Gommersz), 1565–6.
Haarlem Archief Trou Moet Blycken
14 volumes of manuscript plays, marked A–N and Register (vols. H, K and L are lost).

Published Primary Sources and Editions

Aegidius, Petrus. *Hypotheses sive Argumenta Spectaculorum, quae Sereniss. Invictissimo Caes. Carolo Pio, Felici, Inclyto, semper AVG. praeder alia multa & varia Fides et Amor celebratissime civitatis Antuerpiensis antistites (superis favêntibus) sunt edituri.* N.p., 1520.

Aercke, Kristiaan P.G., ed. 'Germanic Sappho: Anna Bijns.' In *Women Writers of the Renaissance and Reformation,* ed. Katharina M. Wilson, 365–97. Athens, Georgia, and London, 1987.

Asselbergs, W.J.M.A., and A.P. Huysmans, eds. *Het spel vanden heilighen sacramente van der Nyeuwervaert.* Zwolle, 1955.

Atkinson, W.E.D., ed. *Acolastvs: A Latin Play of the Sixteenth Century by Gulielmus Grapheus.* London, Ont., 1964.

Barnouw, Adriaan J., ed. *The Mirror of Salvation, A Moral Play of Everyman c1490.* The Hague, 1971.

Bertrijn, Geraard. *Chronijck der stad Antwerpen.* Antwerp, 1879.

Beuken, W.H., ed. *Mariken van Nieumeghen.* Zutphen, 1972.

– ed. *Die Eerste Bliscap van Maria en Die Sevenste Bliscap van Onser Vrouwen.* Noordwijn, 1978.

Bock, E. de, ed. 'Een presentspel van Colijn Cailleu.' *Spiegel der Letteren* 6 (1963), 241–69.

Braght, Thielman van. *The Bloody Theatre or Martyr's Mirror.* Scottdale, PA, 1951.

Brands, G.A., ed. *Tspel van de Cristenkercke.* Utrecht, 1921.

Breen, Joh. C., ed. *Rechtsbronnen der stad Amsterdam.* The Hague, 1902.

Broeckaert, J., ed. *Rederijkersgedichten der XVIe eeuw,* Ghent, 1893.

Bruin, C.C. de, ed. 'Een seer schoon spel van zinnen ghemaeckt by mijn Heer

Johan Wtenhove anno 32 ende is ghespeelt anno 1543.' *JdF* 39–40 (1989–90), 21–94.

Byden Keyser in Zijnen Rade. April 4, 1554. Antwerp, [1554].

Casteleyn, Matthijs de. *Pyramus Ende Thisbe. Schoon retorike amoureus bequame es dit barblijke voor sulcken eersame* [Antwerp, before 1550].

– *De Const van Rhetoriken.* Ghent, 1555.

Cawley, A.C., ed. *Everyman and Medieval Miracle Plays.* 2nd ed. London, 1974.

Cicero, *De Officiis.* Trans. Walter Miller. Loeb Classical Library 30. London, 1913.

Coigneau, Dirk, ed. *Mariken van Nieumeghen.* Hilversum, 1996.

Dale, J.H. van, ed. 'Een spel van zinne van Cornelis Everaert.' *Bijdragen tot de oudheidkunde en geschiedenis inzonderheid van Zeeuwsch-Vlaanderen* 5 (1860), 315–29.

De boom der schriftueren van vi personagien/ ghespelt tot Middelburch in Zeelant den eersten in Augusto in iaer xxxix. n.p., n.d.

Decker, Therese, and Martin W. Walsh, eds. and trans. *Mariken van Nieumeghen: A Bilingual Edition.* Columbia, SC, 1994.

Degroote, Gilbert, ed. *Jan van den Dale: Gekende werken met inleiding, bronnen-studie, aanteekeningen en glossarium.* Antwerp, 1944.

– ed. *Jan Smeken's gedicht op de Feesten ter Eere van het Gulden Vlies te Brussel in 1516.* Antwerp, 1946.

'De rekening der stad Antwerpen van het jaar 1549–1550.' *AA*, old series 1, 17–104.

Die Blyde Incomste den Hertochdomme van Brabant In voortyden by haren Lands-theeren vuleent, ende van Keyser Carolo den V. geconfirmeert ende by Phillippus zynen Sone, den II. Coninck van Spaengnien, etc. solemnelijcken gesworen. Antwerp, [1549].

Dijk, Hans van, et al., eds. 'Plaijerwater: A Sixteenth-century Farce with an English Translation.' *Dutch Crossing* 24 (December 1984), 32–70.

Dillen, J.G. van, ed. *Bronnen tot de geschiedenis van het bedrijfsleven en het gilde-wezen van Amsterdam.* Vol. 1, *1512–1611.* The Hague, 1929.

Dis, L.M. van, ed. *Reformatorische rederijkersspelen uit de eerste helft van de zestiende eeuw.* Haarlem, 1937.

– and B.H. Erné, eds. *De spelen van zinne vertoond op het landjuweel te Gent van 12–23 juni 1539.* Groningen-Antwerpen, 1939.

Dolan, John P., ed. *The Essential Erasmus.* New York, 1964.

Eeghem, William van, ed. Drie scandaleuse spelen (Brussel 1559). Antwerpen, 1937.

Eeghen, I.H. van, ed. *Inventarissen der archieven van de Gilden en van het Brouwerscollege.* Amsterdam, 1951.

330   Bibliography

Een Factie oft spel, Voer de Coninck Philippus onsen ghenadichtste Lantsheere ... van den Violieren binnen Antwerpen gespeelt de xxiij Feb MD.lvj [Antwerp, 1556].

Een Nieuwe Verclaringhe ende gheschiedenisse van onsen edelen vromen Keyser. Antwerp, [1542].

Een Nieuwe zekere ende Warachtighe tijdinghe vanden Tyrannighen Wolf Merten van Rossem. Ende oock van zijnder Bankeroutten. Antwerp, [1542].

Een schone triumphante Godlijcke victorie gheschiet voer dye stadt van Lueuen tegen mertten van Rossom met zijnen adherenten den tweden dach Augusti 1542. Antwerp, 1542.

Een Warachtighe Keyserlijcke victorie/ met der hulpen der Spaniaerden/ voor de stadt van Trenunsijn dwelc conincrijc hi metten bijstant van noch twee ander Coninghen gheconquesteert heeft/ End van des Keysers comste in dese Nederlanden. Antwerp, [1542].

Endepols, H.J.E., ed. *Den spyeghel der salicheyt van Elckerlijc.* Groningen, 1955.

Engen, John van, ed. and trans., *Devotio Moderna: Basic Writings.* New York, 1988.

Erasmus. *La Complainte de la Paix [1525].* Ed. Emile V. Telle. Geneva, 1978.

Erné, B.H., and L.M. van Dis, eds. *De Gentse spelen van 1539.* 2 vols. The Hague, 1982.

Es, G.A. van, ed. *Piramus en Thisbe. Twee rederijkersspelen uit de zestiende eeuw.* Zwolle, 1965.

– ed. *Een esbattement van sMenschen Sin en Verganckelijcke Schoonheit.* Zwolle, 1967.

Friederichs, Julius, ed. *De secte der Loïsten of Antwerpsche Libertijnen (1525–1545): Eligius Pruystinck (Loy de Schaliedecker) en zijn aanhangers.* Ghent and The Hague, 1891.

Galama, E.G.A., ed. *Twee zestiende-eeuwse spelen van de verlooren zoone door Robert Lawet.* Utrecht, 1941.

Génard, P., ed. 'Ordonnantien van het Antwerpsch Magistraat, rakende de godsdienstige geschillen der XVIe eeuw.' *AA*, old series 2, 308–472.

– ed. 'Personen te Antwerpen in de XVI eeuw voor het "feit van religie" gerechtelijk vervolgd.' *AA*, old series 7, 8, 13.

Geus, B. de, J. van der Heijden, A. Maat, and D. den Ouden, eds., *Een Scone Leeringe om Salich te Sterven.* Utrecht, 1985.

Ghistele, Cornelis van. *Een Tragedie ghenaemt Antigone ... door Cornelis van Ghistele.* Antwerp, 1545.

– *Teretius Comedie Nv eerst wt den Latin/ in onser duytscher talen/ door Cornelis van Ghistele/ Rethorikelijck ouer ghesed.* Antwerp, 1549.

Grietens, J., ed. *Antigone van Sophocles, vertaald door Cornelis van Ghistele, gedrukt door Simon Cock in 1556.* Antwerp, 1922.

Grondijs, H.F., ed. *Een spul van sinnen van den Siecke Stadt.* Borculo, 1917.

Haeserijn, Lic. R. 'Oorspronck der cameren van rethorijcke, statuten ende ordonnancien der selve onder den titel Jesus Metter Balsem Bloume.' *Kultureel Jaarboek voor de Provincie Oostvlaanderen* 2 (1960), 1–95.

Happé, Peter, ed. *English Mystery Plays: A Selection*. Harmondsworth, Middlesex, 1975.

Heeroma, K., ed. *Protestantse poëzie der 16de en 17de eeuw*. Brussels, 1940.

Heijden, M.C.A. van der, ed. *Hoort wat men u spelen zal. Toneelstukken uit de middeleeuwen (Spectrum van de Nederlandse letterkunde 5)*. Utrecht-Antwerp, 1968.

Hoebeke, Marcel, ed. *Het spel van de V vroede ende van de V dwaeze Maegden*. 2nd ed. The Hague, 1979.

Horst, Irving B., ed. *Melchior Hoffman. De ordonnantie Gods*. Amsterdam, 1980.

Hullu, J.G. de, ed. *Bescheiden betreffende de hervorming in Overijsel*. Deventer, 1897.

Hummelen, W.M.H., and C. Schmidt, ed. *Naaman, Prinche van Sijrien. Een rederijkersspel uit de zestiende eeuw*. Zutphen, n.d.

'Index der Gebodboeken, berustende der Secretary der Stad Antwerpen, beginnende met 8 February 1489, en eendegende met het jaer 1794.' *AA*, old series 1, 120–464.

Iterson, P.D.J. van, and P.H.J. van der Laan, eds. *Resoluties van de vroedschap van Amsterdam, 1490–1550*. Amsterdam, 1986.

Joldersma, Hermina, ed. 'Anna Bijns.' In *Women Writing in Dutch*, ed. Kristiaan Aercke, 93–146. New York and London, 1994.

Kalff, G., ed. *Trou Moet Blycken: Tooneelstukken der zestiende eeuw*. Groningen, 1889.

King, Peter, ed. 'The Voluptuous Man.' *Dutch Crossing* 28 (April 1986), 53–107.

Kruyskamp, C., ed. 'De klucht van Koster Johannes.' *JdF* 7 (1950), 25–41.

– ed. *Dichten en spelen van Jan van den Berghe*. The Hague, 1950.

– ed. *Het Antwerpse landjuweel van 1561*. Amsterdam, 1962.

– ed. 'Het esbatement vant Gelt.' *JdF* 16 (1966), 59–84.

– ed. 'Het spel van het Cloen van Armoe.' *JdF* 17 (1967), 47–73.

Laan, N. van der, ed. *Rederijkersspelen naar een handschrift ter Bibliotheek van het Leidsche Gemeentearchief*. The Hague, 1932.

– ed. *Uit het Archief der Pellicanisten. Vier zestiende-eeuwse esbatementen*. Leiden, 1938.

– ed. *Noordnederlandse rederijkersspelen*. Amsterdam, 1941.

Lievens, Robrecht, ed. *Tghevecht van Minnen naar de Antwerpse postenkunabel van 1516*. Leuven, 1964.

Luther, Martin. *Luther's Works*. American Edition. St Louis, 1955–76.

Lyna, F., and W. van Eeghem, eds. *De Sotslach: Klucht uit ca. 1550*. Brussels, 1932.

Mak, J.J., ed. *Vier excellente kluchten*. Amsterdam, 1950.

Margolin, Jean-Claude, ed. *Erasme: Guerre et Paix*. Paris, 1973.

McGowan, Margaret M., ed. *L'Entrée de Henri II à Rouen 1550. A Facsimile with an Introduction*. New York, n.d.

Meersch, D.J. vander, ed. 'Kronyk der rederykkamers van Audenaerde.' *Belgisch Museum* 7 (1843), 15–59.

Meertens, P.J., ed. 'Een esbatement ter ere van keizer Karel V (een Leids Rederijkersspel uit 1552).' *JdF* 17 (1967), 75–105.

– ed. 'Het esbatement van de Appelboom. Een volksvertelsel omgewerkt tot esbatement.' *TNTL* 42 (1923), 165–90.

Mierlo, J. van, ed. *Elckerlijc. Nieuwe bijdragen met ge-emendeerde uitgave*. Antwerp, 1949.

Muller, J.W., and L. Scharpé, eds. *Spelen van Cornelis Everaert*. Leiden, 1920.

Pleij, Herman, ed. '*T is al vrouwenwerk. Refreinen van Anna Bijns*. Amsterdam, 1987.

Potter, Robert, and Elsa Streitman, eds. 'Man's Desire and Fleeting Beauty: A Sixteenth-Century Comedy.' *Dutch Crossing* 23 (April 1985), 29–85.

Puys, Remi du. *La tryumphante Entree de Charles Prince des Espagnes en Bruges 1515*. Ed. by Sydney Anglo. New York, 1973.

Raftery, Margaret M., ed. *Mary of Nemmegen*. Leiden, 1991.

Roland, P., ed. 'Inventaris op het archief van het Oud Sint Lucasgild en van de Oud Koninklijke Academie van Antwerpen.' *Antwerpen's oudheidkundige kring* 15 (1939), 42–101.

Rombouts, P., and T. van Lerius, eds. *De liggeren en andere historische archieven der Antwerpsche Sint Lucas gilde, onder zinspreuk wt jonsten versaemt*. 2 vols. Antwerp, 1864–6, repr. Amsterdam, 1961.

Rowen, Herbert H., ed. *The Low Countries in Early Modern Times*. New York, 1972.

Scharpé, L., ed. 'De Rovere's spel van Quiconque vult salvus esse.' *Leuvensche bijdragen* 4 (1900–2), 155–93.

Schotel, G.D.J., ed. *Den boom der schriftueren van VI personagien*. Utrecht, 1870.

Snellaert, F.A., ed. 'Drie spelen van zinne uit den tijd der reformatie.' *Belgisch Museum* 10 (1846), 322–38.

Steenbergen, G. Jo., ed. *De bekeeringe Pauli*. Zwolle, 1953.

Stoet, F.A., ed. *Drie kluchten uit de zestiende eeuw*. Zutphen, 1932.

Straelen, J.B. van der, ed. *Jaerboek der St. Lucas gilde*. Antwerp, 1855.

– ed. *Geschiedenis der Antwerpsche rederijkamers*. Antwerp, 1863.

Vandecasteele, Maurits, ed. 'De Haagse rederijkerskamer "Met Ghenuchten" in 1494.' *JdF* 35–6 (1985–6), 125–48.

Van die blijde Incoemste des aldermachtichsten Conincx van Spaengien ende van

Engelant/ ... binnen die Stadt van Antwerpen/ ende van die triumphe al daer ghedaen. Oock vanden iammerliken ongelucke dat daer doen ter tijt ghebuert is. Antwerp, 1561.

Vloten, J. van, ed. *Het Nederlandsche kluchtspel van de 14ᵉ tot de 18ᵉ eeuw.* Vol. 1, 2nd ed. Haarlem, 1877.

Voolstra, S., ed. 'Een spel van sinnen van de menswerdinge Christo.' *DB* 9 (1983), 53–103.

Vooys, C.G.N. de, ed. 'Een onbekende verzameling refereinen uit de eerste helft van de 16ᵉ eeuw.' *NAK* 21 (1928), 191–232.

Vooys, C.G.N. de, and J.J. Mak, eds. 'Een verloren vastenspel van sinnen uit de XVIᵈᵉ eeuw.' *VMKVA* (1953), 593–650.

Vorrink, J., ed. *Hanneken Leckertant.* The Hague, 1925.

Vos, R., ed. *Den spieghel der salicheit van Elckerlijc.* Groningen, 1925.

Vreese, W.L. de, ed. *Een spel van sinne van Charon, de helsche schippere (1551).* Antwerp, 1896.

Waite, Gary K., ed. and trans. *The Anabaptist Writings of David Joris 1535–1543.* Classics of the Radical Reformation 7. Waterloo, Ont., and Scottdale, PA, 1994.

Waite, Gary K., and Samme Zijlstra, 'Antiochus Revisited: An Anonymous Anabaptist Letter to the Court at the Hague.' *MQR* 66 (1992), 26–46.

Waterschoot, W., ed. *Het esbatement van den Appelboom.* The Hague, 1979.

Willems, J.F., ed. 'Een Factie oft spel, Voer den Coninck Philippus onsen ghenadigste lantsheere, met vele andere Edele Heeren, openbaerlijck van den Violieren binnen Antwerpen gespeelt den xxiii feb. M.D. lvi, tot verhue-ghinghe der ghemeynten, duer de blijde tijdinghe des Bestandts.' *Belgisch Museum* 2 (1838), 242–57.

– ed. 'Tafelspelen.' *Belgisch Museum* 2 (1838), 102–34.

– ed. 'Oorkonden van rederykkamers: 1. Pryskaerte var de rederijkkamer der stad Hulst.' *Belgisch Museum* 4 (1840), 411–23.

Williams, George H., and Angel M. Mergal, eds. *Spiritual and Anabaptist Writers.* Philadelphia, 1957.

Secondary Sources

Alvarez, Manuel Fernández. *Charles V: Elected Emperor and Hereditary Ruler.* London, 1975.

Arnade, P.J. 'Secular Charisma, Sacred Power: Rites of Rebellion in the Ghent Entry of 1467.' *Handelingen der maatschappij voor geschiedenis en oudheidkunde te Gent* 45 (1991), 69–94.

Asselbergs, W.J.M.A. *De stijl van Elkerlyk.* Zwolle, 1968.

Augustijn, Cornelis. 'Anabaptism in the Netherlands: Another Look.' *MQR* 62 (1988), 197–210.

– *Erasmus: His Life, Works, and Influence*. Toronto, 1991.

Autenboer, E. van. *Volksfeesten en rederijkers te Mechelen (1400–1600)*. Ghent, 1962.

– 'Organisties en stedelijke cultuurformen 15de en 16de eeuw.' *VHB* 6–7 (1968), 147–72.

Baere, C. de. 'De deelneming der Brusselse rederijkers aan rhetoricale feesten en wedstrijkden.' *Eigen Schoon & de Brabander* 31 (1948), 8–24 and 49–61.

Barnes, Robin. *Prophecy and Gnosis*. Stanford, 1988.

Barron, Caroline, and Nigel Saul, eds. *England and the Low Countries in the Late Middle Ages*. Stroud and New York, 1995.

Baxandall, Michael. *Painting and Experience in Fifteenth-Century Italy*. Oxford, 1972.

Beemon, F.E. 'The Myth of the Spanish Inquisition and the Preconditions of the Dutch Revolt.' *ARG* 85 (1994), 246–64.

Bemmel, H. Chr. van. 'Toneel in Arnhem van 1500 tot 1565.' In Dibbets and Wackers, *Wat duikers vent is dit!* 121–38.

Bergsma, Wiebe. *Aggaeus van Albada (c.1525–1587), schwenckfeldiaan, staatsman en strijder voor verdraagzaamheid*. Groningen, 1983.

Beyaert, Marc. *Opkomst en bloei van de Gentse rederijkerskamer Marien Theeren*. Ghent, 1978.

Blaauw, C., and A. van Toorn, 'De zin van het spel, rederijkers in moeilijke tijden.' In De Roever and Bakker, *Woelige tijden*, 83–91.

Blasting, Ralph. 'The German *Bruderschaften* as Producers of Late Medieval Vernacular Religious Drama.' *Confraternities in the Renaissance / Les Confraternités à la Renaissance*, ed. William R. Bowen, special issue of *Renaissance and Reformation / Renaissance et Réforme*, 25 (1989), 1–14.

Blommaert, Ph. *Beknopte geschiedenis der kamers van rhetorica te Gent*. Ghent, 1838.

Bock, E. de. *Opstellen over Colijn van Rijssele en andere rederijkers*. Antwerp, 1958.

Boeckel, J. van, and L. van Boeckel. 'Landjuwelen en haagspelen in de XVᵉ en de XVIᵉ eeuw.' *JdF* 18 (1968), 5–27.

Boekhorst, Peter te, Peter Burke, and Willem Frijhoff, eds., *Cultuur en maatschappij in Nederland 1500–1850*. Heerlen, 1992.

Boheemen, F.C. van, and Th. C.J. van der Heijden. *De Delftse rederijkers, Wy rapen gheneucht*. Amsterdam, 1982.

– *De Westlandse rederijkerskamers in de 16e en 17e Eeuw*. Amsterdam, 1985.

Boom, H. ten. *De reformatie in Rotterdam, 1530–1585*. Amsterdam, 1987.

Boomgaard, J.E.A. *Misdaad en straf in Amsterdam*. Zwolle, 1992.

Boon, K.G. 'De glasschilder David Joris, een exponent van het doperse geloof. Zijn kunst en zijn invloed op Dirck Crabeth.' *Mededelingen van de Koninklijke Academy voor Wetenschappen, Letteren en Schone Kunsten van België* 49 (1988), 117–37.

Bonger, H. *Leven en werk van Dirk Volckertsz Coornhert.* Amsterdam, 1978.

Bossy, John. 'Holiness and Society.' *Past and Present* 75 (1977), 119–37.

Brachin, P. 'De Brusselse kamer "Den Boeck" op het Gentse rederijkersfeest van 1539.' *VMKVA* (1959), 105–24.

– 'La Fête de Rhétorique de Gand (1539).' In *Les fêtes et cérémonies de la Renaissance, II, Fêtes et cérémonies du temps de Charles Quint,* ed. J. Jacquot, 255–9. Paris, 1960.

Brady, Thomas A., Jr. *Ruling Class, Regime, and Reformation at Strasbourg, 1520–1555.* Leiden, 1977.

– 'Patricians, Nobles, Merchants: Internal Tensions and Solidarities in South German Urban Ruling Classes at the Close of the Middle Ages.' In *Social Groups and Religious Ideas in the Sixteenth Century,* eds. 'Miriam U. Chrisman and Otto Gründler, 38–45. Kalamazoo, 1978.

– Heiko A. Oberman, and James D. Tracy, eds. *Handbook of European History 1400–1600: Late Middle Ages, Renaissance and Reformation.* 2 vols. Leiden, 1995.

Brandenbarg, Ton. *Heilig Familieleven: Verspreiding en waardering van de Historie van Sint-Anna in de stedelijke cultuur in de Nederlanden en het Rijnland aan het begin van de moderne tijd (15de/16de eeuw).* Nijmegen, 1990.

Brands, G.A. 'Reynier Pouwelsz Tspel van de Cristenkercke en een spul van sinnen van den Siecke Stadt.' *TNLT* 43 (1924), 203–8.

Briggs, Robin. *Witches and Neighbors: The Social and Cultural Context of European Witchcraft.* New York, 1996.

Bristol, Michael D. *Carnival and Theater: Plebeian Culture and the Structure of Authority in Renaissance England.* New York and London, 1985.

Brugmans, H. *Geschiedenis van Amsterdam.* Vol. 1, *Middeleeuwen 1100–1544.* Utrecht, 1972.

Bryant, James C. *Tudor Drama and Religious Controversy.* Macon, Georgia, 1984.

Burke, Peter. *Venice and Amsterdam: A Study of Seventeenth-Century Elites.* London, 1974.

– *Popular Culture in Early Modern Europe.* New York, 1978.

– *The Italian Renaissance.* Princeton, 1986.

Burke, Peter, and Roy Porter, eds. *The Social History of Language.* Cambridge Studies in Oral and Literate Culture 12. Cambridge, 1987.

Burke, Peter, et al. 'Popular Religion.' In Hillerbrand, *Oxford Encyclopedia of the Reformation* 3: 295–316.

Calis, Piet, F.P. Huygens, and B.W.E. Veurman. *Het spel en de knikkers, Kernboek 1. Literatuurgeschiedenis van ca. 800 tot 1880.* Amsterdam, 1977.

Cameron, James K. 'Humanism in the Low Countries.' In *The Impact of Humanism on Western Europe,* ed. Anthony Goodman and Angus MacKay, 137–63. London and New York, 1990.

Caspers, Charles M.A. *De eucharistische vroomheid en het feest van Sacramentsdage in de Nederlanden tijdens de late middeleeuwen.* Leuven, 1992.

Catalogus der bibliotheek van de Maatschappij der Nederlandsche Letterkunde, te Leiden. 3 vols. 1887–9.

Chrisman, Miriam U. *Lay Culture, Learned Culture: Books and Social Change in Strasbourg, 1480–1599.* New Haven and London, 1982.

– *Conflicting Visions of Reform: German Lay Propaganda Pamphlets, 1519–1530.* New Jersey, 1995.

Cohn, Norman. *The Pursuit of the Millenium.* London, 1957; repr. 1970.

Coigneau, Dirk. 'Beschouwingen over de refreinen in het zotte uit de bundel van Jan van Styevoort.' *JdF* 19–20 (1969–70), 37–94, repr. 1972.

– *Refreinen in het zotte bij de rederijkers.* 3 vols. Ghent, 1980.

– 'Liefde en lichaamsbeleving op het rederijkerstoneel.' *JdF* 34 (1984), 115–32.

– 'Matthijs de Castelein (1485?-1550).' *JdF* 35–6 (1985–6), 1–13.

– 'De Evangelische Leeraer: "een spel vul heresien",' *JdF* 39–40 (1989–90), 117–45.

– '"Maer die steden apaert": Over het rederijkerslandjuweel en het haagspel van 1561.' In *Volkscultuur in Brabant,* ed. Fernand Vanhemelryck, 115–41. Brussels, 1994

Couvreur, Walter, et al. *Antwerpen in de XVI^{de} eeuw.* Antwerp, 1976.

Crew, Phyllis Mack. *Calvinist Preaching and Iconoclasm in the Netherlands 1544–1569.* Cambridge, 1978.

Crockett, Bryan. *The Play of Paradox: Stage and Sermon in Renaissance England.* Philadelphia, 1995.

D'Ailly, A.E., ed. *Zeven eeuw Amsterdam,* Vol. 1, *Middeleeuwen en vroege renaissance.* Amsterdam, n.d.

Davidson, Clifford, ed. *The Saint Play in Medieval Europe.* Kalamazoo, 1986.

Davis, Natalie Z. *Society and Culture in Early Modern France.* Stanford, 1975.

– 'The Sacred and the Body Social in Sixteenth-Century Lyon.' *Past and Present* 90 (1981), 40–70.

– 'From "Popular Religion" to Religious Cultures.' In *Reformation Europe: A Guide to Research,* ed. Steven Ozment, 321–41. St Louis, 1982.

Decavele, Johan. *De dageraad van de reformatie in Vlaanderen 1520–1565).* 2 vols. Verhandelingen van de Koninklijke Academie voor Wetenschappen, Letteren en Schone Kunsten van België, vol. 37. Brussels, 1975.

- 'Jan Utenhove en de opvoering van het zinnespel te Roborst in 1543.' *JdF* 39–40 (1989–90), 101–16.
- ed. *Keizer tussen stropdragers. Karel V, 1500–1558.* Leuven, 1990.
- 'Vroege reformatorische bedrijvigheid in de grote Nederlandse steden: Claes van der Elst te Brussel, Antwerpen, Amsterdam en Leiden (1524–1528).' *NAK* 70 (1990), 13–29.

Degroote, G. 'Erasmus en de rederijkers van de XVIe eeuw.' *Belgisch Tijdschrift voor philologie en geschiedenis* 29 (1951), 389–420 and 1029–62.
- *Oude Klanken, nieuwe accenten: de kunst van de rederijkers.* Leiden, 1969.

DeMolen, Richard L. *The Spirituality of Erasmus of Rotterdam.* Nieuwkoop, 1987.

Deppermann, Klaus. 'Melchior Hoffman: Contradictions between Lutheran Loyalty to Government and Apocalyptic Dreams.' In *Profiles of Radical Reformers,* ed. Hans-Jürgen Goertz and Walter Klaassen, 178–90. Kitchener and Scottdale, 1982.
- *Melchior Hoffman: Social Unrest and Apocalyptic Visions in the Age of Reformation.* Trans. Malcolm Wren. London, 1986.

Deursen, A. Th. van. *Plain Lives in a Golden Age: Popular Culture, Religion and Society in Seventeenth-Century Holland.* Trans. Maarten Ultee. Cambridge, 1991.

Dibbets, G.W.R., and P.W.M. Wackers, eds. *Wat duikers vent is dit! Opstellen voor W.M.H. Hummelen.* Wijhe, 1989.

Dieterich, D. Henry. 'Confraternities and Lay Leadership in Sixteenth-Century Liège.' *Confraternities in the Renaissance / Les Confraternités à la Renaissance,* ed. William R. Bowen, special issue of *Renaissance and Reformation / Renaissance et Réforme* 25 (1989), 15–34.

Dijk, Hans van. 'Mariken van Nieumeghen.' *Dutch Crossing* 22 (April 1984), 27–41.

Dijk, Hans van, et al. 'A Survey of Dutch Drama Before the Renaissance.' *Dutch Crossing* 22 (April 1984), 97–131.

Dis, L.M. van. 'Onderzoek naar de invloed van den zestiende-eeuwse concordantie op enkele rederijkersteksten.' In *Bundel opstellen van oud-leerlingen aangeboden an Prof. Dr. C.G.N. de Vooys,* ed B.H. Erné et al., 104–18. Groningen, 1940.

Donnet, Fernand. *Het jonstich versaen der Violieren. Geschiedenis der rederijkkamer de Olijftak sedert 1480.* Antwerp, 1907.

Douglas, Audrey. 'Midsummer in Salisbury: The Tailors' Guild and Confraternity 1444–1642.' *Confraternities in the Renaissance / Les Confraternités à la Renaissance,* ed. William R. Bowen, special issue of *Renaissance and Reformation / Renaissance et Réforme* 25 (1989), 35–51.

Drewes, J.B. 'Het interpreteren van godsdienstige spelen van zinne.' *JdF* 29 (1978–9), 5–124.

– 'Interpretatie van de Gentse spelen van 1539 – Grenzen of onmacht van de filologie.' *TNTL*, 100 (1984), 241–73.

Duke, Alastair C. *Reformation and Revolt in the Low Countries.* London and Ronceverte, 1990.

– 'The Netherlands.' In *The Early Reformation in Europe*, ed. Andrew Pettegree, 142–65. Cambridge, 1992.

Duplessis, Robert S. *Lille and the Dutch Revolt: Urban Stability in an Era of Revolution, 1500–1582.* Cambridge, 1991.

Duyse, P. van. *De Rederijkkamers in Nederland. Hun invloed op letterkundig, politiek en zedelijk gebied.* Ghent, 1900.

Dykema, Peter A., and Heiko A. Oberman eds. *Anticlericalism in Late Medieval and Early Modern Europe.* Leiden, 1994.

Edwards, Mark U., Jr. *Luther's Last Battles: Politics and Polemics 1531–46.* Ithaca and London, 1983.

Eire, Carlos M.N. *War against the Idols. The Reformation of Worship from Erasmus to Calvin.* Cambridge, 1986.

Ellerbroek-Fortuin, E. *Amsterdamse rederijkkersspelen in de zestiende eeuw.* Groningen, 1937.

Elslander, Antonis van. 'Het refreinfeest te Gent in 1539.' *JdF* 2 (1944), 38–57.

– 'Lijst van Noord-Nederlandsche rederijkerskamers uit de XVe en XVIe eeuw.' *JdF* 3 (1945), 24–35.

– 'Lijst van Nederlandse rederijkerskamers uit de XVe en XVIe eeuw.' *JdF* 18 (1968), 29–61.

Erenstein, R.L., et al., eds. *Een theatergeschiedenis der Nederlanden. Tien eeuwen drama en theater in Nederland en Vlaanderen.* Amsterdam, 1996.

Ertborn, J.C.E. Baron van. *Geschiedkundige aenteekeningen aengaende de Ste Lucas Gilde, en de rederijk-kamers van den Olyf-tak, de Violieren en de Goud-bloem, te Antwerp.* 2nd ed., Antwerp, ca.1805.

Es, G.A. van. 'Het drama der rederykers.' In *Geschiedenis van de letterkunde der Nederlanden*, III, *De letterkunde van de Renaissance* ed. F. Baur et al., 276–305 's Hertoghenbosch, 1949.

Fifield, Merle, 'Methods and Modes: The Application of Genre Theory to Descriptions of Moral Plays.' In *Everyman & Company: Essays on the Theme and Structure of the European Moral Play*, ed. Donald Gilman, 8–74. New York, 1989.

Fix, Andrew C. *Prophecy and Reason. The Dutch Collegiants in the Early Enlightenment.* Princeton, 1991.

Forster, Leonard. 'Literary Relations between the Low Countries, England and Germany, 1400–1624.' *Dutch Crossing* 24 (December 1984), 16–31.

Friedrichs, Christopher R. *The Early Modern City, 1450–1750*. London and New York, 1995.

Frijhoff, Willem. 'Het Gelders Antichrist-tractaat (1524) en zijn auteur.' *Archief voor de geschiedenis van de Katholieke Kerk in Nederland* 28 (1986), 192–217.

Gastelaars, Wilma van Engeldorp. *Ic sal u smiten op uwen tant. Geweld tussen man en vrouw in laatmiddeleeuwse kluchten*. Amsterdam, 1984.

Gelder, H.A. Enno van. *Erasmus, schilders en rederijkers*. Groningen, 1959.

Gibson, Gail McMurray. *The Theater of Devotion: East Anglian Drama and Society in the Late Middle Ages*. Chicago, 1989.

Gibson, Walter S. 'Artists and Rederijkers in the Age of Bruegel.' *The Art Bulletin* 63 (September 1981), 426–46.

Gijsen, J.E. van. *Liefde, kosmos en verbeelding mens-en wereldbeeld in Colijn van Rijssels Spiegel der Minnen*. Groningen, 1989.

Gijswijt-Hofstra, Marijke, ed. *Een schijn van verdraagzaamheid. Afwijking en tolerantie in Nederland van de zestiende eeuw tot heden*. Hilversum, 1989.

Gijswijt-Hofstra, M., and W. Frijhoff, eds. *Witchcraft in the Netherlands from the Fourteenth to the Twentieth Century*. Rotterdam, 1991.

Ginzburg, Carlo. *The Cheese and the Worms*. Trans. John and Anne Tedeschi. Harmondsworth, Middlesex, 1982.

– *The Night Battles: Witchcraft and Agrarian Cults in the Sixteenth and Seventeenth Centuries*. Trans. John and Anne Tedeschi. Baltimore, 1983.

Goertz, Hans-Jürgen. *Die Täufer: Geschichte und Deutung*. Munich, 1980.

Gouw, J. ter. *Geschiedenis van Amsterdam*. Vol. 4. Amsterdam, 1884.

Grijp, Louis Peter, Annemies Tamboer, and Everdien Hoek, eds. *De dodendans in de kunsten*. Utrecht, 1989.

Groote, Beatrijs de. 'De overhied en het Gentse rederijkersfeest van 1539.' *JdF* 25 (1975), 105–17.

Hamilton, Alastair. *The Family of Love*. Cambridge, 1981.

– 'The Development of Dutch Anabaptism in the Light of the European Magisterial and Radical Reformation.' In *From Martyr to Muppy: A Historical Introduction to Cultural Assimilation Processes of a Religious Minority in the Netherlands: The Mennonites*, ed. Alastair Hamilton, Sjouke Voolstra, and Piet Visser, 3–14. Amsterdam, 1994.

Herwijnen, G. van. *Bibliografie van de stedengeschiedenis van Nederland*. Leiden, 1978.

Hillerbrand, Hans J. *The Oxford Encyclopedia of the Reformation*. 4 vols. New York and Oxford, 1996.

Hofman, E. 'De Antwerpse drukker Frans Fraeten: De verhouding tussen de vroegste gereformeerde en doopsgezinde liedboeken.' *DB*, new ser, 20 (1994), 71–81.

Hollander, A. den. *De Nederlandse Bijbelvertalingen 1522–1545 / Dutch Translations of the Bible 1522–1545*. Nieuwkoop, 1997.

Horst, Irvin B. 'Menno Simons: The New Man in Community.' In *Profiles of Radical Reformers: Biographical Sketches from Thomas Müntzer to Paracelsus*, ed. Hans-Jürgen Goertz and Walter Klaassen, 203–13. Kitchener, Ont., and Scottdale, PA 1982.

Hsia, R. Po-Chia, ed. *The German People and the Reformation*. Ithaca and London, 1988.

Huizinga, Johann. *The Autumn of the Middle Ages*. Trans. Rodney J. Payton and Ulrich Mammitzsch. Chicago, 1996.

Hummelen, W.M.H. *De sinnekens in het rederijkersdrama*. Groningen, 1958.

– *Repertorium van het rederijkersdrama, 1500 – ca.1620*. Assen, 1960.

– 'Boek N-M uit het archief van "Trou Moet Blijcken".' *JdF* 16 (1966), 85–108.

– 'Types and Methods of the Dutch Rhetoricians' Theatre.' In *The Third Globe*, ed. C. Walter Hodges et al., 164–89. Detroit, 1981.

– 'The Dramatic Structure of the Dutch Morality.' *Dutch Crossing* 22 (April 1984), 17–26.

– 'The Biblical Plays of the Rhetoricians and the Pageants of Oudenaarde and Lille.' In *Modern Dutch Studies: Essays in Honour of Peter King*, 88–104. London and Atlantic Highlands, N.J., 1988.

– 'Het tableau vivant, de "toog," in de toneelspelen van de rederijkers.' *TNTL* 108 (1992), 193–222.

Hüsken, W.N.M. 'Cornelis Everaert en de Troon van Salomon.' *Ons geestelijk erf* 65 (1991), 144–64.

– 'Kroniek van het toneel in Bruges (1468–1556).' *VMKVA* (1992), 219–52.

– 'Politics and Drama: The City of Bruges as Organizer of Drama Festivals.' In Knight, *The Stage as Mirror*, 165–87.

Hylkema, C.B. *Reformateurs: Geschiedkundige studiën over de godsdienstige bewegingen uit de nadagen onzer gouden eeuw*. 1900, Groningen and Amsterdam, 1978.

Hyma, Albert. *The Christian Renaissance*. New York, 1924.

Iansen, S.A.P.J.H. *Verkenningen in Matthijs Casteleins Const van Rhetoriken*. Assen, 1971.

IJsewijn, Jozef. 'The Coming of Humanism to the Low Countries.' In *Itinerarium Italicum: The Profile of the Italian Renaissance in the Mirror of Its European Transformations*, ed. Heiko Oberman and Thomas A. Brady, Jr, 193–301. Leiden, 1975.

Inventaris op het archief van gilden en ambachten [Antwerp]. Antwerp, 1925.

Isaak, Helmut. 'The Struggle for the Evangelical Town.' In *Dutch Dissenters*, ed. Irvin Horst, 66–82. Leiden, 1986.

Jackson, Timothy R. 'Drama and Dialogue in the Service of the Reformation.' In *The Transmission of Ideas in the Lutheran Reformation*, ed. Helga Robinson-Hammerstein, 105–31. Dublin, 1989.

James, Mervyn. 'Ritual, Drama and Social Body in the Late Medieval English Town.' *Past and Present* 98 (1983), 3–29.

Jansma, L.G. 'Crime in the Netherlands in the Sixteenth Century: The Batenburg Bands after 1540.' *MQR* 62 (1988), 221–35.

Johnston, Alexandra F. 'Traders and Playmakers: English Guildsmen and the Low Countries.' In Barron and Saul, *England and the Low Countries*, 99–114.

– 'The Continental Connection: A Reconsideration.' In Knight, *The Stage as Mirror*, 7–24.

Jongh, H. de. *L'ancienne faculté de théologie de Louvain au premier siècle de son existence, 1432–1540*. Louvain, 1911; repr. Utrecht, 1980.

Kalff, G. 'Eenige 16de eeuwische onuitgegeven gedichten van Coornhert, Spiegel en Anderen.' *TNTL* 6 (1886), 309–16.

– 'Handschriften der Universiteitsbibliotheek te Amsterdam.' *TNTL* 9 (1890), 161–89.

– *Geschiedenis der Nederlandsche letterkunde*. 5 vols. Groningen, 1906.

Kaplan, Benjamin J. 'Dutch Particularism and the Calvinist Quest for "Holy Uniformity".' *ARG* 82 (1991), 239–56.

– 'Hubert Duifhuis and the Nature of Dutch Libertinism.' *Tijdschrift voor Geschiedenis* 105 (1992), 1–29.

– 'Remnants of the Papal Yoke: Apathy and Opposition in the Dutch Reformation.' *SCJ* 25 (1994), 653–69.

– *Calvinists and Libertines: Confession and Community in Utrecht, 1578–1620*. Oxford, 1995.

Keersmaekers, A. 'De rederijkerskamers te Antwerpen: kanttekeningen in verband met ontstaan, samenstelling en ondergang.' *VHB* 6–7 (1978), 173–86.

Keirsbilck, G. van. 'Letterkundig leven te Kaprijke in de vijftiende en zestiende eeuw.' *JdF* 14–15 (1964–5), 3–46.

Kernodle, George R. *From Art to Theatre: Form and Convention in the Renaissance*. Chicago, 1970. .

Keyser, H. de. 'Het ontstaan en de werkzaamheden van de Brusselse rederijkerskamers tussen 1400 en 1500.' *Tijdschrift voor Brusselse Geschiedenis* 3 (1986), 65–75.

Keyser, Paul de. 'De Prinsen, de Koningen en de Keizers bij de rederijkers.' *JdF* 3 (1945), 75–98.

– 'Bijdrage tot de blazoenkunde van de rederijkerskamers.' *JdF* 4 (1946–7), 53–66.

Kieckhefer, Richard. *Magic in the Middle Ages*. Cambridge, 1989.

- 'The Specific Rationality of Medieval Magic.' *American Historical Review* 99 (1994), 813–36.

Kipling, Gordon. 'The Idea of the Civic Triumph.' *Dutch Crossing* 22 (April 1984), 60–83.

Kistemaker, Renee, and Roelof van Gelder. *Amsterdam: The Golden Age, 1275–1795.* New York, 1983.

Klaits, Joseph. *Servants of Satan: The Age of the Witch Hunts.* Bloomington and Indianapolis, 1985.

Klötzer, Ralf. *Die Täuferherrschaft von Münster: Stadtreformation und Welterneuerung.* Münster, 1992.

Knight, Alan E. 'Drama and Society in Late Medieval Flanders and Picardy.' *The Chaucer Review* 14 (1980), 379–89.

Knight, Alan E., ed. *The Stage as Mirror: Civic Theatre in Late Medieval Europe.* Cambridge, UK, 1997.

Kölker, A.J. *Alardus Aemstelredamus en Cornelius Crocus. Twee Amsterdamse priester-humanisten.* Nijmegen and Utrecht, 1963.

Kooi, Christine. 'Popish Impudence: The Perseverance of the Roman Catholic Faithful in Calvinist Holland, 1572–1620.' *SCJ* 26 (1995), 75–85.

Kops, Willem. *Schets eener geschiedenisse der rederijkeren.* n.p., n.d. [ca. 1800].

Kruyskamp, C. *Het Antwerpse Landjuweel van 1561.* Amsterdam, 1962.

Laan, N. van der. 'Rederijkersspelen in de Bibliothek van het Leidsche Gemeente-Archief.' *TNTL* 47 (1928), 127–55.

Laan, P.H.J. van der. 'De regering van Amsterdam in de 16de eeuw.' In *Woelige tijden: Amsterdam in de eeuw van de beeldenstorm,* ed. Margriet de Roever and Boudewijn Bakker, 9–30. Amsterdam, 1986.

Ladurie, Emmanuel Le Roy. *Carnival in Romans.* Trans. Mary Feeney. New York, 1979.

Lammerns-Pikhaus, Patricia. 'Het "Tafelspel van een man en een Wachter".' *JdF* 25 (1975), 141–63.

Lennep, O. van. *Beknopte geschiedenis van 'Trou Moet Blycken,' 1503–1922.* N.p., 1922.

Lesger, Cl. 'Tussen stagnatie en expansie. Economische ontwikkeling en levensstandaard tussen 1500 en 1600.' In De Roever and Bakker, *Woelige tijden,* 45–62.

Levack, Brian P. *The Witch-Hunt in Early Modern Europe.* 2nd ed. London and New York, 1995.

Lovett, A.W. *Early Habsburg Spain, 1517–1598.* Oxford, 1986.

Lyna, Frédéric. *Catalogue des manuscrits de la bibliotheque royale de Belgique.* 13 vols. Brussels, 1901–48.

Mak, J.J. *De rederijkers.* Amsterdam, 1944.

Marnef, Guido. *Antwerp in the Age of Reformation*. Baltimore and London, 1996.

Marshall, Sherrin. *The Dutch Gentry, 1500–1650*. New York, 1987.

Martin, J.W. *Religious Radicals in Tudor England*. London and Ronceverte, 1989.

Masure, Thierry. 'De Stadsfinances van Antwerpen, 1531–1571. Een poging tot rekonstruktie.' 2 vols. PhD diss., Rijksuniversiteit Ghent, 1985–6.

Mayer, Susan. 'Cornelis Everaert's *Maria Hoedeken*: A Critique of Popular Piety in Late Medieval Bruges.' PhD field paper, University of New Brunswick, 1994.

McFarlane, I.D. *The Entry of Henri II into Paris 16 June 1549*. Binghamton, 1982.

McGrath, Alister E. *Luther's Theology of the Cross: Martin Luther's Theological Breakthrough*. Oxford, 1985.

Meijer, Reinder P. *Literature of the Low Countries*. Assen, 1971.

Mellink, Albert F. 'Antwerpen als anabaptisten-centrum tot ±1550.' *NAK* 46 (1963–4), 155–68.

– *Amsterdam en de wederdopers*. Nijmegen, 1978.

– *De wederdopers in de Noordelijke Nederlanden*. 2nd ed. Leeuwarden, 1981.

– 'The Beginnings of Dutch Anabaptism in the Light of Recent Research.' *MQR* 62 (1988), 211–20.

Mertens, F.H., and K.L. Torfs. *Geschiedenis van Antwerpen*. Antwerp, 1848.

Mierlo, J. van, S.J. '*Den Boem der Schriftueren*' en het geval Jacob van Middeldonck.' *VMKVA* (1939), 889–905.

Moeller, Bernd. *Imperial Cities and the Reformation*. Ed. and trans. H.C. Erik Midelfort and Mark U. Edwards, Jr. Philadelphia, 1972.

Molhuysen, P.C., and P.J. Block. *Nieuw Nederlandsch biografisch woordenboeck*. 10 vols. Leiden, 1911–37.

Mostert M., and A. Demyttenaere, eds. *De betovering van het middeleeuwse christendom. Studies over ritueel en magie in de middeleeuwen*. Milversum, 1995.

Moxey, Keith P.F. 'Pieter Bruegel and *The Feast of Fools*.' *The Art Bulletin* 64 (December 1982), 640–6.

Muir, Edward. *Civic Ritual in Renaissance Venice*. Princeton, 1981.

– *The Biblical Drama of Medieval Europe*. Cambridge, 1995.

Muir, Lynette R. 'Playing God in Medieval Europe.' In Knight, *The Stage as Mirror*, 25–50.

Muller, J.W. *Cornelis Everaert's spelen als spiegel van de maatschappelijke toestanden zijns tijds*. Verslagen en Mededeelingen der Koninklijke Vlaamsche Academie. Ghent, 1907.

Niccoli, Ottavia. *Prophecy and People in Renaissance Italy*. Trans. Lydia G. Cochrane. Princeton, 1990.

Nicholas, David. *Medieval Flanders*. London and New York, 1992.

Nierop, H.F.K. van. *Van ridders tot regenten: De Hollandse adel in de zestiende en de eerste helft van de zeventiende eeuw.* Amsterdam, 1984.

Nijsten, Gerard. *Volkscultuur in de late middeleeuwen: Feesten, processies en (bij)geloof.* Utrecht and Antwerp, 1994.

– 'Feasts and Public Spectacle: Late Medieval Drama and Performance in the Low Countries.' In Knight, *The Stage as Mirror*, 107–43.

Nissen, Peter. *De Katholieke polemiek tegen de dopers.* Enschede, 1988.

Oberman, Heiko A. 'Teufelsdreck: Eschatology and Scatology in the "Old" Luther.' *SCJ* 19 (1988), 435–50.

– *Luther: Man between God and the Devil.* New Haven and London, 1989.

Oosterman, J.B. 'Anthonis de Roovere. Het werk: overlevering, toeschrijving en plaatsbepaling.' *JdF* 45–6 (1995–6), 29–140.

Packull, Werner O. 'Melchior Hoffman – A Recanted Anabaptist in Schwäbisch-Hall?' *MQR* 57 (1983), 83–111.

– '"The Image of the Common Man" in the Early Pamphlets of the Reformation (1520–1525).' *Historical Reflections / Reflexions Historique* 12 (1985), 253–77.

– 'Hoffman (Hofman), Melchior.' In *Mennonite Encyclopedia* 5: 384–6. Waterloo and Scottdale, 1990.

Paepe, N. de, and L. Roose, eds. *Liber alumnorum Prof. Dr. E. Rombouts.* Leuven, 1968.

Parente, James A., Jr. *Religious Drama and the Humanist Tradition.* Leiden, 1987.

– 'Drama.' In Hillerbrand, *Oxford Encyclopedia of the Reformation* 2: 4–9.

Peeters, L. 'Mariken van Nieumeghen en de Antwerpse volksboekcultuur.' *Spiegel der letteren* 25 (1983), 81–97.

Pikhaus, P. *Het tafelspel bij de rederijkers.* 2 vols. Ghent, 1988.

Pleij, Herman. 'Is de laat-middeleeuwse literatuur in de volkstaal vulgair?' *Amsterdamse smaldelen, I, Populaire literature*, ed. by J. Fontijn, 34–106. Thespa, 1974.

– 'Geladen vermaak. Rederijkerstoneel als politiek instrument van een elite-cultuur.' *JdF* 25 (1975), 75–103.

– *Het Gilde van de Blauwe Schuit. Literatuur, volksfeest en burgermoraal in de late middeleeuwen.* Amsterdam, 1979.

– 'De laatmiddeleeuwse rederijkersliteratuur als vroeg-humanistische over-tuigingskunst.' *JdF* 34 (1984), 65–95.

– 'The Function of Literature in Urban Societies in the Later Middle Ages.' *Dutch Crossing* 29 (August 1986), 3–22.

– *Het literaire leven in de middeleeuwen.* Leiden, 1988.

– 'Van keikoppen en droge jonkers.' In Rooijakkers and Romme, eds. *Charivari in de Nederlanden: Rituele Sancties op deviant gedrag*, 297–315.

– et al., eds. Op belofte van profij. *Stadsliteratuur en burgermoraal in de Neder-landse letterkunde van de middeleeuwen*. Amsterdam, 1991.

Post, R.R. *The Modern Devotion: Confrontation with Reformation and Humanism*. Leiden, 1968.

Potter, Frans de, *Gent van den oudsten tijt tot heden*. Ghent, 1886; repr. Brussels, 1975.

Potter, R.A. 'Morality Play and *Spel van Sinne*: What are the Connections?' *Dutch Crossing* 22 (April 1984), 5–16.

Prevenier, Walter, and Wim Blockmans, *The Burgundian Netherlands*. Cam-bridge, 1986.

In Prims, Floris. 'Cultuurwaarden en cultuurtekorten te Antwerpen in de eer-ste helft van de XVIe eeuw.' *Koninklijke Vlaamsche Academie voor Wetenschap-pen, Leteren en Schoone Kunsten van Belgie* 1 (1939), 15–35.

– *Geschiedenis van Antwerpen*. 11 vols. Brussels, 1927–49; rept. 1981.

Puts, Freddy. 'Geschiedenis van de Antwerpse rederijkerskamer De Goud-bloem.' *JdF* 23–4 (1973–4), 5–34.

Ramakers, B.A.M. 'Maer en beroemt u niet! Het eerste *spel van sinnen van dWerck der Apostelen* van Willem van Haecht.' In Dibbets and Wackers, *Wat duikers vent is dit!* 147–64.

– 'De gespeelde stad: De opvoeringspraktijk van het rederijkerstoneel getoetst aan zeven belegeringsspelen.' *VMKVA* (1993), 180–223.

– *Spelen en figuren: Toneelkunst en processiecultuur in Oudenaarde tussen mid-deleeuwen en moderne tijd*. Amsterdam, 1996.

Ranke, Bert. *Rederijkers in de branding: Het Vlaamsche rederijkerstooneel en de opstand der XVIe eeuw*. Antwerp, 1941.

Reeves, Marjorie. *The Influence of Prophecy in the Later Middle Ages: A Study in Joachism*. Oxford, 1969.

Roberts, Perri Lee. 'Cornelis Buys the Elder's *Seven Works of Mercy*: An Exem-plar of Confraternal Art from Early Sixteenth-Century Northern Europe.' *Confraternities in the Renaissance / Les Confraternités à la Renaissance*, ed. Wil-liam R. Bowen, special issue of *Renaissance and Reformation / Renaissance et Réforme* 25 (1989), 135–49.

Roever, Margriet de, and Boudewijn Bakker, eds. *Woelige tijden: Amsterdam in de eeuw van de beeldenstorm*. Amsterdam, 1986.

Roland, P. 'Inventaris op het Archief van het Oud Sint Lucasgild en van de Oud Koninklijke Academie van Antwerpen.' *Antwerpen's Oudheidkundige Kring* 15 (1939), 42–101.

Rooijakkers, Gerard, and Theo van der Zee, eds. *Religieuze volkscultuur: De spanning tussen de voorgeschreven orde en de geleefde praktijk*. Nijmegen, 1986.

Rooijakkers, Gerard, and Tiny Romme, eds. *Charivari in de Nederlanden: Rituele sancties op deviant gedrag.* Special issue of *Volkskundig bulletin* 15 (October 1989).

Roose, Lode. *Anna Bijns. Een rederijkster uit de hervormingstijd.* Ghent, 1963.

– 'Lof van Retorica. De poetica der rederijkers: Een verkenning.' In *Liber Alumnorum Prof. Dr. E. Rombauts,* eds. N. de Paepe and L. Roose, 111–28. Leuven, 1968.

Roper, Lyndal. *Oedipus and the Devil: Witchcraft, Sexuality and Religion in Early Modern Europe.* London and New York, 1994.

Rothkrug, Lionel. 'Holy Shrines, Religious Dissonance and Satan in the Origins of the German Reformation.' *Historical Reflections/Reflexions Historiques* 14 (1987).

Rowan, Herbert H. 'The Dutch Revolt: What Kind of Revolution?' *Renaissance Quarterly* 43 (1990), 570–90.

Rubin, Miri. *Corpus Christi: The Eucharist in Late Medieval Culture.* Cambridge, 1991.

Rublack, Hans-Christoph. 'Martin Luther and the Urban Social Experience.' *SCJ* 16 (1985), 115–32.

Russell, Paul. *Lay Theology in the Reformation: Popular Pamphleteers in Southwest Germany, 1521–1525.* Cambridge, 1986.

Russell, William R. 'Martin Luther's Understanding of the Pope as the Antichrist.' *ARG* 85 (1994), 32–44.

Schama, Simon. *The Embarrassment of Riches: An Interpretation of Dutch Culture in the Golden Age.* New York, 1988.

Schenkeveld, Maria A. *Dutch Literature in the Age of Rembrandt: Themes and Ideas.* Amsterdam and Philadelphia, 1991.

Schenkeveld-van der Dussen, M.A., et al., eds. *Nederlandse literatuur, een geschiedenis.* Groningen, 1993.

Scribner, Robert W. *For the Sake of Simple Folk: Popular Propaganda for the German Reformation.* Cambridge, 1981.

– *Popular Culture and Popular Movements in Reformation Germany.* London and Ronceverte, 1987.

– 'Ritual and Reformation.' In *The German People and the Reformation,* ed. Hsia, 122–44.

– 'Introduction.' In *Popular Religion in Germany and Central Europe, 1400–1800,* ed. Robert Scribner and Trevor Johnson, 1–15. Houndmills and London, 1996.

Shrag, Dale. 'Erasmian and Grebelian Pacifism: Consistency or Contradiction?' *MQR* 62 (1988), 431–54.

Siegel, Jerrold E. 'Renaissance Humanism: Petrarch and Valla.' In *Renaissance Men and Ideas,* ed. Robert Schwoebel, 1–22. New York, 1971.

Simon, Eckehard, ed. *The Theatre of Medieval Europe: New Research in Early Drama*. Cambridge, 1991.

Slack, Paul, ed. *Rebellion, Popular Protest and the Social Order in Early Modern England*. Cambridge, 1984.

Slee, J.C. van. *De Rijnsburger Collegianten*. 1895; repr. Utrecht, 1980.

Sluijs, P. van den. 'Enkele kanttekeningen met betrekking tot de Bossche rederijkerskamers.' *VHB* 6–7 (1978), 187–203.

Smail, Daniel Lord. 'Predestination and the Ethos of Disinheritance in Sixteenth-Century Calvinist Theater,' *SCJ* 23 (1992), 303–23.

Smits-Veldt, Mieke B. *Het Nederlandse renaissancetoneel*. Utrecht, 1991.

Soly, H. 'Economische vernieuwing en social weerstand: De betekenis en asperaties der Antwerpse middenklasse in de 16de eeuw.' *Tijdschrift voor Geschiedenis* 83 (1970), 520–35.

Spierenburg, Pieter. *De verbroken betovering: Mentaliteitsgeschiedenis van preïndustrieel Europa*. Hilversum, 1990.

Spies, Marijke. '"Op de questye ...": Over de structuur van 16e-eeuwse zinnespelen.' *De nieuwe taalgids* 83 (1990), 139–50.

Spruyt, Bart J. 'Listrius *lutherizans*: His *Epistola theologica adversus Dominicanos Suollensis* (1520).' *SCJ* 22 (1991), 727–51.

Stayer, James M. 'Oldeklooster and Menno.' *SCJ* 9 (1978), 50–67.

– 'Was Dr. Kuehler's Conception of Early Dutch Anabaptism Historically Sound? The Historical Discussion of Anabaptist Münster 450 Years After.' *MQR* 60 (1986), 261–88.

– *The German Peasants' War and Anabaptist Community of Goods*. Montreal and Kingston, 1991.

Steenbergen, G. Jo. 'Het spel der Violieren op het Gentse "Landjuweel".' *JdF* 4 (1946–7), 15–26.

– *Het landjuweel van de rederijkers*. Leuven, 1950.

– 'Willem van Haecht's geschriften voor het Antwerpse Landjuweel.' *JdF* 7 (1950), 78–94.

– 'De apostelspelen van Willem van Haecht.' In De Paepe and Roose, *Liber alumnorum Prof. Dr. E. Rombauts*, 161–77.

Sterck, J.F.M. 'Onder Amsterdamsche humanisten.' *Het Boeck* 6 (1917), 282–96.

– *Onder Amsterdamsche humanisten: Hun opkomst en bloei in de 16e eeuwsche stad*. Hilversum, 1934.

Streitman, Elsa. 'Teach Yourself Art: The Literary Guilds in the Low Countries.' *Dutch Crossing* 29 (August 1986), 75–94.

– 'The Netherlands.' In *The Theatre of Medieval Europe: New Research in Early Drama*, ed. Eckehard Simon, 225–52. Cambridge, 1991.

– 'The Low Countries.' In *The Renaissance in National Context*, ed. Roy Porter and Mikuláš Teich, 68–91. Cambridge, 1992.

Sutton, Anne F., and Livia Visser-Fuchs. 'Choosing a Book in Late Fifteenth-Century England and Burgundy.' In Barron and Saul, *England and the Low Countries*, 61–98.

Torfs, Lodewijk. *Feestalbum van Antwerpen*. Antwerp, 1864.

Tracy, James D. *The Politics of Erasmus: A Pacifist Intellectual and His Political Milieu*. Toronto, 1978.

– *A Financial Revolution in the Habsburg Netherlands: Renten and Renteniers in the County of Holland, 1515–1565*. Berkeley, 1985.

– *Holland under Habsburg Rule, 1506–1566: The Formation of a Body Politic*. Berkeley, 1990.

Trapman, J. 'Delenus en de Bijbel.' *NAK* 56 (1975), 95–113.

– 'Ioannes Sartorius (ca. 1500–1557), Gymnasiarch te Amsterdam en Noordwijk, als Erasmiaan en Spiritualist.' *NAK* 70 (1990), 30–51.

Trexler, Richard C. 'Ritual in Florence: Adolescence and Salvation in the Renaissance.' In *The Pursuit of Holiness in Late Medieval and Renaissance Religion*, ed. Charles Trinkaus and Heiko A. Oberman, 200–64. Leiden, 1974.

Tydeman, William. *The Theatre in the Middle Ages: Western European Stage Conditions, ca. 800–1576*. Cambridge, 1978.

Vandecasteele, Maurits. 'Letterkundig leven te Gent van 1500 tot 1539.' *JdF* 16 (1966), 3–58.

– 'De Haagse rederijkerskamer "Met Ghenuchten" in 1494.' *JdF* 35–6 (1985–6), 125–48.

– 'Het Antwerpse rederijkersfeest van 1496: een onderzoek der bronnen.' *JdF* 35–6 (1985–6), 149–76.

Vanysacker, Dries. *Hekserij in Bruges: De magische leefwereld van een stadsbevolking, 16de–17de eeuw*. Bruges [1988].

Veldman, I.M. *Maartin van Heemskirck and Dutch Humanism in the Sixteenth Century*. Maarssen, 1977.

Verduin, Leonard. 'The Chambers of Rhetoric and Anabaptist Origins in the Low Countries.' *MQR* 34 (1960), 192–6.

Verheyden, A.L.E. *De hervorming in de Zuidelijke Nederlanden in de XVIᵉ eeuw*. Brussels, 1949.

Verheyden, E. *De Vilvoordse koninklijke rederijkerskamer De Goudbloem*. Vilvoorde, 1949.

Visser, Piet. *Broeders in de geest: De doopsgezinde bijdragen van Dierick en Jan Philipsz: Schabaelje tot de nederlandse stichtelijke literatuur in de zeventiende eeuw*. 2 vols. Deventer, 1988.

- *Dat Rijp is moet eens door eygen rijpheydt vallen: Doopsgezinden en de gouden eeuw van De Rijp.* Wormerveer, 1992.

Vooys, C.G.N. de. 'Rederijkersspelen in het archief van "Trou Moet Blijcken".' *TNTL* 45 (1926), 265–86; 47 (1928), 161–201; 49 (1930), 1–25.

- 'Amsterdamsch rederijkersleven in het midden van de 16ᵉ eeuw.' *TNTL* 48 (1929), 133–40.
- 'Twee Rederijkersspelen van Pyramus en Thisbe.' *VMKVA* (1947–9), 5–13.
- 'Een Antwerps sinnespel van Smenschen Gheest door Clodius.' *JdF* 7 (1950), 21–41.

Wagenaar, Jan. *Amsterdam.* 3 vols. Amsterdam, 1760; repr. Alphen aan de Rijn, 1971–2.

Waite, Gary K. 'The Anabaptist Movement in Amsterdam and the Netherlands, 1531–1535: An Initial Investigation into its Genesis and Social Dynamics.' *SCJ* 18 (1987), 249–64.

- 'From Apocalyptic Crusaders to Anabaptist Terrorists: Anabaptist Radicalism after Münster, 1535–1545.' *ARG* 80 (1989), 173–93.
- *David Joris and Dutch Anabaptism 1524–1543.* Waterloo, 1990.
- 'The Longevity of Spiritualistic Anabaptism: The Literary Legacy of David Joris.' *Canadian Journal of History / Annales Canadiennes D'Histoire* 26 (1991), 177–98.
- 'Popular Drama and Radical Religion: The Chambers of Rhetoric and Anabaptism in the Netherlands.' *MQR* 65 (1991), 227–55.
- 'Vernacular Drama and the Early Urban Reformation: The Chambers of Rhetoric in Amsterdam, 1520–1555.' *The Journal of Medieval and Renaissance Studies* 21 (1991), 187–206.
- 'The Dutch Nobility and Anabaptism, 1535–1545.' *SCJ* 23 (1992), 458–85.
- 'The Holy Spirit Speaks Dutch: David Joris and the Promotion of the Dutch Language, 1539–1545.' *Church History* 61 (1992), 47–59.
- 'Reformers on Stage: Rhetorician Drama and Reformation Propaganda in the Netherlands of Charles V, 1519–1556.' *ARG* 83 (1992), 209–39.
- 'Een ketter en zijn stad. David Joris en Delft.' In *Heidenen, papen, libertijnen en fijnen. Artikelen over de kerkgeschiedenis van het zuidwestelijk gedeelte van Zuid-Holland van de voorchristelijke tijd tot heden. Zesde verzameling bijdragen van de Vereniging voor Nederlandse Kerkgeschiedenis,* ed. J.C. Okkema, F.A. van Lieburg, B.J. Spruyt, and G.N.M. Vis, 121–37. Delft, 1994.
- 'David Joris en de opkomst van de sceptische traditie jegens de duivel in de vroeg-moderne Nederlanden.' In *Duivelsbeelden in de Nederlanden,* ed. Gerard Rooijakkers, Lène Dresen-Coenders, and Margreet Geerdes, 216–31. Baarn, 1994.
- '"Man is a Devil to Himself": David Joris and the Rise of a Sceptical Tradi-

tion towards the Devil in the Early Modern Netherlands, 1540–1600.' *NAK* 75 (1995), 1–30.

– 'Talking Animals, Preserved Corpses and Venusberg: The Sixteenth-Century Worldview and Popular Conceptions of the Spiritualist David Joris (1501– 1556).' *Social History* 20 (1995), 137–56.

– 'Demonic Affliction or Divine Chastisement? Conceptions of Illness and Healing among Spiritualists and Mennonites in Holland, ca. 1530–ca. 1630.' In *Illness and Healing Alternatives in Western Europe*, ed. Marijke Gijswijt-Hofstra, Hilary Marland, and Hans de Waardt, 59–79. London, 1997.

– 'Between the Devil and the Inquisitor: Anabaptists, Diabolical Conspiracies and Magical Beliefs in the Sixteenth-Century Netherlands.' In *Radical Reformation Studies*, ed. Werner D. Packull and Geoffrey Dipple. St. Andrews Studies in the Reformation, 120–40. Aldershot, Eng., and Brookfield, VT, 1999.

Walker, Greg. *Plays of Persuasion: Drama and Politics at the Court of Henry VIII*. Cambridge, 1991.

Wandel, Lee Palmer. *Voracious Idols and Violent Hands: Iconoclasm in Reformation Zurich, Strasbourg, and Basel*. New York, 1995.

Waterschoot, Werner. 'De Oudenaardse rederijkers te Gent in 1539.' *JdF* 27–8 (1985–6), 17–32.

– 'De rederijkerskamers en de doorbraak van de reformatie in de Zuidelijk Nederlanden.' *JdF* 45–6 (1995–6), 141–53.

Webber, Ph. E. 'Varieties of Popular Piety Suggested by Netherlandic *Vita Christi* Prayer Cycles.' *Ons geestelijk erf* 64 (1990), 195–226.

Weiler, A.G. 'Recent Historiography on the Modern Devotion: Some Debated Questions.' *Archief voor de Geschiedenis van de Katholieke Kerk in Nederland* 26 (1984), 161–79.

Westgeest, J.P. 'Zeven verborgen Marialoven van Anthonis de Roovere.' *JdF* 45–6 (1995–6), 11–28.

White, Paul Whitfield. *Theatre and Reformation: Protestantism, Patronage, and Playing in Tudor England*. Cambridge, 1992.

Wickham, Glynne. 'The Staging of Saint Plays in England.' In *The Medieval Drama*, ed. Sandro Sticca, 99–119. Albany, 1972.

– *The Medieval Theatre*. 3rd ed. Cambridge, 1987.

Willems, J.F. 'Cornelis Everaert: Tooneeldichter van Bruges.' *Belgisch Museum* 6 (1842), 41–66.

Williams, George H. *The Radical Reformation*. 3rd ed. Kirksville, 1992.

Worp, J.A. *Drama en tooneel*. vol. 1. Rotterdam, 1903.

Yates, Francis A. *Astraea: The Imperial Theme in the Sixteenth Century*. London, 1975.

Zagorin, Perez. *Ways of Lying: Dissimulation, Persecution, and Conformity in Early Modern Europe.* Cambridge, Mass., 1990.

Zieleman, G.C. 'Van Venator tot Duircant. Over het convoluut met Utenhoves spel van zinnen.' *NAK* 71–2 (1991), 157–76.

Zijlstra, Samme. 'Blesdijk's verslag van de bezetting van Oldeklooster.' *DB* 10 (1984), 61–9.

Zika, Charles. 'Hosts, Processions and Pilgrimages: Controlling the Sacred in Fifteenth-Century Germany.' *Past and Present* 118 (1988), 25–64.

Index

For page locations of the rhetoricians' plays examined in this book, please refer to the appendix. Chamber names are listed after their city.